POLICY IN MOTION: an examination and analysis of the representation of Gypsies/Travellers and how this informs and perpetuates their socio-economic exclusion via policy, practice and service delivery with particular reference to Staffordshire

By A Drakakis-Smith

Poolfield Press

2013

First published 2013 by Poolfield Press
Overdale House, 16 Poolfield Avenue, Newcastle-under-Lyme, Staffordshire ST5 2NL
adsads@ntlworld.com

ISBN: 978-0-9564590-4-6

A catalogue record for this book is available from the British Library

Printed by

J H Brookes (Printer)Ltd
Sneyd Street, Stoke-on-Trent

CONTENTS

LIST OF FIGURES

LIST OF MAPS

POLICY IN MOTION : AN EXAMINATION AND ANALYSIS OF THE REPRESENTATION OF GYPSIES/TRAVELLERS AND HOW THIS INFORMS AND PERPETUATES THEIR SOCIO-ECONOMIC EXCLUSION VIA POLICY, PRACTICE AND SERVICE DELIVERY WITH PARTICULAR REFERENCE TO STAFFORDSHIRE

PREFACE

This monograph is the end product of a Ph D Thesis undertaken in the Department of Sociology, Bristol University under the encouraging eye of Professor Tariq Modood and Dr Will Guy. The project was made possible by an ESRC award. The project was completed in 2003. The overall project was an in-depth evaluative area study which sought to examine the relationship between the power group – Local Authorities in Staffordshire (and beyond) – and the target group Gypsies/Travellers who live on sites in, and/or resort to the study area of Staffordshire. The relationship was examined and analysed within three contexts which, when taken together, formed the Gypsy/Traveller situation within this County.

The first context examined and analysed the way in which Gypsies/Travellers have been perceived, identified and represented historically by majority society. In the light of embedded misperceptions and misrepresentations a study was made of the way in which Gypsies/Travellers have been and continue to be treated by Authority via legislation and policy which 'theoretically' assists in the culture making and shaping of the Gypsy/Traveller *habitus*.

The second context explored the way in which the structuring structures of national and local level bureaucracy and the Gypsy/Traveller *habita* have become intertwined and mutually supportive of one another in a helixial configuration which makes it difficult to separate into exclusive and component parts – although not impossible given time and resources. The Gypsy/Traveller-Local Authority interface was examined to reveal the mechanisms used and the game play involved in this construction via legislation, policy, practice and service delivery.

Several analytical theories were utilised to help understand the above processes, not least Bourdieu's notion of *habitus*, Weber's theory of group formation, Simmel's construction of 'The Stranger', the theories of Rational Choice and Game Theory, Barth and Eriksen's contributions re cultural content and boundaries together with the evaluative tools of race and ethnicity, to demonstrate the ways in which groups become politicised, hierarchicised and ultimately represented – and in the case of some Gypsies/Travellers – excluded. How far were theory and reality aligned?

Since agency needs space in which to perform, the Thesis also examined and analysed the Gypsy/Traveller situation in terms of space and place using the DTLR/ODPM and now LGC biannual caravan count data. Thus this third context explored the way in which

1

Gypsies/Travellers can be (mis)represented, how space is enclosed and manipulated and how far Gypsy/Traveller movement and settlement is organised and controlled within it, revealing nomadism to be, in the main, a 'moving myth'.

I would like to thank the following for their invaluable help:

Professor Tariq Modood and Dr Will Guy already mentioned who were my supervisors – always available, supportive and helpful, Dr Derek Hawes and Dr Colin Clark my external examiners who made useful comments on the final draft and who gave a thorough grilling at the Viva which improved the final product.

Grateful thanks is extended to all those who agreed to be interviewed at the national and local level within the DTLR/ODPM, Local Authority Officers and Members of councils in Staffordshire and beyond and who gave of their time so generously during and after interviews. Their patience and stamina was commendable. I would also like to thank all the Gypsy/Traveller families who took the time to answer my questions, gave me cups of tea, loaned me videos and stayed cheerful in adversity.

A warm thank you to Fatih Gungor and his family for their kind hospitality whilst I was in Ankara and to Fatih. especially, for his unfailing patience as a translator and guide around the city. I wish to thank too, Surhan Gum who introduced me to his super parents who showed Fatih and me a wonderful welcome and who provided us with some wonderful meals in their home and useful information on Roma in Ankara.

I would like to thank the Curators of the Scott McPhee Collections at the Sydney Jones Library at Liverpool University, the Archivists at the Staffordshire Record Office and the helpful, obliging staff at Bristol University Library and at Keele University Library. I thank also Elaine Escott, Jackie Bee and Ruth Levitas at the Department of Sociology at Bristol.

I am more than grateful to Keith Mason of Keele University for his guidance and instruction on the wonders of GIS which provided a more useful and insightful analysis of the DTLR/ODPM data and the production of useful maps, which have been updated for this monograph. Thanks also to Andy Lawrence for refining the double helix diagrams and the UK road map.

I would like to thank my children who encouraged me, and my friends for their support – Dr Elsbeth Robson, Professor Ursula Sharma, Dr Douglas Lockhart, Dr Brian Turton and his wife Margaret – to name but a few.

Finally, but not least I would like to thank the ESRC for funding the project and for giving me the opportunity to pursue this topic, and for the pleasure in attending the many useful and interesting courses put on for their Ph D students. I tried not to let them down!

2

CHAPTER ONE

INTRODUCTION

I wish to state at the outset what the Thesis was *not*. The literature indicates that an 'accepted convention' (Watson 1987) has evolved which dictates the way in which Gypsies/Travellers are written about – often governing how they are ultimately treated. The Thesis was not an anthropological investigation following the Gypsy Lorist tradition. Whilst Judith Okely (1994) attempted to move away from the sentimental and romanticised notion of 'the Gypsy' by updating the archival information and questioned whether 'an ethnic group' needed to be 'defined on the basis of its claims to foreign origins and claims to any vestiges of exotic 'culture' (ibid:15), her volume on traveller-Gypsies, nevertheless generated other myths (with Marxist undertones) and inserted other cultural attributes into the archive - not least was their way of earning a living. This she claimed to be 'consciously chosen, and cannot be explained merely as the result of 'prejudice' against Gypsies and their unjust exclusion from the 'opportunities' of the wage-labour market' (ibid:33). This, together with Acton's (1974) 'economic nomadism' and the search for work - taken on board by Okely in 1984 - and in Adams et al in 1975, a somewhat functionalist view is taken, placing a new essentialist 'spin' on the Gypsy/ Traveller economy and mobility. The thesis attempted to show that whilst some families could thrive like 'fish in water' (after Bourdieu 1987) by travelling, for others travelling was often the result of being systemically excluded from space, place and equality of opportunity – which included wage labour and accommodation, even housing.

Neither was it a political treatise depicting a struggle (although struggle and resistance was, is and has been taking place) or a plea-bargaining position for national independence and an independent state along the lines of present-day Israel (Kenrick and Puxon 1972; Acton 1974). Such volumes, whilst encouraging the organisation of UK

3

Gypsies/Travellers and a pan-Roma movement, tended to homogenise the experience and end-play of Gypsies/Travellers. A prevailing emphasis on a single origin via an Indian *diaspora* and a global language tended to exclude (and still does) those who were/are indigenous. It is as likely that any migratory groups, classified (correctly or incorrectly) as Gypsies, might have fitted into an already established mobile way of life in UK if the circumstances and dispositions were right - as much as those who were indigenous might have co-opted 'the Gypsy' way of life. Whichever, the prevailing majority society notion of the Gypsy/Traveller way of life was, and still is, associated with mobility (and usually an ad-mixture of negative, other qualities). Rather, the Ph D project was an area study which sought to move on and away from (if possible) the above approaches and to place Gypsies/Travellers within a wider and more integrated context.

Whilst Gypsies/Travellers for the purpose of the Thesis were the target group, it needs to be stated clearly here that they are not the main focus of the project. The emphasis here is upon the Local Authorities (LAs) in Staffordshire and how their policies and actions impact upon and influence the target group.

Staffordshire was chosen because I have lived and resorted to the area for the past thirty years, I have a background knowledge of the geographical field area and an assimilated knowledge of at least three of the 10 Local Authorities in the County. I had worked in the field of race relations, which entailed working with some families and groups of Gypsies/ Travellers who lived on local permanent and permitted sites. Although the MA study completed in 1997 had extended, deepened and formalised this knowledge, it raised further questions and scenarios which could not be explored then. The Ph D project was an attempt to rectify this. The MA study became a useful background, providing a longitudinal reference point (at least for two LAs: Newcastle-under-Lyme and Stoke-on-Trent – subjects of the MA study).

A change of national government in 1997 indicated that a more enlightened approach, to marginal groups such as mobile Gypsies/Travellers, might be forthcoming given the early rhetoric on exclusion and the discourse on inclusion. However, the 1994 Criminal Justice and Public Order Act (CJPO) remained in place and the pronouncements from the Home Office (under Jack Straw's leadership) were not encouraging at the time.

In fact the stand taken by Paul Boateng against East and Central European Roma begging on London streets and the underground, Jack Straw's speech on the anti-social behaviour of New (any) Travellers and the Conservative Party launch of their 'Common Sense on Travellers' policy (24 August 2000) set a new tone of non-toleration for unauthorised camping and anti-social/unacceptable behaviour, as if these had been 'tolerated' in the past. This appeared to be another c(l)ueing exercise. A Government interpretation of the meaning of 'toleration' as advocated in Circular 18/94 and in Chapter 5 of the Good Practice Guide (1998) quickly followed, together with a revision of Chapter 5. Jack Straw also promised 'tough laws' to enable 'landowners to evict travellers who set up camp and vandalise their property' (The Express on Sunday, 6/11/2000). This was reiterated by the CLG in the Summer of 2013.

The Coalition Government of 2010 comprising the Conservative and Liberal Democrat parties has taken a harder line and once again the duty imposed on Local Authorities to provide sites has been revoked and the grant aid to assist with refurbishing and creating sites, reduced. Although there would appear to be a general softening of attitude towards Gypsy/Traveller sites and a curiosity about the Gypsy/Traveller way of life in terms of radio and television documentary/docudrama and 'reality' programmes and several autobiographies, the recent events at Dale Farm tended to cast the mind back to the 1960s when large-scale evictions took place and many settled families were returned to the road and to mobility – against their will.

In UK the caravan and semi-permanent structure (the 'prefab') were widely utilised, post-war, as cheap, affordable means of accommodation. That people remain in caravans or mobile homes on caravan parks, which proliferate, or take weekend or annual holidays in caravans, is not a cause for concern. The Caravan Club has more than 750,000 active members.[1] These encampments never make headline news in the way that a family with two to five caravans might when they park on a piece of land which is not theirs or they apply for planning permission to set up a site on land they may own. The MA study indicated that not all Gypsies/Travellers in Staffordshire 'travelled', but were penalized when they stopped and settled on land without license. Increasingly, attempts to settle, even on land which families own, had been rebuffed. This begged the questions: why are some groups more accepted than others? Why are some permitted use of land for caravans and others not; and given that provision for caravan dwelling exists, why are alternative arrangements for Gypsies/Travellers necessary?

The Ph D project attempted to discover the breadth of these phenomena in Staffordshire and the reasons why. The Thesis also attempted to challenge some of the 'accepted common-sense knowledge' about Gypsies/Travellers with the intention of creating space into which Gypsies/Travellers might wish to insert their own representations. For too long the Gypsy/Traveller case has been represented by 'others'. The Thesis attempted to examine the power group. The findings are available to strengthen or to enable families to make a case of their own.

Although the race/racism/ethnicity paradigm underpinned the MA project, this discourse, alone, does not adequately explain the often conflictual and exclusionary relationship between Gypsies/Travellers, the State and the housed population. In fact, much of the early race/racism literature either omitted Gypsies/Travellers or mentioned them only in passing, although for centuries they had been subjected to 'the black experience' - in terms of exclusion from access to resources, separation, inequality in terms of opportunity and physical and verbal abuse. In many ways, Gypsies/Travellers are still treated as 'a race' apart – non-belongers, not to be transplanted here (Drakakis-Smith 1997). Given that the majority of Gypsies and Travellers are 'white', they did not fit comfortably into the 'black' discourse. Families did, however, come within the remit of the later discourse on ethnicity, which focussed on other markers of difference such as culture, language, religion and way of life etc.. It was not until 1989 that Gypsies were granted 'ethnic minority' status by case law (CRE vs Dutton) and Irish Travellers were declared an ethnic group in 2000 (Kiely vs Punch Retail). Nevertheless, it is still proving

---

[1] Mainly from Social Classes I and II (The Caravan Club, telephone interview 14/7/2001).

difficult to encapsulate the Gypsy/Traveller situation within this discourse since many Travellers, particularly New Travellers, are indigenous (McKay 1996; Drakakis-Smith 1997, 2003). Some living on sites are not Gypsies, Travellers or New Travellers. The MA project indicated several other theoretical themes which needed elaboration or pursuit, which will be discussed below, in order to attempt to answer the question, 'What is going on here?'

For the purpose of the Thesis the term Gypsy/Traveller was used to include all in Staffordshire who identified themselves as such, and included those who were mobile and those who lived on sites. It also included New Travellers. The Thesis is concerned mainly with those who lived in and/or resort to this County. However, the Gypsy/Traveller experience included those elsewhere in UK and abroad where relevant.

Fast forwarding to 2013, Eastern European Roma have moved to the UK (and to Staffordshire) to add another dimension to the socio-ethnic equation. The families tend to live in houses and many are keen to educate their children to the highest level. They tend not to associate with local Gypsy/Traveller families.

Field work and official records indicated that, at the time of fieldwork, there were no New Travellers living on sites or resorting to Staffordshire.

The Current State of Play And Some Issues to be Addressed
Gypsy/Traveller is an umbrella term for individuals, families and family groups who may or may not live and travel together. Fieldwork revealed that a single caravan is not uncommon, and that like any other family, Gypsies/Travellers appear to disperse easily and to cluster for fairs, family gatherings, religious meetings or 'events'. Identification is either by self-identity or, via mode of transport and/or living unit, by others. The caravan and unauthorised camping appear to be the main ethnic markers for many Local Authority officials who have to 'identify' Gypsies/Travellers for the bi-annual count. Legally, the grouping has already been 'sifted' so that barge dwellers form a separate group as do circus and show people – the latter having separately negotiated rights with

7

the State. New Travellers can either be included or excluded from the Gypsy/Traveller grouping particularly for the purposes of the bi-annual count when Officers may include them or not (see Chapter 5). Whilst some families in the traditional Traveller grouping have distanced themselves from New Travellers (comments made by Gypsies/Travellers during fieldwork in 1997 and 2001), traditional Travellers are themselves separated from majority society for separate and differential consideration. However, with regard to eviction, all are treated in the same way. As several Officers put it, 'When it comes to trespass on *our* land, we don't discriminate'. Chapters 7 and 8 will show how this is translated into policy and practice.

Gypsies/Travellers have tended not to write their own history (Okely 1994) which infers that over time representations by 'others' have created unrealistic 'images' (both negative and positive) of them. It could be said that the history of Gypsies/ Travellers has been one of interference (with apologies to Foucault 1972, 1980). On this basis policies have been drawn up at both national and local levels, with varying enthusiasm and limited success, to both eliminate trespass and to increase and to improve site provision. It has also attempted, via the planning process, to limit the growth and spread of caravan parks generally, which exist parallel to Gypsy/Traveller sites. Earlier research has indicated that in some LAs in Staffordshire (Drakakis-Smith 1997, 2003), and elsewhere (Adams et al 1975), the interaction between Gypsy/Traveller families and Officers has become stylised to a reflex action – a habit, a routine, with eviction and its threat and aftermath forming the basis of a way of life for many. The Thesis explored the extent to which this was so (and still is) in Staffordshire. The conflictual relationship between Gypsies/ Travellers, the State and the housed population is pin-pointed when Gypsies/Travellers stop moving and appear to be settling. The assumption of officialdom (at national and local levels), applied to whatever purpose – ostensibly as reason for not making adequate provision - is that travelling is what Gypsies/Travellers do. This has become an influential perception of Gypsies/Travellers, irrespective of whether it is right/wrong/ rational or contrary to reality.

Interaction/Game Play

The dictum that for every action there is a reaction, is germane here. It could also be said that for every reaction another action is spawned; thus an interplay (game play) develops where each side begins, and attempts to formulate and regulate the rules of the game on its own terms in order to maximise 'utilities'. Encampments, for however long, on land without planning permission and site licenses, are ruled to be unauthorised. The act of making them so is viewed by Gypsies/Travellers to be a hostile reaction. Official action is generally swift and in response to the wishes of local constituents, unauthorized encampments are removed. Eviction by the LA/land owner is construed by some Gypsies/Travellers as a hostile reaction because the notion persists that mobility is *the* Gypsy/Traveller way of life and that they have some right to occupy 'unused' land as part of their right to be, and when they say there is nowhere else for them to go. LA officers claim that sites would be permitted if they were kept clean, they were not in sensitive locations or on private/Council land. Gypsies/Travellers claim that wherever sites occur and irrespective of their cleanliness they are still removed. Whilst some Gypsies/ Travellers have been permitted to remain, the majority are moved on. Both parties lay claim to being 'right' in their actions and their convictions. Each party finds it difficult to see the other's point of view. In some instances both parties resort to unacceptable behaviour which results in zero-sum/lose-lose scenarios. This pattern has become stylised via codification – ultimately written into policies and National, legal Statutes. The game then changes to resistance and counter-resistance producing 'a situation'. Dialogue is reduced to threats and counter-threats to become uncommunicative. The lines of communication close. The two parties become further estranged. This notion of interplay will be demonstrated and developed as the thesis proceeds.

The long history of parallel development, often occasioned by exclusion, of some Gypsies/Travellers from majority society, has led to the adoption of survival, coping strategies. The adoption of the tent, the wagon and latterly the caravan was possibly an imaginative response to the negative and protracted action of exclusion/non-inclusion and constantly being moved on by officialdom (see also McKay 1996 on this topic). However in moving away from potential conflict and pressure from authority (in whatever form) opportunities for negotiation and dialogue are often lost. Where this has not been the case, the relationship between families and authority has been more accommodating and positive. The Ph D project explored the phenomenon of games played between Gypsies/Travellers and authority further in an attempt to fathom how this positive equilibrium could be extended.

The term 'game' used in this thesis adopts the same definition as Luce and Raifa (1957:257) that individual decision-making under uncertainty constitutes 'a game'.

Some Current Assumptions[2]

It would appear that the interaction described above has evolved because attitudes have been underpinned with several sweeping assumptions which I regard to be either erroneous or in need of unpacking and unpicking. These are first, that Gypsies/Travellers choose their way of life; that Gypsies/Travellers do not want to stay/live in one place on sites; that Gypsies/Travellers do not wish to pay to stay/live in one place on sites; that mobility and caravan dwelling is, essentially, a cultural rather than a social and inclusion/exclusion/discrimination issue. The field work and documentation study attempted to test such assumptions. Second, draped around these is a confusion regarding what a 'permanent site' is. The 1960 Caravan Sites and Control of Development Act gave LAs power to create and run sites. When it appeared that LAs in England were being unresponsive and not utilising this power effectively, the Act made it a duty to provide - the intention being to establish a national network of sites in England and Wales where families could safely stop (Circular 6/62) although there appeared to be some ambivalence about families remaining indefinitely. Nevertheless it was acknowledged in Circular 6/62 that many families no longer needed 'to move from place to place for their livelihood and are anxious to settle' (ibid:3). The accommodation needs of Gypsies/Travellers were such that when sites were eventually built they quickly filled and supply did not satisfy demand. Additionally, some Local Authorities created a permanent site in order to accommodate a settled population already existing on 'temporary' sites which had few if any amenities – eg running water, electricity,

---

[2] The assumptions were extrapolated from interviews with paid and elected LA officers.

sewerage or refuse disposal. Thus some Local Authorities took the view that a 'permanent site' was a Council run, or private, site for an already settled group who had been living on an unauthorised site, and no others. Another view was/is that permanent sites are halting places in a specific place through which Gypsies/Travellers can legally pass, or stay, for short periods, en route to somewhere else. A third view represents permanent sites as a half-way measure towards permanent settlement in a house so that sites are used as 'holding' stations until some resolution is made with regard to accommodation of families that no-one seems to know what to do with. Some Officers and Councillors offered the somewhat bleak opinion that if Gypsies/Travellers chose to travel then that is something that they should do and no settlement provision needed to be made. The implication of this view is that Gypsies/Travellers are to be kept moving. Whilst the above are views emanating from policy-makers and practitioners they do not

Figure 1.1 Thought Trajectories – Gypsies/Travellers versus the Official Line of Thought

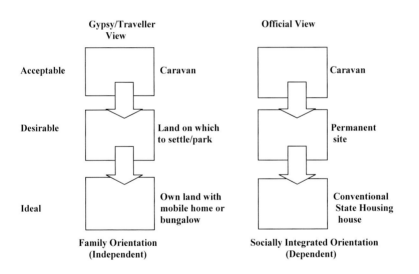

NB. This figure is based on the views expressed during interviews and site visits with Gypsies/Travellers and LA officers in Staffordshire

necessarily represent the views or ideas that Gypsies/Travellers have of permanent sites or settlement. Figure 1.1 attempts to show diagrammatically the two trajectories of thought, which appear not to be converging towards a common target/goal – which suggests a lack of communication between Local Authorities and Gypsies/Travellers.

This Figure can be read in several ways. First, two sets of views exist which are not converging in any useful way, although the end-play is similar: settlement in more permanent structures, often with a more permanent base. Second, that each group has its own view representing what is acceptable, desirable and/or ideal. The official view appears to will Gypsies/Travellers into conventional housing via the permanent site route but within a more socially integrated and dependent setting. Some Gypsies/Travellers on the other hand see settlement on a permanent site as a pathway towards their own land and complete independence. The Gypsy/Traveller trajectory appears to be frustrated by the planning system which refuses planning permission to build or set up sites, particularly in the Green Belt – where some families own land – unless a special case for doing so can be argued (ACERT 1999). This would be quite difficult to achieve in Staffordshire since all Councils expressed the sanctity of their Green Belts and Circular 1/94 had been interpreted to mean the removal of any 'special' privilege re site development. (However, this rule does not appear to be evenly applied in that 'exceptional' cases can be made by anyone building an 'exceptional' home in the Green Belt – ie those with deep pockets. It will be interesting to see if the Localism Act 2011 and the changes to the planning rules will have any impact on this particular game play. That said, some Gypsy/Traveller families appear to frustrate the official trajectory because the 'ideal option' on offer is either social housing or the private market (and whilst the latter scenario is advocated, game play ensures that its reality is checked). Self-help or private provision has become a euphemism for non-provision and for Gypsy/Traveller families to fend for themselves. Whilst some Gypsies/Travellers have invested in the private property market, this would be difficult for many given that a mortgage would be necessary. It would be interesting to discover whether banks or building societies lend to Gypsies/Travellers living on or off sites, who may wish to purchase with a mortgage.[3] A mortgage loan would be problematic for anyone without a

---

[3] Recently (2001) a piece of land in the Southeast was advertised for possible use as a caravan site for £220,000

12

bank account or a permanent address.[4] The solution for some on sites has been to purchase the more affordable 'mobile' chalet or pieces of land cheaply, that would, probably, never attract planning permission. Currently there are indications that those living on sites also own properties elsewhere. Others who live in houses also retain a pitch on a site as an insurance policy. (Fieldwork in Ankara found that some Roma who lived in a gececondu area, also owned a flat or another property in the city. This would equate with those in the majority population, particularly in UK, who own second homes or holiday properties.)

Third, it would appear that the aspirations of some Gypsies/ Travellers are higher than official aspirations for them. Many Gypsies/Travellers do not see social housing as their ideal end-play. Whilst Local Authorities continue to pitch provision and amenities at the lowest level for Gypsies/Travellers, the greater the divergence will be. Although Local Plans in Staffordshire emphasise the need for diversity in provision of accommodation and insist that private developers cater for a diversity of need in their plan, LAs have never entered into negotiations with developers to include Gypsy/Traveller accommodation as part of a planning proposal.[5] Although Gypsy/Traveller pressure groups had canvassed with regard to their needs/wants etc. formal needs surveys by LAs had not been undertaken at the time of writing the Thesis.[6] Part of the problem appeared to be that Gypsies/Travellers were (and still are) perceived not to be represented on a national or regional or even local scale. Thus their voice was often disregarded or their view was not sought by many LAs – at least in Staffordshire. In 2013 some Housing

---

[4] Site wardens and site managers claimed that residents tended not to keep bank accounts. This was supported by a resident on one site who claimed that life savings had been stolen from the caravan.
[5] Trading is now a common negotiation tool in the planning process. It is not unusual for developers to promise to build schools/village halls/roads in exchange for planning permission. In Calgary, Canada the Planning authority trades extra floors to multi-storey complexes in exchange for donations of works of art for the capital's museum. Keele Parish Council was tentatively offered a new village hall and a new village school in exchange for planning permission for house building on land alienated from agriculture after the building of a village by-pass. More recently Section 106 agreements have been a monetary exchange.
[6] Scotland and Northern Ireland have carried out needs surveys. One or two councils in England are beginning to follow suit. Ireland (DOE for Northern Ireland 1999) is returning to the notion of housing after an earlier programme of intermediary housing was abandoned. Then, Travellers were placed in tin huts to get used to living 'in a house'. This reminded me of the programme devised to house Australian Aborigines in the Northern Territory as part of a staged adaptation programme – in tin shacks when temperatures often reached 40C.

Associations who run sites attempt to engage residents with varying levels of success.

That said, the needs of the Gypsy/Traveller grouping, are as diverse as the families within it. Whilst the state attempts to sever 'tribal' affiliations, some families in Staffordshire viewed their group affiliations as an important means of support together with networks which appear important for survival in view of the open hostility from, and rejection by, many in majority society (fieldwork and conversations with families on site during site visits).

At present the State offers few alternatives. However, whilst Figure 1.1 does not intend to typologise all Gypsies/Travellers as desiring settlement, hopefully it does indicate (from observation and fieldwork in Staffordshire) particular moments in what appears to be a Gypsy/Traveller life-stage. In Staffordshire some families had clearly opted to stop travelling (for whatever reason) and some had taken legal action against one LA who was forcing them to move. The Figure also attempts to show a flow, which both sides must see as important if a 'pool' of frustration and log jams are to be avoided.

The 'Pool' of Frustration and the Log Jam

The UK State, via its capitalist mode of production, creates socio-economic hierarchies. At any level detachment from the system can occur when individuals/groups become 'frustrated' and see no advantage to remaining within the system or that it has become impossible for them to do so. Once detached (for whatever reason), individuals and groups are deemed to be 'outside' the system – ie moving from the general *habitus* and into another which either already exists, or the out-going group creates a new one. The notion of *habitus* will be discussed further in Chapter 3. The new/dislocated group has the potential to establish itself as a rival *habitus* which could, if new recruits are attracted in sufficient number, and if it is viewed as a viable alternative, subvert the status quo.[7] In many cases the state attempts to intervene to prevent such detachment/fragmentation from occurring to any great degree. However, in some instances divisions are caused *by* the State, when it ignores some issues until either they are brought (sometimes forcibly) to its attention, as 'a problem' which could threaten political or socio- economic stability.[8] Loyalty to the system (however irrational it might be) is often rewarded whilst 'detachment' is not.

It could be said that the perceived increase in the number of Irish Travellers and the increased size of groups in this category became a cause for concern particularly when encampments occurred in towns or on the outskirts of 'quiet' villages (1970s –1990s) (McKay 1996). Added to this was the perceived increase in numbers of New Travellers particularly in the Southwest of England (the domain of the affluent retired) and south east (the domain of the affluent upwardly mobile), and the advent of raves - again in the countryside (1980s/1990s) (McKay 1996). New Travellers began to increase the need for sites and fuelled by the media, fears grew, that this was a threat to the mainstream. It was not just house-dwellers who feared the new-comers. Aggressive Traveller groups began to displace families who had been on sites for some time, forcing them off and back onto the road (conversations with site residents). None of this pleased local house-dwellers who pressured their local Councils and MPs to remove any unauthorised sites. The issue of Gypsies/Travellers then became elevated to problem status and at a time when National Government was re-examining criminal justice and public order issues in the light of race riots, raves, prisoner protests and rising crime. This was also a period when legislation was being reviewed generally under the guise of being 'updated' (see the Hansard debates of the time).

Prior to the introduction of the CJPO Act (1994), the Department of the Environment, Transport and the Regions (DETR), later the Department of Transport, Local Government and the Regions (DTLR), then the Office of the Deputy Prime Minister (ODPM) and now the Department for Communities and Local Government D(CLG) biannual count figures showed an increase of unauthorised encampments in some areas. Given the slow, and in some cases, lack of response by some local Councils to the 1968 Caravan Sites and Control of Development Act this meant that new groups (New Travellers) were emerging before traditional groups had been satisfactorily accommodated and/or integrated. A need for sites had already been demonstrated in

---

[7] Religious sects, political parties, communes are cases in point.
[8] Rioting attributable to 'race' amongst other exclusionary factors are examples.

some areas, via waiting lists and settled unauthorised encampments. This was so in Staffordshire – as was the scenario whereby some LAs who had provided one site had no intention of providing more. A log jam was building.

Thus, when Gypsies/Travellers are refused planning permission on their own land, they cannot remain in 'unauthorised' occupation. Either families have to revert to Council sites or move on. Those trespassing on land were viewed as squatters and were evicted/moved on continually. Theirs is the choice of Council sites elsewhere or the prospect of remaining on the road. If Gypsies/Travellers remain on LA sites (and some live on sites longer than house dwellers remain in their houses,[9] and new sites or private sites are not built to cater for natural increase or for those coming off the road, saturation point is soon reached. Whilst this situation would not be tolerated in the conventional housing, or any other, sector, it appeared to be largely ignored in terms of accommodation for Gypsies/Travellers. Gypsies/Travellers living on Council sites were not offered the alternative of private site accommodation, other than self-help, when the duty for Local Authorities to provide was revoked and funding to build Council sites was withdrawn. And yet council tenants had this choice. Indeed, Council tenants were encouraged to buy their Council home. The option of buying a plot for Gypsies/ Travellers on Council sites was not contemplated in Staffordshire or elsewhere (Drakakis-Smith 2003). Whilst Housing Associations (HAs) later assumed the responsibility of housing provision from LAs they were not mandated to create caravan sites. They have, however, begun to take over the management of sites (eg Aspire in Newcastle-under-Lyme and the Avalon Housing Association). In many instances in Staffordshire, lack of provision appears to be used as a game, the rule being that it is cheaper and more politically expedient to keep families moving on, and to evict rather than make provision (fieldwork and interviews with LA Officers paid and elected).

---

[9] The ONS Social Trends (2002:172, No 32) found that 11% of English households (ie 2.3 million) had moved house in the past year (2000-2001); 50% of 16-24 year olds had been at their current address for less than one year (ibid:173). One-quarter of households who had moved had done so for job related reasons (Ibid:174). 48% in privately rented accommodation had been there for less than one year; 25% of all tenures had been in their accommodation for between 1-4 years (ibid:173). It would appear that the population in England is mobile. Their mobility is masked by the fact that people move but the house remains; Gypsies/Travellers are more noticeable because they take their homes with them.

This also served to disperse Gypsy/Traveller groups. Chapters 7, 8, 9 will elaborate on how this is achieved. Whilst every Local Plan in Staffordshire has elaborate projections for housing development based on assessment of diverse need, and often in the Green Belt, not one had, at the time of fieldwork, identified a site for Gypsies/Travellers (Local Plans will be discussed in Chapter 7).

Patterns of Mobility and Settlement

Figure 1.2 attempts to show the flow taking place within the Gypsy/Traveller trajectory from the point of view of those who are settled, those who might wish to settle, or who are trying to settle, and those who might not. Figure 1.2 also raises the issue of whether or not the core of Gypsies/Travellers is nomadic or settled. The bi-annual count figures demonstrated at the time, however, that the majority of Gypsies/ Travellers were settled on sites – mainly Council sites - although the number on private sites appeared to be growing. In 2002 the ODPM data for England were as follows: private authorised caravans 4660; Council authorised caravans 6178; unauthorised caravans 2774. If the total number of Gypsies/Travellers is, as estimated by Liegeois and Gheorghe (1995) to be 120,000, then a significant core of Gypsies/Travellers appear to be settled lawfully and

Figure 1.2 To Show the Pattern of Mobility/Settlement of Gypsies/Travellers, Hermeneutically

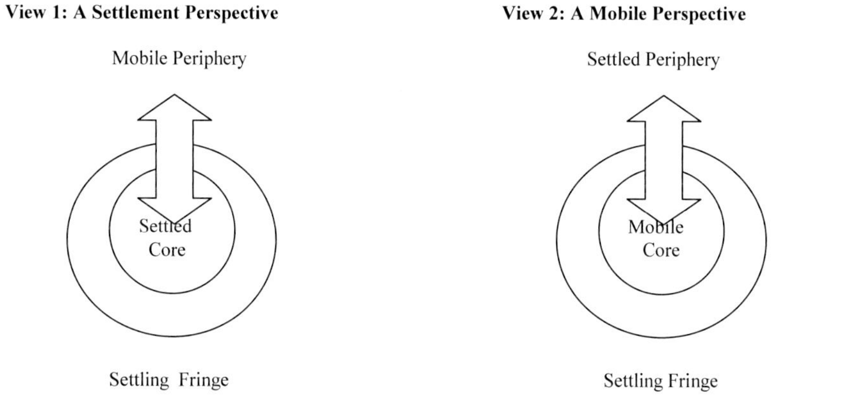

View 1: A Settlement Perspective

Mobile Periphery

Settled Core

Settling Fringe

View 2: A Mobile Perspective

Settled Periphery

Mobile Core

Settling Fringe

are not necessarily 'nomadic'. Chapter 5 will discuss further the ODPM/CLG bi-annual count of Gypsy caravans. It remains to be seen if the core of mobile groups would be reduced if more sites were provided or if planning permissions for caravans/mobile chalets were more forthcoming on privately owned land. The number of Gypsies/ Travellers in conventional housing is not known although more recently rough estimates are being attempted. Whether this settlement and/or mobility is chosen or forced, in Staffordshire, is a matter that the project wished to attempt to establish.

THE ORGANISATION OF THE PROJECT

The Thesis title *Moving On* attempted to encapsulate, first, that the mobility of some Gypsies/ Travellers which is often occasioned by the act of constant moving on and eviction from land, serves mainly to perpetuate socio-economic exclusion and a perceived identity as a mobile grouping. Second, that there is a need to move on and away from the current overall ways in which Gypsies/Travellers are perceived by majority society (often via the media lens), and away from the current negative policies for, and practices and service delivery towards them by all the levels of State. Third, that Gypsies/Travellers, too, have to move on. The world has changed and different strategies and approaches are needed in order to maximise opportunity. The need for useful dialogue, now, is pressing. The title of this monograph - *Policy in Motion* – attempts to point to the way that policy, when shackled by a silo mind set, and when it is in-accurately defined to meet need, and when resources, practice and service delivery are thus less than perfectly aligned then 'movement' takes place – not always in the right direction. Those who analyse policy are aware that often it can be no better than a juddering juggernaut stopping, starting and reversing so that it never quite reaches any destination.

Overall, an attempt was made to link three contexts which appeared to impact upon the Gypsy/Traveller *habitus*. The first context examined the intricate interplay between structure and agency and how each reinforced the other. From this, assumptions and theories were generated which fixed the game and which identified and classified the players. Such classifications, identifications and representations (usually by others) tend to influence the treatment of the target group and its life-world. As structures ossify certain behaviours are encouraged and perpetuated. To this end Bourdieu's notion of *habitus* was explored and discussed as a means of explaining this phenomenon with particular reference to the ways in which *habitus* is created and perpetuated and the ways in which individuals become emotionally attached to what they 'know', rejecting the unfamiliar and the hostile.

As cultures develop 'ways' emerge which may differ from the mainstream. Such norms, if dislocation is extreme, can become construed as 'ethnic'. Ethnicity becomes politicised producing a politics of difference which can lead to classification and stigmatisation. The works of Rex, Miles, Hall and Gilroy are useful here. When classification has been established (and this can often be an arbitrary process) sorting takes place, aided by policy and practice. Thus the second context examined the way in which legislation, policy, practice and service delivery interweaved to control the Gypsy/Traveller identity and *habitus*. An attempt was also made to fathom how far legislation was and is a managing tool and a structuring, culture-shaping exercise, which can, if inexpertly defined and interpreted, exacerbate the very situation it seeks to eliminate (Okely 1994; Murray 1996).

It is impossible to examine the Gypsy/Traveller situation without seeing it in the context of space and exclusion from it. Thus the third context was concerned with the way that Gypsies/Travellers were being organised and controlled within that space and /or excluded from it. Gypsy/Traveller caravans, and by inference Gypsies/Travellers themselves, are monitored in space and place by the bi-annual Gypsy caravan count. Whilst Sibley (1984a; 1984b) and Halfacree (1996) attempted to examine where Gypsies/Travellers were in space and place their geographical analysis was supported mainly by the bi-annual count data which, as Chapter 5 will hopefully demonstrate, provides a picture which is less than detailed or accurate. The data are used by the government Department concerned to test the effectiveness of government policy for Gypsies/Travellers and to assist the Planning Inspectorate in its deliberations when considering planning permission for permanent sites. The question raised was - how far are these figures factual or value laden?

To the above ends, Chapter Two explains and describes the methodology of the research project. Chapter Three assesses the theories which drove the project and which could apply to the Gypsy/Traveller situation, the better to explain it in sociological terms. Chapter Four examines notions of identity and the way in which Gypsies/Travellers are viewed as special cases for treatment. Chapter Five explores the mechanisms which organise space and the way in which Gypsies/Travellers are distributed within it, via an analysis of the Gypsy/Traveller caravan bi-annual count data. Chapters Six and Seven examine and evaluate policy for Gypsies/Travellers at national and local levels, whilst Chapters Eight and Nine evaluate practice, equality of opportunity and service delivery for Gypsies/ Travellers in Staffordshire. Does practice and service delivery match and meld with policy or are important elements lost in translation?

There is no separate literature review chapter. Instead, the literature consulted and the literature on a particular topic will be discussed as those topics arise within the thesis. The remainder of this chapter will locate the Thesis within Staffordshire.

LOCATING THE PROJECT

Locating Staffordshire

Although Staffordshire is associated mainly with the pottery industry, and until recently with the coal mining and iron and steel industries, much of this has taken place in the north and south of the county. Otherwise, Staffordshire is mainly rural. It is situated on the edge of what the local Staffordshire Tourist Boards call the Heart of England, and it lies within the West Midlands Region (see Map 1.1a).

However, the whole of this midland region is crossed by a network of roads which link Birmingham and the Black Country, Liverpool, Manchester Stockport, Leeds, Bradford, Huddersfield, Sheffield, Derby, Nottingham, Leicester – an impressive (black) diamond configuration - to London and the south east. Wales forms the western border of the region. All these roads traverse Staffordshire and historically Staffordshire appeared to be the conduit for the flow of armies, traffic and goods north-south and east-west (Greenslade and Stuart 1998; Maps 1.1a and 1.1b). It would be expected that Gypsies/Travellers would use these routes also.

Map 1.1a To Show The Geographical Location of Staffordshire

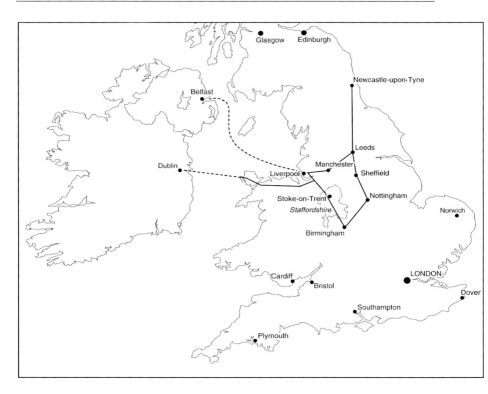

Greenslade and Stuart (ibid) portray Staffordshire as a geographical entity, however, socio-politically and economically it is diverse. The division of the County during the English Civil War has left its mark[10] in that until recently the north was predominantly

---

[10] The Parliamentarians dominated in the north whilst the Royalists held sway in the south.

Labour (mainly old Labour), the south Conservative. Today (2013) there is more of a political mix veering towards Conservative/Liberal Democrat coalitions with some labour strongholds remaining, although reduced, in the north. The more recent Boundary Commission suggested changes might, if realised, further erode the Labour hold in the north. Political orientation and alignment of Local Authorities to that of National

Map 1.1b To Show The Major Routeways Traversing Staffordshire

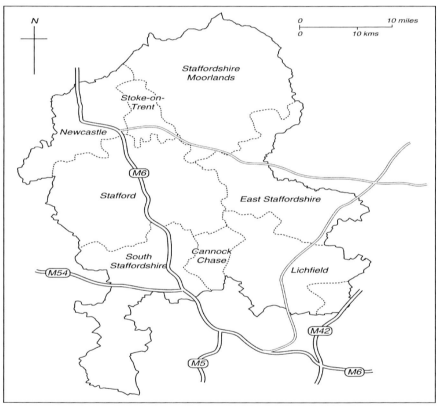

Government is important and can determine co-operation, compliance and where national resources may be allocated first.

For clarification, there are two categories of 'sites': the first refers to the physical location of LA offices and their hinterland. The second to the Gypsy/Traveller sites within these Local Authorities. The following descriptions of the LA 'sites' are based on a 'visual' assessment, combined with information from their various Local Development Plans/Structure Plans, historical and geographical literature, local knowledge and fieldwork. An ultimate assessment would be their acceptance of Gypsies/Travellers and whether or not Gypsies/Travellers would wish to live in or resort to this particular area. The accessibility of LAs was important.

Council Accessibility
The majority of Councils interpreted their accessibility to their constituents via displays of leaflets, pamphlets, newspapers, Local and Development Plans, Minutes of Cabinet and Council meetings, mission statements; small exhibitions in the foyer and in department reception areas; in local newspapers and in their own specially produced news-sheets; and more latterly its web sites[11] as a means to advertise their services. In the main, this literature produced fell into two categories:- the informative: how the Council worked, what its intentions were, how to make planning applications, how to complain, what constituents' rights were, what the 'rules' were (in layman's terms), bus time-tables and What's On etc; and the self-congratulatory: what the Council was doing for its constituents and how well it was doing it. One would need, however, to be literate or own a computer in order to access much of the material. This is imperative in 2013 since much of LA material is now posted on their web site.

More recently physical access for disadvantaged groups - the physically disabled in particular[12] - was being addressed. All but one Council headquarters was situated in the centre of the town. However, Council Offices can still be formidable places for those unfamiliar with bureaucracy and attitudes of some staff can be off-putting.

---

[11] Only Lichfield did not have its own web site at the time.
[12] Many pamphlets on planning and well-being issues had been translated into ethnic minority languages. Some LAs had gone further to produce videos and tape recordings.

Locating The Ten Local Authorities

Staffordshire County Council is based in Stafford, a prosperous market town in the centre of the County. It has two Gypsy/Traveller sites. Their management is devolved to Newcastle-under-Lyme and Stafford Borough Councils respectively. Table 1.1 shows the ethnic breakdown of the Staffordshire population in 2002. Apart from Stoke-on-Trent City Council and East Staffordshire, the ethnic population was very small. Gypsies/Travellers comprise an even smaller sub-grouping.

The economic complexion of Staffordshire is mixed. By the year 2000 mainly all the national coal mines in Stoke-on-Trent, Newcastle-under-Lyme and Cannock had been closed and the pottery industry was in sharp decline. The manufacture of iron and steel was also abandoned in the north. The brewing industry of East Staffordshire was somewhat uncertain (Bass having been taken over by Belgian Interbrew, The Times 15/6/2000) and the silk milling of Staffordshire Moorlands had vanished. (There are current discussions to reintroduce this activity.) Thus Staffordshire suffered high unemployment in areas which were reliant upon those industries. In some cases whole villages and communities found themselves economically 'redundant'.

Table 1:1: Ethnic Breakdown of Population in Staffordshire 2002

Council	Total Population	White %	Ethnic Minority%	Gypsy/Traveller (Caravans)
Staffordshire	1098967	98.2	1.8	265*
Staffs Moorlands	95000	99.6	.4	1
Stoke-on-Trent	254400	96.9	3.1	66
Newcastle-under-Lyme	123000	98.9	1.2	22
Stafford	120000	98.3	1.7	47
Lichfield	97019	99.5	.5	7
Tamworth	76000	98.9	1.1	0
Cannock	106048	99.2	.8	28
South Staffordshire	123770	98.9	1.1	71
East Staffordshire	103730	95.8	4.2	23

Source: The population figures are derived from council web sites as council estimates for 2002 and from Staffordshire County Council projections based on the 2001 Census figures. Ethnic population percentages are derived from the 2001 Census (OPCS). Figures for Gypsies/Travellers are derived from the DTLR Bi-Annual Count January 2002.
* approximately 530 persons based on 2 persons per caravan

All LAs, therefore, were restructuring their economic base. Stoke-on-Trent as a now Unitary Authority and University city, is opting for 'smart', light and service industry. Somewhat belatedly, it is gradually taking on the mantle of a cosmopolitan city. Together with East Staffordshire it has the highest ethnic minority population. Newcastle-under-Lyme, a market town, has had some of its rough edges removed by the presence of an expanding University (Keele), a large teaching hospital and a prosperous rural hinterland. With the additional presence of a busy motorway station, Newcastle-under-Lyme is seemingly prosperous. It is now reliant on light industry, distribution (the shed economy) and services. North Staffordshire was earmarked in the West Midlands Regional Planning Guidance Review (Draft November 2001) as a Regeneration Zone and Agenda for Action Site; an Objective 2 area, a Regional Investment site, a Regional Logistics Centre and a Strategic Centre – all geared towards inward investment and growth. Today (2013) its economy and growth is less assured with the near collapse of the pottery industry and the withdrawal of its Renew funding.

Stafford, in the middle of the County, is the seat of administration accommodating the County Council and the Staffordshire Police Headquarters. It is surrounded by prosperous farming villages. Its history and buildings make it a tourist draw along with Lichfield, a cathedral city. Lichfield has been described as 'the centre of polite society' (Greenslade 1990:3). Tamworth and South Staffordshire have been created from an amalgam of small villages. Tamworth, as a new town, is also a development centre and much of its land is earmarked for development or held speculatively for that purpose. South Staffordshire is a rural overspill area for the Birmingham conurbation. Seventy-five per cent of the South Staffordshire population commuted elsewhere for employment (South Staffordshire Health Authority 1995).

Whilst overall Staffordshire could be construed as economically 'comfortable', pockets of deprivation and poverty exist in varying degrees in the north (Stoke-on-Trent and Newcastle-under-Lyme) and in the southeast (Tamworth, Cannock and Burton-on-Trent). Because of its past industrial base the north west and south east of the County are in a state of flux. It also means that need has been constrained to these areas, leaving a prosperous, green and pleasant central swathe.

Whilst a socio-economic north south divide appears to exist, a political north-south divide has become blurred with time. At the time the research was undertaken, seven Councils in Staffordshire were Labour controlled. The May 2002 local elections reduced the Labour majorities in Newcastle-under-Lyme and Stoke-on-Trent. Both became hung Councils. Of the three remaining Councils, two remained Conservative – South Staffordshire and Lichfield - with reduced majorities; Staffordshire Moorlands Council was run by a joint Rate Payer and Conservative coalition - and this too was a hung Council. The political complexion was likely to change in the following year when the second wave of clean sweep elections would take place in the rest of the County.

Provision of Gypsy/Traveller sites did not necessarily correspond to political persuasion, since the majority of sites occurred in the south where South Staffordshire had 30 per cent of all the sites in the County. However, in terms of site status the majority of private sites were found in the south in South Staffordshire District Council, whilst the majority of Council run/controlled sites were found in the north eg Stoke-on-Trent and Newcastle-under-Lyme. Stafford in the centre had a mixture – one Council site and 4 private sites.

The second category of locations are Gypsy/Traveller sites.

Locating Gypsy/Traveller Sites
At the time there were, 37 authorised sites in Staffordshire. In all, 26 sites were visited between November 1998 and May 1999. Unauthorised sites were visited in Stoke-on-Trent, Newcastle-under-Lyme and Tamworth. I was informed that Lichfield and Staffordshire Moorlands Councils had no sites. Lichfield in fact had two sites - Council Officers no longer regarded them as Gypsy/Traveller sites because of their longevity (Senior Officer, Interview). I was refused permission to visit the private Burton-on-Trent site on the grounds that it might cause trouble! (Officer Interview). Several private sites in South Staffordshire were not visited because they were single pitch sites. It was felt that this omission would not detract from the overall impression of site provision. Some sites were difficult to find and to access. The County accommodates a total of 333 pitches (double and single).

All LA Officers involved kept records of permanent sites and some records of unauthorised sites. The regularity of site visits varied from LA to LA and depended upon whether site licenses needed renewing, or whether complaints about non-compliance with the site regulations/license etc. had been received (Licensing Officer, Interview). Officers also knew the location of 'traditional' stopping places. Until recently the word 'tolerated' was used for sites usually of long duration without planning permission/site licenses. Some objected, rightly, to this tag but its use persisted until recently. They are now termed 'permitted' sites.

'Preventative' work had been undertaken by LAs in order to prohibit illegal encampments - ditching, mounding, fencing, tree planting, bollards, etc. on these sites (see Figure 1:3). Communication is such that few Gypsies/Travellers could remain illegally camped on private or public land for long, without the council or police being informed. Officers claimed that the period was from 2 to 12 hours at the most.

Figure 1.3 LA Preventative Measures

The majority of sites bordered, or were within the Green Belt and tended to be on land which was, for the moment, surplus to development requirements. Some permissions had been granted before Green Belt legislation. The majority were in areas where other 'development' occurred. For example, in Newcastle-under-Lyme the site was located on the edge of a large marl quarry where extraction of clay was still taking place. Today, this quarry has been replaced by a refuse in-fill site. The Stoke-on-Trent site was adjacent to a farm and a working abattoir, set in countryside yet within walking distance of Tunstall, one of the six pottery towns. The Stafford site was the only urban site, fairly close to the town centre, and at the time surrounded by a GEC generator works, old gas works, a traction equipment plant and a Sainsbury supermarket. The other three sites in Stafford Borough were situated in the village of Hopton. Although this was a pleasant, rural location, the sites were adjacent to a large RAF hangar. Local residents in houses also lived in its shadow. In Cannock one site was situated on disused Coal Board land - this was a permitted site without any amenities (apart from a telephone line which had recently been installed by the LA) - and the other was an authorised private site on the grass-verged area of a main road. Unauthorised sites existed on private land adjacent to Sainsbury's, and at regular intervals, which I did not visit. In Tamworth the situation existed whereby a 'tolerated group' (as opposed to a 'tolerated site') were moved on weekly/fortnightly by the Council. They had been in the area for ten years (at least) and wished to stay in the area. In December 1999 I visited them on a disused factory site. In March 2000 they were positioned under a motorway fly-over. They had been removed (via a Local Authority injunction) from Tamworth and had removed to Lichfield where they were about to be removed (December 2001). By 2012 the family had purchased a plot of land and in 2011 had received planning permission for a site. Whilst on holiday the site had been trashed so the family could not use it. Since then they have lived in houses and other rented accommodation in Lichfield and elsewhere (Officer Interview).

Most of the sites in South Staffordshire were on green field sites. A group of sites at Coven were close to the local prison. The site at Cavenswood was close to a disused colliery on the edge of Cannock Chase, although the area had now been landscaped and reclaimed as Chase land. All sites were within an eleven mile radius of the M6, M54 and M5 and A5 (see Map1:1b).

Whilst unauthorised sites are neither liked nor permitted, they appear to be 'tolerated' for a short period of time. The length of time varied from one LA to another and depended upon the toleration levels of local Councillors and whether or not the sites caused 'a nuisance'. This too was dependent upon the proximity to and the sensitivities of local residents. Table 1:2 shows site location, site status and number of sites.

In terms of site management there is a clear division between the north and south of the

Table 1.2   Site Status

Location	Local Authority	Number of Sites	Management
North	Newcastle	1	Housing Trust
North	Staffs Moorlands	1	Private
North	Stoke-on-Trent	2	LA managed with site warden and Gypsy Council
		2	Private
		1	Transit Site
Mid	Stafford	4	1 LA managed 3 private
		1	'tolerated'
	Lichfield	1	Private
Mid		1	'tolerated'
		1	Unauthorised
Mid	East Staffordshire	1	Private
	Tamworth	1	Unauthorised
South			
South	Cannock	2	'tolerated'
		1	Private
South	South Staffordshire	12	Private
		3	Private transit*
		2	Unauthorised
		1	'tolerated'

Source: Fieldwork and County Council records

NB   Unauthorised sites mentioned in the text have not been included.

* One site is purely transit, the other two have transit provision of between 3 and 15 pitches

29

County. In the north, the Stoke-on-Trent and Newcastle-under-Lyme sites were, until recently, Council managed. In April 2000, Newcastle-under-Lyme Housing Department became a private Housing Trust and all Council housing stock, including the permanent Gypsy/Traveller site was transferred to that Trust, now called Aspire Housing (a Housing Association). Similarly in January 1998, Stoke-on-Trent City Council entered into a three-way partnership with the National Gypsy Council and the newly appointed Site Warden (a Traveller) to run their refurbished and extended site at Linehouses which includes a transit site. The extra pitches (12) made this site one of the largest in the country (66 pitches) at the time. The management arrangements for this site were up for renewal in 2012.

In the south of the County, sites were privately owned and mainly family grouped. Some sites were run commercially by Gypsies/Travellers themselves. These were chalet parks which accommodated a mixture of people, namely the elderly and/or retired - the private chalet proving a cheap alternative to conventional housing. Some sites included some provision for Gypsies/Travellers. Whilst in the north the caravan dominated - although over time this had become larger and more luxurious - in the south the mobile chalet was the norm. The transit site in the south was also private.

The chalet parks were laid out in the manner of a small housing estate with tarmacced driveways and roads, street lighting, gardens, tree planting and fencing (see Figure 1:4). The cost of the chalets ranged from £30,000 upwards - although I was informed that a luxurious 'state-of-the-art German or Canadian caravan could cost around £30,000 (Gypsy/Traveller interview).

The reasons for South Staffordshire's high number of caravan parks were: the area's natural beauty - people from the urban areas had always used it as a caravan holiday venue; and historical - the air base in the area had established a precedent and a need for temporary accommodation for a mobile population of service men and their families. Many sites were post war, would have been cheap to establish, and to rehouse a decanted population, whilst the nearby inner city areas, damaged after the Second World War,

Figure 1.4 Private Sites (Gypsy/Traveller Owned) in Staffordshire

were being regenerated and new housing suburbs created in the 1950s and 1960s.
However like most 'temporary' accommodation it had remained. The units have been
upgraded and replaced over time and the sites refurbished so that they remain a desirable
alternative. Part of the up-dating and modernisation of the sites included ownership by
Gypsies/Travellers. On some sites Gypsies/Travellers lived in large brick houses or
bungalows which had been purchased with the site, or built afterwards. On a smaller,
family, private site, the Gypsy/Traveller owner was rebuilding a derelict cottage for his
own use.

Sites and site management will be further discussed in Chapter 9 (Service Delivery).

The Residents

Residents on sites spanned the economic spectrum from very wealthy to very poor.
Those in the south of the County appeared, in the main, to be more affluent than those in
the north. This was demonstrated in their accommodation - large chalets, and their
vehicles - some drove convertible Mercedes or Shogun Land Cruisers with the latest
registration numbers. Some residents, in the north, especially, however, had no vehicle

of their own. This diversity was further reflected in terms of being literate and articulate, although even those who spoke in a different register (see also Bernstein's notion of 'restricted codes' (1960)) were able to get their message across and certainly articulated their needs to me without difficulty. Some were very interested and tried to help whilst others were not and walked away. The residents I met ranged from elderly single to young and middle aged with families; the retired to the employed and self-employed and unemployed; from Irish families to 'traditional' Gypsies, although few used the term Romani unless prompted. Some living on sites were not Gypsies/Travellers at all. Some sites had lots of children whilst others had few. Although rules of sites include the rule that all children will go to school, when I visited there were many children on site - it was not a weekend or a school holiday and they did not appear to be ill.

Some of the caravans/chalets I visited were very comfortable with bathrooms and fitted kitchens, rugs and carpets, washing machines and refrigerators. The interiors were decorated with bone china and crystal glass ornaments - even in the kitchen. There were, however, caravans which had few facilities and it was difficult to see where the occupants sat or slept. For the majority of families, cleanliness was a high priority.

Some residents were not discontent with their lot whilst others wanted or wished for something better. It appeared that those on private sites were more in control of their physical surroundings and residents who owned their site spoke enthusiastically of the facilities and the future plans for the sites. On several of the private sites I visited building and refurbishment were underway. On Council sites, the main complaints were that the Council did not listen, that 'things' needed to be done and that the Council was very slow to carry out this work (Interview with Residents).

CHAPTER TWO

METHODOLOGY

The methodology for the Thesis fell naturally into two parts. One part was the literature/document study which came partly in the form of legislation and policy, which was both historical and contemporary. This was used as a bench mark against which any action and provision could be measured and balanced via the second part – fieldwork - which included interviews and site visits, and participant observation. The policy/ documentation/ literature/historical study was also used as a basis for deconstructing 'accepted' knowledge which has influenced debates past and present.

THE PROJECT

It was recognised that the general hypothesis for the Thesis included two unequal subjects diverse 'groups' of Gypsy/Traveller families, many of whom were 'outside' or inhabited the margins of the system, and LAs, who *were* the system. The latter - the gate-keepers - controlled entry, whilst the former - those at the gate - requested/demanded it. Given the research questions, an investigation seemed necessary of the power vested in LAs, their mechanisms of power formulation via policy, and the ways in which this policy was served to the target group, either as an attempt to satisfy need and/or to keep them in check. As the powerful were in a position to create/change/reverse policy and practice, it was considered that this is where the focus of the study should be, and that Gypsies/ Travellers would act as a witness/focus group where necessary. The thesis takes the Foucauldian view that 'power should be examined in its practice and not just in its intent', that it should be 'a study of power … at the point where it is in direct and immediate relationship with that which … we call its object, its target, its field of application' (Foucault 1980:97).

To this end the project sought evidence[13] which would provide a case to be argued. This would not be a 'trial' (except for the reader) but an inquiry - not into individual behaviour as such, but into the way in which individuals contribute via the roles the powerful are requested or paid to perform within the system. The way, and why, this is done contributes to the ethos/culture of an institution (Stapeley 1996) and to a system of policy, practice and service delivery to Gypsies/Travellers which Councils oversee and express. Bearing in mind that LAs are duty bound to national legislation and National Government agendas, it is not the intention of this project to apportion blame but to identify injustices where they might occur. However, it is often at the local level of operation where injustices are perpetrated. Whilst Staffordshire is spotlighted here, there is evidence to suggest that this County is not alone in its methods or structuring structures which keep some Gypsies/Travellers on the periphery and moving. It is, at this stage, a hypothesis that this structured response contributes to the production of a particular milieu in which Gypsies/Travellers operate – and about which questions need to be asked.

Overall, the project was an in-depth study of the way that Local Authorities in the county of Staffordshire have responded and are responding to their Gypsy/Traveller population who live in and/or resort to the area. The study was opportune given that more responsibility was being devolved to the local level and the abolition of the County tier was being considered at the time in favour of Regional Councils. However, this process which seemed likely to commence in the North East has now, in 2013, appeared to have been removed from the National agenda in favour of 'Localism' and 'The Big Society' - whatever these might mean in practice.

There were ten LAs in all to cover, which included the County Council. Given the amount of information needed to drive the thesis and given that the project's aims - an examination, analysis and evaluation of policy, practice and service delivery within a

---

[13] However in English law there has been 'an exclusionary approach to evidence' (Murphy1995:2). The evidence cited in this thesis will adhere to the types of legal evidence permitted eg direct, circumstantial, hearsay, primary, prima facie, conclusive, oral and documentary.

discreet geographical area - a qualitative approach was taken. However, given some of the statistical information available – for example the bi-annual Gypsy/Traveller caravan count – and given that the sample study for interviewing would be over 30 - it was recognised that the qualitative material could be strengthened by quantitative analysis. More than 80 in-depth interviews were conducted. The shortest was 30 minutes, the longest 3.5 hours (the norm was around 1.5 - 2 hours). Some interviewees were re-contacted for clarification, further or updated information.

Ten formal interviews were conducted with Gypsies/Travellers on five sites in the County (three LA managed and two privately owned and managed) and informal 'conversations' took place during other site visits. Site visits were usually of half a day's duration on each site. Twenty-six sites were visited throughout the County. Some sites were revisited during the course of fieldwork. The 'conversations' were held with site owners, Site Wardens and residents.

Information for the main part of the study was gathered primarily from individuals who made and implemented policy. Given that both the spoken and written word can be charged with as much fact as value, and given that the Interviewer would also be confronted with the 'personal' versus the 'official' view point – and that neither might be reliable – I was aware that such 'evidence' would have to be cross-checked, using other methods. That 'no methodological criteria is capable of guaranteeing the absolute accuracy of research' (Henwood and Pidgeon 1993:23) presented the researcher with a challenge.

Given that two LAs would be revisited this proved an opportunity to set up a (partial) longitudinal comparison. It was therefore decided to treat the MA study as a pilot study and to refine and extend the methodology. This meant maintaining the 'triangulation' method (after Mason 1996a) - of interviews, documentation/historical study, analysis of secondary data and observation. It was felt that this would provide a sufficient methodological variety to support the breadth of the study in terms of time, space, structure and agency.

It was decided that an interview guide would be a starting point to gather 'inside' anecdotal and factual information on how the Council operated; a standard questionnaire was deemed insufficiently robust to deal with the diversity within and between Councils, which had become apparent at the preliminary interview stage. Neither would it provide the detail needed for a proper assessment and analysis of the situation. To become as fully informed as possible, it was necessary to obtain 'deep' information. The preliminary interviews were used to gather first level information and a feel for the game. Although a provisional checklist of topics had been prepared, respondents were given a free hand to 'pack' this stage of 'the conversation'. The formal interview provided an opportunity to 'deepen' the relationship and information. At this point the questions were a general tour of each Council and its operations. These were regarded as basic, practical questions, which would later feed into larger questions, and fell roughly into the following categories:

HOW – how personnel dealt with Gypsies/Travellers and Gypsy/Traveller issues; how are Gypsies/Travellers identified and distinguished from other caravan dwellers?

WHAT - were the Council's policies (if any) and practices; what were the attitudes of Councils and Officers towards Gypsies/Travellers – particularly towards mobile groups; what was the political bias of the Council; what influenced policies and practice for Gypsies/Travellers particularly at the local level; what were the real/perceived problems faced by Council/Officers and Gypsies/Travellers; what provision (if any) was made by the Council for Gypsies/Travellers in Staffordshire?

WHO - dealt with Gypsies/Travellers and these issues within the line-management of the Council; who did personnel perceive their client group to be - ie who did what for whom; who made policy; who translated it into practice?

WHERE - sites were and their status; where the Council targeted its resources for Gypsies/Travellers; where did major problems lie?

WHY - were numbers of Gypsies/Travellers stable in the County/this Council; how deep was any antagonism towards Gypsies/Travellers?

Once collected, a comparison and contrast of the information from each Council was made intra-murally, which would also enable a wider Officer/Council extra-mural comparison. The interview questions grew from the above and were informed by second-tier research questions listed below.

Research Questions to be Addressed by the Fieldwork

It was envisaged that the fieldwork, would attempt to address and inform some of the following research questions – which were general and specific, load-bearing and informing questions. Some of these were raised by the MA study, in which case, the Ph D project assessed the extent to which they applied to the rest of Staffordshire. It was hoped that responses to these would inform even 'bigger' questions:

Policy: What are the policies for and practice and service delivery to Gypsies/Travellers in Staffordshire? How is policy formulated? Does it match National Government policy? How familiar were LAs with National policy?

Does National policy translate easily/faithfully/ into Local policy? Where do problems lie?

To what extent might policy/practice create two categories of Gypsy/Traveller - the traditional/settled (desirable) the new and mobile (undesirable)?

What are the end products of policies/practices and service delivery – inclusion or exclusion? What are its effects on the lives of Gypsies/Travellers?

How does policy, practice and service delivery affect Gypsies/Travellers in terms of space and place within LAs and within the County?

Working relationship: What is the working relationship between Local, National and Regional Government?

What is the working relationship between Gypsies/Travellers and LAs in Staffordshire? What, if any, are the 'games' played by both Gypsies/Travellers and LAs?

Identity: Does policy/practice create/contribute to identity or is identity simply a matter of individual choice? Does identity/identification once expressed affect policy/practice?

Nomadism: Why were Gypsies/Travellers 'nomadic'?

Is this a habit of life – an essentialist quality – as legislation suggests, or an enforced habit, which prevents settlement and integration except on 'the system's' terms?

What influence does this term have, when associated with Gypsies/Travellers, on policy, practice and service delivery?

Rational choices: How rational are choices/decisions made on behalf of and geared towards Gypsies/Travellers, nationally and by Local Councils in Staffordshire? How far do such choices (help to) satisfy need – and whose need? Are LAs aware of Gypsy/Traveller needs?

Socio-economic inclusion/exclusion: How far and in what ways are Gypsies/Travellers socially and economically included/excluded from mainstream society via policy practice and service delivery? Is inclusion/exclusion a matter of choice and which party chooses (the 'them 'or the 'us')?

THE SEMI-STRUCTURED INTERVIEW SCHEDULE AND FIELDWORK
The Informal Pre-Interviews

The preliminary interviews were used to introduce myself and the project to potential respondents and to speak with key LA personnel, informally, about the work they did and the problems and scenarios they encountered when they and Gypsies/Travellers interacted - if they interacted at all. At this stage I needed to know how each LA functioned in relation to Gypsies/ Travellers - ie what was their strategy and line management in terms of policy, practice and service delivery, particularly in the light of current and recent national legislation, Circulars and Guidance and current/pending and recent Local Government re-organisation. I also needed to know who was responsible for policy creation and service delivery. The preliminary interviews were important in that they would provide:

a) information that would enable me (hopefully) to construct a comprehensive and informed suite of questions for mainline interviewing which would be conducted after site visits.

b) The interview would be the basis for beginning a working relationship with the LA and its personnel - paid and elected. From them I would need to obtain, at some point, detailed information - possibly sensitive material which might not be kept on official files (or even on file).

c) It was hoped too, that I would be given names of other staff who dealt with Gypsy/Traveller issues, not necessarily within the LA, i.e. within the Health, Education and Social Service arenas. I was relying therefore on accumulative networking (snow-balling) particularly in LAs where there appeared to be some uncertainty (when cold-calling departmental Secretaries) as to who dealt with what.

Preliminary Interview Set-up

Preliminary interviews were with senior, paid, LA staff who were responsible for Gypsy/Traveller issues. These took place between December 1998 and May 1999. The process began with a standard letter of introduction in October 1998 and a request to each Chief Executive of each LA in Staffordshire (10 in all) for permission to interview staff who dealt with Gypsy/Traveller issues. Some LAs responded promptly and contact was made with those staff. At that time there was only one LA which gave the impression that it did not wish to participate. Later, a telephone conversation was held with a paid member of that Council, which was sufficiently informative to pass for a preliminary interview. I did not site visit in that LA on its request. Where I had to arrange meetings with staff via Secretaries, the assumption was that my interest in Gypsies/Travellers was solely to lodge a complaint against them! During the preliminary interview stage other individuals who also dealt with Gypsy/Travellers issues were identified.

The questions in the interview suite, which formed the main body of the study, grew from the above informal pre-interviews. Interviews were conducted with personnel nominated by the LA who were deemed to 'know' or to be involved with Gypsy/Traveller issues within each Council. From these I learned of others. The pre-interviews were not recorded, but notes were taken. These interviews were either accompanied by site visits then or later. The preliminary interviews assisted with my orientation of the location of the LA geographically, politically and structurally. Each Council was ordered differently, with different departments and levels of personnel dealing with Gypsy/Traveller issues. An attempt was made to accommodate this within the interview schedule. It was also noted how easy (or not) Departments/personnel were to access.

Gypsy/Traveller Site Visits

Site visits were an opportunity for me to *see* for myself what LAs had provided for Gypsies/Travellers or had permitted and to match this with what I would be told during interviews. It was also an opportunity to meet and informally converse with site residents. Their view would balance that given by Council Officers and others in 'the system'. In some, but not all instances, and especially where sites were small, I spoke with most residents, some of whom were owners or site wardens. Some wished to speak at length and air particular grievances and/or concerns.

The visits were also an opportunity to identify sites and residents for more formal interviews.

The site visits - to Council, private and permitted/unauthorised sites - showed the location, standard, variety of site and were systematically recorded on a pro forma sheet. In a less systematic way the socio-economic and 'cultural' differences between residents were also noted. Sites were visited in: Stoke-on-Trent (2) where, the main site, which had recently been extended, comprised a permanent site and a transit site. The third site in Stoke-on-Trent was an unauthorised site. Newcastle-under-Lyme (1 LA managed and 2 unauthorised), Stafford (1 LA managed and 3 private), South Staffordshire (12 all private, 1 private transit), Cannock (1 private and 1 permitted), Tamworth (1) which was an unauthorised site. (see Table 1.2 above). Apart from the Newcastle-under-Lyme authorised site and the Tamworth unauthorised site, I was accompanied by a Local Authority Officer on first visits - the Gypsy Liaison Officer (Stoke-on-Trent), the Planning Enforcement Officer (Cannock), Principal Health and Safety Officer (South Staffordshire), Site Manager (Stafford). Initially it was thought that this might inhibit what residents might have to say. However, in most cases this did not appear so in terms of what some residents had to say about the site/Council. Where residents appeared to have problems with the Council, or where reticence was noted, I returned alone to the site. Description of sites and provision will be discussed further in successive Chapters.

The Interview Suite and Semi-Structured Questionnaire Suite

The final data gathering used the alternative approach of semi-structured in-depth interviews. Different questions were drawn up for different levels of staff in Council management lines (eg Directors of Departments, Enforcement Officers, Site Wardens etc) who would have different fragments of information to place in the Council/system jigsaw. In order to generate data, an attempt was made to include some core questions that all would be able to answer generally and/or collectively (eg all Officers who made the bi-annual caravan count were asked a particular set of questions, which related specifically to what they did). Relevant paid and elected Officers of each Council were interviewed. Questions were gathered under main topic headings in order to orient the respondent – after Foddy's topic/applicablity/perspective (TAP) model- and to assist with the eventual analysis of data. The questions were a mixture of open, closed (Foddy 1992:152) buffer (ibid: 63) and core questions (ibid:129). In this respect questions were both general and specific in the hope that they would allow 'grand and mini-tour' (after Jorgenson 1989) exploration. Description and contrast questions (after Burgess 1984) were also included. In some instances the same questions were placed in different contexts in the interview suite to see if they would elicit a different level of response. The same suite of interview questions was administered to each Council. Respondents were given space for self-evaluation.

The interview attempted to discover not only how structure and agency might impact on target groups (eg. Gypsies/Travellers) when mixed with policy and practice, but how efficient the internal structure was; for example, was the management efficient in terms of passing information up/down the line; how efficient was the translation of legislation into workable policy and what were the mechanisms of practice and service delivery?

The Conduct of Council Interviews

The project was outlined to all respondents – LA personnel and Gypsies/Travellers. Their questions were also invited. It was intended that the interview would be 'active' after the Holstein and Gubrium (1995) model thus the 'interview' was more a 'conversation with a guiding purpose' (ibid:76). Each interview was tape recorded and transcribed, partly to ensure a greater degree of accuracy. The interview could be 'revisited' to check any queries/uncertainties; a language analysis could also be attempted where necessary. It also meant that as in any conversation, supplementary questions could be asked which would be recorded. Each section sought to discover how the respondent understood the key concept of the section eg did they know what the policy for Gypsies/Travellers was Nationally/Locally; what did they understand by equality of opportunity etc.? The section headings were given before questions were asked.

The Interview Sample – Council Officers

The ten LAs studied in Staffordshire were: Staffordshire County Council, Staffordshire Moorlands District Council, Stoke-on-Trent City Council (Unitary Authority), Newcastle-under-Lyme Borough Council, Stafford District Council, Cannock Chase District Council, Lichfield District Council, Tamworth Borough Council, Lichfield District Council, East Staffordshire Borough Council, South Staffordshire District Council.

Respondents from each Council (paid and elected Officers who deal with G/T issues) were interviewed between 1999 and 2000. Chief Executives, relevant DTLR personnel and Staffordshire MPs (who agreed) were interviewed in 2001.

The warm-up questions attempted to discover what experience Officers had with Gypsies/Travellers, whether or not they had received any special training and what their qualifications were. Within the higher ranks at Head of Department and Principle Officer level, Officers had either degrees or diplomas in their field (ie Environmental Health or Planning). All but one of the Senior Officers interviewed were male. One had a Police background. Of the nine Enforcement/Counting Officers two were female.[14] None of the respondents had had any special training in dealing with Gypsies/Travellers. Their knowledge was based on 'experience' of doing the job and/or induction by the previous post-holder.

---

[14] One left the post just after interview and was replaced by a man.

The preliminary interviews had provided a standardised and generalised line-management structure of LAs in Staffordshire (Figure 2:1) despite the recent Local Government Act 2000 which occasioned the re-naming and amalgamation of some departments and activities in some Councils. This set the framework for who would be interviewed in the management line.

Figure 2.1: Diagrams to Show the General Structure and Agency of Staffordshire Councils

a) *General Administrative Structure and Departmental Responsibility for Gypsy/Traveller Issues*

Chief Executives
Directors/Heads of Department/Section
Environmental Health, Planning, Neighbourhood Services, Leisure Services
Senior Officers
Planning, Environmental Health,
Support Officers
Planning enforcement, Environmental Health, Neighbourhood Services, Housing
GLOs
Planning, Environmental Health
Site Wardens
Gypsies/Travellers
Residents on permanent sites, mobile

b) *General Council Structure and **Ideal** Interview Schedule for Each Council (Following (a) above)*

Elected

Leader of Council

(Deputy Leader)
Members of Cabinet
Chairs of Scrutiny Committees
Members of Council

Paid
Chief Executive
Directors of Services
Assistant Directors
Senior Officers
Support Officers
GLOs/Eviction Officers/Rangers
Site Wardens/Managers

An 'ideal' interview schedule was drawn up for each council in order that representatives from each administrative level within each council would be interviewed (see Figure 2.1). This would be accomplished via a combination of snowballing and judgement sampling.

Gypsies/Travellers

Residents on Gypsy/Traveller sites were approached on two LA sites and Site Wardens who were Gypsies/Travellers were interviewed on three further sites (two private and one LA controlled) as 'representatives' because that was how they saw their role. On the two LA sites I was given permission to freely approach residents. On a third site I was advised that this could only be done via the Site Warden and he would choose the respondents. Although the Site Warden was formally interviewed it was decided not to interview residents formally on this site. Here, some were approached in semi-formal 'conversations' during subsequent site visits. Some caravans, particularly those on unauthorised sites, did not have electricity so the interviews were hand-written.

A Wider Context/Contact

The National Gypsy Council (now the Gypsy Council) was contacted but declined to be interviewed. However, their Reports were received so their view could also be considered. Contacts were made via the 'Traveller-Acad' web-site and e-mail 'conversations' were devised to balance the Staffordshire information. GLOs at Doncaster and Kent were also contacted for comparative information. The Coordinator of the Traveller Law Reform Unit (TLRU) at Cardiff University was also interviewed.

Others

To examine more closely the possibilities of economic inclusion of G/Ts, Directors of Small Business and Development Units of Councils were interviewed.

To gain information on equality of opportunity and service delivery, EOP unit representatives were interviewed as were the organisations which delivered services on the Councils' behalf to Gypsies Travellers. These were: the West Midlands Education Service for Traveller Children, Health Visitors, the Police, the Social Services, the then

Health Action Zone (HAZ) project workers and the North Staffordshire Inter-Agency Group now the North Staffordshire HAZ Advisory Group (on Gypsy/Traveller health issues).

Some fieldwork was undertaken in Turkey with a view to conducting a comparative study with Gypsies/Roma in Ankara. Although the idea was abandoned some useful information was obtained and will be used comparatively where relevant.

THE IDEAL VERSUS ACTUALITY

National Government - Towards the end of fieldwork a General Election took place which meant that Departmental names and personnel changed. Since the second (New) Labour Parliament was deemed to be a term of 'delivery', changes at Local Government level proliferated legitimised by the Local Government Act 2000. Changes also occurred to the Race Relations Act (Amendment 2000). The Human Rights Act 1998 (which came into force in 2000) was also introduced, as was The Good Practice Guide (1998) and its Amendment (2001). At the end of 2002 the interim Report on the Condition and Management of Gypsy Sites in England was circulated by the ODPM. Changes to Planning Law were being mooted in a Green Paper in 2002, aimed at stream-lining and speeding up the planning process. Green Belts were to be reviewed. Best Value/Best Performance strategies were being tackled; the Community Strategy and Cabinet-Style administration guidance was being circulated and was in various stages of consideration and enactment by the LAs in Staffordshire and elsewhere. The DTLR was reshuffled in June 2002.[15] Personnel appeared suitably shell-shocked by both the volume of information and the action and change that would be generated. Roles and activities within National Government departments had also changed so that finding who did what and in which Department was time consuming, not always rewarding and some personnel were vague about what they did, and who did what.

The Councils - Whilst a systematic and 'scientific' approach was attempted, it was also acknowledged that society is not a controlled (or always controllable) laboratory. Thus

---

[15] Stephen Byers had been removed, John Prescott reinstated and Transport had been moved to a separate

the researcher worked as systematically as possible within the parameters set by the Councils and other statutory agencies and Gypsies/Travellers. Some Councils were more helpful than others.[16] Some respondents who were not helpful at the beginning became very helpful at a later stage. The sample was not as balanced for each Council as envisaged. LAs with more sites and Gypsies/Travellers 'passing through' tended to have a wider frame of reference and more information to impart and more mechanisms in place to deal with these eventualities. Councillors and Leaders of Council were the most difficult to pin down. Six were interviewed, one of whom was a Shadow Leader of Council). Chief Executives were interviewed and 2 Assistant Directors deputised on the subject of the new Community Strategy Plans. The number of Councillors who were involved with Gypsies/Travellers other than through the planning process - and then only sporadically, was small – 4 agreed to be interviewed. Given their information and that gleaned from other sources, this was not seen as detrimental to the study.

The interview schedule for Directors and Senior Officers was long.[17] Some interviews had to be taken in two parts. On many occasions the 'conversation' extended beyond the formal interview and after the tape was switched off. Some information was also imparted 'off the record'. However, it appeared that within the LA system, what was confidential in one Department/Council was common knowledge in another, so that confidentiality was not as big a problem as feared. Two tapes were spoiled; a General Election meant that some informants lined up for interview were not re-elected so they could not be followed up and their newly appointed counterparts did not wish to be interviewed on the grounds that they were new to the post. These were but minor set-backs. Overall the respondents were obliging, gave me the information they could and the time needed to work through the interview. Their candour and ability to be self-critical and critical of their Council was, at times, surprising.

Gypsies/Travellers – Whilst it had been the intention, before preliminary site visits had taken place, to formally interview all residents on all sites, the site visits revealed that

---

portfolio. The Department was renamed the Office of the Deputy Prime Minister (ODPM)
[16] Whilst some respondents were willing to be interviewed others had to be persuaded and some could not be persuaded at all.

many on site did not wish to be formally interviewed. Given that Gypsies/Travellers were not the focus of the Thesis, this was not deemed to be detrimental to the study. Of those interviewed, some did not necessarily wish to speak about topics on the prescribed list. Also, whilst interviewing one respondent, others – friends, family members, children - would also become involved in the interview.[18] I was faced with the choice of abandoning the formal exercise or utilising their conversation agendas in the hope of getting responses to some of the questions on the formal interview questionnaire. Indeed, more information was gathered via informal conversations with site residents and participant/observation: I was called on to help in the eviction process and learned more from such encounters about the system in action. This helped to balance some of the more 'idealised' accounts of operations described in LA and other interviews.

The small number of Gypsies/Travellers in Staffordshire and the small sample interviewed, and given the diversity of families, meant that it was difficult to present what they had to say as 'the Gypsy/Traveller voice' or as the 'Gypsy/Traveller viewpoint'. However, as this was not the intention, it did not detract from the study. Given that views were expressed, an attempt was made to interweave them throughout the Thesis in order to balance views and to challenge and measure some of the information supplied by Staffordshire LA respondents. Where it was possible to quantify the response from Gypsy/Traveller respondents this, too, has been done.

Site Wardens, who were often at the sharp end of LA rules and service delivery, were also helpful in counterbalancing the 'official' line regarding what bureaucracy chooses to do and/or thinks it is doing for the target group in terms of satisfying need, particularly as some were Gypsies/Travellers. Apart from the (N)GC and a women's group which had just begun as part of the HAZ scheme in North Staffordshire, there seemed to be no other 'organisations' for 'community development'/assistance for Gypsies/ Travellers in this County which could act as a unified or unifying 'voice'. The (N)GC appeared to have a limited constituency within Staffordshire. None of the Gypsies/Travellers spoken to or

---

[17] Especially where respondents spoke at length. Where it was relevant I did not curtail the conversation.
[18] This was not confined to Gypsy/Traveller respondents. In some LAs I was faced with a panel of 2 to 4 - each giving a different view of the same subject.

interviewed claimed to being a 'member'. However, it was noted that the (N)GC was called upon by families on unauthorised sites to assist them, as a last resort. Stoke-on-Trent appeared to be the only Council to be actively working with the (N)GC at the time.

Whilst not all Councils had Equality of Opportunity Units, there were designated personnel who dealt with Equality Opportunity Issues – mainly on the lines of employment and gender. Five were interviewed (the majority were female) and one sent in a cursory response to a postal questionnaire. Two sent their Council's Equality of Opportunity Policy without responding to the questionnaire and two did not respond.

Similarly, some Business/Link Units within Councils were not particularly helpful. Only two agreed to be interviewed, others did not respond some said they were too busy and that 'time was money' and whilst one agreed to be interviewed over the telephone, she could not be persuaded to meet for interview. However, given the responses and the mode of operation of these units it was clear that Gypsy/Traveller businesses would not be included within their remit. Failure to co-operate was not viewed as a threat to the study but was used as an opportunity. The student researcher was a (prospective) client of their service delivery, albeit someone who they might regard as 'non-productive'. As such I was identified and treated accordingly. That treatment contributed to the overall impression of 'the organisation' and gave some indication how other 'non-productive' clients (so identified and perceived) might be treated.

Although a computer package for qualitative data analysis was contemplated (eg NUD.IST) it was decided before the interview schedule was designed that computer packages would not be used.[19] The sample was relatively small and it was concluded that this could be analysed 'manually'. It was necessary to keep a close check on the data and to move within and between Councils in the analysis. Once the tapes were transcribed, key questions were analysed within each section. Responses to each question were transferred onto an analysis sheet. Each Council was allocated an analysis sheet per question, where the responses of tiered personnel were recorded. This meant that responses could be compared within and between Councils. Where uniformity or pattern of response was noted, data were generated and tabulated. A summary sheet for each question was used.

LIBRARY/DOCUMENTATION STUDY

The library study used some of the relevant special resources available such as the Journals of the Gypsy Lore Society (The Scott MacFie Collection, Special Collections, Liverpool University) to examine and analyse the historical representation of Gypsies/Travellers and any bearings these might have on current definitions and treatment of this grouping. The County Archive was similarly scoured (see below). A study of relevant Sociological theory was also made (which will be further discussed in Chapter 3) in an attempt to fathom how this might be applied or might explain the Gypsy/Traveller phenomenon. Both would act as a backdrop to the project as opposed to drivers of the study.

The document study was part of the methodology used to compare what was written as formal intent with what respondents said or thought was written as a guide for action and practice. The documentation study divided into several sections: international, national, local, official, grey and unofficial. At the international level Reports emanating from the Human Rights Commission, the World Bank and the EU were consulted where relevant. European Legislation and Reports, which have a bearing on policy and ultimately practice within UK, were also borne in mind. Texts referring to treatment of Gypsies/Travellers elsewhere in the world (particularly in Eastern Europe) were also noted for the purpose of comparison, contrast and a wider perspective.

Hansard at both the national and local levels was consulted. Any official, national research reports and reports emanating from that research on Gypsies/Travellers in England, Ireland Wales and Scotland were also consulted, particularly those commissioned by the DETR/DTLR. These will be referred to in the text of the Thesis as

---

[19] At the time this package did not appear to have the desired features necessary for what I envisaged doing. I believe that since then new improved software has become available

49

necessary. Academic and 'support' group reports (published and unpublished) were also consulted eg the (N)GC Reports together with relevant web-sites. Some of these came within the 'grey' material available on Gypsies/Travellers and was useful as an 'other' view point. Much of the relevant legislation has also been consulted. The bibliography contains reference to all the information used in this Thesis.

It was assumed that local Councils would have written policies which governed action towards Gypsies/Travellers and that there would be access to them. However, at the time of interview few had written policies as such - other than protocols for eviction/removal. Some were in the process of writing policies for Council approval (this had been at least a three year process in some Councils). Any current policies for Gypsies/Travellers were statements of future conditional intent within the Structure/Local Plans. Gaining access to Council information, other than that produced for 'information/ promotion' purposes proved more difficult than expected. Web sites are now favoured for the dissemination of 'official ' material and the researcher was more often than not directed to these somewhat anodyne sites. But sites change and become defunct and unless this information is also available in hard copy, it might be difficult in future to compile a historical record. Much of the material appeared 'sanitised' for public consumption.

The issue of 'data protection' was often quoted as a reason not to allow access to information, and the Freedom of Information came at a cost. Some Councils said they would oblige if they knew exactly which record/file was wanted. This was difficult for the researcher to know without an index or knowledge of what files a department held. Some information, particularly Police records, are computerised and appeared impossible to retrieve unless as part of a major research project – by the Police. The DTLR was efficient in providing copies of Circulars, Guidance documents and web site references.

The County Archive proved useful for past reports and information on the squatting phenomena in Staffordshire and for documents passed to the archive from local Councils. This has not necessarily been via systematic collection, so there were omissions and not a great deal on Gypsies/Travellers.

The second tier documents were the Structure/Local Plans where policy was formally stated and from these other policy documents emanated. Many of these were placed on deposit and could be used on the Council premises. The Structure Plan for the County and Stoke-on-Trent City Council (as Unitary Authorities) and the Local Plans for all Councils in Staffordshire were read. Some Councils had already commissioned housing needs and future development surveys. Attempts were made to gather information relating to caravan sites and licence agreements, site rules, numbers of caravans in each Council and location maps.[20] Information surrounding unauthorised encampments was more difficult to locate especially if encampments occurred on private land or were not 'full evictions' involving bailiffs etc..

Where retrospective planning had been sought some planning departments had kept records of events, including letters of protest etc.. These were made available to me as a member of the public not necessarily as a Researcher, and appeared to be available (at the time) for public consultation - as advocated by legislation. Such transparency was not available in all Councils.

Local newspapers, particularly their 'treatment' of certain events, proved a useful source of (mis)information and the local newspaper archive was used. Some Councils kept press cuttings, but again this was not systematic collection but depended on individual interest. Some Planning Offices kept fairly extensive records of planning applications so it was possible to follow them through. (Where such records existed, this has been done (see also Case Study A). Others, particularly where refurbishment and removal to new Council buildings had taken place, appeared to have disposed of files, since they were impossible to trace. Some Councils claimed that it might be possible to seek out information but they would have to charge for doing so – and there was no guarantee that the information would be found. This posed problems for the researcher. In light of the Community Strategy, where LAs will be allowed discretion to charge for services,

---

[20] The County Council has collated a geographical record of all permitted and permanent sites

researchers might have to pay for any kind of information which is above and beyond the promotional, in future.

Documents studied thus ranged from 'promotional' to 'informative'. The 'promotional' were readily available in the foyers of most Council offices/departments or on web sites. These were the base line for information existing within the public domain. Mission statements by Councils to its 'clients' proliferated, as did Council and institutional 'newspapers' (eg those printed by the local Health Authorities and the Police; these were generally delivered to householders) which tended to report mainly positive activities. Local newspaper reports, generally negative on their reportage of Gypsy/Traveller issues were also used.

OBSERVATION

I had observed 'nomadic' groups (so-called) in other countries - the Australian Aborigines in fringe camps in Alice Springs and the Northern Territories, squatters in Hong Kong, Singapore, Malaysia and Ankara from fairly close quarters, and more distantly the Bedouin in the State of Israel and the Sami of Finland - which meant that some kind of comparison, however crude, initially, could be made (with caution) with Gypsies/Travellers in UK.

In the main, the purpose of observation as part of the methodology, was to compare written and formal statements and policy, with what was said and executed as practice, or what was happening on the ground. I wished to compare what I had seen for myself with what I was about to be, or had been, told by all parties in the study.

The observation of the Gypsy/Traveller/Local Authority interface, particularly with regard to local sites, has been longitudinal. From childhood days in Cardiff when many came during the summer to the local 'common', to more recent times, as part of a support group within the local REC (where I worked) when site provision issues arose in the local area of Staffordshire, to current observation for this study. Thus change over time has been noted which has allowed comparisons to be made.

Observation took place when a majority of sites in Staffordshire were visited. Officer-Gypsy/Traveller interaction was also observed in terms of unauthorised and authorised sites. The issuing of notices to quit land were observed as were Public Enquiries, Court and Appeal hearings. On these occasions both Gypsy/Traveller and 'official' behaviour were noted. LA behaviour has also been observed in many contexts – at face interviews, over the telephone, responding to requests for information etc. Council meetings - of Cabinet, Planning, Scrutiny; special and Community Strategy meetings etc were also attended in Newcastle-under-Lyme Borough , Stoke City, Stafford Borough and South Staffordshire District.

Training and information days were also attended, sponsored by Stoke-on-Trent CAB/HAZ for agency personnel, Council Officers and the Police who dealt with Gypsy/Traveller issues. TLRU conferences were attended with the researcher acting as participant/observer.

METHODOLOGY FOR THE ANALYSIS OF THE BIANNUAL COUNT DATA

The methodology for the analysis of the secondary, bi-annual count data produced by LAs for the DTLR will appear in Chapter 5. However, the methodology for surveying the Counting Officers in Staffordshire will be discussed here.

Whilst Sibley (1984a; 1984b; 1990) and Halfacree (1996) amongst others have criticised the count in general terms, apart from the 1991 OPCS Report, the mechanics of the count undertaken by LA officers was not reviewed until after 2006 when the responsibilities of the ODPM transferred to the Department for Communities and Local Government (CLG). As part of the research Thesis, the way that data for the DTLR count was collated, was examined. To this end each of the nine Officers in Staffordshire who undertook the count were interviewed in 2000 – almost ten years after the OPCS investigation (see Appendix One for the questionnaire suite). Eight of the officers were interviewed, one officer completed the questionnaire himself and mailed the responses. The results of this section of the research were published in 2001 (Drakakis-Smith and Mason 2001). After interviewing the Officers and observing what happened in practice, the researcher was made aware of how, and in what respects, the data were unreliable and how better to interpret them. This part of the research was undertaken not only to support or refute the DTLR claim that Government Policy for Gypsies/Travellers was working, but also to show how representation could be formulated via data.

ETHICAL ISSUES

It is important to note that the primary target group of this study was not Gypsies/ Travellers, but the LAs in Staffordshire. Thus the intention was not to intrude upon families unnecessarily. The main purpose of the project was to examine the policy practice and service delivery of the Local Authority as an institution of power, to see if and how power was being used to deal with the Gypsy/Traveller situation, and through this to open up a space for constructive dialogue and 'listening' between LAs and families. Thus I had no intention of gathering any information which could further disadvantage Gypsies/Travellers or which could be used as a substitute for LAs making their own enquiries. Where the Thesis might create a space for communicative dialogue, the intention was not for the researcher to insert herself into the space between the power and target group but for the two parties in this Thesis to move forward and use the space constructively. Thus the views of Gypsies/Travellers were sought mainly to balance the information forwarded by LAs and other statutory authorities. The Thesis did not end with solutions or recommendations for policy but exhortations for the power group and Gypsies/Travellers to interact and to usefully discuss some of the important issues which affected their lives in order that they might be better and more accurately defined so that relevant policy could be formulated that might work to satisfy the needs of all parties.

Whilst every attempt was made to conform to the British Sociological Association Ethical Code of Conduct for fieldwork researchers, ethical concerns presented themselves on three levels. First, the MA study revealed how candid some LA personnel could be. Given that I would be revisiting some of them the relationship would begin to deepen and possibly more would be revealed about the institution. 'Inside informants' were also used although not necessarily formally interviewed. It became a question not only of how this information could be, but whether it should be, used – particularly where it explained certain situations. It was also necessary to protect the identity of some respondents who, perhaps unwittingly, were not only damning their institution but also themselves. Thus as far as possible their identity is protected. This had to be balanced against wishing to produce an honest account of affairs in Staffordshire or something more anodyne. Thus to protect their identities rank and date only are given in the text. How the information was gathered is also indicated.

Councils and personnel were only identified when it was useful, helpful and permissible to do so. The intention was not to 'shame' them but to find out what they did to make them aware of the areas where change could be made to improve situations and/or relationships. Some Senior Officers expressed a wish to be informed, if what they were doing was 'wrong', whilst some expressed the view that they had no idea how the present situation could be improved etc. Thus the Thesis was written to inform and hopefully assist those Councils who felt that change/improvement was overdue. It might also assist Gypsies/Travellers (or those who help them) to understand the complexity of the problem and how 'the system' works and where they could usefully interact with it. The study has attempted at all times to give credit where it might be due. Hopefully it also allows Councils to see themselves in relation to other administrations locally, nationally and internationally. The majority of Officers asked to be informed of the outcome of the research. Respondents were asked if they would like a copy of their interview, none did. Nevertheless, several were contacted for further clarification re what they had said or to clarify that what they had said was what they had meant to say etc..

Second, information gained on or from Gypsies/Travellers also had to be treated with similar care. Whilst officialdom would be greatly interested in their 'personal and business affairs' this was a matter between officialdom and Gypsies/Travellers. Indeed, the objective of the study was not to present a plea-bargaining position on behalf of Gypsies/Travellers but to make a space for Gypsies/Travellers to make their own representation and on their own terms. As a vulnerable group it was equally important to preserve their anonymity. As it was, many were reluctant to take even justifiable legal action against LAs for fear of reprisal (and crippling costs). However, this did not prevent them from speaking openly (off the record) about the LA and in front of LA officials!

Since many sites are removed from the public gaze, they are vulnerable places. A map identifying the location of sites in Staffordshire has not been produced in the Thesis, although one was made available to me for use by the County Council.

The details contained within the Case Studies were acquired from Official records and documents which were in the public domain and were on deposit in the LA Planning Office. The use of the Case Studies in the Thesis was an attempt to show the way in which the system worked in practice.

Third, given that I would be working mainly with Councils and Council personnel I had to be clear how I was to be identified. I did not wish to present myself as representing either them or Gypsies/Travellers (although in some instances this was assumed by both sides). I wished to be identified as an impartial researcher, gathering information from all parties involved, in order to address the question - what is going on here. Often this was difficult to achieve particularly when asked by both Gypsies/Travellers and LAs to assist them. On one occasion I found myself in Court on behalf of a family on an unauthorised site because at the last minute they decided not to attend. I went in order to observe the way in which such cases are handled by 'the system'. On another occasion, I was summoned by one LA to give the Gypsy/Traveller 'view' which would have been the LAs stab at Gypsy/Traveller 'consultation'.

Although I knew it would be difficult, before beginning the study, I resolved that I would not become 'emotionally' involved. The relationship with both parties would be 'professional' and I would not attempt to cultivate friendships or relationships in order to obtain 'inside' information. Although LA officials were more obligated (often by law) to give the information I asked for (and not all did) the information from Gypsies/Travellers was of a more 'personal' nature – and in their private possession/ownership, to give or not as they wished. That is not to say I would not utilise already existing friendships/

acquaintance to ask for information. An attempt was made to draw the line between researcher and advocate.

Although a judgmental outcome was not necessarily envisaged, it was hoped that the findings might reconcile both parties to a new method of game play and a more positive game plan.

CHAPTER THREE

ON THE WAGON: GYPSIES/TRAVELLERS IN SEARCH OF A THEORY

MAKING ROOM FOR THEORY

Given that some Gypsies/Travellers are recognised in law as a separate group – an ethnic group - this chapter wishes to examine some of the theories which might apply to the Gypsy/Traveller situation described in Chapter One as a result of that classification. The important element to be explained here is, the stimulus which primarily encourages individuals into alliances or to align with groups already formed and their response – which can take on a life of its own; what keeps them in groups when it is no longer in their interests to remain; and how groups become regarded and treated by Authority. This phenomenon will be discussed in the light of Bourdieu's *habitus* which, as a mega-theory embraces the dynamics and logic of culture-making of power groups and target groups alike. It is not the intention of this Thesis to deconstruct necessarily Bourdieu's theory of habitus. I do wish, however, to examine habitus in terms of the 'logic' of Gypsy/ Traveller and Local Authority 'culture', their development over time via discourse and action, their stylised inter-relationship, and what I am trying to say about it.

Once 'a group' is perceived the processes of identification and evaluation begin whereby the 'new' group is measured against 'the norm'. To this phenomenon the second-tier theories of ethnicity, identity politics and the politics of difference and race/racisms are discussed to explain in finer detail the interaction of structure and agency at ground level. Interweaving, will be the notions of Weber's 'awareness' of action and reaction and the theories which attach to the micro-levels of interaction – game play, dialogue and choice. All of the above will be discussed in Part One of this chapter.

It is the power group which is spot-lighted in this thesis - its perceptions of Gypsies/Travellers which often govern National Legislation and Local Policy; the way in which Gypsy/Traveller groups are treated at the local level in terms of practice and service delivery, which serve to control and guide them towards the 'choices' available. Since Local Authorities (LAs) are mandated and structured to behave in certain ways and to carry out particular tasks/services, these structures will also need to be discussed in theoretical terms - in Part Two of the chapter.

PART ONE: AWARENESS AND INTENT

Does the State intend, via its regulatory legislation, to destroy the Gypsy/Traveller way of life – to 'ethnic cleanse' as Hawes and Perez (1996) have suggested – or to curtail trespass and 'manage' an unwieldy, non-conforming group, for example? Is the breaking up of family groups on a regular basis an attempt to disperse families - to sever 'tribal affiliations'- in order to speed and/or bring about desired 'development'?[21] Or is an attempt being made to separate, segregate, contain and isolate them? Government's awareness of the implications of legislation, of its influence and of any subsequent action is important and this will be explored in Chapter 6. The task of delving into motive and 'the mind' to fathom why agents act in the way that they do has, however, been cordoned off by Psychology and Psychiatry. Nevertheless, there have been Sociological attempts to grapple with this issue. Weber (1978:25) observed that 'in the real world people act in a state of half awareness or total unconsciousness of their 'intended meaning'. Thus 'vague' feelings about meaning rather than knowing or 'making it clear to himself' pervade; in most cases action is on 'impulse or from habit'. Weber believed that 'this is what an analysis of the real world will have to take into account'. This phenomenon will be explored further in this and subsequent chapters.

Bourdieu appears to have taken up this notion via *habitus* (Bourdieu 1977; 1987; 1990; 1992; 993). Habitus attempts to explain the 'logic' of (a) culture in terms of Sociological based rational action and games, of culture in the making as opposed to the economic-

---

[21] In the way that working class neighbourhoods and families were fragmented and dispersed after the Second World War (Young and Wilmott 1962; Donnison 1967)

political theories of Rational Choice and Game Theory,[22] although choice and game playing are ever present. Habitus appears to give a more informed and humanistic account of cultural choice, explaining why individuals remain loyal to a group. It also allows for imposition - important since the Thesis proceeds from the premise that both the State and groups within it follow 'culturally' evolutionary paths which are mutually influential – and the way in which some groups within the Gypsy/Traveller grouping are now not simply 'other' but also 'another,' forging and ultimately possessing a separate 'logic'.

Bourdieu's Claims for Habitus

Bourdieu recognises that culture is not immutable and whilst it may have the 'probability of a science of practices' (Bourdieu 1993:76; Robbins 2000) it escapes 'the formal choice between finalism and mechanism' (ibid). Thus habitus is first defined as 'durable, transposable dispositions, structural structures predisposed to function as structuring structures ie as principles which generate and organise practices and representations that can be objectively adapted to their outcomes without presupposing a conscious aiming at ends or an express mastery of the operation necessary in order to attain them' (1977:72-3). Second, he sees habitus as 'a feel for the game' (1993:128) – as a 'practical sense' that inclines agents to act and react in specific situations in a manner that is not always calculated and that is not a simple question of conscious obedience to rules. Rather it is a set of dispositions which generate practices and perceptions ... (it is) a long process of inculcation beginning in early childhood, which becomes a second sense, a second nature (1993:5; 1990). Third, that it 'represents a theoretical intention to get away from the philosophy of consciousness without doing away with the agent' (1987:10). Fourth, that 'habitus distinguishes factions that are separated by the whole universe of lifestyle' (1993:129). And, finally, 'that habitus was invented in order to account for the paradox of types of behaviour being directed towards certain ends without being directed to those ends or determined by them' (1987:10).

---

[22] These theories have tended in the past to exclude and ignore emotion/gut feeling and habit/half awareness, despite their often over-riding influence on rational action and thought.

At this stage it is unclear whether Bourdieu conceptualises habitus as an adjective describing a universal process, or as a noun and the sum of many parts. I have understood habitus as a noun – and that amoeba-like it is constantly in the process of producing and re-producing. The next section looks at the way in which habitus is structured.

The Structuring Structures of Habitus and Group Formation

Habitus is formed in the following ways. **First** it is '*acquired*' [23] and becomes 'a permanent disposition; it is *historical,* linked to individual history (1993:87). It is '*a product of conditioning*' that leads us to produce the social conditions of our own production, but in a relatively unpredictable way (ibid) – 'a socialised subjectivity' (ibid:126). It is '*a property ... a capital* (1993:87). **Second**, it is '*generative* (unlike habit') thus it is '*reproductive* rather than productive (ibid), *creative and inventive* but within the limits of its structures which produced it (1992:19) with the power of *adaptation* to the external world' (ibid). **Third**, it is '*a structuring mechanism* that operates from within the agent ... the *strategy-generating principle* enabling agents to cope with unforeseen and ever-changing situations (1977:18). It is *shaped* in certain conditions (1993:143). **Fourth,** it is '*a reaction against structuralism*' which reduced the agent to a mere 'bearer' or 'unconscious' expression of structure' (ibid:4). **Fifth**, it is the '*principle of real autonomy* with respect to the immediate determination of 'the situation'. The '*adjustments* that are constantly required by the *necessities of adaptation* to new and unforeseen situations which may bring about *durable transformations* of the habitus but they remain in certain limits ... because habitus *defines the perception of the situation that determines it*' (ibid:87). And **finally**, habitus is '*a virtue made out of necessity*' (1987:11) '*a system of dispositions attuned to the game*' (1993:18). It produces '*strategies* which ... turn out to be *objectively adjusted to the situation*'. In other words, habitus is a set of 'inherited social conditions (Robbins 2000:87) which can be altered by individuals. Perpetuation and alteration rests on the 'feel for the game' which determines 'the success or otherwise the agent will make of the inheritance' (Bourdieu 1987). Such structuring structures could explain how groups, isolated from the

---

[23] The italics are mine.

mainstream, adopt new and different thought trajectories which serve to make social dislocation greater. Their actions are not viewed by them as 'wrong', but the only way to behave given the impact of 'other' structuring structures. Thus different 'logics' emerge as alternatives which can conflict with one another.

Bourdieu further explains habitus and its development by using the notions of *fields* – 'spaces of conflict and competition' (Bourdieu 1992:17), *dispositions* – which are 'transposable' and which 'generate practices … and diverse fields of activity' - which induce actors to play (Bourdieu 1977:5) and *games* and *feel for the game,* all of which intertwine to support habitus structurally. *Codification* – formal rule or law making - which 'ensures calculativity and predictability' to reduce 'the dangers of arbitrariness' which can be 'great' (Bourdieu 1987:84) - acts as an adhesive, binding the whole.

Whilst habitus is comprehensive in terms of 'the logic' of culture formation, Bourdieu plays down the way in which value is added to observable and perceived difference and the conflictual interplay which can result. Also played down is the power-play (in games of uncertainty) between fields, and the way in which groups and individuals shear off to become counter-groups. This indicates that Bourdieu might have perceived society as a whole and habitus as omnipresent rather than viewing society as a molecular structural sum of interconnecting parts where habitus is 'to play for'. If this is so, then he is theorising only one strand of a double helix. Thus an appeal must be made to other theories which might explain diversity and the struggle for hegemony (at most) or participatory power (at least). The lens of race/racisms and ethnicity is more useful in explaining group classification and competition at a more local level.

TO ETHNICITY AND BACK

If the notion of race was problematic in the 1950s/1970s in terms of a black/white dichotomy, which excluded Gypsies/Travellers from its remit, except in passing, then the 1980s onwards saw the problematic rise of ethnicity as it became co-joined with the 'politics of difference' - when ethnic groups competed with each other within and across the 'black/white' divide for resources and access to those resources via equality of opportunity.

Events at home and abroad[24] in recent times have revealed both the width of division and the power and depth of feeling attaching to 'culture', ethnicity and difference. The culture/ethnicity discourse has explored the right of ethnic groups to follow their own cultural path but within the context of a plural 'nation state' (Kymlicka 1995a; Ghai 2001). Invariably ethnicity attached to 'them' and not necessarily to 'us'. The practical and theoretical problems appeared to be how to contain ethnicity (whilst retaining liberalism) within this plural nation state (Kymlicka 1995a; 1995b; Ghai 2001) ie how to get all groups working individually, but together, in relative harmony, but without losing cultural integrity or devolving into separate, self interested and warring factions of the state? Inclusive and participatory democracy became the issue concerning such writers as Kymlicka, Young, Glazer, Gellner, Ericksen, Billig and Sigler, to name but a few. But would this discourse be relevant to the UK Gypsy/Traveller situation (particularly in Staffordshire) and that given Gypsies/Travellers have been an identified group in UK for centuries and who are, more often than not, indigenous? Here 'ethnicity' is focussed on perceived difference of 'way of life', and the Gypsy/Traveller right to lead it irrespective of any consequences. This raises the question, and has implications for other 'ethnic' minorities - how long does one have to remain an 'outsider' or in a 'host' country before full socio-legal acceptance and full citizenship rights are attained? If the Gypsy/Traveller trajectory is pursued, then it appears that value is attributed not only to culture and ethnic group but also to an individual's calibre as a participating citizen and moral fitness to be included in hegemonic society. The group to which one belongs and how it functions, then, is significant as is the number of group members (Crewe 1983). Hegemonic society is to 'play for'.

---

[24] The break-up of the USSR and Yugoslavia, events in Rwanda and South Africa and the global reshuffling of population and groups.

So What is an Ethnic Group?

Bastinier (1994:54) and Rex (1994:30) rightly point out that immigrants/migrants 'do not arrive as ethnic minorities but are created so' - presumably by State mechanisms which create the structures which separate 'them' from 'us'. Parkin's typology for an ethnic group (1974 quoted in Eriksen 1993:44) was that it should be economically self-sufficient, residentially segregated and occupationally specialised. Although this definition, with its economic emphasis, parodies that of socio-economic class (and Weber's status groups), some Gypsy/ Traveller groups would fit (as would some local and national Administrations) - but *why* they became self-sufficient, and *how* they became segregated and occupationally specialised is important here. Later writings attempted to grasp the socio-cultural setting in which individuals were placed either voluntarily or prescriptively. These definitions can be roughly arranged into: (i) those which emphasise the functional aspects of ethnicity and (ii) those which emphasise the conflictual nature of differentiated groupings as a transposed habitus where groups compete for scarce resources and resist being, or not being, classified, hierarchicised and separated from the main body into the individual group habitus - scenarios where choice can be limited and directed. Whilst Kymlicka (1995a:107) claims that 'every way of life is free to attract adherents', not all potential adherents will be welcomed, however. It is at this point that mechanisms/structures are created to prevent 'membership' – the rules of the game, often unwritten - which create and mark boundaries between groups.

Thus an ethnic group, is a 'cultural category' (Wallerstein 1991:77) which has often been (initially) transposed (or believed to be so), which can be 'self' or 'other' defined (Eriksen 1993), which can be 'numerically inferior and culturally different to the majority (Sigler 1983:3; Eriksen 1993), which cannot (for whatever reason) be assimilated into the majority (Balibar 1991:4) and thus becomes 'highly conscious of (its) difference' (Ratcliffe 1994:6). This difference may be perpetuated by 'continuing behaviours that are passed on from generation to generation' (Wallerstein 1991:77; Guiberneau 1996). A 'consciousness' of groupness and difference from other groups must also be registered (Ratcliffe 1994; Billig 1995). However, consciousness can be raised from within the group and by those outside the group who wish to keep it separate.

Status vs Ethnic/Caste Group?

The above theories attempt to explain the impact and processes associated with inward international migration and its impact upon the indigenous majority and its reaction. Whilst this Thesis accepts that an ethnic component exists within the Gypsy/Traveller grouping, it also maintains that ethnicity (for the majority) could be linked more to a prolonged exclusion from the mainstream. Such family groups in the past were, possibly, more akin to status groups (after Weber 1967) with a 'specific life-style' expected of those 'who belonged to the circle' (ibid:187). This placed restrictions on social intercourse (ibid) which leads ultimately to 'endogamous closure' (ibid:188). As group closure becomes more extreme the way of life becomes stylised and ritualised to that of a 'caste' group (ibid). It is possible that the arrival of other recruits from outside UK and beyond deemed 'foreign' advanced the status group to that of ethnic group. Both caste and ethnic communities 'acquire specific occupational traditions, and cultivate a belief in their ethnic community (ibid). They live in a 'diaspora' strictly segregated from all personal intercourse, except of the unavoidable sort, and their situation is legally precarious. Yet by virtue of their economic indispensability, they are tolerated, indeed, frequently privileged, and they live in interspersed political communities' (ibid). Weber gives the Jewish group as an example. Gypsies/Travellers would also fit this typology.

Competition

Groups are neither silent nor passive; they are also economic entities - since groups cannot live by culture alone. This brings elements of competition (Banton 1994), conflict and resistance (James and Harris 1993) into the equation. And indeed, the way in which groups make a living can define some of the cultural content (Okely 1984). But, how groups make a living may also be prescriptive. Often excluded groups 'do what they can' or take whatever opportunities are available. This is particularly so with squatting and excluded groups like Gypsies/Travellers who have to find niche markets in order to survive since many are excluded from the main game. Sway (1983:31-33) claimed Gypsies/Travellers (in USA) to be 'middlemen … who demonstrate a tremendous flexibility ... possessing ... a cultural tradition composed of social and economic mechanisms for survival that have been perfected through a long history of adversity'.[25]

For some groups the choice is whether or not the game is worth playing. Some have no desire to join in, and the State ensures that some groups remain on the periphery. Eriksen (1993:142) claims that 'power dictates when minorities are different' – it also decides which. The game then becomes knowing when groups wish to be included and when they don't, which groups are threatening, which are not etc.. In this respect the State is not always proficient (sometimes deliberately so) – its tacit and sometimes overt rejection of some groups can be internalised by the group. Much also depends on the negotiating skills of the group and how far they are prepared to 'abandon' culture and ethnicity 'the moment it becomes a straightjacket rather than a tool for generating new understanding' (ibid:162). Entry, then, is only partially governed by knowing the rules and/or playing by the rules. Being able to negotiate acceptability, and knowing when to leave one group for another is equally important –as is having a foot in both camps.

Groups, too, have games and rules by which they can strategically play. In this sense, ethnicity can be 'played up or down' (Eriksen: 1993:21; Guy 1975, 1977,2001; Okely 1984) and it is up to the group 'to decide on its significance' (ibid:32). Eriksen also claims that ethnic identities can be consciously manipulated and invested in economic competition' (ibid:20). However, it is 'up to the agent to decide on the importance of ethnicity and its significance in social situations' (ibid: 32). This would indicate potential conflicts of interest between the group and individual group members. Choice then becomes significant. And, once more, the problem becomes differentiating between choice and freedom to choose, forced choice or no choice. Rex and Drury (1994:159) maintain that 'the problem in dealing with ethnic minorities' is 'distinguishing between the ethnicity which is attributed to them and that which they have choosen. A more subtle problem ... is when a particular ethnicity and ethnic classification is attributed. ...Those to whom it is attributed may, either accept the attribution and internalise it for their own reasons and if they have no choice, or reject it and put forward their own self-

---

[25] For some Asian immigrants self-employment via the restaurant and corner shop was their survival

chosen view of their ethnicity'. This however, tends to negate the power of the majority to listen and to be corrected in its view. Is it possible to be 'included' into majority society without losing group integrity or self identity? For Gypsies/Travellers this has become an important consideration. Equally important is what one is being 'included' into.

Discourse on ethnicity is concerned not only with what keeps groups together, but also, and possibly influenced by ideologies of strength in unity which attach to notions of the nation state, [26] on what keeps groups apart. The then emphasis on 'inclusiveness' - transmuted from 'social exclusion' - has influenced the change of emphasis. Thus phenomena such as boundaries and stereotypes are important.

Boundaries and Stereotypes - Boundaries can be constructed of anything. They can be geographical, physical (as in walls and perimeter fences), socio-economic and/or psychological. In the case of Gypsies/Travellers, the caravan and certain behaviours appear to be a barrier to inclusion. Boundaries and stereotypes can be imposed on individuals from within and from outside the group. They can exist at the local level as 'neighbourhood nationalisms' (Back 1996:239) or at regional, national and international levels. And, like groups, they can be real or imagined (Anderson 1983). Power and fear appear to play a major part in their construction and maintenance. Goulbourne (1991: 25) claims that the 'exclusion of minorities from mainstream, majority society ... helps to create a counter exclusivity by ethnic minorities, as a kind of protection'. The result is that members of both 'communities' lock themselves in mutually exclusive social zones and other 'logics'. It appears that from this view point we live our lives in categories – manifestations of the 'ordering tendencies of modernity'[27] (Werbner 1997:2). Who constructs these, how they are constructed and who decides who inhabits which social/economic space, become important questions. However, whilst it is theoretically and ideologically convenient to ascribe individuals and groups to a particular category and whilst a core of a group may always remain within their category, in reality there is a

---

strategy when faced with employment discrimination.
[26] However, it would appear that the notion of the UK nation state might diminish in favour of regionalism and devolution.

fluidity (Bourdieu 1977; 1993; Eriksen 1993:20[28]), particularly at the periphery. Modood et al (1994:119) also claim that 'ethnic identity is far from being some primordial stamp on an individual … the boundaries of groups are unclear and shifting …'. This is particularly so if the habitus was formed under pressure. Once the pressure is removed, individuals, if provided with the freedom and incentives (and/or they have the disposition to do so), can develop an autonomy that could lead to a desire to leave one group for another and to change. Such fluidity could result in the dissolution of one group and in the transformation and/or a creation of a new one. Thus when Gypsies/Travellers begin to settle is this the first processual step to 'change' and how far is local hostility and internal group pressure an impediment to this?

Ethnic Purity

Theoretically, culture has caught up with reality and the state of cultural hybridity is now recognised – which pre-supposes that at one time, like race, a state of cultural purity existed. The latest ONS Census figures show (December 2012) that 80.5 per cent identified themselves as 'white British' as opposed to 87.5 per cent in 2001 and that 1.2 million adults did not use English as their main language (The Guardian 12 December 2012). Gist and Dworkin (1972) believe 'ethnic purity to be a myth'. However, in some groups where group boundary maintenance is strong (for example groups such as the Amish and to a certain extent Jewish groups) a high level of cultural integrity was possible. However, this is only achievable if/when accompanied by high levels of self-sufficiency and/or high levels of isolation. Stringent rules of separation, social and geographical distance, accentuate differences as groups who do not have regular contact with one another lose touch. Separate development and logics occur. But, even in closed groups there are differences of opinion and interpretation. Are these contained by the group or does the core protect itself by removing the fluid periphery where change emanates and could be influential? Even when individuals leave, they do not, necessarily, drop their ethnic identity, it becomes retained in a different way and in a

---

[27] Although 'ordering tendencies' could hardly be called modern.
[28] Eriksen (1993:24) believes that stereotypes are 'crucial in defining boundaries of one's own group – informing members of the virtues of their own group and the vices of others. They can justify privilege and differences in access to society's resources … they can function as self-fulfilling prophecies … can be devoid of truth, morally ambiguous and contested by different parties'.

different context. A pressing question facing Gypsies/Travellers at present is, if individuals cease to travel or move into houses, do they cease being Gypsies/Travellers? This is not a new consideration, however.[29] Pressure can be exerted from both sides of the group divide.

The Gypsy/Traveller Grouping Admixture

That Gypsies/Travellers have been caught up in 19th century discourse and ideologies on poverty and the poor should not pass unremarked. The poor were seen as 'wandering tribes', and 'not English', and as 'nomads', were 'distinguished from civilised man by his repugnance to regular and continuous labour' – and were thus 'alien and predatory' (Mayhew 1851 quoted in Jones 2000:45-47). In many instances the poor and Gypsies/Travellers existed, together, as a homogenous group (divided only into the deserving and underserving) in the minds of majority society and policy makers, with mobile families being regarded as a sub-class of an under-class and undeserving. However, Gypsies/Travellers appear not to have 'moved on' in the minds of many in majority society – with ethnicity/way of life keeping them apart. Mainstream society still believes that Gypsies/Travellers 'cannot belong to us', are not ours but someone else's responsibility (and it is possible that attitudes engendered by the Poor Laws – and early immigration laws dating back to Elizabethan times - live on here (See Yungblut 1996)). Little if any allowance is made for change within the Gypsy/Traveller habitus which means that boundaries/ barriers remain in place. Stereotypical images of Gypsies/Travellers found in history books, ethnography and ancient statutes remain in use today and are proving difficult to shift. Why becomes an obvious question, when in the main differences in UK appear to be the result of segregation, separation and exclusion from the mainstream - the fading ethnic marker, the caravan.

---

[29] In 1890, Simpson berated Sir Walter Scott concerning his idea that 'gypsies ceased to be gypsies by change of habitat … it is perfectly evident that Sir Walter Scott in common with many others never realised the idea … of what a gypsy was or he could never have imagined those only were the gypsy race who followed the tent'. In the 20/21st Century, the tent has given way to the caravan and more latterly the caravan is giving way to the mobile home/chalet.

If ethnicity explained the mechanisms of boundary and group formation and closure, it was the discourse on race and racism which explained the more practical elements of power and control, evaluation and its adjustment. It also illuminated the power struggle at the local level between those who were perceived to be unworthy or inferior on the basis of a difference. This theory of evaluation and the struggle for adjustment (in terms of anti-racism) will now be discussed.

Race and Racisms

Earlier theory concentrated on genetic (race) differences, based on 18th and 19th century group classifications which tended to exclude the experience of some groups who were not always perceptibly, phenotypically different, eg the Jews, Gypsies/Travellers, the Irish (Mac an Ghaill 1999). However, their experience could be equated with the 'black' experience long before that term had been coined (Drakakis-Smith 1997).[30] Through the ages Gypsies/Travellers have been excluded socio-economically and spatially, enslaved, inferiorised and at various times, subjected, like the Jews, to pogroms and attempts at genocide (Hancock 1987; Kenrick 1993; Kenrick and Puxon 1972). This tends to support Wieviorka's notion (1994) that throughout history identifiable and identified groups have been subjected to what are now termed 'racist' practices, accompanying some – possibly through force of habit - into modern times. Whilst Fenton (1999) elaborates on historically located racism(s) in *Ethnicity, Racism, Class and Culture,* Gypsies/Travellers are not mentioned although they became racialised at particular historical junctures.

The rationale for attempts to include Gypsies/Travellers within this debate is that they had often been described as 'black'[31] were perceived as being unable to assimilate, and treated accordingly. Attempts to genetically classify Gypsies/Travellers within the race hierarchy were abandoned by Eugene Pittard in 1932 on the grounds that data were 'too sparse to allow any conclusion as to the origin of Gypsies but there was evidence to

---

[30] I therefore take issue with Bourdieu and others, who advocate that if something is not named it does not/cannot exist.
[31] In parts of Eastern Europe the term black is applied to Roma and other Gypsy groups. In UK 'browness' (George Eliot – *Mill on the Floss;*) and 'tawniness' of skin colour (in Ben Jonson's *The Masque of the Gipsies*) are referred to in literature. Grellmann's infamous Thesis of 1783 also commented on their blackness.

indicate a complex origin' (quoted in Fraser 1992:23).[32] The search began for the 'pure' or 'real' cultural Gypsy.

From Race to Racisms - The UNESCO declaration (UNESCO 1980, Rex 1983), that differences were occasioned by culture rather than biology and that 'race was no more than an ideological tool', opened up the debate. Thus Gypsies/Travellers, along with other minorities, were drawn into a scenario which transferred value from race to ethnicity and culture. Racism - discriminatory practices derived from the false notion of race - soon gave way, to *racisms.* These were explained as discriminatory practices based on difference 'using all kinds of markers for its projects' (Anthias and Yuval-Davis 1993:197) including gender, class, culture, religion, colour, etc. - all of which had been the subject of discrimination in the past. The politics of difference and identity politics assumed importance.

Wieviorka (1994:182) detected two logics of racism: discrimination and segregation - ''the other' as inferior being allocated to a lower place in society and 'the other' as fundamentally different, an invader to be kept at a distance, expelled, possibly destroyed'. He believed that new racism was a combination of both. Thus the race vocabulary, although it persists (Mason 1996b; Miles and Torres 1999), has been over-written by the vocabulary of ethnicity, culture and hybridity - finer tools for the scrutiny and differentiation of smaller entities. The notion of ethnicity embraced all groups – the centred and the peripheralised. It also revealed difference within as well as between (Modood 1996) and exclusions (Miles 1996; Mac an Ghaill (1999). Whilst this may have held out some hope to end the black/white conflictual relationships perceived (euphemistically) as 'race relations situations' (John Rex), Hall's (1992:258) comment that 'we are all ethnically located and our ethnic identities are crucial to our subjective sense of who we are,' channelled energy into the realm of cultural identity. This discourse challenged hegemonic identities/cultures/ethnicities leading to a 'decentering of the white subject' which questioned the British/English, American/ European, white

---

[32] A more recent study in 1968 by the Anthropology Department of Durham University and the Medical Research Council's Department of Serological Population Genetics Unit, was also abandoned (Clark 1971).

identity (Young 1990; Parekh 2000).[33]

This all inclusive mode meant that Gypsies/Travellers re-entered the discourse since the caravan/vehicle and 'mobile way of life' - being the (major) 'cultural markers', as far as majority society was concerned- came within its remit as did language and Grellmann's discovery of place for them. However, despite the Race Relations Act 1976 – a product of the race discourse - and its protection for other ethnic and black groups - and although Gypsies/Travellers in England were declared an ethnic group in 1989,[34] they have, in the main, been excluded from its embrace. This would fit Glazer's (1995:124) notion that 'the law protects some groups more than others'. The Thesis will examine in due course the way in which indirect discrimination and institutional racism, defined in the Act and its amendment after the Macpherson Report (1999), impact on Gypsy/Traveller lives.

The conflictual race/anti-racist discourse of the 1980s in UK, summed up by Cohen (1992:97) as 'not only a minefield of vested interest but a site of powerful structures of feeling – anger, hatred, pain and envy ...' gave way to what was thought might be a more anodyne scrutiny – that of multi-culturalism. Fanon (1970) and Gilroy (1987) were less sanguine and believed new racism to be cultural racism with the language of race recoded in the language of culture. It was described by Gillborn (1995:23) as 'pseudo-biological culturalism', where culture was substituted for race, and heritage for colour' (ibid:18). Language, religion, way of life, food and dress became modes to signify difference; differences became sifted, valued and generally politicised as different groups were targeted as 'movement politics' changed to 'lifestyle politics' (Mac an Ghaill (1999:128). Some groups found their voice and began to fight for equal rights, resisting being relegated to second and third class citizenship. The notion of Human rights assisted with this project. However, for those without a 'home' the struggle began with 'a place to be' (bel hooks 1981 and quoted in Keith and Pile 1993). In the shuffle not to be under-

---

[33] Black authors applied the same deconstruction techniques to 'the West' and its 'culture'. The anti-racist discourse brought about a reversal whereby white groups were demonised as racist and black groups were reified and cast as 'victims' – working on the assumption that 'power + prejudice= racism'. Some confusion arose when it was found that black groups could be equally antagonist towards each other. The equation, perhaps, would have been better expressed as power + prejudice = discrimination.

[34] Irish Travellers were declared a racial group via case law in August 2000 (Kiely vs Punch Retail)

valued and placed at the bottom of the hierarchy of ethnicities/life-styles, the Gypsy/Traveller voice was barely audible. The Gypsy Lorists and more recent 'others' spoke on their behalf (Kenrick and Puxon 1972; Acton 1974; Adams et al 1975; Okely 1984/94; Liegeois 1995). The Thesis later examines the notion of Voice, the way in which, and why, it is sometimes heard, but mainly silenced - in the sense that it is 'assigned no position of enunciation: there is no space from which the subaltern subject can speak ... a blind spot where understanding and knowledge is blocked' (Spivak quoted in Young 1990:164 – with apologies to Spivak 1994[35]).

The theories of habitus, race and ethnicity pertain to the way in which the logic of a group can form and be formed: Gypsies/Travellers are a case in point. Once formed groups are identified and evaluated for treatment. Via research and academic study the system acquaints itself with the groups, using knowledge about them not only in an attempt to understand, but also to control – with control taking multifarious forms.

The next chapter will look more closely at the way in which Gypsies/Travellers have been and have become identified. The remainder of this chapter will now attempt to examine the other strand of the double helix, and explain the logic of policy and the power group which takes decisions and formulates policy for Gypsies/Travellers.

PART TWO: POLICY AND POLICY MAKING IN A THEORETICAL SETTING
Bureaucracy

Weber (1968:75) claimed that bureaucracy was '*the* means of carrying 'community action' over into rationally ordered societal action' and that 'as an instrument for 'societalizing' relations of power, bureaucracy ... is a power instrument of the first order'.[36] Weber also outlined the 'characteristics' of 'modern bureaucracy' which fell into several categories: 'the principle of fixed and official jurisdictional areas, which are generally ordered by rules ... laws or administrative regulations; the principles of office hierarchy and of levels of graded authority' whereby responsibility and supervision is

---

[35] Although Spivak is referring to women, her comments might apply equally to other repressed groups.
[36] He also conceded that 'where the bureaucratization of administration has been completely carried through, a form of power relation is established that is practically unshatterable' (ibid).

ordered' offering the 'governed the possibility of appealing the decision of a lower office to a higher authority' (ibid:67); and where management is underpinned by kept, written documents (files) in 'original and draught form'. In terms of office management, good management relies upon 'thorough and expert training' (ibid:68); that it also demands 'the full working capacity of the official' and that management of the office follows 'general rules which are more or less stable, ... exhaustive and which can be learned'. Weber suggests that knowledge of the rules 'represents a special technical learning which the officials possess ... It involves jurisprudence, or administrative or business management (ibid:69) ie that officials be expert/professional. Whilst this may, in many respects, now represent the 'ideal', all administrations appear to adhere (however loosely) to these principles. Thus all bureaucracies make and follow 'policy' (they say) which guides their activity. Nevertheless, when it does not then policy can be made retrospectively to legitimate action taken.

In response to the question what is policy, Theodolou (1995:3)[37] claims that it is 'a statement of intent with an accomplished end goal as its objective; ... it can be long or short term; ...it is an ongoing process; ... and it involves not only the decision to enact a law but also the subsequent action of implementation, enforcement and evaluation'. A whole raft of processes and procedures governed by a molecular structure is contained within this definition, suggesting that policy-making and policy makers form a habitus of their own, ostensibly, in order to get the job done.

Getting the Job Done? Policy Making Structures and Processes
National Policy is frequently expressed in broad terms leaving scope for interpretation by the Courts, and Local Authorities to fathom the workable detail. However, the gap between theory and practice can be 'filled with contempt' (Minogue 1993:26). Stoker (1991:152) demonstrates this with the way in which Local Authorities can resist central policy via 'implementation gaps' which can be countered by central Government with 'a complex web of assertive strategies' to ensure compliance. In response Local Authorities

---

[37] Although the work of Theodolou and Cahn (1995) is based on the American model of administration it has relevance for UK given the way in which recent heads of UK governments are slowly adopting the US model and presidential style of leadership.

evade compliance by responding with policies which are 'either unknown or unwelcome' to Central Government. This scenario of game-play can become an end in itself and whereby both National and Local Government lose sight of the objective of the policy and even of governance itself. The process of policy making is thus beset by hurdles and obstacles.

Much legislation comes up for renewal or refreshing on a regular basis and as and where necessary creating opportunities to change, expand or abolish certain programmes. Cobb and Elder (1995:111) use the term 'policy windows' – whereby 'open windows' are the 'opportunities to move packages up the decision-making agenda. Windows do not stay open for long'. Sabatier and Mazamanian (1995:12) define the whole process of policy production as 'agenda-setting, formulation, adoption, implementation and evaluation'. However, after evaluation the process returns to agenda-setting and re-formulation and re-evaluation, so the process tends to circularity (rather than being linear) and becomes reinforcing. Theodolou (1995:3) terms this the 'policy cycle theory' or 'a learning system' which is attuned to maintaining the status quo – and often more attentive (if not responsive) to the environment or habitus in which policy is made and must operate than to those for whom the policy is being formulated. Policy and policy making can also be side-tracked by changes in governments[38] and by ideologies which are often located in the past, making the process more jagged than smooth. Policy-making is thus only partly governed by change on the ground.

King and Stoker (1996), Hogwood and Gunn (1995), Atkinson and Robinson (1994), Atkinson and Moon, (1994) Hill et al (1993), Lipsky (1993) and Stoker (1991) cover the policy minefield and the interaction between local and national administrations together

---

[38] After the 2001 General Election the Department of the Environment, Transport and the Regions (DETR) was reshuffled into the Department of Transport Local Government and the Regions (DTLR). Environment issues were dealt with by the Department of Environment, Food and Rural Affairs Gypsy/Traveller issues were overseen by the Department of Housing and Homelessness - which also dealt with anti-social behaviour. This appeared to remove Gypsies/Travellers from a rural setting (and out of the Green Belt?) into an urban context. The Unit which dealt with Gypsy/Traveller issues specifically, had changed from The Gypsy Sites Policy Branch to the Gypsy Policy Branch. It was this Branch that co-ordinated the bi-annual Count of caravans, identified issues and assisted with policy formation.

with the environment in which policy is discussed, formulated and eventually implemented at the local level – which is often fraught. Hogwood and Gunn (1995:238/9) claim that policy at the national level is often crippled before it enters the statute books – if it gets that far. They also claim that 'perfect implementation of policy (at the local level) is unattainable', owing to external circumstances, lack of time and resources, that the underlying theory of the policy may be at fault, that often it is difficult to 'understand and agree objectives for policy, whilst perfect consultation and co-ordination may be lacking as might perfect compliance' (ibid:244). Constraints re policy formulation at the national level are replicated and magnified at the local level where policy is intended for translation and implementation.

Many difficulties arise at the local level (Solomos and Back 1995:201). First, because, 'the policy agenda is set through alliances between emerging political factions' which enter into relationships with key Council Officers' and that it is 'at this interface where the translation, or otherwise, of policy into practice takes place'. Blocking of unpopular National Policy – in the sense of ensuring that it is unworkable - is therefore not uncommon at both national and local levels. Second, at the local level, group representation (particularly) and powerful individuals are important in raising issues and interests for consideration and 'sponsorship'. Solomos and Back (1995:208) state that 'this operates within the framework of a complex balance of influence and patronage which structures the internal dynamics of political institutions'. The corollary to this is that those without any form of, or weak, representation are frequently left out or are totally excluded from the policy-making process. Gypsy/Traveller families appear to comprise one such 'group'. Third, that the responsibility and answerability to local constituents create 'a key dilemma for local politicians' (ibid:209). Pressure at the local level from vocal minorities is quickly and sharply felt. If it is politically expedient, the local 'voice' can be allowed to over-ride policy and frustrate its implementation. Thus it might not be too difficult to fathom why the 1968 Caravan Sites Act did not have the initial impact at the local level that was expected and stated as intent by National Government.

On a More Practical Level …

Neither National nor Local Governments operate in isolation. In theory, and very simply put, National Government empowers a series of Departments and agencies to act on its behalf, to cover the whole gamut of prescribed national and international affairs. An elected Minister is responsible for the overall running/achievements of each Department, assisted by Junior Ministers and Secretaries who are both elected and permanent. Whether elected or employed, all receive payment from the public purse. In effect, constituents are the Employer. The 'voice' of the constituent shadows parliamentary action, in that MPs supposedly voice 'the concerns' of *some* of their constituents in House of Commons debates. Expressed sentiments, however, may not always be their own. The tone and tenor of the discourse influences the content of policy which in turn is predicated on the way in which the target group is identified and valued. As there are few if any Gypsy/Traveller MPs, fact may not often be sifted from value judgments and rhetoric.[39] A spate of well-aimed speeches from the late 1960s to the beginning of the 21st Century (see Hansard extracts in Appendix Two) could be construed as c(l)uing policy. This would compare with Ginsburg's (1992:110) notion of 'common sense racism' which 'informs and nourishes institutional and structural racism via the political and bureaucratic process' and tends to shape a general and lasting view of Gypsies/Travellers – particularly when it is taken up by the media who are an integrated and powerful component of the power group structure (as the more recent 'trial' and tribulations of Rupert Murdoch and Prime Ministers past and present (via various enquiries, the Leveson Enquiry 2012 being the latest) demonstrate.

The Prime Minister takes (or not) the ultimate responsibility for each Department's activities. The sometimes friction between the government in power and 'Whitehall' – the Government amanuensis, which is not without its own powers and controls - is well-known. It too could be regarded as having habitus status and as such has internal structures of its own. Here, Hambleton (2001) found that 'a lack of integration between Whitehall departments creates problems over conflicting objectives, unintended

---

[39] That is not to say that there are not MPs who stand in the House to oppose any negative view during debate.

consequences and contradictory incentives, which contribute strongly to fragmentation.'[40] Thus a need exists for structures, checks, balances and compromises to be implemented within the National Government framework if any policy formation and implementation is to succeed at all. Keene and Scase (1998:2) state that 'checks and balances' are also 'needed in order to ensure a uniformity of service provision and a high degree of procedural and substantive integrity and probity'. Thus National Government aware (or not) of its own shortcomings and practices, also checks local administrations which, given the structuring structures are, in many respects, now microcosms of National Government. This has led Chisholm (2001:48) to comment that 'Whitehall seems to be obsessed with the idea that Local Authorities cannot be trusted'. This view appeared to be reflected back at Whitehall and the National Government by Local Authorities.

Resources

'If a problem is to be tackled in a serious and genuine manner, policies must have adequate inputs' and 'proper resourcing primarily of a financial nature' (Atkinson and Moon 1994:18). 'Few policies can be implemented without public expenditure' (Theodolou 1995:92). (In some instances, street violence has become a means of obtaining positive results and a type of d'accord.) A major 'excuse' for inaction at the local level is a lack of financial resources from central Government - the complaint being that central Government requires local Councils 'to do more and more with less and less' (Leader of Council Interview 2000). Housing provision, although recognised as a basic need in UK has been revamped and downsized in terms of state provision and Local Authority duty to provide. This has had a trickle-down effect on Gypsies/Travellers in terms of site provision. Provision of housing has now been devolved to Housing Associations (HAs), arms-length agencies and more recently to private developers. Gypsy/Traveller sites follow a similar trajectory. This is exemplified in Government's decreasing expenditure patterns. Legislation prevented HAs setting up sites with grant aid from the Housing Corporation because caravans were treated as separate and distinct from housing (even though the majority of caravans in question were stationary/static).

---

[40] With each Department housed in a different building, or a different part of a building, each has the potential to develop a sub/habitus - one not always connecting with another.

Although at the time of writing the Thesis there were no current, state resources for new build Gypsy/Traveller sites in England, grant aid was made available in Scotland to be extended for a further three years (Scottish Executive Ninth Term Report 1998-1999). Grant aid was due to begin in Northern Ireland (Department of the Environment for Northern Ireland 1999). This could be construed as staggered funding, 'rolling out' provision gradually. It also recognised an overdue need in Scotland and Ireland. It could also have been a dispersal mechanism. Eleven years on, grant aid is being provided by the Department of Communities and Local Government on a competitive basis for construction of sites and site refurbishment – although the Coalition Government (2011) has revoked any duty on LAs to provide sites. They can however, identify land suitable for sites in their development plans - based on their Needs Assessment exercises.

The term 'resources' could also include political will. The 1968 Caravan Sites Act demonstrated that even with resources, without political will, full and proper implementation was not guaranteed. Atkinson and Moon (1994:19) are of the view that 'without political will all the declarations of good intent by a government will be worthless'. Similarly the failure to act or to make decisions can also be a statement of intent 'often of greater consequence' than the decisions which are made (Wright-Mills 1995:372). Influencing decisions can also be the threat of non-re-election, particularly where the creation of Gypsy/Traveller sites is concerned and where some Councillors rely on their remuneration for being in Office when that might be their only source of income.

The Time Lag

Events on the ground are often more dynamic than the processes within the system which attempt to deal with them – which can have unintended consequences (Hill 1993). There is a time lag between an issue on the ground gathering momentum, the identification of that issue at the local and national level, policy formulation at the national level and its implementation at the local level. This is accompanied by a tail back of attitudes – often resistant and often linked to historical ideologies and other policies.[41] It is at this point that multiple interests conflict which is a reminder that institutions, however corporate in appearance, are, in reality, a composite of individuals, each with the potential to sabotage the best laid policies and plans – equally, they have the power to fast-forward implementation.

New policies often call for attitudinal change and an agility of mind and procedure which is not always apparent at either national or local levels. Such agility can sometimes be difficult to achieve especially if local administrations are of a different political persuasion to the National Government, or when County Councils differ politically from District Councils. However, where political orientation is the same, LAs may be better placed to make agendas workable.[42] Implementation also depends upon how any policy is translated at the local level. Even within a single Council there is room for disagreement over interpretation and priorities. Thus much hangs on the way in which Local Authorities approach, react to, perceive and interpret National Government legislation, which in turn governs whether or not provision materialises – unless it is ruled as a duty by National Government. For the same reasons, partnership working also has its limitations.

The Right Sort? …

The calibre of Members of Parliament, of local Councils and paid Officers should not be overlooked. Their ability to understand the process of rule-making, to understand and to interpret the rules themselves and to be able to understand the problems being tackled are of importance if policy, practice and service delivery are to seamlessly fuse to deliver desired outcomes. Elmore (1993:313) claims that 'in some instances policies are based on poor and incomplete understandings of the problem they are supposed to address'. When this is mixed with 'the failure of officials to comprehend the ideological nature of (their) own activities … a myopic vision which is thoroughly damaging to public policy

---

[41] Hill (1993:22) noted that 'even with the best intentions policy makers come up against the brick wall of ignorance'.
[42] South Staffordshire District Council - Conservative controlled - for example, during the Thatcher/Major years never levied a Community Charge on its constituents Leader of Council Interview 2000).

itself', can result (Hill 1993:29). Salaries of MPs and allowances for locally elected Council Members have gradually increased, the rationale being to attract better candidates - allegedly. However, the 'expenses' scandals of 2011 and the austerity measures of 2012, highlight that any institution is only as strong as its weakest link. Today, public service is not necessarily the domain of the retired elderly, nor the only motivation of candidates. It is increasingly becoming a 'profession' attractive to the young, upwardly mobile, and a step towards a public profile which could lead to better things, not specifically within the realm of governance.

… vs Human Perversity

It should be mentioned here, that over-riding the above is a whole intrigue of political persuasion and human perversity which can be manipulated to move or block policy. Attempts are made to channel differing and disparate viewpoints of majority society into 'political parties' and forums at both the national and local level. Here, it is envisaged that disagreements can be settled via debate and the ballot box and lobbying rather than by stone throwing, baton charges and terrorism. However, often protest is seen not as a matter for debate but as an issue of law and order and a new type of repression and resistance.

The Factor of Change

In an interview with the Head of the Gypsy Policy Branch at the DTLR, it was clear that the Department had a wide remit. The DTLR was described as being 'the sponsoring government department for local government' which included sponsoring change and development. However, rapid and constant change can also throw policy and foster a laager mentality at the local level.

Many of the changes in legislation at the time of writing the Thesis, were occasioned by the Human Rights Act and the notion of compatibility. Bringing all other legislation into line with the Human Rights Act has revealed the policy maze. These issues will be discussed in the later chapters on National and Local Policy.

Globalisation

National governments are increasingly pressured by global and international concerns which can often over-ride local and national interests. Britain's partial inclusion into the European Community appears to have had some impact on British socio-economic policy, occasioning down-sizing in some areas and out-resourcing in others – Health, Education and Welfare are cases in point. An underlying rationale appears to be that being desirable could trigger massive in/out migrations, given the EU policy of freedom of movement between EU member states.

Policy for Gypsies/ Travellers, therefore, does not stand alone.

(… and An International Aside)

National governments have a wider remit than national affairs with regard to Gypsies/Travellers. National governments link up and sign up to various international agreements and policies. They can also be involved in cross-national initiatives. That national governments exchange information about Gypsies/Travellers which might have 'read across' implications, is important. Of equal importance is the countries/States involved. The UK government in 2001 was involved in a project with the Czech Republic: 'The United Kingdom and Czech Republic Twinning project – Promotion of Racial and Ethnic Equality'. The 'overall object' of this was to 'draw up proposals which will assist the Czech Republic in strengthening government action to combat racial discrimination and improve relations between minorities in particular the Roma and the wider Czech society' (DTLR correspondence 10 August 2001; see also Guy 2001 for the current discourse on Czech Roma). This, at first, might seem encouraging – given that the Czech Republic (and other Eastern European countries have been noted for their harsh treatment of, and discrimination against their Roma population (Ringold 2000; OSCE Report 2000; UNESCCHR 1999; Guy 1975; and Stewart 1997 on Hungarian Roma). However, it is also possible that the motivation to improve human rights for Roma in these countries might have had more to do with gaining swift and smooth passage into the European Community. This view is fostered by the fact that a Prague radio report claimed that British Immigration officials were interviewing Roma families and subsequently preventing some of them from boarding their aeroplanes destined for UK.[43] It would appear that the DTLR and the Home Office were colluding to keep the number of 'foreign' Gypsies/Travellers to a minimum. Alternatively, the Home Office could have been working at cross purposes with the DTLR. This suggests one habitus of many parts, with each sub habitus working independently of the other[44] and for itself.

Dialogue?

Given the mechanisms involved in the structuring structures of habitus and the complexity of the policy making process, effective dialogue is imperative to avert crises. It appeared then (and even now) that little effective, communicative dialogue takes place between the two parties – Authority and Gypsies/Travellers themselves - with many 'conversations' being brokered by others. Thus the notion of 'unequal' conversation and the need for 'communicative action' (Habermas 1991) could also be adapted as a theoretical consideration for the past and current relationship between some Gypsies/Travellers and Authority. For effective communication to take place 'participants come to a common definition of the situation' (ibid:119). This must apply as much between Local and National Governments as between Local Authorities and Gypsies/Travellers. Is the relationship between LAs and Gypsies/Travellers strategic, based on threats, enticements and, ultimately, mutual stand-off? Or is there an understanding which 'specifies the conditions of an agreement to be reached communicatively?' (ibid:136). In the latter, any action carried out is done so on a 'consensual basis' and on 'the basis of some jointly defined action situation' (ibid). Language is an important instrument in the process of influence (Habermas 1981:95). An equal conversation rests upon the notion of shared knowledge or understanding which is

---

[43] The practice was denounced and was initially monitored by members of the Czech and Helsinki Assembly (Radio Prague cr@radio.cz, 6 August 2001). However, the Czech government has now given permission for UK immigration officers 'to resume their practice of screening British-bound flights at Prague airport for asylum seekers ... mostly Gypsies ...'. The scheme is expected to extend to the Balkan States if it proves successful (The Guardian, 28 August 2001).
I was informed at interview that whilst the Home office and the DTLR would liaise and work together on certain issues there are others where they would take unilateral action (Interview 13/9/2001).

predicated on an information exchange and a willingness to compromise, to see the other's point of view. In sum, 'agreement in the communicative practice of everyday life rests simultaneously on intersubjectivity, shared propositional knowledge, on normative accord and on mutual trust' (ibid). It would appear that this state has yet to be reached in UK between National and Local Governments or between Local Authorities and Gypsies/Travellers.

SUMMARY

This chapter has tried not only to anchor the Gypsy/Traveller/Local Authority relationship, and how majority society perceives Gypsies/Travellers as a separate and segregated habitus, to a theoretical base but also to explain how, and possibly why, the LA/Gypsy/Traveller situation might have evolved. It has also attempted to show the mechanics whereby individuals form groups or are assigned to them. Once this process has occurred the group is influenced not just by intra group structuring structures but also by the structuring structures of other, external habita – which can become, knowingly or not, internalised. Although Gypsies/Travellers have been excluded from much sociological theory, or mentioned only in passing, hopefully, it will be seen from the ensuing Thesis and the above, that their situation fits comfortably within mainstream sociological and policy theory.

When groups become identified and 'established', value whether positive or negative becomes added. Theories of race and ethnicity come into play to explain difference in value, the politics of difference, the fear and threat of difference and how difference can be accommodated without fracturing the whole/entity. Theories of race have been applied to Gypsies/Travellers but are only useful when applied in terms of social rather than phenotypical differences. The main, observable markers of difference for Gypsies/Travellers are their mode of dwelling - the caravan - and supposedly their mobility and the agency which has developed around this. Forced mobility produces particular responses and behaviours which then serve to identify 'the group'. This circularity embeds perceptions and fortifies identity.

Whilst theory might describe or attempt to explain and even come to prescribe agency, the complexity of the process produces a mine-field for policy formulation. The strands between agency, policy and implementation are so closely intertwined that they come to form 'a system' not only within the policy-making process itself but also within the institutions which have to formulate, translate and implement policy. Systems formulated and developed, over time, become established and embedded producing what could be viewed as 'a culture', 'an ethos' or 'personality' within that institution – which in turn come to prescribe a way of working and interaction.

Given the many tiers of governance and the numerous rules and personalities involved at each level, it is not surprising that the translation and implementation of policy is often less than perfect sometimes to the point where resulting resolutions produce the opposite to what is intended. This can occur owing to a lack of commensurate dialogue between National and Local Government, between Authority and target groups. A lack of political will and/or a lack of resources are also contributory factors to failure.

The next chapter will explore the processes which pack the notion of identity and the way in which negative identifications make it comfortable for the State to remove and to exclude certain groups judged to be non-belongers, which adds to their 'group' identity.

CHAPTER FOUR

IDENTITY: ARE YOU WHO THEY THINK YOU ARE?

Cornell and Hartmann (1998:xviii) and Craib (1998:7/8) respectively claim that 'identities once established have impacts' and that 'constructed subjects' take on a life of their own'. That life, after identification, can depend on the distance (cultural and geographical) between the (perceived) group and majority society. It also depends on who makes the identification and how far it is contested by those being identified. Young (2000:256) claims that structures of power, exploitation and domination build easily on experience of social and cultural differentiation'. They also determine who will belong and who will not. Identity and identification, then, are not only mechanisms in the process of group formation, but also an important means of sifting, categorising, evaluating and hierachisising groups and individuals into categories which can then be 'managed', manipulated and sometimes excluded.

The last chapter discussed some overarching theoretical principles which help to explain group formation. The notion of identity and identification although taken seriously by some, is often arbitrary and imprecise. Those being identified may contest that assessment. Hence identity is an issue which needs constant re-adjustment and negotiation, particularly since individuals and groups can change and evolve with time and circumstance. This chapter will look at the way in which Gypsies/Travellers are identified by the State and at the local level. The thesis will argue that the way in which Gypsies/Travellers are perceived influences the way in which they are ultimately treated. Once exclusion and exclusivity begins, based on politics of difference, how long is it before exclusion and rejection are internalised to become self-exclusion, spawning a counter-exclusiveness? Those who cease to travel may become integrated, but they do not disappear.[45]

Gypsies/Travellers themselves are aware that their identity is based on what others have said about them. But when asked about Gypsy/Traveller identity, one informant remarked, 'It's whatever we say it is', or 'by the way the group sees us and recognises us'. Although not many said that they were an 'ethnic group', there was a recognition that the group was made up of different families with 'their own ways'. In Staffordshire, English Gypsies/Travellers were anxious to differentiate themselves from Irish Travellers and traditional Gypsies/Travellers wished to disassociate themselves from New Travellers and East European Roma had no desire to associate themselves with UK Gypsies/Travellers (GLO Interview 2013). This suggested that there were genuine or perceived and recognised differences between groups, in addition to differences between Gypsies/Travellers and majority society, which appear not to have been taken into account. That said, the irony is that traditional Roma/Gypsies/Travellers of UK probably have more in common, in terms of shared experience of exclusion and forced mobility with the new wave groups and New Travellers within UK than with their counterparts in Eastern Europe. This would indicate the possibility of greater political scope, rather than less, for national alliances.

National policy appears to recognise that the term *Gypsy* or *Traveller* covers a wide range of groups of different backgrounds. However, it is at the local level that difference is 'felt' most. Some Councils have site policies – overt and covert - which either mix families on site or segregate them.[46] Additionally, mobile groups are separated on sites, from the more permanent residents, where transit sites exist. Speaking with families the general opinion was that they favoured exclusivity on sites – often for the same reasons that majority society excluded mobile unauthorised encampments. Privately owned sites

---

[45] Little or no research has been undertaken to establish what happens to Gypsies/Travellers once they move off sites and into other than conventional housing.
[46] Newcastle-under-Lyme tended not to 'mix' families whilst Stoke-on-Trent did. This is not to say that families do not segregate themselves. When the new Warden at Stoke-on-Trent arrived (an Irish Traveller) Irish families came to fill some of the empty plots. Some of the English families moved off and elsewhere.

in Staffordshire were, in the main exclusive. Thus classifying all Gypsies/Travellers under a single term served to give an appearance of unity when, in reality, individuality and fragmentation, even separation, were the norm.

Gypsies/Travellers have attempted to make the term exclusive to 'known' families who follow the travelling way of life, with their own set of norms. However, way of life can also prescribe norms and modes of adaptation which leads ultimately, and if left unchecked, to separation or exclusion from the mainstream. Hegemonic society and those who co-opt into that way of life attempt to frustrate such efforts. When outsiders refer to Gypsies/Travellers, they call upon a plethora of identities which have, over time, been allocated to this grouping at particular historical moments (Acton 1974). Thus the term appears to incorporate the notion of Gypsies/ Travellers as a status group, an ethnic group, a social movement with utopian overtones, a squatting group, a nomadic group and an affinity group. The common denominator is that Gypsies/Travellers are perceived by majority society as a nomadic non-belonging group with some being more 'ethnic' and mobile than others. The notion of mobility or 'nomadism' has become a term frequently used to describe all Gypsies/Travellers. This term will now be discussed.

Mobility or Stability Denied - Nomadism, the Moving Myth?

Nomadism, as a colonial/imperial notion (Drakakis-Smith 2003; 2007) needs 'unpicking' and deconstructing. With few exceptions, Gypsies/Travellers are described, and some describe themselves, as 'nomads' (Clebert 1963), 'wanderers', 'migrants', 'itinerants', 'Travellers' to name but a few 'other' terms for them, even when they have lived in the same place or a locality for decades. Thus, are such terms accurate descriptions of what Gypsies/ Travellers do, or are they value judgments and/or expedient terms used by others (and internalised by Gypsies/Travellers) for the ease of (mis)appropriation and/or exclusion from land? Indeed, Guy in 1975 queried whether Roma in the Czech republic were migrants rather than 'nomads'. Klimova in 2000 asks the same question and speaks in terms of 'forced nomadism'. Another, related question is, should the treatment of Gypsies/Travellers in UK be seen in isolation or do they form part of a more global whole of de-territorialised/landless groups forced into mobility? The MA thesis looked in more detail at other groups in similar positions, and this information is pertinent here, to examine the structuring structures which have produced other groups – the Inuit, the Sami, Australian Aborigines and the Bedouin of the Negev to name but a few - who have been labelled 'nomadic' in the more recent past to justify (mis)appropriation of land via (mis)perception, policy/rule making/changes (see Shamir 1996; Rowley 1972, Roberts 1978 on this point). This experience was compared to the past and present treatment of UK Gypsies/Travellers, who are often hounded from place to place. It is against the experience of other groups that the claim of nomadism for Gypsies/Travellers can be compared and assessed and hopefully found to be what it really is - a euphemism for power group sleight of hand and as a rationale for removing from land and, space and/or place.[47]

Although 'culturally' each group is different, having adapted to exclusion and de-territorialisation differentially, nomadism has been a particularly virulent colonial tag justifying the (mis)appropriation of land leading to exclusion from the mainstream. Groups are then encouraged to return on less favourable terms. This is expedited via a process of negative identifications and perceptions of some groups who come to be regarded as *persona non grata*, which can make re-inclusion difficult, often impossible. With reference to Gypsies/Travellers the term 'nomadism' has been used to ensure non-settlement and, when linked to notions of ethnic origin, to abrogate citizen rights and privileges. The experience of such groups was compared with that of Gypsies/ Travellers in Staffordshire in particular, many of whom were indigenous to the UK, and where families were constantly moved on and discouraged from settlement (Drakakis-Smith 1997, 2007; Drakakis-Smith and Mason 2001).

Acton (1974) and Okely (1984) redefined 'nomadism' for Gypsies/Travellers in terms of economic purpose, but which left intact the notion that Gypsies/Travellers were nomadic and had no desire to settle. Both Acton and Okely implied that Gypsy/Traveller

---

[47] *The Financial Times* newspaper recently produced an article by John Reed on the way in which Israel is planning to build large urban and military complexes in the Negev Desert which could uproot 40,000 Bedouin Arabs. (28 May 2013)

'nomadism' was based on Gypsy/Traveller agency alone –ie that is what Gypsies/Travellers did to find employment (or wished to do to avoid wage labour (Okely 1984)). However, this would be to ignore other important factors such as exclusion from space and place and discrimination in the work-place, forcing families to move and/or become self-reliant/contained and/or self-employed.[48] This situation can be seen in action, when New Travellers and Gypsy/Traveller families are moved on involuntarily and repetitively, making movement random until new sites and new niches are found. However, once on a mobile trajectory, settlement can become increasingly difficult. Research (Lowe and Shaw 1993; Hetherington 2000; and Webster and Millar 2001) has revealed that even New Travellers are becoming bound increasingly to the economic practice of travelling to find work and travelling in order to find places to live without being harassed. The term 'nomadism', thus, appears to be 'other', and usefully derived, to prevent settlement, which keeps some groups moving and on the periphery.

That said, some Gypsy/Traveller families have adapted to their position as non-belongers and have made a success of State negative action to the point where they now defend their right to travel and/or live in a caravan.[49] New Travellers appear to have co-opted the term as a celebration of freedom of movement (se McKay 1996; Dearling 1998; and Hetherington 2000) and even as a term of defiance. Figure 1:2 in Chapter One attempted to present diagrammatically the duality of perception re settlement/mobility. For the purpose of policy making and service delivery, the issue of mobility needs clarification if the issue is to be resolved so that the needs of all in this grouping can be met satisfactorily.

The Official View – State/Legal Definitions …

Official State definitions of Gypsies/Travellers have attempted to rise above the minutiae of localised difference and refer to 'persons of nomadic habit of life, whatever their race or origin', which points to a melting pot-approach - and the notion that all are 'nomadic'.

---

[48] A more recent study by Ryder and Greenfields (n/d) entitled *Roads to Success: Economic and Social Inclusion for Gypsies and Travellers* (a Report for the Irish Traveller Movement in Britain) examined the Gypsy/Traveller economy and whilst this study was interesting it took the functionalist view of examining what is rather than how this came to be.

However, this fails to address the issue of vulnerability felt by excluded and marginal groups. It also implies that families who have ceased being 'nomadic' or mobile cease being Gypsies/Travellers.[50] This is sometimes the reason given by Planning Inspectors to refuse planning permission for private sites (Kenrick and Clark 1999) – in which case, it also militates against settlement and denies choice to those who wish to cease travelling. That said, the definition was intended to single out those for whom the State would make provision. Given that the State no longer provides, the definition, now, has limited positive use. (Between 2003 and 2010 provision was reinstated by New Labour and once more revoked by the Conservative/Liberal Democrat Coalition government when it came to power.)

... And Closing the Circle?

Welfare Law can be traced back to the Poor Laws and together with planning rules and regulations are remnants of feudal or customary and Manorial Law with its acute sense of boundaries, belonging and negotiated rights,[51] which produced such groups as 'serfs', 'vassals' and slaves, and out groups such as 'vagabonds' and villeins' etc.. After 1300 masterless men or persons no longer having manorial ties were free to respond to the economic market (Beier 1985:12; Comninel 2000). Such changes occurred and were occurring throughout Europe occasioning freedom of movement. Such individuals and families coming from Europe would not be exceptional. Added to this were the criss-crossing crusades, pilgrimages, and traders from west to east and east to west (see Joinville and Villehardouin 2008 for some first-hand accounts of these journeys and of mobility at that time). There were indications, then, that Medieval society was less than static or sedentary as some would imply.

When Manorial Law became overtaken by regal Common Law, the Poor Laws were introduced as a safety net for those displaced, particularly by Enclosures and Clearances,

---

[49] Although the caravan is gradually being replaced on permanent sites with the mobile chalet/home.
[50] Whilst this might apply to some it might not apply to all.
[51] The notion of Commons or Common Land as being free to all is a fallacy. Such lands were used by negotiation between those with rights to, and responsibilities in, the land. Even so, such rights and usage were closely regulated and guarded to prevent exploitation and over usage. For further discussion on this

who became identified as 'the poor'. This category became divided into two groups – 'the deserving' and 'the undeserving' and again into 'the settled poor' and 'the vagrant poor' (Wrightson 1990:141/2; Beier 1985:12). The settled poor had had a recognised place in society and were eligible for poor relief. The vagrant/mobile poor, which could include rogues and vagabonds were deemed to be outside 'the charitable consideration of the authorities' (Wrightson 1990: ibid), 'a threat to the established order' (Beier 1985:xx) and a drain on limited parish resources raised, in the main, by parishioners. 'Peddling' and 'huckstering' became a means to avoid poverty, as did seasonal work. 'More often they were hustled on their way by villagers who feared and suspected them, or whipped out of parishes by constables enforcing the vagrancy laws (Wrightson 1990: ibid). Each parish would support so many 'poor' and no more - the 'excess' were excluded and moved on. Thus administrative rules, mechanisms and practices produced evaluated outcomes. The term 'foreign' was attached to anyone from outside the parish. It is not unlikely that Gypsies/Travellers were perceived to be part of this group and thus co-opted into it if they were not already part of it. The national 'shocked dissociation' (ibid.) permeates legislation and policy and pervades public attitudes today.[52]

Via legal instruments, Gypsies/Travellers appear to have become absorbed into an already existing class of mobile 'wanderers', comprising vagabonds, vagrants, academics, students, surgeons, heathens, criminals etc., some of whom would be classed as non-belongers and 'masterless men' (Beier 1985). The term 'Gypsy' came to re-define a group in the same way that Irish and New Travellers via popular perception fed by the media have come to re-define the term Gypsy. Lucassen et al. (1998:61) suggest that the 'emergence of stigmatised categories and discriminatory legislation aimed at them' induced the very behaviours that legislation was intended to curb.

Thus legal definitions appear to have a history of their own, either originating from identification or in order to exclude by statute (see Fraser 1992 and Mayall 1988) or from the State's attempt to include by making provision. Recent State definitions have

---

issue see (Trevelyan 1964; Hoskins and Stamp 1963; Mingay 1968; Russell 1972; Stevenson 1991; Comninel 2000; Drakakis-Smith 2003)
[52]The recent introduction of legislation for the control of beggars and begging is a case in point.

attempted to rise above the minutiae of localised difference by making reference to 'persons of nomadic *habit* of life whatever their race or origin' (Section 16, Caravan sites Act 1968; Criminal Justice and Public Order Act (CJPO 1994 Part V2(b):62). Geary and O'Shea (1995:169) claim that ethnicity was removed from Gypsies/Travellers by the 1968 Caravan Sites Act, and whilst it gave the appearance of being inclusive and recognizing that not all Gypsies/Travellers were ethnically located, it excluded New Travellers.

Definitions were constructed for a purpose and attempted to sift the category of Gypsy/Traveller in order that only the 'genuine' would be catered for.[53] It needs to be flagged here that the State is also influenced by representations from the local level. Whether the State had any useful exchange with Gypsies/Travellers (particularly those 'on the road') and directly is questionable. Now that the duty to provide has been removed the definition, currently, appears to be used to support the maintenance of policy for existing sites.

However, this definition meant that Gypsies/Travellers were then perceived as a 'status group' (after Weber 1967) and had to prove their 'special' rights if they were to be treated differently from other caravan dwellers, trespassers on or unauthorised users of, land (Kenrick and Clark 1999). The New Traveller phenomenon confused LAs and Planning Inspectors who had to adjudicate on land use. Although New Travellers had co-opted aspects of the Gypsy/Traveller way of life, officialdom refused to provide for them, although they fitted within the Act's non-ethnic (Beale and Geary 1994) and the status group/affinity group definition – it is likely that, at the time, a 'habit of life' had not yet been established for them.

Beale and Geary chart the quest to discover 'the identity of the Gypsy way of life' (ibid:112) which, in the official context, tended to be achieved via the Courts of Law and relied heavily on Judges' interpretations and perceptions of what they construed

---

[53] This might compare with State attempts to discover who are the 'genuine' homeless, who are 'genuine' welfare beneficiaries, asylum seekers etc. – ie an impossible task, yet made necessary by legislation for the allocation of resources

'nomadism', 'habit of life', or 'Gypsies' to be. In this they were influenced by what they had read, by the limits imposed upon them by the State in terms of who would benefit from State resources, from LA feed-back and by those coming before them to seek justice. Thus the basic definitions became fleshed out with judicial refinements which were not always clear or consistent, ebbing and flowing between 'ethnogenesis' – and/or lack of it - (CRE v Dutton (1989) 1 All ER 306 and Mandla v Dowell Lee (1983) All ER 1062); 'tradition' (Berkshire CC v Bird and others (1986) QBD, unreported, September 1986); and 'habit of life' centering around travelling with an economic purpose (R v South Hams DC, ex parte Gibb (CA) (1994) 3 WLR 1151 and R v Gloucester CC, ex parte Dutton (1991) 24 HLR 246). Case law reflects appellants from traditional, Irish and New Traveller backgrounds. This appears to have given rise to the confusions now surrounding identity.

In 1984 the Department of the Environment Gypsy Sites Branch issued a paper entitled, 'Defining a Gypsy'. The paper claimed that 'Hippies, drop-outs and other house dwellers who take to the road are easily distinguishable from gypsies by local authority officials and others who have experience of dealing with gypsies' (Department of the Environment 1984:7). It takes as sufficient and (all-inclusive) the Diplock interpretation that 'a gypsy should be defined as a person without fixed abode who leads a nomadic life, dwelling in tents or other shelter or in caravans or other vehicles' (Mills v Cooper (1967) 2 All ER 100 at 104) which formed the basis for the 1968 Caravan Sites Act definition. Cripps in his Report of 1976 concluded that 'as no-one was inconvenienced in practice by lack of precision in the statutory definition' there was no need to change it (ibid:13). The Department of the Environment also attempted to take on board the issue of ethnicity arising from the Mandla v Dowell Lee case (1983) 1 All ER 1062 at 1066-7) where Lord Fraser seemed to wrestle with the race/ethnicity discourse, declaring eventually that for him ethnic meant '(1) a long shared history, of which the group is conscious as distinguishing it from other groups, and the memory of which it keeps alive; (2) a cultural tradition of its own, including family and social customs and manners, often but not necessarily associated with religious observance'. The Department of the Environment suggested five more characteristics which could be relevant – a common geographical origin or descent from a small number of common ancestors; a common language not necessarily peculiar to the group; a common religion different from that of neighbouring groups or from the general community surrounding it; a common literature peculiar to the group; being a minority or being an oppressed or a dominant group within a larger community' (ibid:14). However, after deliberation it decided that the options left were: to leave the definition as it stood at present; attempt to satisfy the popular idea that a 'real Gypsy' exists and others should be excluded; or make no special provision for those called 'gypsies, letting them make their way as best they can with the rest of the population' (ibid 15). The eventual conclusion was that 'even if it were possible to identify such gypsies as Romanes there was still the question of what provision should be made for caravan dwellers not within the Romani category' (ibid:18). It was, however, noted that 'In eastern Europe the accommodation problem has been tackled by housing gypsies' (ibid). This indicates that ostensibly the problem for officialdom was not one of ethnicity necessarily, but way of life – that it was possibly more inclusive to view families as a status/affinity group as opposed to an ethnic group.

Although the 1994 Criminal Justice and Public Order Act retained the 1968 Caravan Sites Act definition (CJPO Act (1994) Part V 2(b):62), which seems to have ignored the 1989 declaration that 'Gypsies' were an ethnic group (based on CRE v Dutton (cited above) it did not exclude them from any of the inhibiting procedures which related to New Travellers, Ravers and other groups, some of whom were homeless, which were: trespass on land (Part V.61:41), raves (Part V.63:44), disruptive trespasses (Part V.68:49), squatters (Part V.72:54), unauthorised campers (Part V.77:59). Indeed, this Act revoked any positive features that might have accrued to 'traditional' Gypsies/Travellers from earlier legislation, particularly the statutory provision of sites. Thus, in effect, Gypsies/Travellers became, once more, homogenised and levelled on a somewhat un-level field, perceived as a plethora of non-conforming groups, having to compete as best they could with each other and with the rest of the population. Sweeping statements emanating from the Home Office and other political parties – particularly in relation to Roma asylum seekers and refugees, implied that all Gypsies/Travellers were the same, which exacerbated the problems surrounding identity. The persistent reports about trespass, fly-tipping and anti-social behaviour on sites over-rode all other identity claims and provision issues: media reports; Hansard (28/6/1989, 4/11/1992, 15/1/02, 11/6/02); the DTLR Commissioned Good Practice Guidance Report (1998); the Crispin Blunt Private Members Bill (29/1/03) suggested that Gypsies/Travellers were viewed by local populations as a non-deserving status/affinity group with different values to 'the rest' of society with ethnicity being perceived, as not necessarily, a salient feature. The more current spate of 'reality' television programmes (2011/13) focussing on some Gypsy/ Traveller families have tended to reinforce such views.

When the DTLR Department dealing with Gypsies and Travellers re-styled itself as the Department of Housing, Homelessness (and anti-social behaviour) two new definitions crept in – that Gypsies/Travellers on unauthorised sites were 'homeless' and 'anti-social' (House of Lords debate on Provision for Gypsies/Travellers: www.publications.parliament.uk/pa/ld199900/ldhansard/pdvn/lds02/text/20115-07.htm ; House of Commons debate on Trespass: www.parliament.the-stationery-office.co.uk/pa/cm200102/cmhansard/cm0/20115h05.htm; both held on 15 January 2002). Once more the behaviour of the visible few was being interpreted as the behaviour of all. It is not surprising then that increasingly way of life has become confused with certain 'behaviours' and has been attached to Gypsies/Travellers as another essential component of their identity.

Groups Sorted?

To date, it appears that the State offers protection to Gypsies and some Travellers via the 'ethnic' label which has come lately to Gypsies/Travellers in UK.[54] This has resulted, generally, in secondary citizenship/denizenship, and being at the end of any resource distribution queue. Language and the 'discovery' of a place of origin (Grellmann 1782) served (correctly or incorrectly) to locate Gypsies/Travellers within the ethnicity paradigm.[55] This laid the foundation for the 19th and 20th Century notions of the 'True

---

[54] And mainly via the courts – acting as agents of the State.
[55] The discourse on language continues on various levels from global to local – from a 'universal' language to a creole/dialect. The work of Grellmann is scrutinised by Pischell (1908), Grant (1995), Willems 1997, Willems and Lucassen et al 1998; Drakakis-Smith (2003). Although Grellmann' thesis was found wanting in 1787 (Gentleman's Review 1787) his ideas were given substance (and with varying degrees of accuracy)

Gypsy', which has served to excommunicate those who might not compare. Where 'definitions' are made they fall into broad, cross-cutting categories which are often value laden – ie Gypsies – deviant/secretive/alien/ethnic; Tinkers/Irish Travellers – status group/deviant/ethnic; New Travellers – status/behavioural group/subversive etc (with each identification coined by others during a particular historical 'moment'). This appears to connect with the pseudo-scientific procedures of identification utilised in the 18th and 19th Centuries which placed *groups* into (appropriate or otherwise) categories. In the 20th and 21st Centuries identification appears to have become a means of placing *individuals* into the relevant and available categories; the Gypsy/Traveller life has become a recognised habitus; the term Gypsy/Traveller attaching and co-opted by already existing mobile groups in UK, to become an 'umbrella' term. The 2000 English Court ruling that Irish Travellers Constitute an ethnic group (O'Leary and Others vs Allied Domeq and Others 2000 Central London County Court 29 August No CL 950275-79) recognised a group within a group and New Travellers as the newest group could be waiting their turn for inclusion.

The Ph D project fieldwork sought, amongst other things, to discover how policy makers, practitioners and service deliverers identified Gypsies/Travellers at the local level and how heavily they relied upon national and legal definitions. The intention being to assess, ultimately, how precise was the process of identification and how far identification had impacted on policy, practice and service delivery - taking the view that accuracy, particularly when need assessment, the allocation of resources and service delivery are involved - is important. The MA Thesis found that in the two Councils studied (Stoke-on-Trent and Newcastle-under-Lyme) that policy makers appeared not

---

by Rudiger (1782) Sampson (1911), and Bryant who set about collecting and compiling vocabularies, which have been subsequently questioned by Bubenik (1995). Latterly, the language of UK Gypsies/Travellers has been scrutinized in terms of being a 'creole' (Hancock 1970; Arnold 1970) and akin to Yiddish and/or a 'secret language' (Sandford 1973). The most recent edited volumes of the Gypsy Lore Society deal with Romani (Matras 1995, 1998, 1999, 2000), and Irish Gypsy/Traveller languages/dialects are examined by Kirk and OBaoill (2002). The studies appear in conclusive in terms of language origins but shed some light on the way in which vocabularies can be constructed and elevated into language status and/or incorporated into an existing language (eg Irish). The secrecy of the language used by Irish and other Travellers is noted as are the difficulties in obtaining any significant findings without the full cooperation of Gypsies/Travellers themselves (Kirk and OBaoill 2002).

only to be influenced by the target group but also by public opinion, the media - which influences public opinion - and academic findings. The Ph D project sought to discover how widespread this might be in the rest of Staffordshire County.

The Staffordshire Scenario

The semi-structured interview suite administered to Local Authority personnel contained a section on identity, which sought to discover how Officers and other professionals involved with Gypsy/Traveller issues, at the local level, identified their target group. The questions could be gathered under two main headings – social and economic identifications. Social identification involves: ethnicity; identification and methods of identification; treatment and behaviour in the light of ethnicity and identity; the perceived relationship between different groups and the LA, and the housed majority. I wished to see if Local Authorities thought of Gypsies/Travellers in any other terms other than social ie in economic terms – particularly as Acton and Okely viewed them as 'economic nomads'. Did LAs know if they were employed or not and what they did?

A brief rationale of the questions asked and the responses given by LA Officers, Leaders of Council/Councillors and other professionals who deal with Gypsy/ Traveller issues on a regular basis follows.

Identification in Social Terms : Ethnicity

The question 'Are Gypsies/Travellers an ethnic group?' was important in order to gauge whether or not LA personnel viewed Gypsies/Travellers as an ethnic group or as 'something else'. They were also asked where Gypsies/Travellers came from. Were they belongers but different, or were they from elsewhere, distant/'foreign'? The questions also sought to discover if officials were aware of different groups and if they differentiated, and if Gypsy/Traveller identity remained after settlement on sites or in houses. I also wished to know that if Local Authorities viewed Gypsies/Travellers as an ethnic group, whether they also regarded them to be covered by the Race Relations Act 1976. Balancing these responses would be responses from Gypsy/Traveller families.

Fifty-one respondents were interviewed: 27 LA Officers (of whom 14 were senior and 13 were junior); 8 Councillors (of which 4 were Leaders of Council); 5 Site Wardens (two from private sites; three of the Wardens were Gypsies/Travellers); 2 representatives of the Education Consortium for the County; the Editor of the local newspaper and 8 Gypsy/Traveller families on 4 different sites.

Table 4.1 below is a summary of the responses to the question are Gypsies/Travellers an ethnic group. Of the total number of yes responses (26), 12 gave an unequivocal 'yes', 5 an unequivocal 'no' and 2 an unequivocal 'don't know'. The 'yes' responses were, therefore, somewhat modified. The Officers qualified their responses by pointing out that they regarded Gypsies/Travellers to be a 'minority group'; that 'there were different groups within the travelling group'; that 'they are different from us'; to 'it depends how you define ethnic group – does it include Irish?' and 'they are just people who travel'.

Table 4.1 Are Gypsies/Travellers an Ethnic Group (a Staffordshire Perception)

	Yes	No	Possibly	DK
Senior Officers	7	2	-	5
Junior Officers	7	2	-	4
Site Wardens	3	1	-	1
Councillors	5	1	1	1
Others	2	1		-
Gypsies/Travellers	2	2	3	1
Total	26	9	4	12

The Councillors modified their responses with, 'there are differences between groups'; some are proper/real Romanies, some aren't'; that 'those who had settled were no different to anyone else'; to 'they come from all over' and 'I wouldn't say ethnic'.

Of all those questioned, Councillors and Leaders of Council appeared less well-informed regarding change, being more inclined to dwell on notions of ethnicity which related to 'the real Gypsy' (of the past) compared with the groups that their Officers dealt with now. However, Councillors, Officers and Site Wardens were as doubtful (18) as they were sure (22) that Gypsies/Travellers were an ethnic group. Thus within Councils there appeared to be only a loose consensus of view that Gypsies/Travellers belonged to an ethnic group, and no real agreement with regard to what constituted an ethnic group. Diversity within the Gypsy/Traveller grouping, however, was recognised. Would this affect policy, became an interesting question? The Gypsies/Travellers commented that

'We belong to our own families'.

'We have our own ways'.

'We're different to other people. We're a separate group. We stick together'.

'There are Gypsies everywhere'.

'It's in your blood, it's your background and that's what I am'.

'There's no difference between Gypsies and Travellers. You know one when you see one. There isn't anything like a true Gypsy. I don't know any. There's thousands of Travellers in big houses who have settled down and then there's ordinary ones who hasn't been lucky enough to have big businesses so they just go along as they are. They're known amongst Gypsies and Travellers once they've settled down even in a house.'

The majority of Gypsies/Travellers asked this question indicated that they, too, were unsure about 'ethnicity'. The term 'ethnicity' was alien to some. However, difference appeared to be internalised and respondents were aware that they were different 'in their ways' and set apart from majority society. I was shown a book which documented the history of well-known Gypsy/Traveller families, which the young owner regarded as Gypsy/Traveller history and therefore important. Thus for Gypsies/Travellers, identity and affiliation is not necessarily concerned with group but with family, kin and friendship networks – along the lines of a clan (Scottish) or band (Aboriginal Australian) system.[56] Whilst the Officers and Councillors spoke in terms of 'them', Gypsies/Travellers spoke in terms of 'us'. The response of the Gypsies/Travellers to this question was more in line with the views expressed by the lesser informed Councillors, tending to indicate that neither group thought too deeply about the subject.

---

[56] When new members signed onto the then Trav.net system and said that they were Gypsies/Travellers the first questions asked were who are you related to and who do you know, in order to establish proof of belonging.

The question regarding national origins was intended to draw out the geographical distance contained within the ethnic label. Table 4.2 shows the multiple responses

Table 4.2 Perceived Origins of Gypsies/Travellers in Staffordshire	
Europe/Eastern Europe	9
Ireland	10
Romania	10
Egypt	2
India	7
Don't Know	10

given. The majority who felt they knew, saw Gypsies/Travellers as having a European/East European origin. Of the European origins, Ireland was as dominant as Romania. A significant number felt they did not know. This could either reflect general confusion or a lack of interest in wanting to know or to find out. The number who thought that they came from India was significant - these replies being given by Senior Officers (none of the Junior Officers or Councillors mentioned India) and the Gypsies/Travellers interviewed. The fact that there is a substantial Indian/Pakistani/ Bangladeshi population in Staffordshire who are regarded to be 'ethnic' by Local Authority officials and the fact that Senior Officers have read or have heard that Gypsies/Travellers originated in India, could account for their high number of 'yes' responses to the question on ethnicity.[57] Of the Gypsies/Travellers, 3 mentioned India (one volunteered that they knew because they had read it in a book) one mentioned England and another said 'elsewhere', which implied 'not here'. When asked where their parents and grand parents came from all came from within UK and some had been local. It was the Councillor category that mentioned Egypt. The Site Wardens were less than specific mentioning 'all over the world' or 'abroad' but it was difficult to know if they were referring to those on site or making a general reference to Gypsies/Travellers. It is likely that the East European origin was uppermost in the mind of some respondents because the local press had recently made much of asylum-seeking Roma and East European refugees, some of whom had been settled in the local area.

---

[57] On all the training days attended, the Indian origin was stressed as fact and usually in the first sentence of any lecture/literature.

Officers (27) were asked if those on permanent sites were still regarded to be Gypsies/Travellers. Twenty said yes, 2 said possibly, 2 said no and 3 said they didn't know. The majority of Gypsies/Travellers said yes. This indicated that being a Gypsy/Traveller was about more than just mobility. The yes responses were elaborated with comments such as: 'they are proud of it and want to hang on to their way of life'. The no's felt that 'it could be debated if the new generation had been brought up on a site'; and 'they tend not to get up and go from a site'. Some recognised the problem by stating that 'They have to have somewhere to live'. Nevertheless, the crisp affirmative response was unexpected given the general lack of decisiveness in the responses to the questions on ethnicity and national origins. Similarly affirmative were the responses to the question whether or not Gypsies/Travellers remained so if they lived in houses. Clearly, changed circumstances would not change identification or perception easily. One elderly settled Gypsy/Traveller commented, 'I believe in being separate. I cast them out if they go to live in houses. They should be in a caravan' (Gypsy/Traveller Interview).

When Councillors were asked, in this section, if Gypsies/Travellers were covered by the Race Relations Act 1976 there appeared to be no real consensus (4 said 'yes', 2 said 'no' and 2 did not know). (This issue will be dealt with in later chapters.) The somewhat ambivalent responses, however, tended to fit in with the ambivalence reflected in the responses to the questions on ethnic group and national origins. The Gypsies/Travellers when asked said that they had not heard of the Race Relations Act.

Methods of Social Identification
Given that most of the respondents recognised difference, this section sought to discover official methods of recognition and what those differences were. Officers were asked, generally, how they identified Gypsies/Travellers for the purposes of the DTLR bi-annual Count. This was an attempt to discover how Gypsies/Travellers were differentiated from other caravan dwellers who, despite their way of life, remain part of majority society. Multiple responses were allowed. Responses to the question how are Gypsies/Travellers identified are set out in Table 4.3. This demonstrated more clearly the different factors

which influenced recognition varying from the cultural to the physical, the factual to the evaluative. Overall, the most influential markers appeared to be, lifestyle, accent, being

Table 4.3 How do you Identify Gypsies/Travellers

Officers		Councillors	
Lifestyle/nomadism/mobility	9	Travellers move all the time	3
By van or vehicle	7	They live in caravans	2
Occupation of illegal sites	6	Use legal definitions	2
Accent	6	We don't	2
Follow DETR guidelines	6	Romanies live on sites	1
Just know	5		
Different temperaments	3		
They describe themselves as such/ask them	3		
Their mobility	2		
Physical features	2		
Language (non English vocabulary)	2		
Affluence	1		
Names	1		
China in their vans	1		
Assume	1		
Don't know	2		

illegally on sites, the type of vehicle or caravan occupied and DTLR guidelines. Officers appeared to be more aware than Councillors of the nuances that 'created' difference. To narrow the identification further, officers were asked how they differentiated between Gypsy and Traveller families. Multiple responses were allowed and these are shown in Table 4.4 (a) and (b).

These responses were qualified with comments such as 'we don't see many Gypsies any more'; 'Gypsies are pleasant people, they don't leave a mess'. When the responses of Councillors in Table 4.3 and 4.4 were taken together an impression was given that

Table 4.4 (a) How Does Council Identify Gypsies*

By caravan	4
They are mobile	2
We ask them	1
They live on sites	1
They are friendly	1
They are a nuisance	1

Gypsies were partially settled and that Travellers were not. It was also interesting to note that Irish is associated with the Traveller and not the Gypsy category. Since New Travellers did not seem to frequent Staffordshire, the term Traveller was used by respondents to identify Irish Travellers.

Table 4.4 (b) How Does Council Identify Travellers

By vehicle or van	3
They are Irish	3
They are irresponsible	2
Way of life	1
They leave rubbish	1
They are a nuisance	1

* Only Councillors were asked this question. NB Staffordshire only

The image of the Traveller group was more negative than that for the Gypsy group. The responses at this level were also more evaluative/judgmental – the term 'nuisance' was used to describe both groups. 'Different temperaments' was mentioned and several Officers, at the interface level, said that Irish Travellers were more aggressive. Given that the respondents perceived differences between the groups, when Officers were asked if they treated Gypsies and Travellers differently, of the 27 responses, 26 said no. All Councillors said that they did not.

To balance these accounts, the Gypsy/Traveller families were asked how they would describe a 'typical Gypsy' and themselves (Table 4.5).[58] Of these responses none mentioned mobility. However later in the interview one (who lived on a permanent site and did not travel) did mention that Travellers are always on the move (although it was unclear whether the reference was made in respect of New Travellers, Irish Travellers or whether there were two groups of Gypsies – those who travelled and those who did not – or whether mobility was forced or voluntary.) Some responses were given in terms of what they were not whilst others indicated socio-cultural markers. Only one reference

---

[58] Although the number of respondents was small to get an overall picture, the responses did give an insight into a view on the matter. More politicised Gypsies/Travellers might have responded differently. Lomax et al (2000:14) in their study of Scottish Traveller views came to a similar conclusion : 4 9% claimed they were Scottish Travellers, 8% that they were Romani; and 23% said 'other'.

Table 4.5 How Gypsies/Travellers in Staffordshire Described Themselves

The way they are brought up	1
Different breeds/families	1
We only mix with our own kind	2
We're not different to anyone else	1
Dark hair/blue eyes	1
We're not cheeky	1
We know who are not Gypsies	1
Someone like me	1

was made to phenotypical differences/similarities. Behaviour was mentioned in terms of upbringing and 'not being cheeky'. Also, of some significance, was their separateness – 'we only mix with our own kind' coupled with their non-difference ie 'we're not different to anyone else'. This begged the question, do Gypsies/Travellers 'mix with their own kind' because they are prevented from mixing with others by exclusionary processes –ie sites being detached from main settlements? These responses were elaborated with such comments as: 'Gypsies are nothing to do with Travellers'; 'there is no difference between us' and 'outsiders, they just think we're different'; 'we're different to your kind of people, we're not New Travellers, we're different' - which tended to emphasise an awareness of difference. However, there seemed to be an inability or unwillingness to pin-point or to articulate further what 'the differences' were, or who was making the distinction – given that there was also an awareness of 'being the same but being thought of as different'. In comparing the responses of Officers and Councillors with those of Gypsies/Travellers it appeared that Officers and Councillors had different notions of what constituted difference. However, just as Officers claimed 'they just knew' who Gypsies/Travellers were, Gypsies/ Travellers also claimed they 'just knew'.

To clarify the identification muddle, Officers and Councillors were asked if the legal definitions were correct. Of the 27 Officers asked this question, 11 did not know, 3 said they were not, 6 said they were, 6 claimed they did not know what they were, one did not wish to respond. The majority of Councillors did not know what the legal definitions were. Responses were qualified by 'we follow them' to 'they are very confusing'. It appeared that legal definitions were yet another stratum of confusion to what was already a confused and confusing issue, but in the main, Officers, Councillors and Gypsies/ Travellers gave the impression that legal definitions were not of great concern to them.

The final question in this section was, 'Do you think that the Gypsy/Traveller way of life is chosen?' The MA findings (1997) suggested that the two LAs interviewed assumed that the Gypsy/Traveller way of life was chosen and that families could change life-style at will. Responses for the Ph D project (2003) suggested that this view was County wide, (and remains current), with 17 of the 27 Officers claiming that it was – 8 thought not and 2 didn't know. All the Councillors believed that their life-style was chosen, whilst the majority of Site Wardens believed otherwise. When Gypsies/Travellers were asked this question some responded in terms of their parents and ancestry – the family had always been on the road and they knew 'no other way'. Where officialdom perceived that choice had been made, their reaction was *'c'est la vie'*. No-one drew a distinction between voluntary and enforced movement.

Social Relationships Between Groups

This question sought to discover how Officers perceived their relationship with different groups, how different groups interacted with each other (in order to assess how cohesive they thought the group to be, given that more often than not no distinctions between groups were made and that different groups were often placed or encouraged to share existing sites. Thus, in terms of need assessment and resource allocation, relationships become important. Not all Officers came into contact with mobile groups thus only 24 responded to this question. The majority of Officers (18) thought that their relationship with settled groups was good. Six did not know what the relationship was. The majority of Councillors also felt that the relationship between settled families and themselves/LA was good. The relationship with mobile groups, however, was described as dire/poor/bad by 11; 4 thought it was good and 9 didn't know. The response to the relationship between settled and mobile Gypsy/Traveller groups was: 3 Officers thought it was good, 11 that it was bad and 10 didn't know.[59] None of the Councillors knew what the relationship between settled and mobile groups was. The 'don't know' category is significant here and has implications for need assessment and site provision. Does this mean that settled and mobile groups will/do not mix? Is there a real (or artificial) dichotomy between those now settled and mobile groups which serves as another division between the Gypsy/ Traveller grouping – and how far is this division manufactured? What happens if mobile Gypsies/Travellers wish to settle – are they doubly disadvantaged by LAs *and* the Gypsy/Traveller groups already settled?

An Economic Identity?
From the above it would appear that Gypsies/Travellers were viewed in social terms – ie in terms of culture, ethnicity, way of life, behaviour etc. This seems to overshadow the economic aspects of Gypsy/Traveller life. The majority of sites I visited were hives of activity. The fact that some families are very successful, and appear like Bourdieu's 'fish in water' in this habitus, begged the question – do LAs see Gypsies/Travellers as having an economic identity/worth? In this context, I wished to know, therefore, how Councils treated small in-coming business people and whether or not Gypsies/ Travellers were included within this category. All LAs in Staffordshire claimed that they actively encouraged small businesses in their area, at the time, offering incentives for start-up and expansion programmes, actively canvassing for newcomers. Big players were actively assisted to apply for EU and other grant aid. When Officers were asked if their LA supported new businesses coming into the area, of the 22 replies, 19 said that they did, or were sure that they did, and 3 said they did not know. This issue will be discussed further in Chapter 9.

The majority of responses by Officers and Site Wardens to the question 'Are Gypsies/Travellers regarded as small businessmen by this Council', was no. The few yes responses were qualified with such comments as: 'we accept that they have certain trades' (Senior Officer Interview); 'running a caravan site is a business' (Senior Officer Interview); 'yes, by default'(Junior Officer Interview). Officers modified the majority 'no' responses with 'they are just local residents'(Senior Officer Interview); 'they are

---

[59] In conversation with those on private sites, the impression given was that mobile groups were often threatening and aggressive to those settled on sites and attempts had been made to take over some sites.

trespassers on land'(Junior Officer Interview); 'they are just Gypsies, nuisances' (Junior Officer Interview); 'they might be tolerated if they were' (Junior Officer Interview). Councillors, some of whom run or are part of small businesses, commented: 'they are people carrying out their way of life as they want to, but they don't contribute in the same way as other businessmen'; 'they carry out odd jobs'; 'if they conducted themselves in a different manner they would be accepted by the Public' (Leader of Council).

The responses in Table 4.6 indicated that Gypsies/Travellers were seen in negative economic terms, comparable to the way in which squatters were viewed by governments in 'developing' countries in Southeast Asia in the 1960s – as playing no great part in the

Table 4.6 Are Gypsies/Travellers identified as Small Businessmen by Local Authorities in Staffordshire

	Yes	No	Don't Know
Officers	6	15	6
Councillors	3	3	2
Site Wardens	3	-	2
Total	**11**	**18**	**10**

wider economy (McGee 1967; Mangin 1968). The social and behavioural terms which were used to judge Gypsies/Travellers appeared to overshadow any other 'identification'. How not playing the game appeared to over-ride any contributions that were made by doing so, and to the point where apparent exclusion from the 'official' game resulted. Officers and Councillors were then asked if Gypsy/Travellers were employed (Table 4.7) and about the kind of work families did (Table 4.8).

Table 4.7 Are Gypsies/Travellers Employed/Self-employed

	Yes	No	Don't Know
Officers	23	-	4
Wardens	4	-	1
Councillors	1	2	7
Total	**28**	**2**	**12**

This was a difficult question to answer because LAs appeared not to keep records of employment status – although information is kept if families receive welfare benefits and are settled on sites. One way of knowing was by the work vehicles which were either on site or which accompanied mobile groups. The responses, therefore, were based primarily on assumptions made by Officers who saw vehicles on site or on encampments. Wardens would be more au fait with the employment status of settled families. In the south of the county, those living on private sites tended to be employed. The general responses were qualified by such statements as: 'a growing number are in conventional occupations' (Senior Officer Interview); 'yes, until they come to pay their tax' (Councillor Interview). One family who ran a private site as an economic venture was only too happy to show me their 'paper work' and were proud of the fact that they paid VAT. It would appear that paperwork was related to the scale of the business enterprise and whether or not the family was settled. Respondents were then asked the type of work that Gypsies/ Travellers did – see Tables 4.8 and 4.9 below:

Table 4.8 Occupational List of Gypsies/Travellers in Staffordshire 2003.

Unskilled/casual	Tree pruning/hedge cutting/landscape gardening
Double glazing UPVC	Garden clearance/rubbish collection (tyres)
Carpet sales	Scrap collecting
IT Equipment	Home repairs/roofing
Block paving	Tarmaccing
Owning/Managing permanent caravan sites	Factory work (pottery industry)
Horses	Trotting
Bare Knuckle Fighting	Greyhound racing

This list was born out by vehicles with trades written on the sides, by the debris left after sites had been vacated, by items on permanent sites. Employment also took place abroad and elsewhere. Although only one of the Officers mentioned specifically running caravan sites, this appeared to be an occupation of long standing for the better off. This activity was not mentioned by Okely (1984/1994), although it must have been in evidence as an informal/if not formal activity in the 1960s/1970s where Gypsies/ Travellers owned land. From the lists below it should be noted how occupations have changed over time and in line with a changing economy and changing demand for certain types of job. Perhaps the notion of 'traditional' occupations should now be challenged.

None of the Officers mentioned economic activity relating to horses – even though some families keep horses in fields adjacent to some permanent sites,[60] which some officers claimed to be a problem on occasion. Clearly more research is needed on Gypsy/ Traveller adaptation in changing economic circumstances.

Table 4.9 Changes in Occupation Over time

MHLG Report 1967	**Acton 1974**	**Okely, Adams et al 1975**	
Dealing	Dealing	Scrap dealing	Crazy paving
Agriculture/horticulture	Labouring	Hawking	Knife grinding
Hawking	Factory work	Fortune telling	Cart construction
Labouring	Building work	Tarmaccing	Painting
Tarmaccing	Building work	Selling/Linen	Lace
Building work	Logging	Carpets	Antiques
	Landscaping	Charms/flowers	Building
		Logging	Logging
		Tree-pruning	Roofing

Sibley 1981	**Webster and Millar 2001 (New Travellers)**
Scrap collecting/dealing	Factory work
Rag collection	Crop picking
Hawking	Festivals
Tarmaccing	Self-employed mechanics
Gardening	Temporary agency work
Craft goods	Unemployed
Antique dealing	

Drakakis-Smith 2012

Carpets	Horse dealing	Scrap collecting/scrap yard owners
Horticulture	Farming	Festivals/fairs
Gardening	Caravan site owners	Local market stalls
Landscaping	Antiques and furniture	The Law
Tree surgery	Tarmaccing	College/University teaching
Factory Work	Farm work	Nursery nurses/teaching assistants
Cleaning	Odd job work	Dog breeding
Retail	Boxing	

NB: Some of these activities would require a permanent address.

The last group of questions in this section on identification attempted to discover how Gypsies/Travellers were treated on arrival and to fathom what Gypsies/Travellers had to

---

[60] Trotting is a leisure pursuit but it could equally have economic links in terms of horse breeding/training/competition/horse dealing etc.. Horse fairs are still a popular part of the culture and are held regularly throughout the year. Bare knuckle fighting, dog and cock fighting could also be considered to be economic activities.

do in order to become more acceptable. How could Local Authorities and Gypsies/ Travellers make life easier for each other?

Acceptance

LA Officers did not admit to recognising that Gypsies/Travellers entering their Authority might wish to remain. Their responses are tabulated below in Table 4.10 and multiple replies were allowed. The responses indicated that Gypsies/Travellers were not welcomed regardless of why they had come. There also appeared to be little scope for families to decide whether or not they would like to remain. Some Councils took a more liberal approach than others and this was reflected in their responses. However, despite the negativity in the overall response, many Councils appeared to turn a blind eye to families on unauthorised sites if they were not causing an obstruction or a nuisance to others, kept the site clean and tidy and if there were no complaints from the public. As one officer stated: 'They usually stay the weekend, but they will stay as long as they are tolerated'. There seemed to be little effort to find out what could be done if Gypsies/Travellers wished to remain. Most Councils 'managed' the situation. Families

Table 4.10 How does the LA know if Gypsies/Travellers wish to remain

Officer Response

We don't	9
We don't ask or presume	6
They may want to but they can't	2
We ask them	2
They tell us	2
They never say they want to stay	1
Some have purchased land	1
As there is no place to stay that's legal they are just moving through	1
We assume they are passing through	1
They have settled on sites	1
If they are on an unauthorised site we move them on	1

Councillor Response

Only by asking and we don't do that	3
We don't know until we've got a problem	2
It doesn't arise if they are only here for a few days	1
Don't know unless they ask us	2

were moved on irrespective of whether or not they had links (via family ties) with the area. The only way they could remain was if they were to challenge decisions in Court and even then a successful outcome was uncertain.

Only Councillors, as policy makers, were asked the question 'what must Gypsies/ Travellers do to be more accepted?' and they were allowed multiple responses. Table 4.10 demonstrated the way in which non-conformity is viewed as the greatest barrier to acceptance, and reads like the 10 Commandments – thou shall not ... . In the main the list is weighted with references to behaviour – and in the main Gypsy/Traveller behaviour was viewed as negative and seen in terms of a minority of *mobile* groups who behave badly.

When later in the interview Officers and Councillors were questioned about settled groups, they claimed (unanimously) that they had no problems with settled groups. This was borne out by their positive response to the relationship they had with settled groups. If Gypsies/Travellers did none of the things alleged below it would be interesting to see if

Table 4.10 Councillor Response to the Question What Must Gypsies/Travellers do to be Accepted

Conform	3
Not trespass on private business land	1
Pay their way	1
Not travel in large numbers	1
Not work on site	1
Have driving licenses	1
Keep the law	1
Not leave litter/rubbish	1
Not steal	1

they would still be accepted. When asked if Gypsies/Travellers moved/lived in barrel-topped wagons their way of life would be more accepted, 4 said yes, 2 said no and 2 said possibly.

Councillors were then asked how they could make life easier for Gypsies/Travellers. The majority said create more sites; other comments related to 'educating Gypsies/Travellers in the ways of the planning system'; or the more vague response of 'doing more for them'. Such comments begged the question that if Councillors, as policy makers, know what needs to be done, why wasn't it being done? As a corollary to this the final question asked both Councillors and Officers how they thought Gypsies/Travellers should be accommodated. The term 'accommodated' was used in the questionnaire in its broadest term and Officers and Councillors were left to interpret it as they wished - some used the broader term and others the narrower interpretation of housing etc.. Multiple comments were allowed and these are listed in Table 4.11. The responses divided themselves into positive and negative. In doing so it became clear that the negative responses displayed

Table 4.11 How Should Gypsies/Travellers be Accommodated

Councillors

Positive:

Create a reasonable site and ensure they keep their side of the bargain	3
In a caravan if that's what they want	1
However they want to be accommodated	1
If it was a statutory duty then we would have to accommodate them	1
They have never come to the Council to say we want land	1

Negative:

They can't be that's the problem	1
If they don't intend staying how can we accommodate them	1
They are breaking the law when they are trespassing	1
We have no land	1

Officers

Positive:

More provision	13
Short-term sites	6
On their own land	5
Need for a national strategy	3

Negative:

Don't know	3
Don't know what they want	2
We don't accommodate them	2
Offer them a house	1
They can't be accommodated under the present legislation	1

an unacceptable level of apathy and lack of concern which, if transferred to other 'special needs' groups, could be construed as discriminatory and a cause for concern. The positive responses from Officers were practical and summed up what needed to be done in order to accommodate Gypsies/Travellers. The 'positive' responses from Councillors were more circumspect, suggesting that it was up to the Gypsy/Traveller groups to come up with suggestions for accommodation need. This gave the impression that the Council was not going to take the lead, and indeed, could or would only do so if it was a statutory obligation. However, when this opportunity had arisen in the past, Councils had not taken it. Given that Councillors are policy makers their responses suggested that little would be done for Gypsies/Travellers unless families or National Government pressed the matter. There was also an indication that Councillors were reluctant to do anything for mobile Gypsies/Travellers, viewing them as 'non-deserving' non-belongers, and that there was no real intention of doing a great deal for those settled on sites unless they asked - and even then it was doubtful that requests would be taken seriously.

Overall, there appeared to be a pre-disposition against Gypsies/Travellers settling who came into the area.

SUMMARY

Identity and identification of groups and individuals occurs at many levels, ranging from the global to the local; 'identities' can also be internally and externally derived. The individual can be identified with reference to the whole group and vice versa. In this process quantum leaps and inaccurate assumptions are made about individuals and groups, producing a tension between 'other' and 'self' identification. This constructs a baseline for the contestation of the space between 'self' and 'other' representations. The process then becomes one of thrust and parry in an attempt to arrive at a more enlightened and agreed view. If no dialogue takes place the majority, view of 'other' (which is often negative) can become embedded as a politics or strategy of exclusion (Bloul 1999). At the group level Bloul (1999:7) claims that a distinction needs to be made between 'collective self-affirmation – which still allows for alliances with others – and exclusionary politics of identity', which does not. Unless communicative dialogue takes place on a regular basis, power groups can (and do) insert their own (mis)perceptions as fact and minorities lose control over their self-determination and their life-script.

A consequence of perceived difference, is that Gypsies/Travellers appear not to have 'moved on' in the minds of many in majority society. Mainstream society appears to believe that Gypsies/Travellers 'cannot belong to us', are not ours, but someone else's responsibility (and attitudes engendered by Feudalism and the Poor Laws, live on here). Little if any allowance is made for change within the Gypsy/Traveller habitus, which means that boundaries and barriers remain in place. Once representation and identities have been established, they are difficult to shift. The identification of Gypsies/Travellers as 'nomads' is a case in point and has been used to ensure non-settlement and, when linked to notions of foreign origin, to abrogate not only citizens rights and privileges but also to absolve the State from any responsibility in terms of provision, equality of opportunity and fair treatment (as Chapters 7, 8. and 9 will show). Identity and identification, then, is a process in the game which can single out specific groups and individuals for particular differential and/or exclusionary treatment. Interaction, in the form of games, stimulus and response begins the structure-making processes which produce a double helix configuration each strand supporting the other (see Figure 4.1) which can make change a difficult and often painful process.

Bourdieu's notion of cultural formation via habitus goes some way to explain the way in which cultures are established, even from humble negative beginnings, which can advance to take on positive lives of their own. The main markers of difference have, supposedly, been Gypsy/Traveller mobility, mode of dwelling and being, and language. However, if historical records are examined carefully much of the mobility turns on policies of eviction and the prevention of settlement. The question then becomes how far does constant eviction and enforced removal impose 'nomadism'? And is mobility as an important component of Gypsy/Traveller-ness a response to policy and constant, enforced removal? Given that families have been settled for generations clearly there is more to being a Gypsy/Traveller, for some, than mobility or living in a caravan would imply.

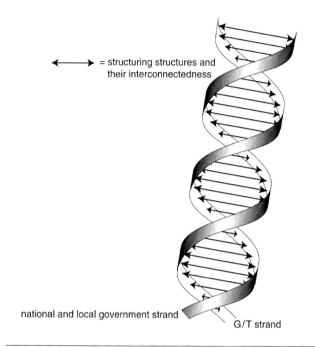

= structuring structures and their interconnectedness

national and local government strand

G/T strand

Figure 4.1   To Show the Supporting Structures Between Gypsies/Travellers and Authority as a Double Helixial Configuration (Adapted from Watson (1968))

Whilst finer tuning could be construed as politically divisive, viewing Gypsies/Travellers as a homogenous group denies the different needs and aspirations of each family group. The term Gypsy/Traveller is suitably vague to encompass those who do not live in conventional housing and yet it does not refer to *all* who live in caravans. This indicates that the State is not *in*tolerant of *all* caravan dwellers. Currently, service provision is based on the assumption that all Gypsies/ Travellers wants/needs are the same – and assumptions are made concerning not only what those wants/needs are, but also what they should be.

The fieldwork and responses to the questionnaire on identity have attempted to show that the processes of identification and identity, at least in Staffordshire, are far from the precise, rational processes that dictionary definitions and theory would suggest. Indeed here it is found to be messy, confusing fact with value judgments, often allowing emotion and gut-feeling to override evidence which makes it difficult for policy to move on - which in turn keeps Gypsies/Travellers moving.

Even if Gypsies/Travellers stopped travelling and settled on sites or in houses, they would still be perceived as Gypsies/Travellers – and presumably treated accordingly by majority society. Gypsies/Travellers, therefore, appear to be living in a parallel habitus, which has been detached from the main, by a series of structures, stimuli and responses which have been predicated on identity and identification. In response to the question - 'are Gypsies/ Travellers an ethnic group'? whilst many were thought to be 'ethnic' it appeared that 'ethnic' was used to denote, not necessarily foreignness in a geographical locational sense (except for some), but in the sense of difference which has grown from the process of protracted separation/exclusion/non-inclusion from, and the lack of a commensurate dialogue and real exchange with, mainstream society. Thus differences in terms of custom/values, language/accent, economic activity etc., merge to emerge to significance. Should Gypsies/Travellers be regarded then, not just as an ethnic group but as a national minority? That this discourse was current between various Gypsy/Traveller groups and individuals, at the time, was significant (see Liegeois1994; Gheorghe 1997; Mirga and Gheorghe 1997). In 2002 there was a burgeoning Euro movement to unite Roma in order to press their ethnicity claim. However, in UK, where the number of Roma are fewer than in other European countries this would tend to separate and divide even further what is already a fragmented grouping in UK. There was such a call for Gypsy/Traveller groups to unite in UK, and for a short while, which met with only a limited response.

The next chapter will analyse the DTLR/ODPM/CLG bi-annual Count data to examine another kind of representation - that via official data.

CHAPTER FIVE

SPACED OUT: AN ANALYSIS OF THE BI-ANNUAL COUNT DATA - OR READING THE RUNES?[61]

The National Government bi-annual Count of Gypsy/Traveller caravans in England and Wales had become instrumental for the support and perpetuation of Government policy/ legislation for Gypsies/Travellers – which in 2003 was enshrined in the Criminal Justice and Public Order Act (CJPO) 1994, and the more recent Housing Act of 2004. Over time, and despite its shortcomings, the count has assumed significance as a representation of Gypsy/Traveller existence in space and place. Whilst it has undergone several refinements since 1979, its function remains the same – ostensibly to inform policy, to keep track of caravan numbers and their spatial distribution and, seemingly, to satisfy identified need. Whilst in Scotland and Eire the data appear more concerned with people, in England Wales and Northern Ireland the data appear more concerned with caravans and where they should or should not be.

This chapter will attempt to analyse the data collected by the National Government, from each LA in England which makes a survey of caravans each January and July. It will also look at the data collected in Wales, Northern Ireland Eire and Scotland in an attempt to see if a national UK figure for Gypsies/Travellers can be arrived at. Scotland and Ireland carry out their own census. Wales ceased counting in 1994 when the duty to provide was revoked by the CJPO Act 1994. Wales resumed counting in 2004 when the Welsh National Assembly commissioned a needs survey.

The questions that need to be raised here are formulated in terms of accuracy and fair play. Do the data, for example, accurately reflect what is happening on the ground?

Whilst they might imply an even-handed game does action taken by LAs suggest a manipulation to give the appearance of compliance with National Government directives and any targets set? This chapter will move across several time periods comparing the present with the past and using present day data together with that used for the Ph D Thesis at the beginning of the 21st Century. To avoid confusion past and present data will be clearly identified.

The Count and Its Mechanisms
Why Count?

It needs to be noted that Gypsies/Travellers living on sites, as opposed to housing had been separated from the main for enumeration until the 2011 Census. The precedent for separate enumeration was set in 1965 when the first 'census' of Gypsies/Travellers in modern times was carried out by the Ministry of Housing and Local Government (HMLG 1967) to sift Gypsies/Travellers from others living in caravans in order to assess the need/demand for accommodation. The findings supported the strengthening of the 1960 Caravan Sites and Control of Development Act via the 1968 Caravan Sites Act which made it a duty for LAs to both close and provide sites. The figure then for the Gypsy/Traveller population in England and Wales was enumerated as 15,000 although this was declared to be an underestimation by Acton (1974) and Adams et al (1975).

A rationale to continue separate enumeration emerged when public money entered the equation in 1978: to assist LAs in their duty to provide sites, and as a vehicle to ostensibly monitor the working (or otherwise) of the 1968 Act. The reason for the first bi-annual Count in 1978/9 was then need assessment/satisfaction in terms of provision – via sites, presumably. When the 1994 CJPO Act revoked the duty to provide, the count continued and the 'need' then became couched in planning terms – 'to assist Planning Authorities with planning and the Planning Inspectorate in its deliberations' (Letter DETR 1997). In 2001 the need for counting caravans was to support the usefulness and to demonstrate the success of the 1994 Act (Interview, Senior Officer, DTLR 2001) via

---

[61] I would like to acknowledge the assistance given to me by Keith Mason, School of Physical and Geographical Sciences, Keele University for producing the maps for this chapter.

private provision of sites and the reduction of unauthorised sites. Associated with provision was the exercise of defining who, or who was not, a Gypsy/Traveller in order to target those who would qualify for any State provision.

Whilst the bi-annual Count has been criticised for being inaccurate and an underestimate (by Sibley 1984a; 1984b; Halfacree 1996; and by Drakakis-Smith and Mason 2001) it remains the only longitudinal record of the distribution of Gypsy/Traveller *caravans* in England providing a useful snapshot. However, its usefulness as a means of surveillance, keeping track and control of numbers and the distribution and redistribution of caravans should not be ignored.[62]

Who/What is Included?

In Scotland (2001) and Northern Ireland (1993), *people* were included in the count, which made for a more comprehensive and useful analysis. Although the DTLR count pro forma did ask for information on people/families, this was not published in England, making it difficult to draw comparisons and to compute an accurate total Gypsy/ Traveller population for UK. The Count also tended to misrepresent. An increase in number of caravans does not necessarily mean an increase in the number of *people*. Separate caravans are used for cooking, storage, eating and sleeping. It can, however, indicate 'flourishing' - ie children growing up on site and needing a space of their own. It could also indicate a growing prosperity to support extra caravans.

In England, because caravans are counted the Gypsy/Traveller situation has tended to become objectified and codified as planning, land-use, health and environment problems rather than as social/human issues. It is morally easier to justify the removal of caravans; the term 'unauthorised' being easier to attach to vehicles than it is to people (Drakakis-Smith and Mason 2001; Drakakis-Smith 2003). Whilst in Scotland there is a tendency to include New Travellers, in England the situation is more confused. No New Traveller vehicles were counted in Staffordshire in 2000 and a significant number of counting

---

[62] Clark (2001) in his study of the mechanisms of counting Central and Eastern European Roma suggested political and discriminatory undertones.

Officers claimed that they would not include them even if they were present - although the legal definition is broad enough to include New Travellers and the DTLR guidelines advocate inclusion. (See Drakakis-Smith and Mason 2001 for the way in which the Count operates and who is included) Neither were Show/Circus people included or barge dwellers or other non-Gypsy/Traveller caravan/mobile home dwellers - which suggested a constant sifting and sieving of the mobile/Gypsy/Traveller grouping. Whilst this could imply that different groups had different needs, it was possibly more about reducing 'need' to a minimum level.

The Count Mechanics

It was found that each Counting Officer in Staffordshire had a different method which did not make for a standardised or reliable count (see Drakakis-Smith and Mason 2001 for the full findings with regard to the count methodology). An added complication was the change, over time, in the way the data were presented by the responsible Government Department and the way in which administrative boundaries have been changed by National Government via the Boundary Commission, making longitudinal analysis difficult, although not impossible. More recently, extra categories of legal (or not) status for caravans have been introduced such as "unauthorised 'tolerated'" and Gypsy/Traveller caravans 'not/on own land tolerated/not tolerated' etc.).

Added to this were the seeming inaccuracies - eg differences between some of the regional totals (particularly between 1998 and 2000).[63] Other complications and errors also affect the data. First, although records were kept of authorised counts and the number of licensed pitches on each site, it was found that extra caravans on private sites were not counted as unauthorised (which technically they were). This tended to *inflate* the number of caravans on authorised private sites in some counts in Staffordshire (Interview Principal Officer, 2001). Second, with regard to unauthorised sites, the count took place on two days per year in January and July. Unauthorised sites can occur (at least in Staffordshire) throughout the year (LA records). Caravans 'on the road' on either

---

[63] The single annual returns differed from the collected 'last five counts returns'.: 2 errors were detected in 1998, at least 5 in 1999, 4 in 2000. Some of the differences were around 100 or more caravans. The change in government seemed not to make a difference except that more errors were detected after 1996.

of these days, would not be counted. Neither were unauthorised caravans on private land always recorded by LAs. Third, caravans counted as unauthorised might be in transit (ie families on holiday) and might have a permanent pitch elsewhere. There appears to be no mechanism to gather and sift this information. Thus the count has tended to underestimate the number of unauthorised caravans. Added to this were the errors of transcription. Often figures are transposed and others placed in the wrong column. In Staffordshire it was discovered that in 1999 the total for the county had been recorded officially as 228. When all the figures were added the total was 253. In January 1999 East Staffordshire had 23 authorised caravans on a private site not recorded in the DETR return. In July 1999 Cannock recorded 22 caravans on an authorised Council site when the site was private. Lichfield regularly did not count 4 caravans (2 on an authorised and 2 on an unauthorised site) preferring to submit a nil return. In January 2000 Stafford Borough Council returned 31 caravans on their authorised site and 32 on an unauthorised private site when 11 caravans were on the authorised Council site and 52 were on the authorised private site.[64] When LAs failed to make a return, the DTLR estimated the number based on past submissions. This continues to the present. Non recording of unauthorised caravans can, however, be an attempt to disguise provision need. Such examples show both a possible political tinkering and human error, and when multiplied by the number of LAs in UK, this could make for a large margin of inaccuracy. Since writing the Ph D the way in which the count takes place has been 'reviewed' and recommendations for improvement were made (ODPM 2006).

The Sum Total of the Count and Beyond – An Overview

Although comparatively and nationally the Gypsy/Traveller population is small it is extensive, and its impact at the local level can be great. It would therefore be remiss not to speak of Gypsies/Travellers in terms of land, space and place. Liegeois (1995) estimated a total UK population (which presumably included house dwellers) of around 120,000. Clements (2001) suggested 150 –200,000. As neither provided a methodology for the computation of these figures they remain evaluative, possibly political, rather than

---

[64] These corrections are from my own findings and from consultations with the County who keep their own records on certain sites.

factual. Whilst in the past and to highlight the Gypsy/Traveller plight, the politicisation of numbers might have been necessary, things have moved on slightly to the point where, given the current emphasis on need, some LAs are recognising the importance of accuracy in data collection to inform local policy, service delivery and satisfaction of need, particularly as it is difficult to 'hide' caravans.

The results of the 2011 National Census, which, for the first time, included Gypsies/Travellers in the ethnic question, has thrown some light on Gypsy/Traveller families who live in caravans and who are settled in houses. In the past and for whatever reason, not all Gypsies/Travellers would have received or completed a census form (Drakakis-Smith and Mason 2001) nor would they have been easily distinguished from others living in mobile accommodation. The 2011 Census attempted to be inclusive and efforts were made to include all known Gypsy/Traveller sites. Results available in 2012 revealed that there were approximately 62,492 in UK who identified themselves as Gypsies/Travellers comprising 0.15 per cent of the total population for England and Wales. However, as with other groups, the percentages of Gypsies/Travellers were higher at the local level in some areas: for example in Fenland, Basildon, Canterbury and Maidstone they were 0.5 per cent of the total populations. In Staffordshire, Gypsies/Travellers comprised 0.2 per cent of the total population of the County. It would appear that the 'politicised' figures are an over-estimate of Gypsies/Travellers or that a large number of families no longer consider themselves to belong to this group.

Whilst the bi-annual Count tends to reinforce the myth that *all* Gypsies/Travellers are 'nomadic', the bigger picture demonstrates that not all Gypsies/Travellers *are* 'nomadic'. When compared with the 2011 Census figures, the bi-annual count showed that totals for England were 32688, the count for Scotland 2120, for Wales 1857, Northern Ireland 1710 and Eire 29573 (totals provided by National Government Departments). This provided a total of 67948 persons. Based on previous data from Wales and Scotland which collected family numbers it was possible to estimate that there were approximately 2.4 people per caravan. (increased to 3.1 for Northern Ireland and Eire, where families tended to be larger (Centre for Housing Research 2008). The 2011 Census figure of 62492 suggested that a majority of families who identify themselves as Gypsies/Travellers were settled on authorised sites or were housed indicating that they might not be 'nomadic'. Later chapters will attempt to fathom if this is by choice or owing to a lack of alternatives and adequate provision and service delivery.

The following section examines the data supplied by the constituent 'States' of the UK. Since the constituent States gather different data for different purposes and at different times, what is examined here is what was available at the time of writing this volume, which, whilst not perfect, provides a stab at a national picture.[65]

England

A GIS package was used to produce maps which show a general distribution based on the count data for the relevant dates.

Currently, the National Government bi-annual Count of caravans in England provides a snapshot of their number and situation. In January 2002 the count revealed a total of 13612 caravans in England. Of these 10838 were 'authorised' and situated 'permanently' on sites; 2774 were recorded as 'unauthorised' and having no permanent place in space. This would give a total of those living in caravans as 32668 persons in England. In January 2012, the figures were as follows: the total for England was 18750 caravans suggesting a population total for England living in caravans as 45000. Of the total caravans 15900 were on authorised LA/Registered State Landlord (RSL) or private sites, and 2850 were on unauthorised sites. Of the unauthorised number 1395 were 'not tolerated' with 914 being 'not tolerated' on their own land, and 481 being 'not tolerated' and not on their own land – ie they were trespassing. In terms of people this would give an approximate figure of 38160 persons living on authorised sites and 6840 living on unauthorised sites. Map 5.1 shows the distribution of Gypsy/Traveller caravans in England.

---

[65] In order to present the data in map form a GIS package was used working the data through MINITAB.

Between 2002 and 2012, whilst the numbers of total caravans have increased by 5138, the number of unauthorised caravans has increased by only 76. This phenomenon would need further in-depth investigation to explain. It does show, however, that in 2012, 85 per cent of caravans were on authorised sites and that 15 per cent were not. The highest numbers of caravans were found in the South East, the South West and the east of

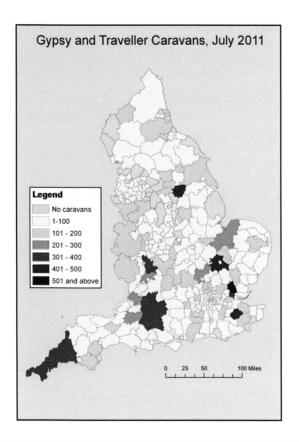

Gypsy and Traveller Caravans, July 2011

Legend

	No caravans
	1-100
	101 - 200
	201 - 300
	301 - 400
	401 - 500
	501 and above

0   25   50   100 Miles

Map 5.1 The Distribution of Gypsy/Traveller Caravans, July 2011

Source: Based on data provided through EDINA UKBORDERS with the support of the ESRC and JISC boundary material which is the copyright of the Crown, and CLG Bi-annual Count of Gypsy/Traveller caravan data

England (see Map 5.1). The count data show that in July 2011, the total in the South East was 3967, the East of England 4672, West Midlands 1852, East Midlands 1308, Southwest 2702, Yorkshire and Humberside 1613 and the North West 1303. In England it would appear that the axes of distribution followed the axes of the major routeways, namely the M4 in the southern part of England and the A5 and M56 in the north. This was supported by reports that many of the Travellers resorting to England came from Ireland.

The main purpose for the count in England, as stated by the CLG, is for use 'by other Government Departments, Local Authorities and essential services to plan service delivery' and 'for tackling unauthorised encampments and developments' – which suggested that the emphasis here was to indicate where families might not go rather than where they might. It was difficult to work out pitch capacity nationally for England from the official data provided. The English data and that for Staffordshire will be discussed in more detail and analysed in greater depth later in this chapter.

Scotland
The Scottish Government has stated that its reason for reintroducing the bi-annual count was to 'establish standardised and consistent estimates across Scotland' and that its purpose was 'to better understand the characteristics of this population and to assist and inform the development of public policies and services for Gypsies/Travellers both nationally and locally (Scottish Government Social Research, Count Number 16 July 2009:4) – which suggests that in theory at least, a more humanist approach was being taken.

The Scottish Census of Gypsy/Traveller families in July 2009 (ibid) claimed that there were 684 households living on sites of all tenures, amounting to around 2120 persons. Of this total, 294 were on Council and registered sites, 229 were on unauthorised sites and 161 lived on private sites. Of the 31 sites created in Scotland, only 8 operated to full capacity. The sites in North Lanarkshire and Glasgow remained unused. At the time the greatest number of families tended to live in Fife, South Lanark and Highlands, Dumfries and Galloway with these four LAs accounting for 46 per cent of the total July Gypsy/ Traveller population. The LAs with the fewest families were Clackmannanshire, South Ayrshire, East/Midlothian, North Lanarkshire and Stirling which had fewer than 10 households at the time of the count. The greatest increases in household numbers occurred in Dumfries and Galloway (+28 per cent), and Edinburgh (+17 per cent). It was reported that several sites used by families had been 'secured' which meant that they had to go elsewhere. The LAs with no caravans were East Dunbarton, East Renfrewshire, Eilean Siar, Glasgow, Orkney and Shetland. In 2008 three sites were empty and not available for letting: Aberdeenshire (Greenbanks), Highland (Newtonmore) and Scottish Borders (Innerleithen) amounting to 37 pitches which were set aside for seasonal use and there were, overall, 23 pitches unfit for use with vandalism being given as the cause in two of the LAs concerned. Overall there were 81 applicants on waiting lists for Council and RSL sites (19 per cent of available pitches). The waiting lists were longest in Angus (17 names), Fife (17 names) and South Lanarkshire (20 names) some of these were fairly settled sites with minimum on/off movement. Twenty nine per cent of families had held tenancies on the same site for more than five years, with 70 per cent holding tenancies for over one year. Forty five per cent of the total population counted lived on LA or RSL sites Tenancy changes were highest in Fife, Scottish Borders and West Lothian. (All data were obtained from the Scottish Government Social Research Centre Count- No 15: January and Count No 16: July 2009).

Wales

The most recent caravan Counts for Wales were collected by the Welsh Assembly Government in January 2012, when, 774 caravans were reported on the 71 sites then identified across Wales. Using the above formula this would equate to around 1857 persons. Of the 22 LAs in Wales, 18 responded to the survey held in July 2010. Of these LAs, the number of caravans on sites varied between one and 95. Of the total number of LAs that responded, 465 caravans (69 per cent) were on socially rented authorised sites and 208 (31 per cent) on private sites. There were 52 caravans on unauthorised sites and on land not owned by the families. Given the response, there were 346 pitches on sites provided by LAs – 351 were residential and 21 were transit pitches. The total number of pitches had reduced by 21 (6 per cent) since July 2010. Caravans were distributed mainly in Wrexham/Flintshire, with some (25) appearing in Anglesey (as tolerated). Maps 5.2 and 5.3) show the distribution and changes over a one year period. In South Wales distribution extended from Newport to Pembrokeshire, the majority of which were in the industrial and former industrial areas. Cardiff and Pembroke had the highest numbers mainly on socially rented sites (143 and 112 respectively). As can be seen from the two maps, there is a north and south distribution with very few in the middle – which tends to

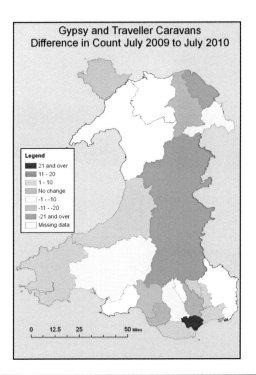

Map 5.2 Difference in Distribution and Numbers Between 2009 and 2010 Based on Biannual Counts

Source : Source: Based on data provided through EDINA UKBORDERS with the support of the ESRC and JISC boundary material which is the copyright of the Crown, and CLG Bi-annual Count of Gypsy/Traveller caravan data

reflect the general population distribution for Wales. Map 5.3 shows a more even distribution with less of a concentration around Cardiff/Newport which could suggest policy implementation re removal or redistribution. Given the route map in Chapter One it would appear also that distribution follows the major route-ways, with settlement occurring along the way – this would be the A5 from Holyhead in the North and from Fishguard along the M4 in the south. The Cardiff site on the fringes of the Cardiff Bay

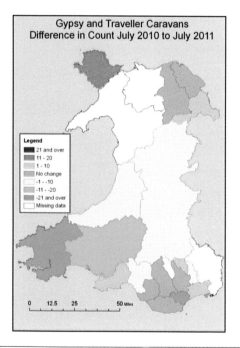

Map 5.3 Difference in Distribution and Number Between 2010 and 2011 Based on Biannual Counts
Source: Source: Based on data provided through EDINA UKBORDERS with the support of the ESRC and JISC boundary material which is the copyright of the Crown, and CLG Bi-annual Count of Gypsy/Traveller caravan data

development is one of the largest in the UK. (All the data for Wales came from the Welsh Government, Statistics for Wales Unit, Cardiff, 2010.)

Northern Ireland

Northern Ireland which has the same latitude as borderland Scotland and north England has tended to concentrate on housing, as in group housing, and halting sites as a response to accommodating its Traveller population. The 2011 UK Census reported that there were 1710 Travellers in Northern Ireland at the time, a figure comparable with those of Scotland and Wales. The highest number (294) were found in Newry and Armagh, Belfast West (188), Foyle (170), Mid Ulster and West Tyrone (168), Upper Bann (150), Fermanagh and South Tyrone (118). The lowest numbers were in East Antrim (16), East Belfast (19), Strangford and South Antrim (20), Lagan Valley and North Down (21). Of the sample it was found that 98 per cent were Irish Travellers. Spatially, caravans were concentrated around Newry, Armagh and Belfast West, suggesting work and travel opportunities and access to locations beyond Ireland. The 2008 Northern Ireland Housing Executive (NIHE) found that 41 per cent preferred group housing, an initiative that Northern Ireland and Eire have pioneered, 28 per cent preferred social housing and that 28 per cent preferred serviced sites. Indeed, in Northern Ireland, 59 per cent of the sample lived in settled accommodation, with 43 per cent stating that they needed proper housing. Forty eight per cent thought that accommodation issues were most important, with 35 per cent saying that racism/discrimination was an issue (NIHE 2008) and possibly an obstacle to settled accommodation in conventional housing.

Eire

Eire like Northern Ireland has concentrated on providing group housing and halting sites as a means of accommodating its Traveller population as a response to demand by families (NIHE 2009). At least this is where the greatest expenditure has been made (in 2005 £18,245,165 had been spent by LAs on halting sites and £14,833,203 on group housing (Centre for Housing Research 2008: p58).

The 2011 Census for Eire claimed a total population of Travellers of 29573. The highest number was found in Leinster with 14854, with Munster at 6665, Connacht with 6617, Dublin with 5935 (37 per cent in South Dublin), and Galway with 4143. The areas with the lowest were Leitrim with 264, Monaghan with 258 and Waterford City with 259 and

Waterford County with 152. Eighty four per cent of Irish Travellers lived in permanent housing, with 12 per cent in caravans or mobile homes. The data gathered by Eire's Centre for Housing research (2008) appeared to be within the context of targets to be met, provision and expenditure per head needed or utilised to meet them.

The Eire Census of 2008 found that Travellers made up 0.6 per cent of the total population. Of this percentage, 21.1 per cent lived in their own homes, 24.9 per cent lived in caravans or mobile homes, 51.2 per cent rented from LAs and that 69.1 per cent lived in permanent accommodation. (Data obtained from the Eire Census 2011 and the Centre for Housing Research, Traveller Accommodation in Ireland: A Review of Policy and Practice 2008.)

From this 'global' round-up it can be seen that in the UK States (Scotland, Wales, Northern Ireland where numbers are fewer and where the climate is less favourable, the tendency is for Gypsy/Traveller families to live in more permanent accommodation. Also where national populations are lower more resources appear to be allocated to the needs of Gypsy/Traveller families. Eire which had a comparatively high number of Travellers but a comparatively smaller national population also allocated more resources to the needs of Travellers and had attempted to cater more imaginatively for their needs – group housing could be regarded as an example of this. More families also appeared to want to live in conventional housing. England, by comparison, saw sites as the main avenue for the satisfaction of Gypsy/Traveller accommodation needs, with the settlement of caravans being more important than the integration of families into mainstream society. And whilst not all families wanted live in houses or to integrate, those that did often met opposition. These issues, mechanisms and game play will be examined more closely in later chapters and at the local level, where they tend to manifest themselves more overtly.

A CLOSER LOOK AT THE BI-ANNUAL COUNT DATA FOR ENGLAND

This section, will examine the bi-annual count data for England since these are the most complete over time and uninterrupted from their inception in 1979 - although from time to time the format has changed and extra status of caravan categories have been introduced.

Preamble

As already mentioned above, such data, whilst useful, must be handled with caution. It was realised that the greater the scale, the least useful and, possibly, less accurate the data, other than to indicate broad trends for England, and even then this information needed careful handling. Thus I would concur with David Sibley (1984; 1990) that when working with the national data, notice needed to be taken re what was happening at the local level, and on the ground. To this end the data for Staffordshire will be examined in greater detail. The data for Staffordshire were analysed in 2000 using the ONS Classification of Local and Health Authorities in Great Britain (1996) thus figures were used, in the main, up to this date. More broadly, where it is useful to do so, the most recent figures are also used as comparators. In some instances an average of the January and July data are used in order to capture those settled for the winter and those travelling during the summer. However, whilst the January and July figures, seen together, show seasonal changes, such movements are not always voluntary. For example in Southport a large number of families were, at the time, 'allowed' to use an out-of-town car park on waste ground on the edge of Southport over the winter months. In summer when the car park was used by tourists, the caravans were moved on. The area has since been developed, so Gypsies/Travellers have had to seek an alternative site. A similar scenario operated in Cardiff when families were allowed to use Leckwith Common in summer. Such examples weaken Sibley's (1984) seasonal variation explanation as a natural or cultural phenomenon, and that seasonal forced movement is now but one aspect of several factors which inform Gypsy/Traveller mobility, not least being a search for work, and to which forced removal can be added.

Back to the Future – An Overview of Caravan Numbers in England 1979-2012

The Findings of the 2002 Analysis of the Data

Generally, the bi-annual count over this period in England, showed an increase in the number of caravans. However, as stated above this might not necessarily be an increase in number of people over and above natural increase. When the data were analysed in 2002, as in 2012, they showed large regional variations. For example, in 2002 within East England, Kent had the largest total (1262) of caravans, followed by Cambridgeshire with a total of 1060. The highest totals for the east Midlands was Lincolnshire with 362. In the West Midlands, Warwickshire had 381. The South West had the highest number of caravans in Somerset with 565. High concentrations at the time were found in East Anglia, Cambridgeshire and Doncaster.[66] The areas where there were few or no caravans were often adjacent to areas with high numbers (see Figure 5.1 for examples of this

Figure 5.1: Some Examples of Caravan Highs and Lows in 2000

High	Low	High	Low
South Cambridge	East Herts	Wychavon	Cotswolds
Huntingdonshire	North Herts	Tewksbury	Cheltenham
East Cambridge	S Edmonds Bury	South Gloucester	Gloucester
			Stroud
			West Wilts
			Bath and
			Somerset
Congleton	Macclesfield	Darlington	Teesdale
	High Peak	Carlisle	Tyneside
	Staffs Moorlands		Alnwick
	Crewe and Nantwich		
Lancaster	Wyre	Bradford	Pendle
	Fylde		Burnely
Kerrier	Penwith	Newark	Gedling
Carrick	Restormil		Mansfield
Hinckley	Charnwood	Thurruck	Castlepoint
	Melton	Basildon	Rochford
		Chelmford	Maldon
Salisbury	Kennet	Waverley	Rushmoor
			East Hampshire

---

[66] Doncaster had approximately 400 caravans which was equivalent in size to Keele Village, Staffordshire.

phenomenon). An examination of the data then revealed, over time, that where figures had been high (or low) they had tended to remain so. That said, a general increase in caravan totals was noted despite the 1994 CJPO Act. Greater London showed a gradual decline from 1989 (1034) to 1996 (713) but then increased again in 2000 (to 995). However, by January 2002 the figure had reduced to 812 – lower than the figure for 1979). The South East also peaked in 1992/1993 (with 2314 and 2231 caravans respectively) but had reduced by 1996 (2104) to its almost 1989 figure (2117). By 2000 the number of caravans had further reduced to 1948 (bi-annual count data for those years). Whilst this might indicate a preference for certain areas it could also mean 'red lining' (after Sarre et al 1989) and the operation of other exclusionary mechanisms.

The stability in some areas and fluctuations in others, also suggested a management of 'numbers'. However, overall, it appeared that the CJPO Act 1994 had had a limited and, in some regions, a short-lived impact. Whilst some fluctuations could have been attributable to boundary changes[67] this would not have affected the overall totals.

The increases in private authorised caravans between 1989 and 2002 were a result of already existing unauthorised temporary sites being granted planning permission as private sites rather than making extra provision (this certainly occurred in South Staffordshire and Stafford).[68] Some permitted but unauthorised sites were created as Council sites before government grant aid was revoked in 1994 (eg the Newcastle-under-Lyme site). When privatisation was advocated in 1994 (CJPO Act) some Council sites in Staffordshire were transferred to private partnerships (although some Councils maintained a managerial interest). Thus it appeared that the increases could be attributable more to paper conversions than to actual increases in provision.[69] Although some Councils in Staffordshire denied the existence of 'quotas' others conceded that they

---

[67] These have been taken into account when producing the maps.
[68] It is likely, too, that a percentage of caravans recorded as unauthorised in the count would be settled on an unauthorised or permitted/temporary site. Giving the family permission would regularise the site, making it official and private. This could be the case particularly if the family owned the land.
[69] And already it has been shown how data have been manipulated via method of data collection.

did work to 'figures' devised at the County level (in 1979). More extensive research was necessary in order to provide a more robust national picture.

It was also noted that some LAs with a history of no caravans had, by 2002, begun to record unauthorised encampments. These appeared in small numbers and occurred in the July counts – and were found, mainly, in sea-side and rural areas. This could point to summer/working holidays. This was supported by site visit conversations. This is not to say that families were not evicted on arrival. Possible, too, is, that with the removal of designation (1994 CJPO Act), families were now accessing these once 'no-go' areas.

If numbers had been inflated by in-coming Irish and New Travellers then it would be possible to hypothesise that the road axes from the ferry ports of Fishguard, Holyhead and Liverpool might be the lines which took them eastward, particularly if they were moved on arrival. The data indicate concentrations along these axes. Fairs and racecourses might also provide a reason for certain concentrations and geographical locations of caravans. However taking a broader perspective, these were the axes historically used by travellers and the 'vagrant poor' (Wrightson 1990:141; see also Chapter 4). Beier (1985:33) also found that from 1250 onwards the 'Southeast drew contingents from most parts of Britain and abroad ...' but ' ... most transients originated in the region itself ... with London being the main direction of flow' Generally 'the flow was west-east' (ibid:34). Thus, if history, geography and social science are melded then it seems likely that new arrivals to an already mobile grouping – eg 'Gypsies' (in the 14th Century) would follow the same or similar paths. Similarly, New Travellers might be expected to concentrate in areas close to significant monuments such as Stonehenge, Avebury and where festivals take place eg Glastonbury.

Whilst the maps and data might provide a visual distribution of change over time, they do not indicate whether change is forced or voluntary. Neither do they explain concentrations in some areas and the sharp increases and decreases in others. Clearly there were reasons for this mobility which went beyond the convenient and 'conventional' theories of 'nomadism', and forced movement.

Examination and Analysis of the Data since 2002

When the data were revisited for this volume, the greatest increase in caravan numbers in England appeared to have been between 1999 and 2009 (see Table 5.1) – 4806 caravans. Table 5.2 shows the regional distribution of all caravans in 2012 and totals by broad status. Table 5.3 shows the percentage changes in caravan status over the same periods of time, indicating the decrease in caravans on unauthorised sites and the increase in

Table 5.1 Total Gypsy/Traveller Caravan Numbers Over Time

1979	1989	1999	2009	2012
8358	11321	13007	17813	18746

Source: CLG Bi-annual Gypsy/Traveller Caravan Count Data for England, January 2012

caravans on private authorised sites. From an even split in 1979 between authorised and unauthorised, the 2012 data show that authorised caravans now form a majority (84.8 per cent) with a significant increase in caravans on private sites (from 14.3 per cent in 1979 to 48.5 per cent in 2012). Whilst the caravans in the socially rented category had

Table 5.2 Regional Variation of Caravan Numbers by Classification January 2012

Region	All Caravans	Authorised	Unauthorised
North West	1303	1135	168
North East	543	496	47
Yorks/Humberside	1492	1350	142
West Midlands	1951	1673	278
East Midlands	1569	1367	202
East England	4250	3581	669
Southwest	2651	2030	621
South East	4157	3555	602
London	830	709	121
Total	18746	15896	2850

Source: CLG Bi-annual Gypsy/Traveller Caravan Count Data for England, January 2012

increased between 1989 and 1999 by 2012 that percentage had reverted almost to 1979 levels of 35.7 per cent.

Table 5.4 shows the gradual changes between 1979 and 2012 of authorised caravans, the greatest increase occurring between 1999 and 2009, which would equate to an annual increase of about 374 during that decade. Whilst the data in Table 5.4 indicate increases

Table 5.3 Percentage Changes Over Time to Caravan Status Between 1979 and 2012

	Unauthorised Percentages	Authorised Socially Rented	Private	Total Authorised
1979	50%	35.7%	14.3%	50%
1989	33%	45.6%	21.4%	67%
1999	19.7%	47.4%	32.9%	80.3%
2009	20.4%	38.1%	41.5%	79.6%
2012	15.2%	36.3%	48.5%	84.8%

Source: Table Produced by CLG Statistics Section Bi-annual Gypsy/Traveller Caravan Count Data for England, January 2012

over the decades and in some regions these are greater than in others, however, when the changes per decade are examined it will be seen in Table 5.5 that there has been a decline – sometimes sharp - in almost all regions. In some regions such declines might be attributable to socio-economic circumstances and triggers, boundary changes and

Table 5.4 Changes Over Time by Region Between 1979 and 2012: Authorised Caravans

	1979	1989	1999	2009	2012
North East	186	308	410	475	496
North West	440	628	873	1193	1135
Yorks/Humberside	277	564	1103	1291	1350
East Midlands	337	584	867	1150	1367
West Midlands	563	780	1156	1492	1673
East England	609	1472	2649	3405	3581
London	457	507	667	745	709
South East	750	1311	1608	2788	3555
South West	563	742	1108	1646	2030
Total	4182	6896	10441	14185	15896

Source: CLG: Bi-annual Gypsy/Traveller Caravan Count Data for England, 1979-2012

climate change (colder Winters and wetter Summers). The only relatively stable regions appeared to be East Midlands, West Midlands and London although the trend in these regions still tended to be downward. The greatest decreases have occurred in the North

West (-58) and London (-36). The deep recession which began to bite in 2009, the Olympic Games effect and climate change could be reasons, also, for a north to south

Table 5.5 Changes per Decade by Region of Authorised Caravans

	1979-89	1989-99	1999-09	2009-2012
North East	122	102	65	21
North West	188	245	320	- 58
Yorks/Humberside	287	539	188	59
East Midlands	247	283	283	217
West Midlands	217	376	336	181
East of England	863	1222	756	176
London	50	160	78	-36
South East	561	297	1180	767
South West	179	366	538	384

Source: CLG Biannual Gypsy/Traveller Caravan Count Data for England, 1979-2012

movement. The caravan site clearances in and around the Olympic Games site should not be ignored. The data for London might have been affected by the fact that the 'Greater London' category for collection of the bi-annual count data became reduced to 'London' - which could also account for the spike in numbers in East England and the South East regions. The greatest increases between 1979 and 2012 have occurred in the South East (2805 caravans), East England (2972), and the South West (1467). The overall total increase in authorised caravans in the same period (1979-2012) was 11714 suggesting an annual average increase of 355 caravans over the past 33 years. However, as can be seen from the above tables these increases are not even temporally or evenly spread geographically. The fact that a majority of caravans are authorised, which presumably means with permission/authorisation/licences, suggested a form of stability with a space being 'granted'/found, so that settlement could take place. It was then important to examine the situation with regard to unauthorised caravans - the corollary being that as they are classified as 'unauthorised' they have yet to find space or a place to be and if sites were not being created to cope with this demand, then numbers of unauthorised caravans would increase.

Table 5.6 gives an overview over time and by region of unauthorised caravans. It is noted that there is no overall discernible pattern although prima facie the trend appears

Table 5.6 Changes Over Time by Region Between 1979-2012 Unauthorised Caravans

	1979	1989	1999	2009	2012
North East	258	117	30	7	47
North West	263	249	151	139	168
Yorks/Humberside	552	411	157	242	142
East Midlands	236	202	212	385	203
West Midlands	404	579	460	324	278
East England	998	1040	588	973	669
London	376	328	213	121	121
South East	819	669	424	569	602
South West	270	289	333	841	621
Total	4176	3884	2568	3628	2851

Source: CLG: Bi-annual Gypsy/Traveller Caravan Count Data for England, 1979-2012

downward in several of the regions – namely in the North East, Yorkshire and Humberside and West Midlands. A noticeable increase occurs in the South West.

Table 5.7 shows the downward regional trend more clearly, with some regional figures implying a rebalancing after a notable spike in the number of unauthorised caravans. This could be brought about by policy changes, removal or regularising unauthorised caravans, some of which are permitted, and some are permitted on Gypsy/Travellers' own land, resulting in planning permission being granted eventually. This tended to indicate that the term 'unauthorised' has begun to assume various nuances of acceptance/ belonging, at least geographically. Since the reasons for movement, destination, or where caravans have come from are not collected it would be difficult to know whether or not unauthorised caravans have a place to be or not. This means that the current data are unable to support further useful in-depth analysis along such causal lines. Overall, these data indicated that government policies were working. When the reality of this assumption was tested, nothing of any significance emerged using standard deviation as a method of analysis.[70] Whilst this suggests that legislation might be working to reduce unauthorised caravans it was not significant. In terms of provision it was noted that, using the same analysis, although provision was being made, and the number of unauthorised caravans was reducing, compared with numbers on authorised Council sites,

Table 5.7 Change per Decade from 1979 – 2012 of Unauthorised Caravans

	1979-1989	1989-1999	1999-2009	2009-2012
North East	-81	-87	-23	40
North West	-14	-98	-12	29
Yorks/Humberside	- 141	-254	85	-100
East Midlands	-34	10	173	-182
West Midlands	175	-119	-136	-46
East England	42	-452	385	-304
London	-48	-115	-92	0
South East	-150	-245	145	33
South West	-19	44	508	-220
Total	-292	1316	1060	-777

Source: CLG Bi-annual Gypsy/Traveller Caravan Count Data, 1979-2012

the correlation was weak enough to have occurred by chance (-0.056). Would there be a greater correlation between the increase of caravans on authorised private sites and the decreasing number of caravans on unauthorised sites? Again the result showed a weak correlation (0.102). Clearly different questions needed to be asked.

Moving with the assumption that Gypsies/Travellers are small business people and that Acton (1974; Acton and Mundy 1997) and Okely (1984/1994) have claimed that movement was for economic reasons as opposed to randomness, it was decided that an examination of *areas* might prove useful. To do this the Office of National Statistics (ONS) Classification of Local and Health Authorities in Great Britain (1996) was utilised.[71] This classification was used for the 'identification of specific types of area for public policy or commercial purposes. (ibid 2:1.6). It also claimed that the district level classification was 'useful' in the coding of geographically sparse data to an area typology for further classification and for pairing or grouping Authorities for comparative studies' (ibid 3:1.7). LAs were classified into 6 socio-economic Families: Prospering Areas, Rural Areas, Maturer Areas, Mining/Industrial Areas, Urban Centres and Inner London. This classification system is explained briefly in Figure 5.2.

---

[70] Spearman's Rank analysis was used to test if a relationship existed between unauthorised caravans and total change. A weak correlation was found (-0.188 compared with a 0.05 level of significance).
[71] Using such terms as 'squared Euclidean distance', Ward's hierarchical clustering algorithms' and 'centroids' it was irresistible!

Figure 5.2 ONS Classification

Area Type	Profile
Prospering Areas:	Satellite towns, growth corridors, areas of transient populations, metropolitan overspill, market towns/ concentrations of prosperity, established high status
Rural Areas:	Uplands and agriculture, remoter England and Wales, Heritage coast, accessible amenity, towns in country Industrial margins,
Maturer Areas:	University towns, suburbs, traditional seaside towns, Smaller seas-side towns, retirement
Mining/Industrial Areas:	Ports, coalfields, areas with inner city characteristics, Mining, former mining areas, areas with concentrations of public sector housing
Urban Centres:	Mixed economies, manufacturing, established service centres, New and expanding towns, areas with large ethnic minority groupings

Further Interpretation

Whilst the above analysis of the bi-annual data might be of interest, without context it did not fully explain why Gypsies/Travellers lived in or frequented/frequent certain areas. This is important because areas attractive to Gypsies/Travellers should also have the level of accommodation commensurate with demand. Without this Gypsies/Travellers would be excluded unless they were to camp illegally. Thus a context via the ONS Classification was applied to the bi-annual count data. The expectation, extrapolated from the literature, was that scores would be highest in Rural Areas and Urban Centres and possibly Mining/Industrial areas now in decline where land (Green and Brown) would be more readily available for encampments and/or authorised sites. To determine preference for area type the expected figures based on the number of Local Authorities falling within each ONS family group was calculated. Deviations between the expected and actual numbers might be taken to reveal a preference for, or an avoidance of, certain area types. The summary results are shown in Table 5.8. The grouping with the most caravans was the Prospering Area, which had caravans in excess of expected numbers.[72]

---

[72] If adjustments had been made for physical size of Local Authority then the difference between observation and expectation might have been even greater.

Table 5.8 To Show the Distribution of Total Caravans in England in 1995 and 2000 According to their ONS Family Grouping

Family Grouping	1995	2000	*Expected*	Percentage Change(1995-00)
Prospering	4537	5220	*3960*	15.0
Rural	3061	2978	*3355*	- 2.7
Urban Centres	1814	1857	*2197*	2.4
Industrial/Mining	1472	1454	*1526*	- 1.2
Maturer	679	1097	*1494*	61.6
Inner London	455	507	*592*	11.4
Total	**12018**	**13113**		**9.1**
	(12572)	**(13134)**		

Source: DTLR Bi-annual Count Gypsy/Traveller Count data for 1995 and 2000 based on totals for January only. Totals in brackets are the DTLR totals and show a data error

The Rural Areas had fewer caravans than expected in 1995 and even fewer by 2000.
The Rural Areas had fewer caravans than expected in 1995 and even fewer by 2000.
Urban Centres had more caravans than expected (in 2000) but the difference was less
Pronounced than that for the Prospering category. Although the Maturer Areas category
had fewer caravans than might be expected from the number of Local Authorities making
up this class, it showed the greatest percentage increase in caravans over the last five
years, relegating the Prospering Area category to second place in terms of recent patterns
of growth. It would appear that the caravan distribution reflected the economic
fluctuations of areas and their economic relevance to Gypsies/Travellers. This would
account for the reduction in caravan numbers in Mining/Industrial Areas.

To test this hypothesis further, the number of unauthorised caravans was checked against
the ONS classification to see if a correlation existed between Prospering Areas and
unauthorised encampments on the premise that mobile groups would not be tied to any
particular geographical location. Table 5.9 showed a decrease in unauthorised caravans
overall (-16%) between January 1995 and 2000, the decreases occurring in the
Mining/Industrial Areas, Urban Centres and Rural Areas. Increases occurred in
Prospering, Maturer Areas and Inner London. This indicated a correlation.

Table 5.9 The Distribution of Unauthorised Caravans Within the ONS Groupings Between the Period January 1995 and January 2000

ONS Classification	1995	2000	Percentage Change
Prospering	880	970	10.2
Rural	798	589	-26.2
Urban Centres	585	385	-34.2
Mining/Industrial	493	201	-59.2
Maturer	149	236	58.4
Inner London	38	91	39.5
Total	2943	2471	-16.0
	(3143)	(2516)	

Source: DTLR Bi-annual Gypsy/Traveller Count data for January 1995 and 2000. The figures in brackets are the DTLR total figures (data error)

It would appear, then, that like the housed population, Gypsies/Travellers were drawn to the more affluent parts of the country, which resulted in competition for place and space not only between Gypsy/Traveller groups but also between Gypsies/Travellers and the rest of society. The National Trends Survey (ONS 2002:32) indicated that for the national population, the highest gains via inter-regional migration occurred in London, the South East and East. However, given that when Gypsies/Travellers move they take their homes with them, they are able to access the prosperity trail faster than other minority groups and faster than majority society allows.[73] They are able to move into and to be closer to these areas, to take advantage of what is on offer, without having to save to buy property - which probably offsets being unable to access credit/mortgage facilities. Some will remain as long as they are permitted or until the economic climate changes. Tables 5.8 and 5.9 also indicate a core of 'settled' caravans across all the Family Groupings, which suggests other reasons for remaining in a particular area, and permanence. Such findings challenge the notions of 'nomadism' and suggest, instead, a strong pull towards economic opportunities, more readily available in some areas. The next section will look at the local level, ie Staffordshire, using local knowledge and fieldwork research in an attempt to explain some of the phenomena mentioned above and to see how they are played out locally.

The Bi-Annual Count and Staffordshire Under the Microscope

Staffordshire and the West Midlands - A Comparison

In January 2002, at the time of fieldwork, there was a recorded total of 265 caravans in Staffordshire. Of these, 245 caravans were authorised (148 were authorised private) leaving 20[74] as unauthorised. There were approximately 37 sites within the County, three of which were overseen by District Councils on behalf of the County Council. The rest were run by Gypsies/Travellers themselves and were private.

The Staffordshire figures followed the national trend towards an increase in private provision. Tables 5.10 and 5.11 show how these figures compared regionally and over time, and the percentage changes within Staffordshire. Whilst the 1994 CJPO Act might have had some influence regionally, initially, by 1999 this appears to have dissipated. Whilst overall in Staffordshire there had been a 53.4 per cent increase since 1979, and a general increase to 1999 there had been a decrease in caravan numbers between 1999 and 2002, with some LAs replicating their 1979 totals (Table 5.11).

Table 5.10 The Total Number of Caravans in Staffordshire and the West Midlands Region between 1979 and 2002

	1979	1989	%Change 1979-89	1999	% Change 1989-99	2002	Total % Change 1979-2002
West Midlands	967	1393	44.1	1024	-26.5	1485	**53.4**
Staffordshire	183	236	29.0	320	35.6	265	**44.8**
Staffordshire as a % of West Midlands total	18.9%	16.9%		31.3%		17.8%	

Source: DTLR Bi-annual Gypsy/Traveller Caravan Count data 1979 to 2002. The totals for Staffordshire include Stoke-on-Trent, which was made a Unitary Authority in 1999.

---

[73] Their mobility is more visible – although it might be no greater than that of the so-called settled housed population.
[74] However, in the north of the County, LAs had records which showed more than 100 had 'passed through'.

Table 5.11 The Total Distribution of Caravans in Staffordshire from January 1979 - 2002

Local Authority	1979	1989	1999	2000	2001	2002
Staffordshire Moorlands	-	-	1	1	-	1
Stoke-on-Trent	36	35	66	74	75	66
Newcastle-under-Lyme	27	21	23	26	23	22
Stafford	35	24	61	67	60	47
Cannock	26	19	64	31	28	28
Lichfield	-	-	12	2	3	7
Tamworth	-	-	12	3	-	-
South Staffordshire	35	103	68	78	65	71
East Staffordshire	24	19	23	21	23	23
Total	**183**	**236**	**320**	**303**	**277**	**265**
% Change		29%	36%	-5.3%	- 8.6%	-4.3%

Source: DTLR Bi-annual Gypsy/Traveller Caravan Count data 1979-2002 (the figures for 2000 have been amended)

Distribution within Staffordshire

Table 5.11 shows the local distribution of caravans and fluctuations over time in Staffordshire. The data show concentrations in the north middle and south of the County. Between 1979 and 1989 there had been reductions in all the Staffordshire LAs, except South Staffordshire, which suggested limited provision and consequent removal of unauthorised caravans. (Given the geographical position of Staffordshire, the County could also act as a conduit through which families pass in order to access other and more lucrative areas.) By 1999, Stoke-on-Trent, Stafford and Cannock showed significant increases although percentage decreases were observable. Other LAs such as Newcastle-under-Lyme, East Staffordshire and Staffordshire Moorlands show a consistency of numbers throughout. In 1999 an upward 'spike' is observable from which a majority of LAs 'recovered' by 2000. Staffordshire Moorlands, Lichfield and Tamworth had the fewest number of caravans. Lichfield a cathedral town, Staffordshire Moorlands, an area of stark natural beauty, and Tamworth which claimed it had no appropriate land for sites. This would preclude and severely limit choice for Gypsy/Traveller families who might wish to settle. A history of resorting to certain areas might not always indicate preference for a location, but also could indicate exclusion from other areas. Thus a history and habit of removal/non-admittance in some LAs is also a salient factor in the distribution of caravans. The later chapters dealing with local policy, practice and service delivery will deal with such issues.

Higher and consistent numbers recorded, demonstrated where provision had been delivered. This was shown to be in the form of Council provision in the north, private provision in South Staffordshire and a mixture of both in Stafford (in the centre). Where sites were provided, Gypsy/Traveller expectation might have been raised so that chain migration then became a factor inflating numbers of unauthorised caravans. Nevertheless, overall, there has been a general decrease in the number of caravans in Staffordshire with unauthorised caravans, suggesting a continued need for some kind of provision. Between 2005 and 2007 a needs survey was undertaken in Staffordshire covering East Staffordshire Borough, Newcastle-under-Lyme Borough, Stafford Borough, Staffordshire Moorlands District and Stoke-on-Trent. This admitted a need for 76 pitches in Stafford Borough. In a recent report by Newcastle-under-Lyme Planning Committee (19 February 2013) Stafford Borough had yet to produce a needs 'update' or 'successor documents' and until it did, provision could not be delivered on the grounds that 'A new study could recommend a reduction in the provision of pitches and this could in theory result in an increase in our own provision requirements' (ibid, page 35). Whilst Newcastle-under-Lyme prevaricates, Stoke-on-Trent, however, is about to create another site and a planning application was pending in December 2012.

The data in Table 5.12 demonstrate not only change over time, but also the way that provision has been effected. Stoke-on-Trent and Stafford can be seen as providers. Unauthorised figures (for 1979) have been transformed to authorised (mainly Council sites) by 1989 under the remit of the 1968 Caravans Sites Act. A similar scenario is demonstrated in Stoke-on-Trent between 1999-2000 and 2000-2002 when the permanent site was enlarged and a transit caravan site was created in 1999. The transit site absorbed the unauthorised site and those not wishing to take up accommodation on either of the sites were moved on or families moved of their own accord. Table 5.13 shows the way

Table 5.12 The Number and Distribution of Unauthorised Caravans in Staffordshire from January 1979- 2002

Local Authority	1979		1989		1999		2000		2002		2012	
	U	A*	U	A	U	A	U	A	U	A	U	A
Staffs Moorlands	-	-	-	-	-	-	-	-	-	1	4	4
Stoke-on-Trent	7	29	-	35	30	36	5	69	-	66	-	63
Newcastle-u-Lyme	-	27	-	21	-	23	1	25	-	22	-	25
Stafford	35	-	12	12	28	33	4	63	3	44	-	69
Lichfield	-	-	15	-	-	2	-	2	7	(2)	2	4
Cannock	11	15	4	15	33	31	8	23	8	20	-	43
Tamworth	-	-	-	-	12	-	3	-	-	-	-	-
South Staffordshire	2	33	23	80	-	68	16	62	2	69	29	109
East Staffordshire	4	20	-	19	-	23	-	21	-	23	-	13
Total	59	124	54	182	103	216	37	265	20	247	35	330

Source: DTLR Bi-annual Gypsy/Traveller Caravan Count data from 1979-2002
- Key: U = unauthorised; A = authorised
- The figure in brackets represents the number of caravans that exist but were not recorded in the count

in which temporary sites have, over time, been issued with licences to become permanent, private sites. This has occurred particularly in the south of the County where there have been more private sites but no Council provision as a matter of policy. It also needs to be noted that most of these sites were granted permission on Appeal. Newcastle-under-Lyme had had a permitted site which was moved and made permanent in 1993/4 (somewhat belatedly under the 1968 Caravan Sites Act and just before government funding was revoked). Stability in numbers in Newcastle-under-Lyme are probably attributable to provision being made for those on the existing permitted site only, and all in-coming unauthorised caravans were and still are, sometimes swiftly, removed. Unauthorised caravans, as already mentioned, do not always show on this LA's bi-annual counts.

The planning permission for private sites in Stafford meant that the unauthorised caravans became authorised in line with the remit of the 1994 CJPO Act and Housing policy. East Staffordshire has similar eviction practices to Newcastle-under-Lyme hence, possibly, the stability in their figures and lack of unauthorised sites. Tamworth also removed all unauthorised encampments. In the interests of Best Value (operational

Table 5.13 Planning Permissions Granted to Temporary or Permitted Sites Since the 1968 Caravan Sites and Control of Development Act in South Staffordshire

1980	1981	1987	1988	1991	1996
	1 Temp (a)	-------------	1 Perm (t)		
1 Temp (a)	------------	-------------	-----------	1 Perm (t)	
			1 Perm (a)	1 Perm (a)	
	1 Temp (a)	-------------	------------	1 Perm (t)	
	1 Temp (a)--	1 Perm (t)			
					1 Perm (a)
				1 Perm (a)	

Source : Staffordshire County Council records
Key: (a) denotes on appeal
     (t) denotes status change from temporary to permanent of the same site
Note: One site was granted established use status (no date)

at the time) this Local Authority served an injunction on a family in 2001 (after moving them weekly around the Borough for ten years) who, at the time of writing the Thesis, were recorded as unauthorised in Lichfield and were about to be evicted. These were not seasonal movements related to employment as the data alone might imply. However, it shows how exclusionary action by one LA affects spatial distribution and the data. Such instances also point to the fact that not all Gypsies/Travellers are passing through – there are families who wish to remain. Whether or not they are permitted to do so is another matter and well-rehearsed mechanisms and practices ensure that they are kept moving. South Staffordshire has mainly private sites which are family run and these are subject to changes in ownership.[75] Some owners who run sites as business ventures refuse families they do not know. Gypsy/Traveller families can be squeezed off when site upgrades occur. Additionally, if planning permission for a private site is refused, the family usually disperses and moves elsewhere.

---

[75] One private site visited had been abandoned, its amenities vandalised.

The transmogrifications effected when unauthorised sites become authorised or when LA sites become privatised, is not necessarily an indication of more provision, so much as a regularisation of some caravans which moves them into more acceptable categories which fit National Government criteria. Much of the provision has been in response to waiting groups who had settled in an area. Apart from Stoke-on-Trent and a small transit site in South Staffordshire there appeared to be little or no extra provision or space allocated to take up new or in-coming families. If there are no spaces on authorised sites then families must remain illegally. Whilst the data might support the view that the 1994 CJPO Act had worked in that there had been increased private provision and a reduction in unauthorised encampments, this has not been in the ways, probably, envisaged. That said, Table 5.12 does show a general increase in caravans which could be accounted for via a redistribution from elsewhere and a possible easing up of the moving on process.

The Attraction of Staffordshire

In line with the national data for England the distribution of caravans in Staffordshire was examined using the ONS Family grouping criteria, using the DTLR data for January 1995, 2000 and 2002. Table 5.14 shows that Staffordshire has a range of categories for useful analysis. Table 5.14 and 5.15 show that Staffordshire followed the national trend

Table 5.14 Total Numbers of Caravans Allocated to ONS Family Groupings in Staffordshire in January 1995 and 2002

ONS Family Classification	1995	2000	2002
Prospering	146	145	125
Rural	69	79	74
Mining/Industrial	87	74	66
Urban Centre	5	3	0
Total	**307**	**301**	**265**

Source: DTLR Bi-annual Gypsy/Traveller Caravan Count data for January 1995, 2000 and 2002

in that there were more caravans in the Prospering Area category than in any other, and more than expected. However, South Staffordshire showed a big decrease after 1995 and

Stafford a large increase.[76] The increase in Stafford could be attributable to planning permission being granted for several adjacent private sites.

Table 5.15 Total Number of Caravans in Staffordshire and Their Distribution within the ONS Family Grouping for January 1995 and 2000

Local Authority	ONS Class	1995				2000			
		T	U	C	P	T	U	C	P
Staffordshire Moorlands	Rural	-	-	-	-	1	-	-	1
Stoke-on-Trent	Mining/Industrial	87	53	34	-	74	5	65	4
Newcastle-under-Lyme	Rural	23	4	19	-	26	1	25	-
Stafford	Prospering	44	18	13	13	67	4	31	32
Cannock	Rural	21	4	-	17	31	8	-	23
Lichfield	Prospering	-	-	-	-	-	-	-	-
Tamworth	Urban Centre	5	5	-	-	3	3	-	-
South Staffordshire	Prospering	102	20	-	82	78	16	-	62
East Staffordshire	Rural	26	-	-	26	21	-	-	21

Source :DTLR Bi-annual Gypsy/Traveller Caravan Count data for January 1995 and 2000.
Key: T = total; U= unauthorised; C = authorised Council; P = authorised private

Although Cannock and Newcastle-under-Lyme and East Staffordshire are classified as Rural, they lean towards the Prospering Area Category. When the Prospering area is Grouped and Clustered, the Grouping is that of 'growth area' and the Cluster is 'market town'. Thus Gypsies/Travellers frequenting the Rural Areas in Staffordshire, might do so for other than its rural qualities.

Lichfield as a Prospering Area and a Cathedral city, has developed as a tourist centre and appears to be an exception. Whilst Officers claimed that their area attracted few Gypsies/Travellers, the LA made no provision under the 1968 Caravan Sites Act yet employed a part time Eviction Officer. Whilst Lichfield might be 'off the beaten track' for Gypsies/Travellers, it might also be out of bounds. However, ability to pay could make a difference – as it has in South Staffordshire. Since writing the Thesis, Lichfield has undergone a process of housing development and general enlargement. In January 2012, Lichfield recorded 6 Gypsy/Traveller caravans – 4 private and 2 unauthorised but 'not tolerated' (see table 5.12). However the numbers of caravans 'permitted' are proportionately, and considerably, fewer than for the number of newly built houses.

---

[76] Some of the land in Stafford had changed hands and planning permission had been granted for a private site. When ownership changes, an exodus can result. Also new groups coming into an area can 'remove'

The Mining/Industrial category has shown a decline in numbers probably linked to the reduced mining/industrial activity in Stoke-on-Trent and North Staffordshire, generally. The emphasis now is on 'smart' and service industries. However, given the unofficial figures for Stoke-on-Trent for unauthorised caravans resorting to the area the 'reduction' might be linked to the fact that now Stoke-on-Trent has enlarged its site and created transit accommodation, the Council, as part of its 'proportionate response', removes any unauthorised caravans promptly if families refuse the transit site. Newcastle-under-Lyme has a tendency to remove any unauthorised encampments, usually to Stoke-on-Trent.[77]

Table 5.16 shows how unauthorised caravans are distributed through the ONS classifications. This follows the national trend in that prospering Areas are being favoured. However, the Prospering Areas show a significant decrease together with Mining/Industrial and the Urban Centre group. The decreases here are likely to be attributable to non provision and eviction. The Urban Centre decrease – ie the Tamworth scenario - has already been discussed.

Table 5.16 Total Number of Unauthorised Caravans Allocated to ONS Family Groupings in Staffordshire in 1995 and 2000

ONS Family Classification	1995	2000	% Change 1995-2000	2002	% Change 2000-2002
Prospering	38	20	- 47.4	12	- 40
Rural	8	9	12.5	8	-11
Mining/Industrial	53	5	- 90.6	0	-100
Urban Centre	5	3	- 40.0	0	-100
Total	**104**	**37**	**- 64.4**	**20**	**-45.9**

Source: DTLR Bi-annual Gypsy/Traveller Caravan Count data for January, 1995 -2002

Apart from the Urban Centre classification, other categories showed a core of 'settled' caravans. The instability in the unauthorised figures could partly be attributable to

---

existing families.
[77] Because the permanent site is full, when families refuse this offer, they are issued with an Order 24. Neither can they be regarded as homeless once this offer has been refused - emergency housing is not, therefore, an option.

groups moving in an out voluntarily, but largely it would appear that the main mechanisms could be forced movement and eviction.

SUMMARY

The accuracy of the DTLR bi-annual Count data have often been challenged, although it does not prevent successive governments using it as a basis for policy and forward planning. This chapter has attempted to pin-point where the inaccuracies lie. It has also attempted to show how these data as presented, form a representation of Gypsies/Travellers which may not be entirely correct. To this end, this chapter has attempted to sift fact from value within a statistical frame.

The raw longitudinal data, taken at face value, appear to show that, nationally, Government Policy re private site provision is working and that the CJPO Act 1994 has reduced unauthorised camping. These figures are used by Government to support its legislation and to dismiss calls for change (DTLR Interview 2001). This chapter demonstrates how the data can be manipulated at the local and national levels by changing the status of caravans and sites, and by moving and redistributing caravans and families, often against their will.

Overall, whilst the figures show a broad distribution for England, the East, Southeast and East Midlands regions have the largest numbers of caravans and this appears to be a historical trend rather than a recent phenomenon. The west–east flow also mirrors that of majority society, which presents competition for space and place. Legislation, to deal with dispersal and removal from these areas, has been used which has had the effect of re-mobilising families who were once settled, and by keeping families who wish to settle, out and mobile. Whilst the data may suggest 'nomadism', policies and practices on the ground when examined, together with evictions and moving on, appear to have caused much of the random movement in Staffordshire, giving the appearance of 'nomadism'. When broadly compared to majority society, Gypsy/Traveller movement (particularly for those on sites) in Staffordshire is not excessive and the reasons for movement are broadly similar.[78] Eviction, however, might be disproportionate. Nevertheless, some families on the road have permanent pitches elsewhere. This is an area that needs further research in order to properly and more accurately assess need.

Gypsies/Travellers, like majority society, are attracted to Prospering Areas. It could be that some are attempting to move away from unsatisfactory sites/areas and in search of a better place to be and more lucrative 'markets' and or employment. Majority society objects to this since 'place' and 'space' must be earned/purchased. There was evidence to suggest that families were being removed from the better areas to those more 'in keeping' with their perceived status. Unauthorised caravans could also signify resistance.

Eviction causes disproportionate mobility – more visible with Gypsies/Travellers since when families move they take their homes with them. The notion of free and seasonal movement (ie 'nomadism') could thus be challenged –even for those who claim to be 'nomadic', and will be held questionable as being the *only* explanation of Gypsy/Traveller mobility. The magnitude and rapidity of change, visible in the data raise the question of voluntary versus forced movement. Chapters 6 and 7 will demonstrate the way in which exclusionary policies and practices by LAs in their interpretation of national policy tend to cause mobility – often forced. The recent Dale Farm evictions and the clearance of the Olympic village site bear this out. However, where groups are settled illegally on land or where licenses exist and are breached or exceeded, then the alternatives for some families, given the past and present state of play, are bleak.

---

[78] See Hogarth and Daniels (1988) on the increased mobility of the 'settled' community.

CHAPTER SIX

THE POLICY TRAIN

PART ONE – NATIONAL INTENT VIA LEGISLATION?

Chapters 3, 4 and 5 have explored the ways in which the mechanisms of identity and identification, myth, prejudice, interpretation of data and the way in which it is collected, what is collected and assumptions generated within power groups combine to exert pressure which can influence the structure and development direction of minority groups. Such pressure can be covert or overt, and via encouragement and/or legislation/ regulation. This chapter examines some of the significant policies for Gypsies/Travellers in recent history and the way in which these have acted as a theoretical guide for official action at the national and local levels. Although the MA Thesis suggested a strong alignment between policy and practice, in order to examine what is a very complex process, these are separated here. Policy has also been subdivided into National and Local Policy for closer scrutiny.

Overall, this chapter wishes to chart the attempts by National Government to find 'solutions' to the perceived 'problem'. How far does the policy formulation process contribute to the' them/us' syndrome not only between groups but also between levels of administration and their constituents? Individuals and groups are constantly splitting away from the main, forming and reforming in response to external (even internal) stimuli (political parties and religions are particularly prone to this). Are the mechanisms of exclusion embedded in legislation and policy – if so where, how and why? The research for this chapter involved interviews with policy makers and implementers at national and local levels. It also involved an examination of national policy as it could apply to and impact upon the Gypsy/Traveller grouping over time. The main research questions were: who is National Policy for and what is its intent; has it been and is it likely to be effectively translated into Local Policy and practice; have governments learned from previous policy shortcomings?

Who is National Legislation For?

Chapter 5 demonstrated that if 'political' estimates and data are taken as valid then the majority of Gypsies/ Travellers are settled in conventional ways. Those who are settled are subject to the benefits and prohibitions contained within *all* legislation – allegedly. Those who are mobile are excluded from space making it difficult to access rights and privileges. They become the prime recipients of regulatory legislation and policy, which in turn produces a vicious cycle of negative game play. Legislation and policy for Gypsies/Travellers, then, concentrates on the regulation and attempted control of a relatively small number of mobile families in its attempt to arbitrate between two perceived different lifestyles/value systems.

Given the then, limited, positive action and lack of resources it appeared that best value for National and Local Government was to continually keep families/groups moving. National Government expressed this as wishing 'to minimise the disruption that arises from illegal camping' (DTLR Interview, 2001). However, government suggested, that within that there is 'a whole policy ambit of site provision and good practice guidance' (ibid) – and the presumption that everyone concerned will play their part. Taken at face value it appeared that National Government was not averse to people travelling but to the disruption caused by unauthorised settlement and trespass, which has become part of the 'accepted' travelling way of life, which raises the questions, is this way of life a cultural trait, or an evolved expediency linked to exclusion, a lack of provision and enforced mobility which has become 'a way of life'? One Gypsy/Traveller interviewee commented: 'You've got to have somewhere stable haven't you? When you move is to go on holiday or on business'. And another: 'When it's open land it's anybody's. You don't ask who it belongs to'.

The MA research (Drakakis-Smith 1997) indicated that via policy and practice Gypsies/Travellers were being divided into two groups – the settled (The Good) and the mobile (The Bad). Additionally, different groups were being evaluated into the 'more deserving' and the 'less deserving'. However, whilst regulatory legislation is intended for a minority (within a minority) in practice it is equally applied to all within the group.

National Policy as Future History and Intent?

Legislation is a set of rules governing action, it relies on precedent (it has a history), rarely stands alone and it is usually linked or has compatibility with other legislation, presenting the reader with a legal labyrinth leading backwards into medieval law. Angus Fraser's history (1992) and David Mayall's (1988;1995) history of state policy from the 16-19th Centuries and the Gypsy Lore Journals are catalogues of eviction and exclusion of those who were unable or unwilling for whatever reason, to negotiate settlement and belonging. Since UK legislation relies upon precedent, present-day Social Policy has built and re-mixed past policy with surprisingly little innovation (see Jones 2000; Glennerster 2000 for more recent evaluations and the evolution of Social Policy in UK).

Policy Mix

National Policy is multifarious. However, the two main strands which primarily affect Gypsies/Travellers are Social Policy (which includes housing policy) and Planning Policy. Social Policy has regard for the welfare of Gypsy/Traveller *families* in terms of their right as citizens to access health care and education. Planning Policy, on the other hand, is concerned with *caravans* and where to put them. Housing Policy includes policy for caravan sites – mainly for those who are not Gypsies/Travellers, although Gypsy/Traveller sites are implicated within it. The emphasis of Planning Policy is on the allocation of space and the legitimate and rightful use of land. The 1968 Caravan Sites Act attempted to address this by combining the two policy strands by making planned provision for caravans so that families could benefit from the product of Social (and at the time Welfare) Policy. The boundary was redrawn by the 1994 Criminal Justice and Public Order Act - which revoked provision and resources. This was viewed, generally, as regressive. Clements (2002) attempted to reverse the situation in his Private Members Law Reform Bill by combining welfare and planning issues.

Restructuring Structures

At the time the Thesis was being written, the DTLR was described as being 'the sponsoring Government Department for Local Government' which included sponsoring change and development. The Gypsy Policy Branch (previously the Gypsy Policy Sites Branch) became a sub-unit of the Housing and Homelessness Department (which also dealt with anti-social behaviour) which in turn was but one Department comprising the full remit of the DTLR which also covered Transport and the Regions, which before the Thesis was completed, became the Office of the Deputy Prime Minister (ODPM). It is the Gypsy Policy Branch which collates the bi-annual Gypsy caravan count. Today (2013), dealings with Gypsy/Travellers are spread across 16 Departments within the Department of Communities and Local Government (CLG).

The role of Government, too, has changed over recent decades as UK moves from a paternal/welfare state to that of a managerial/self-help/partnership-driven model. The language of Governance has also changed being more closely aligned to that of corporate business. EU membership has meant that the UK Parliament in its own law-making is subject to a higher authority – that of the European Parliament and many of its directives. Many of the more recent legislative innovations, shifts and alignments have been in response to EU requirements (eg The European Commission Reports on Economic and Social Cohesion 1996; 2001; the EU Social Protection Committee Reports 2001; and more latterly the various edicts from the European Commission on Human Rights and the rulings emanating from the European Court of Human Rights, particularly with regard to minority and vulnerable ethnic groups- to name but a few). The European Fundamental Rights Agency (FRA) established in October 2010, has recently adopted steps specifically for the Roma grouping. In April 2011 the European Commission published an EU Framework for National Integration Strategies up to 2020 which is accompanied by EU funding of 26.5 billion Euros and is available for Roma social inclusion in the most disadvantaged regions. Unfortunately the UK failed to meet the deadline for their submission, claiming that it was mainstreaming its own policy framework requirements (TAT News Spring 2012:20).

Such shifts have entailed changes to National Legislation and Local Policy, as attempts are made to 'modernise' UK governance and policy. Although the system of a Local Development Framework (driven by a Regional Plan) which sought to replace the County/Unitary Structure Plans was introduced by the Blair (New Labour) Administration, this was overturned by the more recent Conservative/Liberal Democrat Coalition. Nevertheless, Community Strategies were supposedly intended to bring social well-being and land-use planning closer together. The current Localism Act (2012). Is an attempt to stream-line and to 'simplify' planning rules making development easier and the planning system more accessible, the intention being to fast track the planning decision process - which may, however, result in over-riding social and local community considerations. Thus it will be interesting to see how these ultimately balance, if at all. In terms of its effects on Gypsies/Travellers, enforcement is suggested against those who 'try wilfully to avoid planning controls' (2.7 and 5.68-70) and a 'punitive charge for retrospective applications' is being contemplated.

Such changes are not always adequately explained to, or readily taken on board by LAs who must implement change at ground level. Rules are not always fully explained to or understood by the target group at the local level, thus the assumption that 'everyone knows the rules' is often false. Attitudinal change does not necessarily flow from National Government rulings. Thus some legislation can exist within a time warp – its opportunities ignored by both LAs and the target group. This could be said of the 1960 Caravan Sites and Control of Development Acts and the 1968 Caravan Sites Act.

Into the 21st Century – The National Legislative Train Evaluated

The Caravan Sites and Control of Development Act 1960 …

Evaluations of the Caravan Sites and Control of Development Act 1960 and the Caravan Sites Act 1968 have already been academically (Swingler 1969; Acton 1974; Adams et al 1975; Brand 1985, 1986; Home 1993; Okely 1994) and officially (the Cripps Report 1977, the Wibberley report 1986; Todd and Clark 1991) sifted. The main findings were that any good intentions for Gypsies/Travellers were off-set by poor management and control at the national level leading to non-compliance and resistance at the local levels aligned to a lack of resources when the Act was first introduced. With hindsight it appears that these Acts were not so much 'starting afresh' suggested by Hawes and Perez (1996:31) as a half- hearted and inclusionary 'blip' to accommodate Gypsies/Travellers in what had been a cycle of exclusionary legislation, with built-in mechanisms, which assured non-settlement, particularly of perceived non-conforming families.

The statement of intent[79] for the 1960 Caravan Sites and Control of Development Act appeared, mainly, to bring all non-permanent accommodation into line with housing and under State control in an attempt to hasten provision to improve conditions (Donnison 1967) and to reduce the post war squatting/homeless population. LAs were thus given the power to both provide and prohibit.[80] Gypsies/Travellers were not singled out at this stage for special provision but existed as a group within a plethora of 'groups' not living in conventional housing. This Act began the sifting process on the one hand and the removal of squatting groups on the other, from land, some of which was needed for development.[81] As such the Act began an enclosure of open land and a redefinition of the built environment in line with post-war planning ideologies of space organization and zoning (Sibley 1981,1990; Simmie 2001).[82] It also attempted to stem the process of 'assarting'.[83]

The Act was reviewed in its relation to accommodation for Gypsies/Travellers in 1967 (MHLG 1967) and found that since more sites had closed than were created the situation of homelessness had been exacerbated. It claimed that Gypsies/Travellers had different

---

[79] 'to make further provision for the licensing and control of caravan sites; to authorise local authorities to provide and to operate caravan sites; to amend the law relating to enforcement notices and certain other notices under Part 3 of the Town and Country Planning Act (1974)'.

[80] Every caravan site had to be licensed (Pt.1.s3.3); all caravan sites had to be regulated in terms of health and safety and layout (Pt.1.s.5-6); the use of commons for camping (23.s.1); and to authorise the LAs to purchase land for sites and to provide facilities on those sites (24.s1-5).

[81] The advent of the motorway, more and faster traffic meant that the roadsides were no longer safe places to camp.

[82] In this respect Gypsies/Travellers were difficult to accommodate since they worked where they lived. The new health and safety regulations separated these two functions.

[83] A medieval term whereby land was usurped by 'cottagers' and others by a gradual encroachment into the countryside. Its modern-day equivalent would be additional encroachment into both the Green Belt and the countryside. Although the term is no longer used, the act of encroachment occurs and is carefully controlled by planning authorities and residents.

accommodation needs.[84] However, the Report barely touched on the issue that Gypsy/Traveller families were being barred from established caravan sites. This happens today (site visit conversations) and appears to be a matter that has not been, or is not being addressed.[85]

Although Gypsies/Travellers had agitated for sites in 1967 (Swingler 1969:987) and despite Government Circular 6/62 only 37 out of 62 County Councils had undertaken a needs assessment exercise in their area and only 15 sites (in addition to those already created) were provided between 1960 and 1968 (DTLR data 2001). However both Acts appeared to work well for dispersal and removal. The fact that no time limits had been set, only a power and not a duty to provide had been placed on LAs and that no extra financial resources had been provided from National Government served as expedient mechanisms by some LAs not to provide.[86]

The Caravan Sites Act 1968[87]

This came into force as a response to the representation by Gypsies/Travellers and their advocates, and was a strengthening of the 1960 Act. That some sites had been created gave National Government some leeway to regulate further with regard to illegal encampments and squatting. It also offered both inducements (to LAs) to provide and punitive measures for non-compliance. To this effect, if LAs provided sites then 'designation' would follow whereby 'surplus' caravans could be moved on. Although it was not intended that individual LAs would apply for designation (Lord Avebury Interview 2001), this is what happened. Some began to unofficially self-designate. Circular 28/77 (23) attempted to clarify the position by stating that, 'designation must be

---

[84] In terms of 'ethnicity and a deep rooted habit of nomadism and way of life' (MHLG 1967:17)
[85] A desk top exercise was undertaken of caravan sites in Staffordshire. More than 1000 pitches were provided for non Gypsies/Travellers (permanent and holiday accommodation). Some sites closed during the winter months. Thus it would appear that although pitches are available Gypsy/Traveller families are not allowed access to them . Such sites were thus seen as 'not for them' (Gypsy/Traveller interview).
[86] Some LAs were reluctant to commit public funds to projects for 'non-belongers' or the non deserving. Feudal boundaries for some were firmly in place, still.
[87] Its stated intent was 'to restrict the eviction from some caravan sites of occupiers of caravans and make other provision for the benefit of such occupiers; to ensure the establishment of such sites by local authorities for the use of gypsies and other persons of nomadic habit; and to control in certain areas the unauthorized occupation of land by such persons; to amend the definition of caravans' (Caravan Sites Act 1968).

seen only as a means of acquiring additional powers to ensure gypsies use the accommodation available to them' (quoted in Brand 1985:977). The instrument of 'mandamus' was threatened in order to force/instruct recalcitrant LAs to comply with the Act. However, it was rarely used during the life of this Act.

The Act also provided a definition of the beneficiaries of the Act – thus creating a group where one might not have existed. It also provided many loop-holes to LAs (see Caravan Sites Act 1968: Part Two (a); 6 (1); 6(2)a; 7(1); 10(1); Part Three (5)).

Although the Act's failings have been discussed over time (Acton 1974; Adams et al 1975; the Cripps Report 1977; Brand 1985; Todd and Clark 1991; Home 1993; Okely 1994; Clements 1997) its confusions have been left in obscurity. First, the term *permanent* crept into the LA vocabulary and its meaning was differentially interpreted and disputed as permanent sites intended for a mobile population passing through; or permanent sites for those who no longer wished to travel who wished to reside permanently in an area; or as permanent sites for those already settled on 'permitted' or 'tolerated' sites – ie those who were settling, and no others. Second, 100 per cent funding did not accompany the Act until after 1980 (Local Government Planning and Land Act 1980); and that once sites were established LAs had the financial responsibility of raising capital for their management and maintenance at a time of high inflation and reduced spending. Third, funding for site provision was only gradually rolled out, first in England and Wales and then to Scotland,[88] and was only recently made available in Northern Ireland (at the time of writing the Thesis). Whether this staggering was a matter of economy or an attempt to regulate an over-provision of sites in order to 'produce an artificial demand (Home 1993:14; Todd and Clark 1991) was never made clear.[89]

---

[88] Although grant aid was available in Scotland from 1971, a duty to provide was never imposed. Lomax (2000) found that there was little to choose between an imposed duty and persuasion in terms of response when Scotland was compared to England and Wales.
[89] No research appears to have been carried out to gauge whether or not the creation of sites in England and Wales led to an outmigration in search of sites from Scotland and Ireland. Scottish and Irish families were found on LA sites in Staffordshire and were of long-standing.

Additional problems were more systemic in that the County had the responsibility of deciding where sites would be provided (Caravan sites Act 1968 Part 2:7(1). The relationship between County and Borough Councils was akin to the relationship between National and Local Government in that a heavy reliance was placed on 'good will'. County Councillors were, often, also Borough Councillors. It would be unlikely that they would jeopardise their position by allocating sites on their own patch or scarce resources to those deemed undeserving by their constituents. In this, Party Politics also played a part. National Government tends not to interfere, unduly, in local affairs. Thus political will at the local level is often absent and public relations management re such issues has been far from satisfactory (Wills 1991:16: Todd and Clark 1991; Drakakis-Smith and Mason 2001; Drakakis-Smith 2007)). Thus the provisional instruments of the 1968 Act were lightly implemented, rarely enforced and contained sufficient inherent weaknesses and caveats to make any initiative less than a national success.

Despite such difficulties, sites *were* created. In addition to the sites already in existence, 105 new sites were provided during the 1970s, and 105 were created during the 1980s. Whilst Halfacree (1996) suggests that the DETR data showed that the Act was successful – and certainly provision did accelerate in the later years of its life, this could have been the result of paper transactions (see Chapter 5) whereby private sites were taken over by LAs and temporary, unauthorised sites of long standing became authorised public or private sites. Nevertheless, site creation where it existed was destined to be short-lived. Already in Parliament, c(l)uing debates were being initiated which suggested that the end of statutory provision and grant aid was nigh (Hansard 13 March 1987; 15 June 1989; 4 November 1992; 24 March 1993). New waves of Travellers at the time (Irish and New Travellers) produced fertile ground for more regulatory legislation.

Regulatory Legislation for Unauthorised Encampments vs Human Rights
(a) Planning and Control
The then National Government policy, which affected Gypsies/Travellers who were mobile and who lived in caravans on unauthorised sites was enshrined in the CJPO Act 1994, the Crime and Disorder Act 1998, The Good Practice Guide (1998), its Amended

Chapter 5, Circulars 1/94 and 18/94, Planning Law (and Health and Safety rules and regulations), The Human Rights Act 1998. The Race Relations Act 1976 (as amended 2001) also includes 'traditional' and Irish Gypsies/Travellers within its remit. The Human Rights Act (1998) could impact on the lives of this group and New Travellers but in 2003 was only beginning to be tested in the UK Courts and in the European Court of Human Rights. This raft of legislation will now be discussed.

The Criminal Justice and Public Order Act 1994 – Although this Act appeared as a *volte face* and a jagged backwards leap from the 1968 Caravan Sites Act, when seen in context, it appeared to be linked to the UK forward plan of privatisation and self-help and the dismantling of the Welfare State. As such the Act was part of a historical continuum – a non-acceptance and criminalisation of 'mobile' groups which included Gypsies/Travellers who trespassed. In many ways it codified the often un-official practices that had been taking place on the ground well before the 1960/68 Acts and after the eviction and moving on of families who were attempting to settle, for however long. The CJPO Act (1994) has been discussed by legal and policy critics and has generally been viewed as an infringement of human rights – notably the right to travel and an entitlement to a culture which involved travelling, and the criminalisation of a 'nomadic' way of life (Campbell 1995; O'Nions 1995; Homes 1995; Hawes and Perez 1996; Murdoch 1998; Morris and Clements 1999).

The Act was conceived as a prohibition against mass trespass and 'raves' by middle-class youth and the advent of New Travellers, who, for economic and other reasons, were taking to the road (see Murdoch 1998). Some were university educated, who happened to be caught up in the Conservative Party Policies of the 1980s which produced large-scale unemployment coupled with the removal of the welfare safety net for the unemployed – and for students. Others, like the Eco-Warriors and Road Protesters (some of whom, were of middle class parentage) travelled from one protest site to another, and were part of a burgeoning Social Movement/protest phenomenon of the 1980s/1990s (see also

McKay 1996 on this issue).[90] Whilst for some being 'on the road' was a rational choice, for others the choice was forced – the alternatives being training and work schemes of a dubious nature, bed and breakfast hostels, living at home or in a 'cardboard city'. The increasing number of those being squeezed out, or leaving 'the system' became a law and order concern (see A Widdicombe comments in Hansard 15 June 1989). It was feared that a new under- and a protesting- class was being created to challenge the status quo (comparable to 15/16th Century concerns).

The CJPO Act 1994 was not, therefore, particularly aimed at Gypsies/Travellers. As one MP put it, 'they became caught up in the side wind' (Staffordshire MP Interview, 2001). Indeed only Part V: 80 mentions Gypsies – repealing the LA duty to provide for them (1) and the resources to do so (5). LAs still had the power to provide if they so wished (and one Council in Staffordshire did so). However, Part V of the Act *implicates* Gypsies/Travellers in 'Collective Trespass or Nuisance on Land' Part V: 61) since nuisance can have many interpretations. Section 61 empowers the Police to remove trespassers. That said, in Staffordshire, Section 61 of the CJPO Act 1994 had been used only rarely (and only once in Stoke-on-Trent) and then, it was claimed, only reluctantly by the local Police Force, who did not wish to assume this role or become involved directly in this kind of activity, particularly if the end game was imprisonment. As one Police Officer stated, 'From a practical point of view, we don't have the space to impound caravans and where would we put everyone? (LPU Interview 2001). However, working within their Equal Opportunities Policies (EOPs) LAs claimed that they removed *all* trespassers.

This Act, like any other, is open to interpretation and if LAs chose to see Gypsies/ Travellers as mass trespassers or squatters they could, since Gypsies/Travellers were not specifically excluded from the Act. Indeed, they had become, by virtue of rhetoric in the House of Commons and particularly the media, bound up with the new waves of mobile groups. Some say that the Act was a cynical approach by the then Government to deal

---

[90] Whereby individuals rallied around a particular issue then disbanded. Some however, moved from issue to issue but without forming an 'official' pressure group or political party.

with all mobile groups (TLRU Interview, 2000). And yet, underpinning it is not necessarily the notion of prohibition of mobility for Gypsies/Travellers, but prohibition of settlement via trespass on land (CJPO Act 1994, Section 77-79).

The CJPO Act 1994 raised the question of human rights – particularly the right of Gypsies/Travellers to live on their own land. However, this issue was clouded by the fact that some families set up sites without planning permission and in the Green Belt. Local Authorities claimed that this was/is a back-door route to intrude into the Green Belt and is a contravention of Planning Law. Circular 1/94 removed any apparent 'favour' in this respect. Whilst the Report by ACERT (1999) demonstrated that overall the planning permissions granted to Gypsies/Travellers were fewer than those granted to others, it also found that 32 per cent of the refusals related to applications for sites in the Green Belt, 97 per cent to land in the countryside and 11 per cent in Areas of Outstanding Natural Beauty (ANOBs) and Special Sites of Scientific Interest (SSSIs) (ibid: IV). Of the fifty applicants seeking planning permission who were interviewed for that study, all except one had applied for planning permission retrospectively (ibid:VIII). Some families have attempted to assert their right to remain (eg Buckley v United Kingdom discussed by Barnett 1996:1628). It would appear that the Buckley case failed because the family had been offered an alternative site and under the terms of the CJPO Act 1994 it was no longer the duty of the Local Authority to provide.[91] Fearing exclusion from land, clearly, Gypsies/ Travellers were attempting to include themselves. And indeed, in conversation, Gypsies/Travellers maintain that unless they use the tactic of retrospective planning they would never get permission via the legal route of making a planning application first (site interviews, site conversations, e-mail conversations).

...And More Regulatory Structures

*The Crime and Disorder Act 1998 (*CJPO – the study on Monitoring the Good Practice Guidance on Managing Unauthorised Camping (DTLR: Housing Research summary 150, November 2001) revealed that little use was being made of the Crime and Disorder Act

---

[91] Had this been the case then the family might have succeeded. (On this point the Court found by '10 votes to 7 that Article 8 of the Convention had not been violated' (Adjudication transcript of Buckley vs UK 20/01/2001:24).

1998 either through the inclusion of unauthorised camping in initial local Crime and Disorder strategies or the use of Anti-Social Behaviour strategies'. It does, however, concede, 'more effective working relationships between Local Authorities and the Police' (ibid: 2). This appeared to be manifesting as stream-lined protocols between the two, at the local level. National Government also recommended a wider use of anti-social behaviour orders (ASBOs) (ibid) to curb anti-social behaviour on sites.

(b) Bridging the Regulatory Legislation/Human Rights Gap

In the then absence of a Human Rights Act in UK, National Government sought to temper the seeming excesses of the CJPO Act 1994 and the way it impacted on Gypsy/Traveller lives - particularly as some families were appealing to the European Court of Human Rights.

Circulars 1/94 and 18/94

Although the Buckley case was dismissed by the European Court of Human Rights it did raise the question of 'a fair balance between the interests of individuals and those of the community as a whole' and the notion of 'proportionality'. This entails that 'the measures taken in pursuit of a legitimate goal must be in proportion to the goal' (Barnett 1996:1629; see also Galtung 1994). This ruling would surely have had implications for the 1994 CJPO Act since the UK is a signatory to the European Convention on Human Rights. This could account for the seeming easing of the Act by Circular 18/94 (Gypsy Sites Policy and Unauthorised Camping) and Circular 1/94 (Gypsy Sites and Planning). Circular 18/94 advocated 'a policy of toleration towards unauthorised gypsy encampments' (6) and that 'local authorities should not use their powers to evict gypsies needlessly (9). It also advocated providing temporary sites with basic services for those resorting to the area. LAs were reminded, too, of their obligations under other legislation, for example Welfare and Health (11, 13).[92] The transfer of management of Council run sites was also discussed (19-22).

---

[92] However, the police in any enactment of S61 are not obliged or bound by a duty of care (Barclay 2003:7).

Circular 1/94 alerted LAs to 'occupational and planning needs of gypsies having regard to their statutory duties, including those in respect of homelessness under Part III of the Housing Act 1985)' (6). It also warned that 'the repeal of local authorities' duty to provide is expected to lead to more applications for private gypsy sites' (4). Thus LAs were duly warned that development plans would need to take account of this 'through appropriate use of locational and/or criteria-based policies (9) and that local plans should, 'wherever possible identify locations suitable for gypsy sites, whether local authority or private sites' and 'where this is not possible, they should set out clear, realistic criteria for suitable locations' (12). However, it is interesting to note that locations suggested were 'outside existing settlements', 'on the outskirts of built-up areas' and that 'the best and most versatile agricultural land' should be 'protected (14) as should the Green Belt' (13).[93]

Whilst the above appeared to be a rational approach to deal with the 'side-wind' effect of the CJPO Act on Gypsies/Travellers, embedded in the legislation were several games. First, national policy, in terms of the CJPO Act, recognised that it had been too 'all inclusive' in its negative terms, and that it had disadvantaged 'traditional' groups of Gypsies/Travellers, thus contravening the European Court of Human Rights legislation, particularly with regard to ethnic minorities. Circulars 1/94 and 18/94 attempted to rectify this and to appease critics of the Act and to make the Act more humane for some groups. However, the effect has been to give LAs two sets of rules – one statutory, the other discretionary – to follow and interpret, without resources. Whilst National Government might have *hoped* that some LAs would comply, they must surely have *known* that the majority would follow the letter of the law and not the spirit of Circular and/or Guidance.

Second, that National Government tended to assume simplicity of implementation at the local level re site creation despite the evidence which suggested otherwise and some LAs'

---

[93] In the then new Local and Structure/Regional Plans being drawn up, new categories of land to be protected were being introduced to add to the already lengthy list of where development of any kind might not take place, thus making it even more problematic for 'suitable' land to be found for Gypsy/Traveller accommodation.

reluctance to comply. This could be construed as an attempt by National Government to pass the buck, placing local Councillors (and as it transpired MPs) in the voting firing line, whilst the National Government washed its hands of the political mayhem at the local level. Gypsies/Travellers, too, were expected to take on the role of developer to set up sites as a workable solution. Whilst for some families this was a tall order, some were able to rise to the financial and legal challenges. This remains the case in 2013.

Third, underpinning the Act appeared to be the message to certain families to 'come in' and conform or remain outside the system (where the weight of the law/authority can be heavy). This is equally ingenuous since it appeared to shift blame and place it upon Gypsy/Traveller families for being outside the law/system when it was the system which had outlawed them (McKay 1996). Thus the CJPO Act was less than 'clear cut' as the authors of the Good Practice Guide (1998:7) might have suggested.

The Good Practice Guide (1998 ...)

Circulars 1/94 and 18/94 were attempts to humanise the CJPO Act 1994. The Good Practice Guide attempted to advise LAs on good practice with regard to encampments in England. Whilst there was much in the Report which attempted to exhort LAs to be even-handed in adopting a 'balanced approach' in the management of unauthorised encampments, the under-tow was the removal and exclusion of nuisance groups. Nevertheless, the Report made useful recommendations. However, most if not all, recommendations suggested a more stream-lined approach to removal and a closer relationship with the Police in terms of protocols and strategies.[94] Few if any of the recommendations suggested dialogue/liaison with Gypsies/Travellers themselves, although liaison with Gypsy/Traveller representatives was advocated (3.6). In the main, the Guidance was for LAs and their personnel to pass on information down the management line so that eventually it would reach Gypsies/Travellers. Unfortunately, the line did not always extend that far. Thus a game with imperfect information became the norm and the Habermasian notion of non-communicative dialogue the reality. The

---

[94] At the time of writing the Thesis, the police, at least in Staffordshire, were resisting any greater involvement in the eviction process, other than a watching presence, if necessary.

overall tone of the Niner Report was one of tightening the management and control of unauthorised encampments. It also defined the term 'toleration' more clearly in the revised Chapter 5.

... And Its Amendment (Chapter 5)

On 26 July 2000 the DETR issued a letter to all LAs in England and Wales entitled 'Revision of Advice on Toleration'. This Circular replaced paragraphs 6-9 of Circular 18/94 and provided 'revised guidance on the provisions in Section 77-79 of the CJPO Act 1994. The Circular claimed that the 'advice on 'toleration' had been wrongly interpreted by some LAs to mean that they must tolerate all types of unauthorised camping, regardless of the amount of criminal or anti-social activity that might be associated with the encampment. Such behavior should not be tolerated in any circumstances' ... LAs should ... 'draw a clear distinction between unauthorised camping where there are no problems and no criminal offence, and where there is anti-social or criminal behaviour'. The revised Chapter 5 insisted that 'Standards of behavior expected of Gypsies and Travellers should be those expected of the settled community' (2000:5.1). However, as Chapter 9 will show, Gypsies/Travellers were, and are, not afforded the same back-up and support as the 'settled' community. Both the Guide and its amended Chapter 5 appear to be carefully worded. Whilst it intimated that LAs were doing and would do everything in their power to accommodate 'good' unauthorised encampments *temporarily* and that recalcitrance and non-cooperation lay with Gypsy/Traveller groups, it was equally aware that not all Councils would or did comply and that not all Gypsy/Traveller encampments were a nuisance. It also assumed that there was a useful and communicative dialogue between LAs and mobile groups.

Whilst it exhorted all parties involved to cooperate and assist one another, the Guidance appeared to take for granted that such encampments would be of short duration and that settlement was neither desired nor was it an option. Even 'good' encampments, which did not cause a nuisance, were only permitted for a short and agreed time period (ibid:5.11; 5.13). From this an underpinning notion that those on the road were/are not looking for permanent sites can be drawn, or because sites for permanent residents were/are full 'extra' families cannot remain. Although designation had been revoked it would appear to have arisen in a new context serving, as it always had, as a dispersal and exclusion mechanism. Such 'informal' practices meet up with Policy which makes them officially acceptable. This raised the question of how far the Good Practice Guide was an amalgam and advocacy of exclusionary bad practice (given the National Government emphasis on inclusion) perpetuating a system of intolerance? As the researchers themselves acknowledged, 'nothing was 'solved' by moving encampments on'.[95] At best, the Guidance could be construed as an attempt to soften the hard, entrenched attitudes of some LAs, pressured to act by hostile constituents – often where action might not be justified. Such action could be construed as pressure to discriminate which would contravene the Human Rights Legislation and the Race Relations Act 1976 and its (Amendment).

As the issue had been improperly understood/perceived the Policy was confused and the Guidance and Circulars intended to clarify matters often exacerbated that confusion. At about this time an 'alternative' was forwarded by the Traveller Law Reform Unit (TLRU) based at Cardiff University, which will now be discussed.

A Workable Alternative?

A Private Members Traveller Law Reform Bill, drafted by Luke Clements of the Cardiff Law School was submitted in January 2002 which attempted to restore LA responsibility to ensure adequate provision of accommodation whilst removing from 'the political stage decisions concerning site provision and site toleration (Clements and Morris 2001:7) A Gypsy and Traveller Accommodation Commission would decide what provision should be made (ibid). Nevertheless, it retained the more punitive measures of S61 of the CJPO Act 1994 – namely Clause 13.[96] This Bill appeared to be recombining *social* and

---

[95] There is also acknowledgement at the national level that the 'basic conflict underlying the 'problem' of unauthorised camping is between Gypsies/Travellers who want to stay in an area for a period of time but have nowhere to legally camp, and the settled community who, by and large, do not want to have Gypsies/Travellers camped in their midst' (Housing Research Summary No 91:1998 DETR).
[96] Clements, explains this away by claiming to 'strengthen the wording by '... reverting to the wording of the original provision in the 1986 Act' which emphasises ' that the powers can only be used in cases of mass trespass (12 or more persons or 12 or more vehicles) and subject to stringent obligations on the police

170

planning legislation in that it included Education, accommodation provision, aspects of criminal justice, grant aid to Travellers, non-discrimination and rights to a 'nomadic way of life'. Whilst in spirit it might have been commendable, its title suggested that in the past there had been separate legislation for Gypsies/Travellers which was in need of amendment, which was not the case. Creating specific legislation for specific groups has its dangers (Hanafin and Williams 1999). Whilst its intention was to be 'a drop-down menu' (TLRU Interview, 2001) for provision in other legislation – eg Education, accommodation etc - the outcome, had it been accepted as law, would, possibly, have distanced families further from the mainstream. Socio-economic and education needs should surely be incorporated within the mainstream (legislation) given that Gypsies/Travellers are a recognised (and protected) group. Already their wider needs were being overlooked because provision for them had been separated – in terms of accommodation and education, or ignored in terms of employment. The most useful clause in the Bill was that pertaining to the Housing Corporation and Housing Associations (HAs) as major providers of 'social' accommodation. The Bill disclosed that the legal remit of HAs did not extend beyond permanent dwellings (Clause 15) – which, surely, must be construed as discriminatory and exclusionary and in need of amendment.

The recommended 'Gypsy and Traveller Accommodation Commission' (Clause 2) appeared to equate with Scotland's Advisory Committee on Travellers and might have been a way to kick-start land being identified for sites, although this was criticised by Charles Smith of the Gypsy Council.[97] Such criticism of a national initiative would 'fit' National Government objectives which were described in interview as being 'to pull away from hands-on control of Local Government' (DTLR Interview 2001), because LAs

---

both as to service of notices, the recording of reasons for the use of the powers and statutory defenses for failing to comply to such an order' (Explanatory Notes to the First Draft 4/9/00)

[97] In his submission to the Labour Party Conference in 1997 (p3) he stated 'We don't want a Gypsy Sites Advisory Committee for England and Wales. We believe that policies should be developed in the local area involving local Gypsies and Travellers so that their views inform policy makers. Every area is different, many Traveller groups have different views'. This has been reiterated by the Roma Rights and Access to Justice in Europe (RrAJE) (http://eumc.eu.int/publications/equalvoices/ev07/ev07-6_en.htm (6/202) which concluded that responsibility should be kept at the local level. Whilst this may be so, it is interesting to note that the Chair of the meeting was from the Home Office.

are 'best placed to tackle issues and deliver services locally and democratically. They know the ground much better than Central Government' (ibid). Whilst the rhetoric states that LAs should be 'allowed to sort out their priorities through various strategies', and to decide where 'blocks of money should be spent' (ibid), an increasing amount of Government money granted to LAs is 'ring fenced' for the particular projects that National Government wishes Local Government to expedite. The failure of the 1968 Act is testament to National Government non-responsibility and LA inaction (in too many cases). Unless a National Government initiative on this issue is taken then the buck-passing between Local and National Government will continue (as later chapters will show). The Bill was endorsed by a Conservative Party MP David Atkinson and was due to be read as a ten-minute Bill at the beginning of July 2002 – with amendments. It was tracked by a Trespassers on Land (Liability for Damage and Eviction) (England and Wales) Bill (Hansard 15 January 2002), and was due a second reading in May 2002 (http://www.expolitix.com/Data/Web Minister/Images/crispin-blunt-bill.html). This advocated amending the CJPO Act 1994 to include making 'a person liable for any damage caused by any person to land or property on that land, on which he (sic) is trespassing for the purpose of residing there'. This appeared to combine S61 and S77-79 by enabling LAs to instruct a Chief Constable to issue direction to leave and/or 'remove any such vehicles or other property … and the Chief Constable shall comply with any such request (Northern Ireland was similarly amending the CJPO Act 1994 with regard to trespass on land). This evoked the déjà vu of police involvement in evictions in the 1960s/1970s. It was also doubtful that this legislation would be workable in Staffordshire. Ultimately, both Bills fell and were not enacted.

Whilst a head of steam was building around reform of the CJPO Act 1994, several pieces of protective legislation were being introduced and/or amended. These will now be discussed.

(c) Protective Legislation
The Human Rights Act 1998
This came into force in October 2000. Whilst the Human Rights Task Force Secretariat

hailed the Human Rights Act as 'the most significant piece of constitutional legislation enacted in the United Kingdom' (1:3) like any other, its effectiveness relied on interpretation. It could also have been construed as a contract between the citizen and the State. The Secretariat claimed that 'The Government's broad aim in introducing the Act is to help create a society in which people's rights and responsibilities are properly balanced and where an awareness of the Convention Rights permeates our government and legal systems at all levels'. Its immediate benefit was that alleged cases of Human Rights infringements could now be heard in the UK rather than in Strasbourg (3:3) and that it placed 'new responsibilities' on the public authorities 'to act compatibly with the Convention Rights' (ibid). The Human Rights Act (HRA) incorporated provisions from the European Convention on Human Rights into UK law' (ibid 2.6:4) 'making it unlawful for a public authority to act incompatibly'... (p 4) and thus '... providing a new basis for the protection of fundamental rights of every citizen' (ibid 5.32:16). It would be 'unlawful for a public authority to act (or fail to act) in a way which is incompatible with a Convention right' (ibid 5.39:16). Amongst other things a public authority would have to ask itself 'whether the rights or obligations of individuals may be affected in the performance of a duty and whether an individual may be deprived of some legitimate expectation in performance of the duty' (ibid 4.20:12). Convention rights were formulated in three ways in that some were absolute, some were limited and some were qualified (4.21-24:13). The concepts of 'proportionality', 'victim' and 'margin of appreciation' also had to be taken into account. Morris (1998) claims that 'the Human Rights Act is a 'quasi-constitutional' document, not a 'clear constitutional mandate to make judicial decisions which might limit the powers of parliament'. However, it has the overall effect in UK of removing 'the system of 'precedent' in the Courts, whereby past decisions are usually followed wherever possible' (ibid).

Ravi Low-Beer (2001) suggested that 'the relevant provisions of the convention for Gypsies facing eviction were likely to be:

    a.   Article 3 – freedom from inhuman and degrading treatment;
    b.   Article 8 – right to respect for private and family life, home and correspondence;
    c.   Article 14 – freedom from discrimination in respect of rights protected by the Convention;
    d.   Article 1 of the First protocol – right to peaceful enjoyment of possessions;

e. Article 2 of the First Protocol – right to education.'

Indeed, all the above Articles were applied to the Buckley vs UK and Chapman and Others vs UK adjudication (ECHR 2001).[98] With regard to the Chapman and Others v UK case, one of the Judges (Bonello) felt obliged to give an individual opinion on the case which highlighted the interconnectedness between policy and practice and the effects this had on the target group:

> 'A public authority owes as great an obligation to comply with the law as any individual. Its responsibility is eminently more than that of individuals belonging to vulnerable classes who are virtually forced to disregard the law in order to be able to exercise their fundamental right to a private family life —individuals who have to contravene the law due to an operation of the prior failures of the public authorities. In the present case, both the public authorities and the individual had undoubtedly trespassed the boundaries of legality. But it was the public authority's default in observing the law that precipitated and induced the subsequent default by the individual. Why the human rights court should look with more sympathy at the far-reaching breach of law committed by the powerful, than at that forced on the weak, has not yet been properly explained.' (Cited in Jones 2001:4).

It was believed (Morris 1999) that the HRA would challenge the lawfulness of raids on encampments, and the constant evictions by LAs 'where no 'toleration' is given or site provision made'. Lack of security of tenure on sites could also be challenged as could planning refusals. The law of trespass and the right to 'exclusive enjoyment' with regard to uncultivated land could also be threatened as landowners would have to argue 'a significant hampering of the owner's right to peaceful enjoyment' (Clements, quoted in Morris 1999). LAs would thus find it more difficult to obtain 'immediate possession orders' (ibid). At the time of writing the Thesis, trespass via unauthorised sites, particularly on private land, was untested in the Courts in terms of the consideration of 'proportionality' [99]

---

[98] Low-Beer believed that had Mrs Buckley not been offered a site as an alternative then 'planning enforcement measures requiring the eviction' would not have been proportionate and would likely have contravened Article 8 (ibid:5; and transcript of the adjudication cited above).

[99] Some permissions had been granted at appeal to families on their *own* land using the Human Rights Act 1998 – eg Wrexham v Berry (31/10/02)

At the local level, in Staffordshire (and seemingly elsewhere), many Local Authorities appeared to have taken the ultimate precaution of closing sites and ensuring that the numbers of Gypsies/Travellers resorting to their area were reduced to a minimum by harsh non-toleration protocols and constant eviction. In the Summer of 2001, all LAs in Staffordshire reported evictions of unauthorised encampments in their area. By 2002 the number had reduced considerably with some LAs reporting none.

The Race Relations Act 1976

This has grown and developed from the 1965 and 1968 Acts. The 1965 Act set up the Race Relations board to examine cases of discrimination in 'places of public resort'; the 1968 Act directed attention to housing and employment (see Ben Tovim et al 1986 for a critique).

Overall the Acts attempted to 'make fresh provision with respect to discrimination on racial grounds and to make provisions with respect to relations between people of different racial origins' (25 October 1968). In the absence of Human Rights legislation in UK, the Race Relations Act 1976 was an attempt to protect ethnic minority groups from racial discrimination in the spheres of employment (s78), training and related matters: education (s14, s17, s18, s19, s57), the provision of goods, facilities and services (s20) in the disposal and management of premises where 'premises' also includes *land* (my italics) (s.21, s.22, s.23, s.24) and clubs and associations (s.25). The Act defined two types of discrimination, direct (s.1(1)(a) and indirect (s.1(1)(b). The Act also extended its remit to discriminatory practices (s.28), discriminatory advertisements (s.29), instructions to discriminate (s.30), pressure to discriminate (s.31), indirect access to benefits (s.49), discriminatory terms in contracts (s72) and incitement to racial hatred (s.70). The Act applied to Local Authorities 'in the same way as it applies to acts done by private persons' (A Guide to the Race Relations Act 1976: 28). It 'imposes a duty on all local authorities to make appropriate arrangements with a view to securing that their various functions are carried out with due regard to the need: to eliminate racial discrimination; and to promote equality of opportunity and good relations between persons of different racial groups' (ibid). Up to the present, few Gypsies/Travellers have availed themselves of the protection afforded by this Act, particularly in respect of discrimination regarding services and land issues.

Whilst it was generally acknowledged that the Act was 'comprehensive' it had obvious limitations (MacEwen 1994:359).[100] With regard to Gypsies/Travellers, it tended to overlook their plight in all but a cursory way, because up until 1989 this grouping was not considered to be an 'ethnic group' and thus were not protected by the Act, although much of the Act could be applied to the Gypsy/Traveller experience. Race Equality Councils and the CRE itself were slow to take up the cause of Gypsies/Travellers, other than to admonish pubs and traders who put 'No Traveller' signs in their windows or who refused to serve them. The fact that Gypsies/Travellers were being removed from land or that people were refusing to sell land for sites either to Gypsies/Travellers themselves or to LAs seemed to pass. The CRE cannot be blamed entirely for this since the system was complaint-led with an underlying assumption that those being discriminated against would not only be aware of it but would also know the rules of the game in order to play effectively. Given that the CRE takes on mainly *prima facie* cases[101] trespass would, for the CRE, clearly cloud the issue. The CRE and RECs would also have been tackling Local Authorities head on - difficult for the latter since Local Authorities heavily subsidised them. Indeed, only since Gypsies/Travellers were declared an ethnic group in 1989 has the CRE been able to include them within their remit. Ireland declared its Travellers to be an ethnic group in 2000 and Scotland's Equal Opportunities Committee has decided that Gypsies/Travellers should 'be regarded as a racial group for the purposes of framing legislation and policies relating to public services' after a Report by the Equal Opportunities Committee in Scotland on 27 June 2001. Whilst this is to be welcomed it appears somewhat belatedly. Classifying them as a 'racial' group, however, might cause some confusion.[102]

---

[100] The structures in which the CRE and RECs operated made effectiveness difficult (Bourn 1996; Young 1992: Anwar 1990; Cairns 1988; Gay and Young 1988). There were also claims that their very structure set them up to fail (BenTovim 1986)

[101] ie those that could be proved without doubt, having no other extenuating circumstances.

[102] if the line is taken that many families are indigenous.

The reform of the Race Relations Act had not produced, at the time of writing the Thesis, 'a comprehensive reform of Race and Equality Acts ... a coherent user-friendly joined–up framework' as Lord Lester had recommended, to take up 'the scattered pieces of legislation and combine them in a single comprehensive Equalities Act with an Equalities Commission' (http://www.cre.gov.uk/publs/connections/conn olsu_lester). Nevertheless, its reforms substantially extended the Act. The changes recognised the 'shift' and 'changes' within 'Race Relations' since the 1976 Act given that 'new identities, new priorities and social forms have emerged, new terms and understandings have developed' (ibid). He also acknowledged that the legislation too 'has changed' having been 'restricted or expanded in scope by court decisions' (ibid) and EU directives (ibid).[103] Then, the 2000 Race Relations (Amendment) Act (see below) had to suffice. Its continued existence as a separate entity from other types of discrimination, however, was not guaranteed. Indeed the Commission of Racial Equality became subsumed under the umbrella of the new Equalities Commission in 2010.

The three Race Equality Councils in Staffordshire, when asked in 2001 if they took up Gypsy/Traveller issues, claimed that they kept only a watching brief, which was not to say that they would not take up issues if Gypsies/Travellers approached them.

The Amendment – and LA Duty

The Race Relations (Amendment) Act 2000 claimed to 'provide new laws for race equality' - 'the first significant Amendment in 25 years' (Home Office Fact Sheet, December 2000), to strengthen the Race Relations Act of 1976, and to complement the Crime and Disorder Act 1998 which made specific offences of racist violence and harassment'(ibid) unlawful. Influenced by the Macpherson Report (1998), the recommendation was that 'there must be a co-ordinated effort to prevent 'racism

---

[103] Article 13 of the Amsterdam Treaty, for example, recommended a strengthening of the Race Relations Act 1976 so that Gypsies/Travellers would be protected in the sphere of employment, 'where different treatment' would be allowed 'on racial or ethnic grounds where a particular occupation activity justifies this'. The Race Relations Act would have to contain the 'new definitions of indirect discrimination and harassment' and provide 'protection' in areas which were not covered by the present Act including 'access to self-employment or occupation', together with the 'full scope of 'social advantages' and 'social protection' where the race directive proposes protection (www.erope.org.uk/info).

177

growing, which needs 'to go well beyond the police services … it is incumbent upon every institution to examine their policies and practices to guard against disadvantage in any section of our communities' (Home Office 2000). To this end the 'full force of race relations legislation' now applies to the Police; outlaws race discrimination in all public functions'; and 'places a positive duty on public authorities to actively promote race equality – that is, to avoid race discrimination before it occurs' (ibid).

The Home Office also warned that:

> Local Authorities 'will need … to ensure that they consult ethnic minority representatives, monitor the impact of policies and services, and put things right when they are unfair or unlawful. As employers they will need … to monitor ethnic composition of their workforces and employment practices to ensure that the procedures and practices are fair so that the public sector can better reflect the society that it serves' (ibid).

To this end, the CRE was empowered to issue a Code of Practice to Local Authorities. In line with the 1976 Act it remained 'a general duty for Local Authorities to work towards the elimination of unlawful discrimination' (www.homeoffice.gov.uk/reu/cpsusummary.htm) However, as Lord Lester commented, the issue 'is more about leadership and political will than it is about law … legislation is not a panacea' (www.cre.gov.uk/publs/connections/ conn_olsu_lester.html). Legislation is only meaningful if it is used by those it is seeking to protect – and that those in need of protection know the rules.

21st Century Legislation/Intent

The problem of progress or lack of it was, perhaps, summed up by a UK Government Senior Officer who claimed that there was 'quite a cohesive policy at National level but the delivery on the ground rests with Local Authorities' (DTLR Interview 2001). National Government also felt that via *The Good Practice Guide* (GPG 1998) 'good practice on approaches is disseminated' (ibid). An interim research project was then circulated for comment (ODPM December 2002) entitled *The Provision and Condition of Local Authority Gypsy/Traveller Sites in England* – its intent, to inform future policy and research. The project was undertaken by Pat Niner who had produced T*he Good Practice Guide.* In the meantime the government supplied a funding scheme for site refurbishment and LAs could apply competitively for a share of the £17 million which would be spread over a three year period. The scope of the scheme was to 'extend the useful life of existing Council sites, bringing under-used or unused sites back into full commission; and or/improve the quality of life for residents my modernising or improving sub-standard facilities and /or providing new facilities … The relocation of sites would only be considered in the second and third year of the scheme (DTLR 625/01); www.housing.dtlr.gov.uk/information/gypsy/index.htm). However, the grant would only meet 75 per cent of the costs up to a fixed sum (ibid). Up until 2010 LAs were still empowered to make provision. In June 2002, LAs were advised that they could apply for aid for site provision in addition to maintaining existing provision and to facilitate 'the management' of illegal encampments at the local level. Neither was it the intention to reduce the number of pitches: 'We would want a strong justification (for this) … We aim to maintain what's there. … Local Authorities will have to make a good case to reduce (DTLR Interview 2002). Nevertheless, sites were being closed and threatened with closure (DTLR data 2001) especially those which were established as 'tolerated' sites (ie sites where families had settled on their own land for a number of years but who did not have planning permission or the correct permission – eg Mid Bedfordshire, South Bedfordshire, Epping, Maidstone, Basildon, to name but a few (National Civil Rights Movement (South West), ncrmsouthwest@aol.com:17 April 2001).

At the time of writing the Thesis, these were the National Legislation and National initiatives in place some of which referred to or implicated Gypsies/Travellers. However, not all were geared towards implementation.

…But That Was Then, This is Now

And the question is, in 2013, have things changed as a result of the above legislation? Speaking in terms of rapid change, the answer must be no. However, there have been small step changes in policy which have attempted to include Gypsies/Traveller accommodation (and inclusion) within existing legislation. Circular 01/2006 dismantled Regional Strategies and with it targets for pitch provision on the one hand, whilst introducing security of tenure for Gypsies/Travellers on Local Authority sites on the other. This ironed out any anomalies between tenants in social housing and Gypsies/Travellers on Local Authority sites. Unfortunately, this was revoked by the Coalition Government in March 2012 who promised to replace it with 'light touch' Guidance and Planning Policy. Prior to the change of National Government, LAs were required to draw up accommodation needs assessments for Gypsies/Travellers, under the terms of the Housing Act of 2004, which could be used in future Local Development Plans. Furthermore, LAs were expected to develop strategies and policies to meet those needs.

The most significant policy to be enacted since 2003 which has the potential to have a positive impact on Gypsy/Traveller lives is the Localism Act 2011 and the National Planning Policy Framework (NPPF) published in March 2012.

The Localism Act (2011) claims to streamline Planning Policy. It also predisposes the system to granting permissions for development whilst limiting refusal and rights to protest against infrastructure projects in particular. With regard to Gypsies/Travellers, LAs can set their own targets for Gypsy/Traveller sites and provision. However, the duty imposed on LAs to assess Gypsy/Traveller site needs remains (S125 Housing Act 2004) and 'the evidence on which RS figures are assessed will remain a material consideration until more up-to-date studies are carried out in accordance with that duty' (TAT News Spring Edition 2012). The loophole of retrospective planning applications has been closed, denying retrospective planning applications where an enforcement on the land exists and where it was issued before the application was received (S123LA 2011 and Section 70 (c) inserted into the Town and Country Planning Act (TCPA 1990). In effect this forces Gypsy/Traveller families to take the 'formal' route to planning applications for their land. It will be interesting to see how this plays out given the provision for community right to challenge (Part 5 Chapter 2), local referendums and neighbourhood development orders (Schedule 9 Part 1), and since the problem with the creation of sites and accommodation for Gypsy/Traveller families has often stalled at the community level. That said the Act does provide opportunities for Gypsies/Travellers to take over the running and management of Local Authority sites (which already happens in some

LAs). It also has the potential to ensure that sites cannot be blocked from receiving planning permission by neighbourhood development orders - provided that these sites are contained within Development Plans and Site Allocation Policies (see above).

National Government claims that the NPPF will streamline Planning Policy. In relation to Gypsies/Travellers it advocated that (a) Local Authorities should identify and update annually a supply of specifically deliverable sites sufficient to supply 5 years' worth of sites against their locally set targets, (b) identify a supply of specific developable sites or broad locations for growth for 6 -10 years, and where possible for 11-15 years (Paragraph 9). If, however, an LPA could not demonstrate an up-to-date 5 year supply of developable sites then this should be a significant material consideration in any subsequent planning decision where an applications for the grant of temporary planning permission was being considered (Paragraph 25). Whether Local Authorities will comply with this in their Site Allocation Policies, currently going through the consultation process in some LAs, remains to be seen. If the Newcastle-under-Lyme Draft Policy is an example of the LA response to the NPPF then it is far from encouraging. The efficacy of the streamlined planning laws, remain to be tested.

And the Future? …

The Squatters Act came into force on 1 September 2012 which criminalises squatting on private property: 'The new offence will be committed where a person is in a residential building as a trespasser having entered as a trespasser, knows or ought to know that he or she is a trespasser and is living in the building or intends to live there for any period' (p.36). Campaigners argued that since land around derelict and commercial property in urban areas is often used for temporary stops by Gypsies/Travellers, they could be adversely affected. Consequently the government ruled that, 'having noted the concerns of groups representing Gypsies and Travellers that any new offence could criminalise Gypsy and Traveller encampments on land ancillary to the buildings protected by any new offence … The Government has decided to limit the offence to residential buildings, however, it will not extend to the land ancillary to those buildings at this stage' (p.38).

At the moment the Caravan Sites Bill 2012 is currently working its way through Parliament. It received its first hearing in the House of Lords in 2011 and its second is awaited. Whilst it harks back to the 1968 Caravan Sites Act it does attempt to build on recent positive developments. For example: Section 1 (2) facilitates the provision of sites to include identifying land for sites where other organisations or individuals can seek to set up a site; Section 1 (3) introduces a duty to cooperate which enables Local Authorities to work together in the process of site provision; Section 1 (4) directs LAs to have regard to their recently acquired accommodation needs assessments; and Section 1 (5) and (6) reintroduces the power of Ministers to step in if LAs fail in this duty. Unfortunately, the Bill does not have the support of the Coalition Government so it is feared that it will fall. Nevertheless, there is 'some agreement' that there should now be adequate authorised site provision, both permanent and temporary. And much hangs on the word 'adequate'

So whilst there is some movement this is slow, seemingly circular and not always forward moving. The problem does not always lie in National Policy itself but in the way that it is interpreted and implemented (or not) at the local level. National Government often finds it difficult to communicate with individuals at the local level, thus groups 'pop up' to oblige in the process of 'representation'. Such groups often have their own agendas. Whilst this may assist with the process of raising the Gypsy/Traveller cause to National attention the 'voice' may be far from pure and thus by the time it reaches National Policy makers, it may be altered to an extent that the individual once more becomes side-lined. Unless this National/Local disjuncture can be resolved then much of National Policy - whilst it might tick the boxes for campaigners in the UK, the watchdogs in the European Parliament and the Human Rights Commission – it might not be implemented. Thus many Gypsy/Traveller families remain in limbo – waiting.

SUMMARY

This chapter has attempted an evaluation of past and current Policy and its amendments via Guidance and Circulars which have impacted on Gypsy/Traveller lives to date. It has also attempted to show the various short-comings and mechanisms which can frustrate, temper or thwart Policy and its successful implementation. The numerous processes through which policy formulation passes - not least Parliamentary debates which attempt to ensure a liberal and 'fair' end product – can produce anodyne and counter-productive instruction in the form of laws and rules which are difficult to implement satisfactorily. Whilst case law provides refinements to definitions and interpretations of Statutes, it can also complicate and confuse (see Chapter 4). How the target group is perceived and how attitudes towards the target group become mediated and crystalised via local and national media to become 'common knowledge' are also important factors when it comes to the acceptance or rejection of groups and the type of Legislation/Policy drawn up.

Workable legislation needs action and input from all sides and is usually a sum total of multiple interests and concerns. It also needs resources. Since the advent of the EU much of National Policy has become aligned to EU directives often derived at via consensus, and conventions which have been ratified by Member States (and not all Member States sign up to all of these). This, however, does not prevent National Legislation from providing an overarching framework of intent and rules which provide a blueprint and structure for Local Policy, practice and service delivery. Within the legislation which had implications for Gypsies/Travellers via their caravans, there was scope for provision – albeit tempered by rule and regulation. How National and Local Government and Gypsies/Travellers played the game became important. The seemingly balanced and broad remit of most legislation, allows room for manoeuvre and interpretation by all sides, which leaves 'gaps' that are often filled with contempt and resistance. In many instances regulation can make redistribution and provision problematic to become a recipe for inaction and inertia. This can also happen when local and National Administrations 'work together' - even collude - to prevent issues from being resolved.

Whilst there have been calls for specific National Legislation for Gypsies/Travellers there is a danger that no matter how well intentioned, this could result in Policy which disconnects families further from the mainstream. Overall, it would appear that the

Policy cycle for National Legislation affecting Gypsies/Travellers since 1968 has moved in a circle to resume its habit of regulation and control. Plus ca change …. .

Further comments on Policy will be made at the end of the next chapter.

CHAPTER SEVEN

PART TWO: LOCAL POLICY AND A LOCAL RESPONSE TO NATIONAL
LEGISLATION

This chapter examines the way in which Staffordshire LAs have responded to National
Legislation, Circulars and Guidance for Gypsies/Travellers and the way that these have
been translated into Local Policy. It will also examine the then recent and pending
changes made by National Government which affected LA structures and the implication
that these could have for Gypsies/Travellers. Examined are some of the issues which
arose from this and from National and Local Planning Policy in Staffordshire and the
Structure Local/Plans which enshrine hegemonic will and attitudes at both the local and
national levels. Overall, this chapter seeks to investigate the working relationship
between National and Local Government, and to examine the influences which inform
practice and service delivery to Gypsies/Travellers. Was the then discussed joined-up
thinking a reality and how was it interpreted at the local level – if at all?

The National/Local Government Partnership as a Blueprint for Action – A Kantian
Utopia or Utopian Cant?

Weber, influenced by Kant's notion of rational governance, viewed ideal bureaucracy as
a rational, stream-lined process based on the principles of legislation and rules; an official
hierarchy whereby the higher officials sanction and supervise the actions of the lower; the
technical and professional knowledge of Officers; and the maintenance of documentation/
files (Weber 1968). Weber also believed that the bureaucracy was '*the* means of
carrying 'community action' over into rationally ordered 'societal action' (ibid:75) . His
view was that a 'societal action' which is 'methodologically ordered and led, is superior
to every resistance of 'mass' or even 'communal action' (ibid). He also believed that

when governments change, the bureaucracy remains- only those Officers at the top need to be replaced (ibid: 76-77) which indicates the endurance of 'the system' and the difficulty of bringing about radical change. The modern English bureaucracy of government appears to have adopted, with some tweaking, the above principles. Over time, Orwellian doublespeak has tempered the intransigence of such a system cushioning it with notions of 'listening to' and 'hearing', particularly at the grass roots level.

LAs are required by law to function specifically within certain rules and to perform certain tasks on behalf of national government. They are often prescribed roles to ensure the successful implementation of national policy at the local level (DTLR Interview 2001); Guidance Document 11/6/01 http://www.local-regions.dtlr.gov.uk/consult /lgbill 99/pcdraft/o4.htm). Their role as junior partner (with leeway) whilst understood at national level, was not always obvious at the local level. Other roles, over time, have become superimposed and added – eg community leaders, community strategists, agenda setters who must initiate coincidental National and Local Agendas, empowerers and promoters of well-being (see Figure 7.1).

The intended end product was, presumably, a stream-lined, cost-effective mode of governance, leading to quicker policy deliverance and its implementation. Important projects of the national administration at the time were inclusion in the light of increasing diversity in the UK national demographic, the need for outcomes, accountability and information exchange. However, sceptics might suggest that for invisible or excluded groups this was utopian cant rather than a realisation of a Kantian utopia of a perfect civic society where individuals live in liberal harmony. Inclusion for excluded groups such as Gypsies/Travellers meant developing strategies at the national level which safeguarded their interests so that they did not become disadvantaged to the point where inclusion was impossible and to the point where some groups were operating in a parallel society.

The National Will Imposed?
It was claimed that the DTLR had a good relationship with LAs (DTLR Interview 2001) and that this had improved since new Labour came to power. 'We have a more inclusive climate between central and local government so that if central government is proposing

Figure 7.1 Ascribed Local Government Roles

Roles	Function	Intended Outcome
CommunityLeaders (Keane and Scase(1998; Cochrane (2001)	empowerment; enabling; managing leadership, adoption of cabinet-style administration	breakdown of 'tribalism' extended partnerships, speedier implementation of national policy, joined up thinking
Community Strategists	to produce a community strategy plan; to promote the socio-economic and environmental well-being of all communities; provision of information and advice to promote/support any involvement; establish 'a vision' via resources and activity analyses	integrated, sustainable development, social inclusion equality of opportunity production of an Action Plan
Promoters of Well-Being	consultation with local communities re service needs; devising strategies to meet needs of housing/health/ education/transport/crime prevention; environment/culture/leisure	coordinate/streamline/ rationalise activity; charge for discretionary services; 'trade' in goods and services; not to act *ultra vires*; deliver best value
Monitoring Performance*	to promote more business-like practices; more targeted service delivery	accountability; best value

Source: * **Local Government Act 2000; DTLR Guidance Document t 11.2.01**

legislation it will *often* (my italics) consult at the local level if only because they will have to put it into practice. We want to be sure it is workable at the local level. It's a question of a shared aim between Central and Local Government. We consult on how it's framed to ensure it's 'workable' (ibid). Whilst this sounded somewhat utopian, some elected Members at the local level viewed this as cant and signified a loss of their role as policy makers. The Government viewed LAs as a 'vital tool for delivery of National Policies (ibid). Thus National Government would have a vested interest in maintaining a good relationship with them. To this end National Government provided, I was told, 'an overarching framework in terms of National Policies … rather than tell them what to do. We want to ensure a balanced approach' (ibid).

With regard to Gypsies/Travellers National Government still provides 'Guidance which totally exhorts Local Authorities to ...adopt largely good practice' and 'to facilitate this (ibid). In line with Government's then current ideology, the Department was looking to improve strategic partnership working with Local Authorities and other local stakeholders', so that they had 'policies, protocols and clear strategies for and in relation to Gypsies/Travellers' (ibid). The Good Practice Guide (GPG) was produced by the Department to 'guide Local Authorities' to formulate policies which address the need and importance for site provision. 'Local Authorities know ... the problems that arise if this doesn't happen' (ibid). Whilst a mutual dependency is recognised, the issue is one of balance: 'centralised tyranny' has generally been offset by 'local government resistance' (Elcock 1994). The ODPM whilst not unaware of the problems that LAs experience with regard to site provision, distances itself from the local fray. The apparent free hand that National Government claims to award LAs is often tempered by ring fencing government grants to LAs for specific and 'pet' Government approved projects (this was mentioned by a Local Council elected Member). Clearly Local Authorities cannot be trusted by National Government to do the 'right thing' and given Local Authority form when it comes to Gypsies/Travellers this is an area where National Government intervention is deemed to be necessary and for the foreseeable future if any real progress is to be made.

Section 32 (in the draft Guidance to LAs for Preparing Community Strategies (http://www.local-regional.dtlr.gov.uk/consult/lgbill99/pcdraft/04.htm) stated that, 'Where deprivation and social exclusion are significant factors for any community, the Community Strategy will need to address how these are to be tackled and how the quality of life of those in deprived communities is to be improved'. This, if taken seriously at the local level, would have implications for Gypsies/Travellers. However, this had yet to be included in local Community Strategies in Staffordshire at the time of writing the Thesis. Where references were made to Gypsies/Travellers, it was in the vaguest of terms.

Local Authority Structure and Functions

LAs have two masters – national government and the local electorate – which places them in a, sometimes, uncomfortable position. Additionally, their activities then were governed by the Regional Office, and they have to work with and aver to the County Council if they are not a Unitary Authority. Although the County Council currently presumes an overarching position over District Councils, and despite its seemingly weakening in Staffordshire in 2002, Staffordshire County Council in 2012 has been strengthened in its authority and it has taken over more functions from District Councils to maintain a higher position in the local governance hierarchy. To this end it now commands the lion share of the Community Charge – Newcastle Borough Council then received a similar amount to that of the police and the fire service. Today, 2013, the Police receive slightly more than LAs. And whilst regional devolution appeared to be on the National Government agenda in 2002, in 2012 it has, it seems, fallen under the radar. Some Regional Offices together with Regional Plans have been disbanded. Added to this, European Parliamentary legislation which has begun to change the way in which National Governments operate within the EU, is now gradually beginning to filter down to the local level so that partnership working and sharing of resources (together with a certain notion of consensus) is becoming more acceptable locally, although to some extent this was tending to happen anyway. Over the past twenty years such changes have meant that Local Councils no longer provide but are required to take on other roles for which some seem unsuited and are uncomfortable with, and given that many Councillors are returned term after term, and some Officers remain in post for decades, many felt ill-equipped to deal with the constant changes which had, and still are, taking place. Many thus felt that their roles had been reduced and their authority eroded. This tended to demonstrate that when National Government wanted things done it did not prevaricate or take into too much consideration the finer feelings at the local level. However, to maintain good will trade-offs occur so that compromises take place on both sides and on certain issues. None of the LAs in Staffordshire viewed Gypsies/Travellers as 'an issue' thus they did not appear on many Council agendas and neither did they appear to be being considered for any special provision other than in passing in Housing Strategies. Indeed, many Officers seemed not to know what to do with them or where to put them in terms of policy.

Interviews took place in 1999 -2001 just as Cabinet-style administration was being introduced at the local level. Some felt that this had been thrust upon them by National Government, thus the ten Councils in Staffordshire were at various stages of conversion. Only one Council showed resistance. Some junior Officers and one senior Officer interviewed seemed unaware of the changeover (see Table 7.1. below). Elected Members interviewed were critical of the new structure, fearful that it would erode the democratic process – now that decision-making was devolved to a core group of Councillors (the Cabinet). One elected Member claimed that the ruling party were hard pressed to find portfolio Chairs of a suitable calibre within their own group (Elected Member Interview) and that some Councillors found the process of scrutiny, particularly of their own party policy and decisions, difficult (Senior Officer Interview). Where additional departmental change and amalgamation had occurred some Officers no longer knew who their line managers were.

Table 7.1 Responses To The Question Has Cabinet-style Administration Been Adopted By This Council Yet?

	Yes	No	Don't Know	Not Yet	Total
Senior Officers	6	4	-	2	12
Junior Officers	5	3	3	-	11
Leaders of Council	5	1	-	-	6
Members of council	4	-	-	-	4
Total	**20**	**8**	**3**	**2**	**33**

Local Line Management

All Officers acknowledged the formal structural hierarchy of their organisation and line management system operating, which appeared to conform to the Weberian model (see Chapter Six). There appeared to be formal rules for dealing with Gypsy/Traveller sites. Where authorised sites existed and where unauthorised sites were frequent, Officers allocated to deal with them operated within separate units and seemed to have more discretionary powers for 'getting the job done', particularly eviction. In such units the line management was described as 'informal'.

Formality of the system however, did not guarantee efficiency and several line managers confirmed this. Nevertheless, all Officers and Councillors claimed that it was not difficult to get Gypsy/Traveller issues onto Agendas. They could not remember, however, the last time such an issue had appeared. The objective of having a special Officer to deal with Gypsy/Traveller issues ensured that problems were 'sorted' or 'buried' before they reached issue status. All but one of the elected Councillors, and all Leaders of Council who were interviewed, claimed that theoretically theirs was not a 'hands-on' approach and that paid Officers were 'allowed to get on with their job'. Respondents considered that elected Councillors did not figure in the line management of Council – except that Councillors *set* Policy and that Officers *implemented* it. However, from observation and interviews this distinction was somewhat blurred since Officers have to translate national policy into workable implementation and service delivery strategies. Issues are raised at the local level although often 'nudged' into existence by National Government, particularly if funding streams come with them. Elcock held the view that Members and Officers interacted in order to take decisions and to control the affairs of their Authority, which tended to ensure that 'the roles of Councillors and their senior Officers are, and must, therefore, be integrated' (Elcock 1994:90). To this end National Policy is often formulated on the 'ground-swell' emanating from the local level. Officers and Councillors become engaged in identifying issues and bringing these to the attention of the Council and the public. However, which issues are identified and highlighted can depend on what Councillors and Officers regard to be important. In this respect 'street level bureaucrats' (SLBs) (Lipsky 1993) can raise, advance, or block issues emanating from the ground. When applied to the issue of Gypsies/Travellers, Councillor input, constituent-led, tends to escalate when unauthorised encampments occur. After the police, the second line of contact is, often, the local Council/Councillor who is pressured to have the encampment removed. The responsible Officer is then bound to act (Senior/Officer Interview).

The Staffordshire LA Response to National Legislation

The CJPO Act 1994

LA respondents claimed that the CJPO Act 1994 had not been an improvement on the 1968 Caravan Sites Act. The responses varied between 'National policy is a disaster, we no longer provide anything' (Junior Officer Interview) to 'We don't know, we've never tested it (Senior Officer Interview), or as one Member of Council stated, 'We adhere to Local Policy whatever it is, whatever it says' (Leader of Council Interview). Others did not know what the CJPO Act was about. However, via this question, concerns and rationalisations were expressed thus:

> We ignored it, it was unworkable. We couldn't fulfil the requirements of the Act. The enforcement powers evaporated so it was better to use old Orders, where you don't have to make anywhere near the same level of social enquiries.

> We used it as a stick …We were in a stronger position to remove.

> We don't use the CJPO Act, never have and never would do. We use Order 24, it's an easier route to go down. The CJPO Act was too open ended. Travellers could have challenged and appealed and been allowed to remain.

> We don't rate it highly because there is no finance to back it ... National Government is not at the sharp end dealing with problems, we are.

> We looked at the CJPO Act. It formalised what we were doing before. It probably structured how we were doing it.

> The CJPO Act had an impact in that it speeded up the process. We could evict in under a week. It strengthened our arm I that it is a tool for local authorities and the police to deal with unauthorised encampments. National policy doesn't seem to address the problem at all.

> The eviction process is now too long.

> It's been useful in dealing with unauthorised sites but planning law is strong anyway. Everything else is a side issue.

> The CJPO Act is unwieldy and the police dumped their responsibility onto Local Authorities.

Neither did they think that it had had any effect on practice (18 thought not). Twelve respondents claimed that is was never used. Table 7.2 demonstrates in the response to the question 'Did this Council use the CJPO Act?' that there was no clear consensus

Table 7.2 Does This Council Use The CJPO Act?

	Yes	No	Don't Know	Total
Senior Officers	6	4	2	12
Junior Officers	2	7	2	11
Leaders of Council	4	2	-	6
Members of Council	2	1	1	4
Total	**14**	**14**	**5**	**33**

between Officers and Members or between Councils. A significant number felt that whilst National Policy did not work, Local Policy did and was better. Overall, Councils tended to use the punitive instruments of the CJPO Act (ie its powers to remove) but avoided using the more lengthy route of S61 and S77/78 because, it was claimed, that these took too long. Instead, the majority of Councils opted to use Order 24 of Planning Law which did not require Circular 18/94 to be taken into account. Stoke-on-Trent admitted using S61 of the CJPO Act only once. Thus the CJPO Act 1994 appeared to be working (particularly for removal) but not in the manner envisaged by National Government. Court adjudications had also honed Council procedures in Staffordshire, so that provided these were followed to the letter of the law and attention was paid to the Circulars and proof of this was provided, then removal could be justified.

Respondents were then asked if Local Policy fed up to the National Government level to influence Policy (see Table 7.3). The number of senior Officers and Members who claimed they did not know was significant since it is at this level that representation to National Government would be formulated and sent up the information line. Whilst it

Table 7.3 Does Local Policy Feed Into National Policy?

	Yes	No	Don't Know	We have Mechanisms	We try	Total
Senior Officers	4	2	3	2	1	12
Junior Officers	1	2	7	1	-	11
Leaders of Council	-	-	1	3	2	6
Members of Council	2	-	-	-	2	4
Total	**7**	**4**	**11**	**6**	**5**	**33**

might be expected that junior Officers would feed information from the ground into the system via line management it might also be expected that senior Officers would pass it on. There are mechanisms in the form of Local Government Associations etc. and Leaders of Council said that they made direct representation to National Government; the Officers interviewed at the then DTLR mentioned the size of their post bags from LAs with regard to Gypsy/Traveller issues (DTLR Interview 2001). Nevertheless, the response reflected the feeling that National Government was either not listening or not doing enough – or not doing what LAs wanted them to do. Of the 'yes' respondents the additional information volunteered was that they were not sure what use their representation was. It was also mentioned that responses were made when National Government asked for feed-back but National Government did not always reciprocate. Feed-back – in possibly modified form – tended to return to the local level in terms of done-and- dusted Legislation, Guidance and Circulars which tended to legitimate local practice (see Chapter Eight). Nevertheless, during the Blair administration, and on the issue of Gypsies/Travellers, Circulars and Guidance tended to come as a response to and in support of local practices of removal tempering some Council enthusiasm for removal by suggesting leniency.

… To Circulars

To assess whether or not LAs complied with Government Circulars and Guidance, Officers who had direct contact with mobile Gypsies/Travellers were asked if they followed Circular 18/94. Of the nine Officers (Eviction/Enforcement Officers/Gypsy Liaison Officers) involved, 6 claimed that they did, 2 did not know and one stated categorically, 'No', we just go for Orders'. Of the two who did not know, from responses to other questions, it appeared that their Council did. In policy terms, it appeared that more attention was paid to Circular 18/94 than expected. However, the way in which Officers made social enquiries would affect any take up by families.

… To the GPG

When interviews took place the Good Practice Guide (GPG) 1998 had been in circulation for almost two years. LA staff were asked what action their Council had taken to implement its recommendations. Some Officers and Councillors said that they had not heard of it, others said that it had been implemented in part, whilst some thought that their Council had not implemented it at all. Only one Council appeared to be in tune with the then Government thinking and had Policies in place for unauthorised sites before the GPG was issued. Some responses demonstrated complacency:

> I've heard of it but I haven't seen it.

> The GPG went into the Chief Executive's office and hasn't been seen since.

> It's been to committee but I don't think it's been adopted. I haven't done much with it.

> If I don't implement it then nothing gets done. It depends whether I get the time to do it.

> It hasn't been put into practice here.

> Often things aren't taken to committee but we note the content.

> I've not been instructed to implement it.

Some showed defiance:

> It's cloud cuckoo land. The GPG is not workable. That's my personal view. The basic need is to get Travellers to be responsible for their own actions. If we had an invasion of Travellers who brought their own skips and portable toilets with them and controlled their children and showed that they weren't there to cause problems, then I think that other things could follow from the GPG. There would be more toleration if there were less problems. (Officer Interview)

And non-acceptance:

> We don't really follow guidance. If it doesn't fit in with what the locals want then it's ignored.

> We say we may take it into account, we may not.

> It goes back to toleration when the local view isn't tolerant.
> The council will pay lip service to some of it – the bits that concentrate on eviction.

> I am going to have to persuade members that all this legislation applies to everyone including Travellers. Our policy needs reviewing … a more balanced approach is needed.

> The toleration side (of the document) might not be useful.

Several respondents offered that without resources little would be implemented. It was also implied that if an Officer was not appointed to take on the issue then it would not be a priority. However, all Councils appeared to be formulating 'non-toleration' Policies – if they hadn't done so already. It is important to note that whilst all respondents had heard of the Race Relations Act 1976, some claimed, however, that it had nothing to do with their work or with the issue of Gypsies/Travellers (despite some of the responses on ethnicity – see Chapter Four). Overall, it appeared that some LAs had some difficulty in joining up the various pieces of Legislation, Circulars and Guidance to the work that they did with, or with Policies that were made for, Gypsies/Travellers.

Local Policy – Getting the Job Done in Staffordshire

A Formal Policy?

Given the plethora of National Policy, when Officers and Councillors were asked if they had a formal Policy for Gypsies/Travellers, and given the corporate ethos of most Councils a uniform, affirmative response was expected, particularly from those who dealt with Gypsies/Travellers on a regular basis. Table 7.4 below indicates that more than half

Table 7.4 Does This Council Have a Formal Policy For Gypsies/Travellers?

	Yes	No	Don't Know	Number of Respondents
Senior Officers	7	4	1	12
Junior Officers	4	4	3	11
Leaders of Council	3	3	-	6
Elected Members	1	2	1	4
Total	**15**	**13**	**5**	**3**

thought not, with more than half of junior Officers claiming that either they did not know or that a Policy did not exist. When pressed, only two Councils were unanimous that there was a formal Policy. Of those who had said yes, 5 claimed that their Council's Policy was enshrined in the Local Plan; 8 said that their Council did not have so much a Policy as a 'removal strategy' or 'protocol'. Three mentioned a Policy which dealt with unauthorised camping. As additional information, one Officer claimed that although they had a written Policy it had not been accepted by full Council, and 2 respondents claimed that Gypsies/Travellers were treated 'the same as anyone else when they trespassed'.

When asked if Local Policy conformed to National Policy, 16 said yes, 3 said no, 14 did not know. Of this number 4 asked what National Policy was (see Table 7.5 below). However, all respondent categories felt that there was no clear National Policy. In the yes category, concern was expressed that it was difficult to implement National Policy at the local level in that Policy, Guidance and Circulars from National Government tended

Table 7.5 Does Local Policy Follow National Policy For Gypsies/Travellers?

	Yes	No	Don't Know	Number of Respondents
Senior Officers	9	-	3	12
Junior Officers	3	1	7	11
Leaders of Council	4	1	1	6
Elected Members	-	1	3	4
Total	**16**	**3**	**14**	**33**

to conflict. Senior Officers were aware that Local Policy had to be set in a framework of National Policy. However, they were equally aware that in the confusion between statutory Policy and Guidance there was room for discretion at the local level - to act or not.

Respondents were then asked what their Policy was for dealing with unauthorised sites. In terms of formal Policy for unauthorised camping, some junior Officers did not know if it was formal or not. Clearly some Councils had no written Policy and Officers followed 'standard' and 'usual' practice of their Council, governed by legal guidelines. Overall, 18 respondents claimed unequivocally that their Policy for unauthorised encampments was 'non-toleration'. Twelve respondents believed that they were complying with National Policy – which they believed to be a non-toleration Policy. However, in the same reply, some Officers and Councillors asked, 'What is National Policy these days?' Of interest was that out of the 10 Councils interviewed, all senior Officers spoke of 'Policy' – some claimed that it was written and formal, others (a minority) that it was draft or written but not yet accepted by Council. All junior Officers spoke (presumably about the same Policy) as 'procedures', 'mechanisms' or 'protocols' for removal/eviction. The majority of Officers were aware that Council Policy meant 'non-toleration'/removal. Within this response, some Officers claimed that if 'Gypsies/ Travellers camped on unauthorised sites but the site was 'not a nuisance' and no complaints had been received then official notice to quit was slower in coming.

However, the term 'nuisance' was open to interpretation and could cover visual as well as physical nuisance.

Only one Council claimed that its Policies were 'balanced in approach', in line with National Government's advocacy of a 'proportional response' as stated in the GPG (DTLR 1998) and Circular 1/94. But even this Council had stepped up its practice of removal from unauthorised sites after it had provided a transit site.

Despite the above responses, in fact, *all* Councils had Policies (other than removal/eviction policies) in their Local Plans/Structure Plan. However, despite the County Council Structure Plan and the GPG (DETR 1998) all the LAs had evaded the issue of provision in their Local Plans. These Policies together with Plan Guidance will be discussed below. However, first, the question - Does this Council make its Policies for Gypsies/Travellers known to them? (See Table 7.6) – needed to be asked.

Table 7.6 Does This Council Make its Policies for Gypsies/Travellers Known to Them?

	Yes	No	Don't know	Evasive Response
Senior Officers	3	4	1	4
Junior Officers	4	4	1	2
Leaders of Council	1	2	-	3
Members of Council	2	1	-	1
Total	**10**	**11**	**2**	**10**

Of the total number of respondents only 3 gave an unequivocal yes response to this question. The evasive replies warranted a separate column. Only one Council claimed that it made its Policies known to Gypsies/Travellers, two were ambivalent and two were adamant that they did not. Overall, the Leaders and Members of Council were more optimistic that Gypsies/Travellers knew what the relevant Policy and rules of engagement were. Some of the responses termed 'evasions' are noted below:

> They are supposed to be.
>
> I think they could tell us. I think they know all about it.
>
> I'm not sure if (named officer) advises groups. There are various bodies that advise them.

Not directly. I can't recall if contact was made with them on the first round of the Local Plan, but it would be on the next. They must have representatives looking at the Development Plan and scrutinising the development plan system irrespective of whether or not we consult them or not.

Every time they turn up they are told what the policies and rules are.

I don't think so. They're on the receiving end of policy.

In a lot of cases the conversation if you've got three days to get off this land. Sometimes they use stalling tactics – they know their rights – but a lot accept it as a way of life and move on their way.

We don't actively publicise our policies

We only tell them when we are removing them, They are resigned and just say how long have we got. The majority are very reasonable about it. Some swear and let their dogs loose.

We would when they are done.

You go and ask a Gypsy what the laws are an they'll tell you better than we can tell them.

The assumption appeared to be that Gypsies/Travellers 'know' what the Policy is (and this referred primarily to the eviction process). However, in speaking with Gypsies/Travellers during site visits (and e-mail conversations) it was clear that unless they had been through the legal process (working with Barristers or Solicitors who were working on their behalf) they did not. Any knowledge of the rules appeared to be based on the experience of being evicted/removed and what they had learned from that and from the experiences of others on what not/to do. Similarly, local, housed residents do not, generally, know what the rules are and believe that Councils can remove/evict immediately. Thus it appeared somewhat disingenuous to suppose that Gypsies/ Travellers had any superior knowledge of Council rules and practices.

National Legislation, Guidance and Circulars are thus the current framework for Local Policy which should translate into workable action at the Local Level. Much of Local Policy is now bound up with sustainable development in the spheres of Housing, Transport, Employment, Health , Education, Social Services and Planning in some form or other. Who pays creates a game of inter and intra play not only between National and Local Government but also between service deliverers who are increasingly contracted by Local Authorities to provide. Broadly speaking, National Government has its own policy priorities. Needless to say not all national priorities match with local priorities and some do not even apply – for example problems in large cities needing urgent intervention might be non-existent at the more local and rural levels, yet scarce resources have to be expended on 'going through the motions' of compliance. The allocation of National Resources to accompany policy is often an indication of political will, serious intent and urgency with regard to implementation. When resources are absent, Local Authorities have to make a strong case to justify to their electorate the allocation of their own funds to projects which might be in competition with hospitals, schools, etc.. Unfortunately, Gypsy/Traveller sites do not come high on many Agendas.

The priorities for Local Authorities tend to be set out in Local/Structure Plans. At the time of writing the Thesis, Regional Plans were being drafted. The next section will examine these Plans in relation to Gypsies/Travellers and Staffordshire.

Ground Force: National (Land Use) Plan Policy for Gypsy/Traveller Sites – A Case For a Makeover?

In the past, planning has been seen in terms of the duality of *development* and *control.* Some LA departments call themselves 'planning control departments'. The tension inherent here, in practical terms, is obvious. Plan policy thus has to balance the paradox. The 2002 Government Green Paper entitled *Planning: Delivering a Fundamental Change*

Table 7.7 Staffordshire LA Score Against BV 112*

LA	Percentage Score	Average Score
Staffordshire County	33	62.6
Staffordshire Moorlands	33	62.6
Stoke-on-Trent	80	62.6
Newcastle-under-Lyme	44	62.6
Stafford	56	62.6
Cannock	50	62.6
Lichfield	70	62.6
Tamworth	60	62.6
East Staffordshire	50	62.6
South Staffordshire	55.6	62.6

Source: ODPM Data 3/1/03
*BV211 = Score against a checklist of planning best practice (max 100%)

---

was an attempt to speed up and streamline the whole process, not least by establishing a more standard form of planning Best Practice since indications suggested that Local Planning Authorities (LPAs) were underperforming. This certainly appeared to be the case in Staffordshire for several Councils (see Table 7.7).

There are added difficulties in setting up Gypsy/Traveller sites which have never been satisfactorily resolved in some LAs, which place Gypsies/Travellers in additional legal binds which also need to be addressed.

First, the 'fundamentals' of UK planning and control are based on the 1947 Town and Country Act (Simmie 2001:387) which zoned land use, separating industrial, residential and leisure space. Such notions were linked to the 18th and 19th Century health and safety responses to the indiscriminate spread of heavy industry during and after the Industrial Revolution. Currently Gypsies/Travellers, particularly on unauthorised sites, live and work in the same spaces and thus contravene health and safety regulations and planning regulations unless the site is licensed. Site licence rules however, preclude families from working on site. The notion and practice of placing sites in mixed land-use zones, appears unnecessary today. Additionally, land used for sites could also be used for housing, thus Gypsies/Travellers compete with housing and other developers of land. These were some of the reasons given by LAs for the difficulty in finding suitable sites for Gypsies/Travellers under the 1968 Caravan Sites Act. However, there appear to be many instances where housing and industry co-exist which points to arbitrariness in the planning system and where planning rules can be used to exclude rather than include. Attendance at Planning Committee meetings demonstrated that it was possible to work around the Local Plan and planning rules. Some large developers appear to do this with alacrity, using appeals, and teams of planning lawyers in order to get their development through and often on their own terms. All this raises questions about equality of opportunity and value. Studies have shown that the planning system is not above discriminating against ethnic groups resulting in institutionalised discrimination as well as direct and indirect discrimination (Ousley n/d; Elson and Ford 1996; Thomas and

Krishnarayan 1995). Accusations of corruption are not unknown. Since the CJPO Act 1994 and the reintroduction of legal chastisement for trespass, Gypsies/Travellers have been encouraged to engage with the planning system. Their lack of success has added to the knowledge bank of discrimination (Home 1993, 1995, Morris 1998; ACERT 1999; Drakakis-Smith 2003).

Albrecht and Denayer 2001:379) claim that Planners decide who will belong to the community and who will not'. Belonging to a group is, therefore, important as is the definition, perception and status of that group, particularly if it is accepted that 'Planners act on behalf of and have an interest in the social order' (ibid:380). Some Planning Officers in their defence, claimed that Gypsy/Traveller families wishing to set up sites on their own land did not approach the Planning Office prior to purchasing land or making an application before settlement. Gypsies/Travellers claimed that if they were to take the legal route they 'wouldn't stand a chance' (e-mail conversations). Whilst this might not make any difference to the outcome, unless Gypsies/Travellers test the system, and highlight its inadequacies by engagement with it at an early stage, exclusion is often the predictable outcome.

Second, politics – power relations and the competition for space (in this context) – is another dimension in the planning process (Atkinson and Moon 1994; Simmie 2001; Albrecht and Denayer 2001). Small developers do not have the same resources as large developers to fight their cause within the planning arena, since large developers have more to offer LAs who depend upon payment via Section 106 Agreements, and fees accompanying planning applications and much more from developers to provide revenue. One large development can raise a six figure sum, at least, for the Local Authority. Consequently, bargaining and deal making is now an important feature of the Planning Process. In fact Albrecht and Denayer (2001:367) claim that Planners are now 'more deal makers than regulators of the rise of entrepreneurism' and the local Planning Office has become the first stage in that negotiating process. The Planning Office is also a first stage sounding board for those 'with plans'. It was noted that small-scale plans were dealt with more publicly in the foyer of the Planning Office, larger-scale plans in a separate interview room and large-scale plans were debated in more opulent surroundings elsewhere. Officers claimed that the Planning Office was not frequented by Gypsies/ Travellers. During site visits Gypsies/Travellers who were asked, said that they 'never went to the Council'.

Third, a fear of Gypsies/Travellers and what they might/not do can influence local Planning decisions and local perceptions of any application. The media, too, plays a part in coordinating and whipping up public feeling. Public opposition to a planning application carries weight particularly if formal objections are made during the planning process. This fear was exemplified in a then planning refusal by Stoke-on-Trent City Council on the grounds that the applicant *might* be a Gypsy (4 January 2002). This particular application was different in that the applicant was not living on the land at the time of the application, the family was appropriately represented, the objections which gave rise to the refusal were addressed, a reapplication was made, and the Plan was then passed.

It would thus appear that the planning system is not as impartial or un-political as LAs would like constituents to believe, and despite how LAs may be instructed by National Rules and Guidance to conduct the Plan and Policy process. This will now be discussed in relation to Gypsies/Travellers.

Plan Policy – Toeing the National Line?

Guidance is issued by both National Government and County Councils to Local and Statutory Authorities which they are 'expected' to follow. Policy Planning Guidance (PPG) 12 (DTLR December 1999) and PPG3 (March 2000) were relevant at the time of writing the Thesis.

PPG 12 is clear that Development Plans 'provide an essential framework for planning decisions (1.6: Pp,7). It is equally clear that 'social progress' concerns 'recognising the needs of everyone' – which includes 'ethnic minorities, religious groups, the elderly, and disabled, women, single parent families, students and disadvantaged people living in deprived areas' (ibid). Those involved in the process, were also exhorted to consider the extent to which the issues of social exclusion through land use Planning Policies could be addressed (ibid). Affordable housing was mentioned (4.14). This section also pointed to Circular 1/94 'which makes clear' that:

> 'Plans should wherever possible identify locations suitable for gypsy sites whether Local Authority sites or private sites. Where this is not possible they should set out clear realistic criteria for suitable locations as a basis for site provision policies. They should also identify existing sites which have planning permission, whether occupied or not and should make quantitative assessment of the amount of accommodation required'.

PPG 3 (March 2000) underlines National Government's intent regarding social inclusion:

> 'Government intends that everyone should have the opportunity of a decent home … they further intend that there should be greater choice of housing. The housing needs of all in the community should be recognised and that housing should not reinforce social distinction. The housing needs of all in the community should be recognised including those in need of affordable or special housing in both urban and rural areas' (1).

PPG 3 also reminded LAs of their power of compulsory purchase (15), of the need to 'provide wider housing opportunity and choice' (2), to 'encourage the provision of housing to meet the needs of specific groups (11), and that 'assessments of housing need' should be undertaken 'to underpin local Housing Strategies and Local Plan Policies' (13). Whether by accident or design, the term 'housing' was used as opposed to 'accommodation'. Nevertheless, recognition of diversity was stressed in that the assessment process should include 'the range of needs for different types and sizes of housing across all tenures in their areas. This should include affordable housing and housing to help the needs of specific groups 'which includes 'travellers and occupiers of mobile homes' (13). Some confusion was evident between PPG 12 and PPG 3 in that one spoke in terms of sites and the other of housing. It was unclear whether 'housing' was a pseudonym for accommodation – but even if it was not and the intent of National Government was 'suitable' housing for Gypsies/Travellers, here was an opportunity for imaginative and inclusive LAs to use the above Guidance to make a strong case for site provision, albeit private, if they so wished, and in the countryside (with justification). At National level, the tools have always been present to enable LAs to make provision for Gypsies/Travellers via private or public means. Not all Councils in Staffordshire availed themselves of this opportunity. Whilst this Planning Guidance is not new, and is regularly updated, it appeared that LAs 'generally ignore(d) it' (Home 1995:1005). This might be overstating the case, however, since LPAs appear also to work *around* it.

When asked why accommodation for Gypsies/Travellers was being excluded from Local Plans, one senior Planning Officer volunteered that 'Local Authorities have a right to approve their own Local Plans themselves. Government or independent persons can object but as long as they are in general conformity with the Structure Plan the Inspector will approve them'. LAs have 'to go through a series of hoops in the preparation process – eg consultation (Senior Officer Interview). If they do not then they can be challenged legally, but that depends on local interested parties. It is open to question whether or not placing a copy of the Draft Plan in the Council foyer or the local library is sufficient 'consultation'. It appears that LAs do not have to consult either the County or the National Government re their Local Plan – only the public. However, the Local Plan must receive a Certificate of Approval for its conformity to the Structure Plan from the County Council. This is described as a 'weak exercise' and 'provided that housing and employment plans at the local level come within 10 per cent of the Structure Plan projections, a Certificate is generally issued'(ibid). As the respondent commented, 'At the end of the day the Structure Plan is not enforceable. A likely source of objection is the Government Office but it depends how Government feels at the time'. Re Gypsy caravan sites, I was informed that in Planning Law they were in the same land use class as general caravan sites. The difference occurred in Environment Law. Here specific conditions were applied to Gypsy/Traveller site licenses. One Officer claimed that Gypsies/Travellers were too honest in stating on planning applications for sites that it was for a Gypsy/Traveller site. He felt that if they did not use this identifier the outcome might be different. The Stoke-on-Trent case, however suggested that it made no difference, since people 'find out'. In effect, LAs in Staffordshire relied on precedent in terms of their treatment of Gypsies/Travellers and anything 'new' could be easily side-stepped if a Council so wished (see the Staffordshire Habit section below).

The Staffordshire Structure Plan Policy Response

At the time of fieldwork, all Councils in Staffordshire were at different stages of revising their Local/Structure Plans. All LAs had a Plan Policy for Gypsies/Travellers – usually placed at the end of the Housing Policy section and after the section on Affordable Housing and the need for diversity in provision. This placed policy provision for Gypsies/Travellers into perspective. Both the County and Stoke-on-Trent took an overarching view of Plan Policy and simply indicated what Local Plans should contain in terms of development policy. In terms of Gypsy/Traveller provision it stated that:

> 'Adequate sites to meet an identified demand for gypsies residing or resorting to the Plan area should be available for both long and short term accommodation needs. The detailed criteria for suitable locations will be set out in local plans but in general sites should:
>
>> a) not be located in areas of open land where development is severely restricted;
>> b) not be permitted in areas of Outstanding natural Beauty, Sites of Special Scientific Interest or in the Green Belt (H1)
>
> This policy covers persons of nomadic habit of life, whatever their race or origin and includes persons living in largely static or mobile homes that have either ethnic or cultural associations with the historic travelling community' (7.53)
>
> The provision of sites for gypsies is a form of affordable housing provision and additional authority provision is the most effective means of ameliorating the difficulties for owners, neighbours and gypsies alike, that arise from unauthorised encampments. The levels of proposals should broadly relate to the number of unauthorised encampments shown in official counts over the last few years but must further be further informed by discussion with representatives of the travelling community and providers of education, social services and health services to them. The locational criteria should reflect government guidance. The current criteria are stated in Circular 1/94 and are reflected in the policy (7.54).

The above is quoted (almost) in full because, like National Government Policy, it takes a seemingly 'can do', overall approach to accommodation for Gypsies/Travellers assuming that what they are asking Local Authorities to do is not problematic and doable- which , in a perfect world, it should be. The Policy appears to recognise that site provision is a form of affordable accommodation. Nevertheless, clauses (a) and (b) alert the reader to the fact that this policy indicates only where sites should *not* be, leaving little scope for where they *should* or *could* be. There is thus an implied negative emphasis and a loophole through which Local Authorities with no desire to provide can slip. And this is not a stand-alone Policy. When read in conjunction with PPG 3 and Housing Policy, the comparison leaves any Policy for Gypsies/Travellers wanting.

Structure Plan Policy for housing states that:

> Good quality housing is a basic human requirement which everyone has a right to expect. The planning system has a role to play in ensuring a continuous supply of land which is adequate to meet housing need, having regard to market demand and government policy … (7.1)

> The 'balancing act' occurs across all concerns of planning, but the position of housing as a basic human need and as the largest built use of land makes it a particularly important issue (7.2)

The first sentence throws into relief the statement that 'adequate sites' for Gypsies/ Travellers are sufficient. With regard to Affordable Housing the County claims that housing needs studies were 'currently in preparation by several District Councils which may determine the requirement (7.15). However, with regard to accommodation needs for Gypsies/Travellers, the requirement here is for 'discussion with representatives of the travelling community to further inform the level of provision'. The number of houses required for the Plan period is specific – 70400 (7.5) and already 51800 have been built. Stoke-on-Trent estimated that it had over-provided 814 dwellings and the over-provision for the County was around 5000 (Senior Planning Officer Interview). A discussion document prepared as a 'background paper to the Structure Plan Policy (n/d –possibly 1998) concluded that:

> ' … the provision of additional authorised pitches is the best method of reducing the problems that arise from unauthorised encampments (1:Pp11); that 'there is an existing shortfall of about 45 caravan standings and a similar number of transit pitches. There is a need to have available accommodation for 323-424 caravans by the end of the plan period. The Structure Plan is unable to state a distribution of pitches between districts. Co-ordination between districts in setting the distribution is desirable. These decisions should be informed by discussion with Gypsy representatives and providers of services to them, and should take account of locational preferences (3. Pp11).

Unfortunately, this information which might have concentrated the minds of some District Councils was omitted from the Structure Plan Explanatory Memorandum. All this taken together suggests an inequality of consideration, of provision and need satisfaction. Despite the emphasis on diversity of need within the housing sector, there is no mention of diversity of need for Gypsy/Traveller accommodation, the choice being between permanent or transit sites. Whilst the Structure Plan suggested that an accommodation needs assessment was currently underway, Gypsies/Travellers did not appear to be included. Failure to include at this stage could mean another generation excluded and with needs unmet.

During the course of interviewing it emerged that several LAs were adhering to the County Council Policy for Gypsy/Traveller Caravan Sites in Staffordshire 1979 and in the absence of any other. This document was drawn up in response to the 1968 Caravan Sites Act and the expected duty of LAs to provide. The document stated that the County would 'provide and encourage the provision and development of a total quota of some 90 pitches to meet the accommodation needs of gypsies in the County, in addition to 120 pitches on existing sites'. (1979: 2.8). The total County allocation would thus be 210. The allocations for some Councils are low and some LAs have exceeded them. For example the allocation for Stoke-on-Trent/Newcastle-under-Lyme was 20; Central Staffordshire 30; East Staffordshire 10; and South Staffordshire 30. The same Policy advocated where sites should be. A notable criteria was that sites should be 'within reasonable distance of urban areas or other settlements although not immediately adjoining housing areas (2.12). Such criteria set Gypsies/Travellers apart from, rather than making them a part of any local community.

How far Structure Plans and Policy (past and present) influence Local Plans will now be discussed.

Local Plans/Community Strategies
All Plans and Strategies whether National or Local are statements of intent and cover a period of between five or ten years. The Plan process takes several years to complete and

there is usually a refresh every five years. These Plans map out priorities, land use and where resources will be channelled. Local Plans are presented as a local menu and the assumption is that anyone can 'buy' in to what is on offer. They are also weighted and supported by an armature of precedent, ideology, politics, will, financial resources and negotiation, so that some will have a better chance than others of being part of 'the game' and successful re their implementation.

With regard to Gypsies/Travellers broad National Policy has to be fleshed out at the local level, tie in with the Structure Plans and be workable. The National Government intent for Gypsies/Travellers was that 'adequate sites should be provided'. Wilson (1998:18) found that of the total number of LAs (364) 54 per cent were criteria based, with some criteria being so stringent that 'they gave more opportunities' for LAs 'to refuse proposals on policy grounds' (ibid:10). The DETR in a letter dated 19 November 1999 attempted to close this bolt-hole reminding LAs of Circular 1/94 (Gypsy Sites and Planning) which emphasised 'identifying suitable locations for Gypsy sites in Plans, wherever possible'. It also expressed concern that LAs were 'placing too much emphasis' on pursuing criteria-based policies' and that 'criteria-based policies which' (in the view of Gypsy representatives in a meeting with the Minister) were being drawn too tightly, 'with the result that applications for private sites were being refused'. However, Wilson pointed out that 'nowhere in Circular 1/94 does it state a Policy to promote more Gypsy site provision through the planning system' (Wilson 1998:11) – even though a need had been identified, and via the bi-annual count, quantified. At the time of writing the Thesis, Community Strategies were being proposed and hurriedly formulated to meet the Spring 2003 deadline. The intention here was that the Community Strategy would inform and drive the Local Plan. After interviews with some Chief Executives it was apparent that Gypsies/Travellers were not going to be included in any meaningful way because 'they were not an issue.' The Local Plans and how they relate to Gypsies/Travellers will now be discussed.

Local Policy – Workable?

Whilst all Councils had at least a statement in their Local Plan re Gypsies/Travellers, intention varied. When asked if the Policy reflected the needs of Gypsies/Travellers the response of interviewees was largely negative (see Table 7.8 below). Five Officers felt that Policy did not reflect need in the sense that: 'no need had been expressed to them by families; 'We don't provide anything'; 'There are no sites because there is no demand for them'; 'Does anyone know what their needs are?';' They ask us we don't go out and ask them.'; 'They don't tie into anything' (Officer and Member Interviews). One County respondent claimed that, 'We are limited in what we can do. We can't dictate to District Councils. They come to us with a set of criteria (in Plan Policy) which don't address needs. National Policy says that we should. We can't deliver to moving groups' (Senior Officer Interview). Some felt that having provided one site, all obligations had been met. Another Council felt that its 'quota' based on County Council figures (1979) had been met.

Table 7.8 Does This Council's Policy Reflect the Needs of Gypsies/Travellers?

	Yes	Yes But	No	Don't' Know	Total
Senior Officers	2	-	8	2	12
Junior Officers	2	4	5	-	11
Leaders of Council	2	1	2	1	6
Members of Council	1	-	3	-	4
Total	**7**	**5**	**18**	**3**	**33**

When asked if there were channels for Gypsies/Travellers to articulate their needs a majority thought not (see Table 7.9 below). Three Site Wardens also responded to this question, thus the total responses to this question were 36.

Table 7.9 Are There Channels for Gypsies/Travellers to Articulate Their Needs?

	Yes	No	No Response	Total
Senior Officers	4	7	1	12
Junior Officers	3	8	-	11
Leaders of Council	-	2	4	6
Members of Council	-	-	4	4
Site Wardens	3	-	-	3
Total	**10**	**17**	**9**	**36**

Some interviewees claimed that there were no formal channels, whilst others said that the formal channel was via the Local Plan process. Of those that claimed there were formal channels these were for site residents rather than mobile groups and even here it was questionable if the line of communication between Gypsies/Travellers and problem solvers at the LA level were open. One Senior Officer said that their complaints procedure had changed in that people were now invited to 'make comments' rather than to 'complain'. This process was questionable since in performance tests and the rating of LAs the number of complaints (or not) played a significant part. One Site Warden claimed that he referred complaints to the Gypsy Liaison Officer or to the National Gypsy Council. To make any formal complaint forms have to be completed and knowing the rules and how to formulate complaints is required if they are to be taken seriously. Another Site Warden claimed that 'things were put to the Council but they never said anything'. Some of the responses to this question are listed below:

'We have a complaints procedure but we don't hand them out. It's rare that Travellers come in.

We have no procedure for complaints. We don't get any.

We have no contact with Travellers therefore we don't know if they are aware of procedures for complaint. We have never had any need expressed to us.

I doubt if Travellers are aware of complaints procedures.

We don't assess need. We would need a needs survey of Travellers in the area but in reality it's only a lip service thing.

If they asked for a complaints form I wouldn't give any out.

We make no assessment of need. We don't provide sites.'

Gypsy Site Provision vs Other Provision

Although site provision is included as part of the housing section in each Local Plan it is treated as being apart from housing re diversity and special accommodation needs. Whilst it is important to stress the needs of disadvantaged groups in theory, it is equally important not to separate them from the whole in practice. Although LAs were not then statutorily obliged to provide, the delivery of suitable accommodation for all and development were still their responsibility. Only one Council used its *power* to provide. The mistaken assumption appeared to be that provision is no longer an LA *responsibility* either. Provision has been delegated to Housing Associations, Registered Landlords and developers, but LAs were still duty-bound to oversee such activities to ensure that the Local Plan and Structure Plans were being implemented and that these arms-length Agencies were carrying out the duties laid upon LAs re equality of opportunity, well-being etc.. Local Plans become fuzzy when they include Gypsies/Travellers because they tended not to specify how and where they were to be included within the Plan. The wording was/is suitably vague in each policy so that Gypsies/Travellers and their legal representatives would be hard pressed to seek legal redress for a Council's failure to comply with the Plan Policy in terms of site identification.

Green Belts are often a contentious issue. Whilst LAs defended the sanctity of their Green Belt Policy, the County Structure Plan 1996-2011 (6.11:36) advocated that in order to meet its projections 1275 gross hectares of land for employment use alone would have to be taken from the Green Belt. The projection for housing during the same period was claimed to be 51800 houses in the 'countryside' and in rural areas where development would not be permitted in the Green Belt except in 'exceptional circumstances' (D5B:30). This suggested that incursions into the Green Belt and the countryside would have to be made. The areas identified were located mainly in the south of the County – where much of the Green Belt land was – and the north. The Plan stated that 'General locations where substantial incursions into the Green Belt may be required are identified in the appropriate Structure Plan Policies, to be defined and taken forward in Local Plans (ibid 5.25:30). For Staffordshire, the areas identified were 'around Tamworth, southern Staffordshire and Stoke-on-Trent in the north. The Structure Plan called for a redefinition of the Green Belt, in an area in the south of the County 'where the boundary has been drawn too tightly (ibid:20). Clearly, then, the Green Belt is a moveable feast and its edges are routinely nibbled and replenished at will by Councils. Whilst attempts are made to safeguard the Green Belt from incursion, Councils recognise that for the sake of sustainability of some areas, that development within it needs to take place. However, it is Councils and the locality who ultimately decide *which* developments take place and any contentious applications by 'others' are easily ruled out (see Table 7.10 below).

An additional problem was that Draft Regional Planning Guidance (November 2001) suggested that whereas Development Plans should concentrate residential development mainly in existing towns and villages and should not be allowed in the 'open countryside', there were exceptions: 'the only exception to this Policy are agricultural workers' dwellings and appropriate sites for Gypsies/Travellers (Policy RR7:43). Policy CF6:56 encouraged the development of mixed communities and that such plans 'should ensure that adequate provision is made for suitable sites to accommodate gypsies and other travellers'. Equally, Section 6.38-56 recognised that in terms of site provision there appeared to be a 20-25 per cent short-fall, that LAs 'take account of this legitimate need for accommodation in carrying out their assessments of housing need and reflected it in

Table 7.10 BV 108 The Number of Advertised Departures From The Statutory Plan Approved By The Local Authority as a Percentage of Permissions Granted in Staffordshire

LA	Score	Average	Average by LA Type
Staffordshire County	**1.2%**	**1.1%**	**6.1**
Staffordshire Moorlands	1.2%	1.1%	0.6
Stoke-on-Trent	0.5%	1.1%	0.5
Newcastle-under-Lyme	0.3%	1.1%	0.6
Stafford	0.1%	1.1%	0.6
Cannock	0.0%	1.1%	0.6
Lichfield	0.2%	1.1%	0.6
Tamworth	0.0%	1.1%	0.6
East Staffordshire	0.3%	1.1%	0.6
South Staffordshire	1.3%	1.1%	0.6

Source: ODPM Data 3/1/03

their Development Plan provision'. However, the Spatial Strategy Plans suggested development of the major urban areas which fall to the north and south of the County – where the majority of Gypsies/Travellers lived and/or resorted (ibid 28/29). Similarly, the patterns of need suggested a need in the south of the County (ibid:18) so that both areas were targeted as 'communities of the future' (ibid:60/61) and regeneration centres. Although the overall Plan suggested 'prosperity for all' (ibid: Chapter 7) it will be interesting to see if the needs of Gypsies/Travellers will be considered and realised in the competition for space and place. It is now 2013 and current plans are no further forward, despite needs assessments for Gypsies/Travellers having been undertaken in parts of the County in 2005. In a recent County Council Election flyer the identification of sites was 'threatened' (a UKIP prospective candidate, April 2013).

Overall, it would appear that Gypsies/Travellers were either being squeezed out of Development Plans, or included in a somewhat cursory way, then and now. Unless sites or land are included in the Local Plan then LAs are simply paying lip service to any National Government Guidance. Many of the Plans state a need for assessment of need but unless Gypsies/Travellers and/or their representatives challenge and push for this, then this will remain rhetoric. Whilst Circular 1/94 revoked 'special privileges' for Gypsy sites being given planning permission in the Green Belt, a precedent has been set by LAs who have already removed land from the Green Belt for housing, commercial and other uses, so such caveats could be regarded as discriminatory. Gypsies/Travellers also need to make representation at the Draft Local Plan and refresh stages. The next Section deals with the self-evaluation of Policies for Gypsies/Travellers by LAs.

Giving Councils Their Say

Councils were given the opportunity to evaluate their Policies for Gypsies/Travellers. They were also challenged, given their expertise in the field, to formulate their own Policy. Table 7.11 summarises the responses to the question: 'In the light of your own experience, if you were formulating Policy for Gypsies/Travellers what would it be?' Only Officers were asked this question since Councillors already make Policy.

Table 7.11 If You Were Formulating Policy For Gypsies/Travellers What Would It Be?

More Sites	5
Transit Sites	5
A National Regional Network of sites	4
More Consultation/Research	2
What we have works	4
Non-toleration	2

Several respondents volunteered the information that the families they came into contact with 'wouldn't want to be on a site. If we provided a transit site would they use it?' Other suggestions were:

A free hand – no toleration whatsoever

I would like a transit site near traffic routes. It would make the enforcement issue easier.

I would want to work more closely with the police to remove them.

A transit site. We have sites for touring caravans but I don't think Gypsies would be admitted.

They wouldn't be encouraged to stay. I've never met any groups that said they wanted to stay here. I don't think council would approve any site.

It's a national thing. It needs a regional policy.

There is reference to a site in the Local Plan but no commitment to it. People tend to avoid the issue.

Respondents were then asked to evaluate their Council's Policies in the light of being fair/unfair, inclusive/exclusionary. Table 7.12 below summarises that response.

Table 7.12 Are this Council's Policies for Gypsies/Travellers Fair/Unfair; Inclusive/Exclusionary

	Fair	Unfair	Neither	Don't Know
Senior Officer	5	2	3	3
Junior Officer	4	3	-	4
Leaders of Council	2	-	-	-
Members of Council	2	-	-	-
Total	**13**	**5**	**3**	**7**

NB There were 5 non-responses to this question

	Inclusive	Exclusionary	Neither	Don't Know
Senior Officers	-	6	2	3
Junior Officers	-	8	3	3
Leaders of Council	-	2	-	3
Members of Council	-	2	-	-
Total	**0**	**18**	**2**	**9**

NB There were 4 non-responses to this question

Additional comments were made which indicated that Councillors and Officers knew that whilst Policies might sound fair, they were exclusionary for mobile groups. Settled families on authorised sites appeared to be viewed in a slightly different way. One Council claimed that its Policies were 'harsh and very direct and very consistent' when dealing with mobile groups (Senior Officer Interview). A Member of Council asked, 'How can you include a section of society that lives by a different set of rules and regulations to the rest? There's got to be give and take' (Leader of Council Interview). One Officer stated, 'We're not setting Policies for the benefit of mobile groups'. There were also suggestions that the Policies were fair to constituents and that they 'agreed wholeheartedly' with what the Council was doing. Any solution was expressed in National rather than Local terms for resolution. Only a minority of respondents appeared to be aware of the connection between unfair Policies and exclusion.

Although both Officers and Councillors have recourse to action other than removal, removal was the quickest and cheapest solution – and in the face of public protest and pressure – the line of least resistance. This should not surprise since a precedent for removal appears historic in Staffordshire and a habit (see Table 7.13 and Chapters 8 and 9 for further elaboration of these points).

The Staffordshire Habit

A County Council Report entitled *Gypsies and Other Nomads* (1952/53) indicated a long-standing 'tradition'/habit of eviction and moving on. It quoted 1900 evictions for the year with 1154 of them taking place in the south of the County. Table 7.13 is reworked to show the eviction rates throughout the County and in the District Councils which remain within the County today. It was estimated that within Staffordshire around 80 families travelled through the south of the County and that overall there were between 100 and 150 'nomadic' families giving a population of between 400 and 500 (ibid:12). However, no distinction was made between the post-war homeless living in caravans and Gypsies/Travellers. The same caravan was moved on 'two or three times within a few days' which led 'to the feeling of not belonging to the normal community which is at the root of the problem' (ibid: 13). The number of sites permanently occupied was 10 whilst

120 were temporarily occupied. However it was unclear whether the sites were temporary because the land did not belong to the families so they were constantly moved on thus preventing permanent settlement. It seemed that few Councils admitted to a permanent population, although some sites were on land owned by the family which suggested permanence. Many of the sites were on waste ground or in fields; others were close to refuse tips, on backyard sites, in old quarries or by the roadside. It is not known how many of these sites were made permanent under the later 1968 Caravan Sites Act. Such constant eviction tends to militate against the notion of 'traditional' sites and

Table 7.13 To Show the Distribution and Eviction Rates of Caravans Within Staffordshire 1952/53

District	Permanent Occupation	Temporary Occupation	Number of Caravans	Number of Evictions
Boroughs				
Lichfield	-	-	-	-
Newcastle-under-Lyme	-	5	13	37
Stafford	-	-	-	-
Tamworth	-	3	4	20
Totals	**0**	**8**	**17**	**57**
Urban Districts				
Biddulph	-	1	4	4
Cannock	-	2	3	11
Kidsgrove	-	1	2	-
Leek	-	2	2	4
Stone	-	-	-	-
Uttoxeter	-	2	10	8
Totals	**0**	**8**	**21**	**27**
Rural Districts				
Cannock	-	-	-	-
Cheadle	-	1	4	10
Leek	-	-	-	-
Lichfield	1	-	5	148
Newcastle-under-Lyme	-	-	-	-
Stafford	-	9	1	56
Stone	-	-	-	-
Tutbury	-	4	2	48
Uttoxeter	-	7	2	40
Totals	**1**	**21**	**14**	**302**
CountyBoroughs				
Burton-on-Trent	-	5	3	39
Stoke-on-Trent	-	10	20	54
Totals	**-**	**15**	**23**	**93**

Source: Adapted from the 1953 Staffordshire County Council Report: County Record Office

stopping places. Instead it seems that families tended to stop wherever they could and with or without permission in order to remain. The Table also demonstrates the long history of non-toleration and expulsion of caravans and mobile families within this County.

It was noticeable that those Councils with the highest number of evictions were Councils with the lowest number of caravans today – Lichfield, Tamworth, Burton-on-Trent, Cannock. The Table also shows that the Rural District Councils with the fewest caravans (35) carried out the most evictions (302). The Urban District Councils (29 caravans) carried out the fewest evictions (27) when compared with the Borough Councils (38 caravans and 93 evictions). The number of caravans suggest small family groups being evicted continually when in fact they wished to remain or perhaps they lived permanently in the area but no longer in a permanent dwelling. Thus, 'displaced persons' as opposed to being termed 'nomads' might have been a more appropriate descriptor.

A Local Gypsy/Traveller Responsorial View
Overall, Gypsies/Travellers spoken with and interviewed were of the opinion that LAs did not do much for them. As one respondent commented: 'because we're Gypsies they just don't care. They think we're scum, but we're not. They think it's all right living like this, but it's not'. However, when asked if they approached their LA or local Councillor their responses ranged from 'Yes, we're always asking for things but we never get them' to 'I don't know who the local Councillor is. I can't write or do anything like that so I don't vote in elections'; or 'We don't want any bother'; and 'We're used to being treated badly'.

SUMMARY
The last two Chapters, together, have attempted to show the Policy train for Gypsies/Travellers, by examining the relevant National Legislation and how this is translated into Policy at the local level in Staffordshire. I have also attempted to show the

structural milieu in which Policy is advanced or frustrated, interpreted for implementation - or not.

Contained within Legislation and Policy is the potential to shape not only what is happening on the ground but also future direction and the moulding/changing of attitudes. Codification within Policy and accompanying resources (or not) can convey the urgency of the Policy to the local level, which often determines whether or not implementation will occur. Structures within the Policy and within institutions can effect failure as can individual perversity and irrationality. At the time of writing the Thesis National Policy for Gypsies/ Travellers was somewhat ambiguous. On the one hand the CJPO Act 1994 prohibited trespass, and whilst Circular 1/94 removed any special treatment for settlement within the Green Belt or the countryside, Circular 18/94 and the Good Practice Guide advocated clemency. This tended to allow both National and Local Government off the hook, and a lens to find loopholes in the Policy to justify non- compliance – unless the target group and its advocates pressed for change or compliance via the Courts. It could also be construed as an example of an inability to 'do' (or want to do) joined-up thinking.

Constant Policy and structural changes at National and Local levels can turn LAs into habita for themselves so that their purpose becomes distracted to that of resistance and adaptation to change in order for the institution to survive with some employing a defensive avoidance of change and real and/or perceived threats. However, as it is in no-one's interest within institutions to lose the good will of partners, practice is codified to ensure that some, if not all of Policy, is doable, and within the capabilities of LAs. Being seen to attempt to do 'the right thing' at the National level is often more important than implementation on the ground. At the Local level there is less desire to embrace unpopular causes or issues since here public reaction can be harsh. There are also few mechanisms to challenge Local Authorities other than via the instrument of maladministration, gross misconduct, or (partially) via the ballot box. Additionally, any challenge carries with it the implication that the rules are known. This demands a high level of literacy, knowledge of the legal process and the Law. Few Gypsy/Traveller families attempt this challenge and few win where they do unless the legal profession is paid to act on their behalf. Thus many families become caught up in the legal bind which prohibits settlement and keeps them moving. Equally, a significant number of Officers claimed that they, themselves, did not know what the rules were precisely, and that new rules took some time to filter down to the delivery level. At this level the practice appeared to be to do whatever it takes. When this is repeated and honed it is not long before it becomes converted and enshrined in Law and Policy. Hence the Good Practice Guide does not surprise in that it is based largely on the practice of exclusion and removal albeit with a nod to clemency and common sense re not removing families needlessly. However, considering that the Guide had been in circulation for more than two years, there were many Officers who had not heard of it or knew in detail what it advocated.

Officers, when asked how they would resolve the situation, knew that more permanent and temporary sites and fewer evictions were an answer. Despite the furore around settlement Gypsies/Travellers do live in houses and families have become part of mainstream society. Those settled on authorised sites and who can afford it are living in mobile chalets and some who have been granted permission for a site on their own land are building conventional houses. It would appear that those who can, negotiate entry into the mainstream successfully. The less conforming are relegated to the 'fringes'. The difficulty comes when families park their homes on land not their own, and without planning permission – which is at the crux of the issue and will be discussed further in the next chapter.

The last two chapters have attempted to show that Social and Plan policy would appear to contain embedded inequalities which inherently divide Gypsies/Travellers into two groups the settled 'the Good' and the mobile' the Bad'- and this is how they become identified. Much of the Policy which is applied to Gypsies/Travellers is prohibitive and applied to manage and control the latter grouping. At the local level this becomes translated as non-acceptance and exclusion. Mobility then becomes proscriptive especially when linked to other types of exclusions – eg from employment, education and health care. The overarching assumption is that Gypsies/Travellers move. This is not questioned even when families wish to stay and some wish to settle on land that they own, or they have lived in a locality for generations. Whilst some families adapt to mobility like fish in water (Bourdieu 1993b, 1987) others cling precariously to 'the edge' in all senses of the word- wishing to settle, but they are pressured to keep moving on.

Policy for mobile groups has rarely been inclusionary. Negative attitudes towards 'outsiders' can be traced back to Feudal and the Manorial system when non-belongers were quickly identified as 'other' and expelled. This was bound up with the responsibility of care by the Lord of the Manor (later the community) and the notion of contribution of some kind for that care and protection (Dyer 2002; Beier 1985). Policy identifies in order to protect and provide for those who are deemed to contribute and to belong. It excludes the rests who are or who have become 'outsiders' (Simmel 1971). The 1968 Caravan Sites Act and the CJPO Act 1994 are part of this continuum.

Evaluating their own Policies, many respondents were not only clear that they were unfair and exclusive, but they also knew what needed to be done to remedy this. However, solutions and responsibilities for any change tended to be seen in terms of National rather than Local initiatives. And so the circle is closed. Perhaps it is Policy that needs to be moved on.

In 2013 and ten years since the Thesis was written, there have been small step changes such as security of tenure for those on Local Authority run sites. Needs surveys have been undertaken nationally and competitive Government funding is available for new sites and for the refurbishment of old sites. However, to date few if any Councils in Staffordshire have identified land or sites in their Site Allocation Plans. The next step is awaited, as Development Framework Plans are working their way through the system. It will be interesting to see how Staffordshire fares in this process. The pressure in England has eased since Ireland, Scotland and Wales are now implementing their own National Policies and earmarking funding for the creation of accommodation for Gypsies/ Travellers. The recent high profile evictions in Essex and Bedfordshire and from the Olympic site in the southeast demonstrate that as far as local attitudes are concerned there is still much work to be done with regard to the equalities agenda as it applies to Gypsy/ Traveller families. These issues will now be discussed in the next two chapters.

CHAPTER 8
IMPLEMENTING POLICY: THE THIRD WAY?

This chapter seeks to discover how LAs in Staffordshire tackle the implementation of National Policy, given its apparent lack of clarity, its perceived negative bias and its stated hands-off approach to Gypsy/Traveller issues at the Local administrative level. Since Policy informs any implementation at the Local level and indicates how LAs are permitted to act in certain situations it would be of interest to discover if implementation ultimately could contribute to the intended solution – given the half-hearted inclusion in the Local Plan Policy and the non-toleration Policies of LAs in Staffordshire for any Gypsy/Traveller settlement. The interviews also sought to discover how far 'workable' practice at the local level influenced the delivery of services with outcomes informing National Policy, thus closing the Policy Circle, which tends to ensure that there is nowhere else to go.

The information in this chapter is based on fieldwork – ie site visits, site conversations, interviews and participant observation undertaken between 1999 and 2002.

Policy into Practice – the Staffordshire Scene
The Problem
Chapter 7 showed how Local Plan Policies for provision were vague suggesting only that 'should' a need arise action 'might' be taken. The Plan system at the time was and still is demand-led. The onus rests on the assumption and practice that Gypsies/Travellers will come forward with planning proposals for land deemed suitable for sites within any Local Plan. Whilst some can afford to buy land and employ legal representation, many are out of this league. Thus many obstacles face Gypsy/Traveller families who wish to settle. First, proposals for caravan sites of any kind compete in planning terms with housing

development. Not only is there a predisposition in favour of conventional housing, but housing developers and professional builders are the competition for space/land. Second, the success rate of planning permissions submitted by Gypsies/Travellers is also low owing to the strength, in part, of local opposition. The land purchased by some families is often accommodation land or land in the Green Belt which might never attract planning permission, hence its affordability. Retrospective planning permissions are also few and far between and these are often the permissions that are sought by Gypsies/Travellers who settle first and then make an application to create a site later. A third variable in this equation is that few LAs today provide housing for tenants and it is unlikely that they will 'give' land for sites – which some families appear to believe would be the case. If Circular 1/94 removed any special situations pertaining to Gypsy/Traveller sites, subsequent legislation has closed any loop-holes within the planning system thus Gypsy/Sites and social housing are now more on a par with each other and gypsies/Travellers are placed in the same category as any developer. Any sites are expected to be provided by the private sector, Gypsies/Travellers themselves or Housing Associations. Fourth, the term 'affordable housing' was introduced in 2000 with the expectation that developments over a certain size would include a percentage of affordable units for shared purchase or rent. To date, this has never been applied to include Gypsy/Traveller accommodation.

In Staffordshire, whilst the 'quota' for housing supply had been over-subscribed at the time of writing the Thesis, the demonstrated need for Gypsy/Traveller sites, from the data available and site waiting lists appeared to be in deficit. This tended to make a nonsense of the Good Practice Guide, Circulars 1/94 and 18/94. The situation also appeared to frustrate National Government intent for private provision and a more inclusive society. It also ensured that a series of counter-productive zero-sum games were being played out between some LAs and some Gypsy/Traveller families – producing an end-play of reduction in trust and confidence on all sides and negative equity in the longer term.

So, how far was National Policy effective in practice in 2001? This question was asked of LA Officers and Members (see Table 8.1). A majority said that it was not (18) with senior Officers who have to implement it (8) and junior Officers who have to enforce it (6) being the most certain of its ineffectiveness. The Case Studies at the end of this chapter confirm these responses. There was an almost even split between the 'don't knows' and the 'Yes/No' category. The opinion of this latter group was that the Policy might be working in ways that either it shouldn't, or in ways that were not envisaged. When asked to elaborate, it was revealed that there was confusion as to what the Policy was, and that without a clear strategy, practice was difficult. It was also apparent that some Officers and Members were still under the impression that either the duty remained to provide or that the Guidance and Circulars advocated provision when the duty to do so had been revoked. LAs said that they attempted to 'do the right thing' by following the letter of the Law – particularly amongst those who thought that it allowed them off the provision hook. The general feeling was that a perfect 'fit' between National Policy and

Table 8.1: Is National Policy Effective in Practice

	Yes	No	Yes/No	Don't Know
Senior Officers	1	8	1	2
Junior Officers	-	6	3	2
Leaders of Council	-	3	1	2
Members of Council	1	1	1	1
Total	**2**	**18**	**6**	**7**

Muddled:	It's not practical to use it.
	It's not realistic, it's out of step with local views.
	It's incredibly muddled.
	Different facets of different policies are going around and are open to different interpretations by different local authorities.
Dilemma:	We don't know what to do.
	It expects toleration and making enquiries before you do anything. It doesn't accept the reality of what is expected of you from the settled community.
	Very little is done in practice although a lot is written down.
	It's a disaster. It needs a complete overhaul. It says local authorities are not required to provide anything – that actually makes things worse.
	There is a serious dilemma between what the Guidance wants us to do and what the local community and other legislation force us to do. Resources have to be put in if anything is going to happen.
What is policy?	I don't know anything about national policy. It hasn't come down to the local level or I'd have heard about it

local practice was difficult to forge. Some of the responses, all of which went beyond yes and no, are set out in Table 8.1 and could be divided roughly into three groups: those who thought the Policy/practice issue muddled; that Policy in practice presented practitioners with a dilemma; that no-one was sure any longer what National Policy was.

LAs have to do what is right in terms of National Legislation, its local residents and Gypsy/Traveller families, particularly those settled on sites. They also have to do what they are 'told' or paid to do. At all levels they can be challenged for not getting it right (or what is thought to be right). Few underestimated the difficulty in finding practical solutions which would please everyone. Some did not even try. For others, self-help removal methods were used (eg barricading Gypsies/Travellers into their unauthorised sites). It was claimed that this method, usually utilised by private landowners, cleared the site quicker than an Order 24 or via the Magistrate's Court. Order 24 was described as 'an old fashioned protection, in many ways, of ownership of land' (LA Solicitor Interview), and did not have a strong role for Circular 18/94. When Newcastle-under-Lyme Council adopted this practice, it was halted prematurely by the local Police who claimed it to be unlawful. The LA Officer claimed that he had had the full support of Councillors. A representative from the Legal Department of the same Council said that his Department 'would advise any Department on its action. We would advise them proactively. They would not normally go against this advice. Generally speaking we find that our advice is accepted'. Thus the Council appeared to have fully supported this kind of action as 'good' (and even legally correct) practice. Table 8.1 also indicated that LAs will interpret any vagueness in National Policy to their own advantage. Similarly Gypsies/Travellers will attempt to minimise and avoid any measure damaging to their interests. To succeed, Legislation/Policy requires positive participation and agreement from many quarters (Theodolou and Cahn 1995). However, just because people and agencies sign up to such Policy, this does not make bad Policy and bad practice right or just.

Officers were then asked what the practical problems were in dealing with Gypsies/ Travellers. This was an open question but the majority sought to respond in terms of unauthorised encampments and mobile groups. It was made clear by a majority who thought that settled families posed few, if any, problems. The responses were gathered under two headings: communication and behaviour.

Communication

Officers felt, mainly, that they did not know how to communicate with groups that they did not know. Underpinning this was a fear of the reception that Enforcement Officers would receive. Several claimed that they had been abused verbally and physically, dogs had been set on them and children had thrown stones. A physical fear was a precursor to any contact. Gypsies/Travellers were equally afraid of the reception they might receive not only from Officers but also from the police and local residents. Families are often afforded little or no protection or respect. On one particular site, frequently used for unauthorised encampments, local residents were in the habit of stoning the caravans. It was difficult to know if the families complained but the response from one Officer was that 'it moves them on quicker than we could' (Enforcement Officer, Interview). Thus it would be unlikely that any action against the stone-throwers would be taken. Three Enforcement Officers said that they negotiated and where this was a first response, confrontation and aggression were minimised on both sides, making it possible to amicably agree a length of stay – but, usually, only as long as the legal process of removal would allow.

Communicating need is another problem (see also Thomas and Campbell 1992 on this point). Whilst some families may be asked if they need Education/Health or Social Services, they are not always asked if they need basic facilities such as a safe place to be, rubbish skips/plastic rubbish bags, water or lavatories. When speaking with families on unauthorised sites, they claimed that they had not been asked. One group who formerly lived on a 'permitted site' claimed that they had been provided with port-a-loos but the company had not serviced them so they were not used. There appeared to be no collective action on site for the families to do this themselves. Thus need is communicated in other ways. Some families asked housed residents for water - which then becomes contentious. Gypsies/Travellers attempt to resolve these issues by choosing sites where these facilities are more readily available – eg supermarket and leisure centre and hotel car parks, industrial estates or disused factory sites. Such sites also have the advantage of hard-standing and there is close proximity to shops. Such sites are also highly visible and therefore in some respects safer. Conversely, they are also sites where a lengthy stay would not be permitted. When a group came and parked on a supermarket car park in Newcastle-under-Lyme (when fieldwork was being undertaken) they did not cause a nuisance other than that 15 caravans took up parking space and the manager claimed that the store lost a considerable amount of money because shoppers began to go elsewhere. The Manager said that he was forced to take action (Interview 2000). The site was close to the town centre. The incident was reminiscent of medieval descriptions in Fraser (1992) where families arrived in towns and set up in the market place – and were promptly removed.

Behaviour

Behaviour had become a dominant factor used for the removal of unauthorised sites. A majority of Officers were concerned about anti-social behaviour. Many Officers intimated that they would take a more lenient view of the site if the behaviour of families was more socially acceptable. However, what is acceptable for one group may not be acceptable to another. The number of complaints received by LAs about the unauthorised sites governed how long that site would be permitted. Even if no complaints had been received LAs would know that the site was there. Officers reported that the main stress points which occasioned complaints were: barking dogs, horses, noisy generators, unruly children, blockages of footpaths and route ways, litter, trade and human waste building up and left behind after departure, and criminal activity. Whilst all these activities would not occur on all sites, the majority of Officers claimed that some activities such as rubbish, tended to be the rule rather than the exception. One Officer said that, 'We try to find out what they do re toilet facilities and where they get water, but they won't tell us. Even if we give out plastic bags the litter is still strewn around. The simplest thing would be to put a skip on site but it's down to money and there isn't a budget for it. Perhaps when Best Value comes along people will look at things in an entirely different way. What nobody wants to be seen doing is condoning someone being there when they shouldn't be' (LA Senior Officer Interview). Another stated that, 'Sometimes, they ask for skips but they don't get them – only bin bags' (LA Enforcement Officer Interview). Officers claimed that, overall, rubbish was left behind on 'a vast majority of sites'. Although a litany of misdemeanours was quoted, some Officers were anxious to point out that not all families behaved in this way. However, irrespective of behaviour, all appeared to be treated in the same way in terms of removal from unauthorised sites, which suggested that some responses were less 'proportionate' than they might have been. The visibility and safety of unauthorised sites was also a factor used for removal – ie on the side of major highways etc.). The location of early 'permanent' sites, many of which exist still under fly-overs, next to gas works and infill sites etc. appeared to be overlooked.

Procedures

The County Council had a strict policy regarding trespass and District Councils were authorised to act on its behalf in repossessing land. Although the County Council advocated following Court procedures for any trespass, it also called for discretion. There was no guarantee, however, that District Councils would comply. The County's Policy claimed to 'hand out rules to anyone they are thinking of evicting on an unauthorised encampment (LA Senior Officer Interview). At the time this did not appear to be a general practice.

Local Councils fell into two camps: those with frequent encampments and those that had none or few. In the latter case, Councils tended to take a harder line to ensure that encampments were infrequent. One Council with few or no encampments claimed that when caravans did arrive Officers hassled them until they left or stayed there until they did (LA Eviction Officer Interview). If families refused, vehicles were brought to tow them off. The Officer claimed that he 'did not have to evict them because they left of their own accord'. One Officer said that he 'visited the site twice per day until they left' (LA Eviction Officer). Some Councils with few or no sites claimed that it was because 'word had got round'. Where Councils took a more sympathetic approach (and this depended on the location of the site and complaints received) families could remain provided that they had permission from the land owner and whilst formal eviction procedures took their course (LA Senior Officer Interview). This could take up to eight weeks. This procedure was also the exception rather than the rule, and the removal time depended on the Legal procedure followed. Whilst there appeared to be a variety of procedures followed within the County, the overall response to unauthorised encampments was to 'take action immediately to get them off'. This is not to say that all families were moved on immediately.

The Eviction/Unsettlement Procedure

Officers were asked what their procedures were from the point of entry to the time that the families moved. Procedures were similar and the outcomes for most Councils appeared to be to repossess 'their' land as quickly as possible and to 'regularise' the situation – which appeared to be moving the family on as quickly as the Law would allow and securing the site against further trespass. If it appeared that families wished to remain, other than serve an injunction, the process then became one of legal attrition. Generally, the procedures were that once an unauthorised encampment had been brought to the Councils' attention – usually by members of the public – the site was inspected and Officers would attempt to discover when the family would be moving on. If the land was in private hands, the owners were located, and it then became their responsibility to evict. If they did not they would become subject to legal action themselves. If requested, Councils would give legal advice. Only one Council covered all legal and clearance costs of the landowner. Some owners applied to the Courts for a Repossession Order whilst others used 'self-help' methods.

Given the haste that was expected and given that some Councils did not have a formal Policy, Officers were asked if they used informal procedures to evict. The majority of respondents claimed that they followed Court procedures and strict Policies/Protocols for trespass and eviction (18). One Officer stated that the Council preferred to negotiate rather than take the legal route. When asked if Councils tolerated unauthorised sites the majority (21) said that there was no toleration. Six Officers thought that there was toleration, three suggested it was toleration by default since the legal process could take up to two weeks and the families were allowed to stay during this time. Three claimed that they did not know. Officers in the same Council gave conflicting responses. However, overall, it appeared that all Councils did not 'tolerate' unauthorised sites – describing them as 'invasions'/'incursions'. The notion of a 'proportional response' was recognised by only one Council. Families interviewed on unauthorised sites claimed that LAs were treating them unfairly, some also knew that they need not move on until an 'Order' was issued, others said they wanted to stay in the area.

The length of stay appeared to depend on factors such as numbers of complaints received, the size of the site, behaviour and cleanliness of the group, location of the site, the length taken by the legal process and other extraneous factors such as foot and mouth (at the time) where movement would be discouraged. Illness, health/education needs and other factors requiring clemency suggested by Circular 18/94 did not always carry weight. Nevertheless, when asked if Officers worked to Circular 18/94 six of the nine Enforcement Officers said that they did, one said 'no' and two did not know.

To the question 'Do Gypsies/Travellers wish to remain?' the majority response was that 'We don't ask that question'. Respondents were then asked under what circumstances families could do so. The majority response was that they could not (see below):

Numbers are small, they don't make a mess and we don't get complaints about them.

We have to adhere to our policies

I've never known a case where they say I want to settle down and get a job. They just move to the nearest place where the job is and when the job's worked out they move on.

They can only remain on council land on health grounds. Some say don't send education and welfare down, but we do.

If they want to stay permanently I mention that they should approach housing. If they want to stay in a van they contact the site manager and go on the waiting list.

Only with planning permission.

Their only recourse is the court. If they want to plead in court, that's their right. They've never appealed against a Court Order yet.

They can't.

It's the bailiffs or the police.

We could advise them about land which they might legally occupy as a caravan site. We'd be happy to do that but it's never happened. They would be told where the sites are in the borough that might have available pitches. It never happens in practice.

If they wanted to stay they could go into housing but they would have to prove a local connection.

It has never arisen. They would need planning permission.

I don't know that that has ever happened.

It's not possible for them to remain.

even if they wanted to. Only a minority of responses suggested assisting Gypsies/ Travellers to remain. When asked if the Council encouraged families to move into houses the response was 'Only if they want to'. Whilst they were not excluded from housing waiting lists, the lists were over-subscribed and where families would wait would be a problem. Keeping in touch with Housing Departments would be difficult and almost impossible without a fixed address given that if an offer came and was not responded to quickly the assumption would be that the offer had not been accepted and the name would be removed from the list (Housing Officer Interview). The ability to read and write and reasons for being in the area were also factors in the application process. Despite these obstacles where there are permanent sites, Officers did report that there was a steady trickle from the site into houses. This possibility was reduced in LAs where there were no sites. In LAs where private sites were the norm, Gypsy/Traveller families owned their own homes and building in bricks and mortar was taking place. Where families lived on permanent sites and they could afford it, the mobile chalet home was replacing the caravan. Records of the movement of families from sites into houses are not kept, but research into this area would prove useful if only to ascertain if need was being met. One lady who had been on a permanent site for a long time claimed that she now wanted something 'posher ... a better site or a bungalow in a field'. This activity and expression of interest in more permanent structures suggest that the findings of Thomas and Campbell (1992) in their Cardiff study which claimed that Gypsies/Travellers had an aversion to bricks and mortar, might not necessarily be a universal view.

Elected Members of Councils, only, were asked: 'What happens to families after eviction/being moved on?' – on the grounds that they were Policy makers and might feel some responsibility for what happened next and given the rhetoric around 'responsible governance'. Whilst some said that they didn't know, others responded in the following way:

> I think they have scouts out looking for the next site. I think tracks are kept of where they move to – we did that with New Age Travellers (in one area).

> They move on and around. How many hundreds of years has that been going on and no-one's come up with a right scheme. We put a mound up so they can't do it again.

> We just move them onto the road. Some Local Authorities escort them to the boundary by the police.

> They often have another site lined up. I've never asked where they're going.

> They move on somewhere else and become someone else's problem.

> No idea. I read in the newspaper that they move on and set up another site.

> I don't know where they go. They're probably evicted by someone else. There's a bush telegraph where one Council will ring up another and say we're moving X number of caravans, look out for them in your area. We do dig trenches to prevent them getting on.

> I don't know they just disappear overnight.

The general attitude of Councils appeared to be that either there was no problem or the problem was not theirs. That most families did not resist either demonstrated a fatalism re being allowed to remain or that they lived elsewhere on a site or in a house. However, not all families entering the County could be 'just passing through'. They did know that if they did not move on then the bailiffs would be summoned. The usual practice was to leave the day before. In this way the families were not forcibly removed and the LA could say that an eviction had not taken place. There were no mechanisms to sift 'visitors' from families wishing to remain. Only the families determined to remain and who could afford a Barrister had any chance of doing so. Without proper legal representation families were out of their depth in Court (observation/fieldwork). Many of them did not turn up at Court to hear their case and this was also held against them.

Officers were asked if they found the process of eviction/moving on stressful and most agreed that it was 'not an aspect of the job that they 'enjoyed''. At the time, bailiffs were employed to carry out the task. Others said that they had no qualms about serving notices – that was what they were paid to do – they did not refuse to do it. Some found it difficult wearing two hats where they were employed as both Gypsy/Traveller Liaison Officer and Enforcement Officer since this tended to complicate their task, particularly when welfare checks were carried out. It was unlikely that families would be prepared to give them the information they needed if that person had the power and authority to move them on. Certainly families being moved on found the experience stressful. The families living on unauthorised sites said that they were 'living on their nerves'.

The Practice of Police Involvement

In spite of National Government insistence, more police involvement was not welcomed by Officers or Members of Councils (see Table 8.2). For some Councils who did not have a problem with frequent or large encampments, more police involvement was regarded as unnecessary given their presence at evictions. It was understood that they would come if called. A liaison role and the sharing of costs, however, was welcomed. The feeling tended to be that families 'knew what the law allows, how long they can stay and what they can get away with. They play the game and we play the game' (LPU Officer Interview). One leader of Council suggested that a police presence could 'inflame the situation'. Some Councils wanted more help and assistance from the police so that families could be moved more quickly. It was recognised that partnership working was necessary to ensure that all parties worked within the law.

Table 8.2: Would You Welcome More Involvement by the Police

	Yes	No	Sufficient	Don't know
Senior Officers	4	8	-	-
Junior Officers	4	5	2	-
Leaders of Council	1	5	-	-
Members of Council	2	2	-	-
Total	**11**	**20**	**2**	-

Liaison

When asked if LAs liaised with each other the response was mainly 'yes' but in an informal way. The process is currently being formalised. (An Inter-agency group had been established in North Staffordshire for information exchanges). Where there was liaison, this occurred over certain issues – unlawful encampments, policies to encourage joined-up thinking (a buzz word at the time), site management issues and Council services available (or not), intelligence over movement, and Best Value. Joint protocols between the Police, Councils and other agencies were being drawn up for the streamlined management of unauthorised sites. At the time of interviewing in 2001 only one Council had an agreed protocol in place.

The Practice of Need Satisfaction?

In recognising need, Councils fell into two groups. One group acknowledged that Gypsies/Travellers had special needs. One Council viewed sites as cheap, affordable alternatives to houses – although' Planning does not like caravans irrespective of who occupies them'. Another claimed that it needed to make proper provision. One Council saw this in terms of transit sites, although the realisation of this was deemed 'unlikely'. Where need was identified it was interpreted, mainly, in terms of site provision, which could not be achieved 'at a cost to (the rest of) the community. We don't get any extra money to provide extra sites or to tidy up after families have left. Therefore we need to prevent them from misusing property' (Senior LA Officer Interview). This group of Councils placed themselves in a dilemma – recognising need but feeling that there were factors that prevented them from satisfying that need, especially from families who came from outside the area. The second group of Councils either were 'oblivious' to need because they said that they 'did not go out looking to see what we can do,' or that Gypsies/Travellers had 'not expressed any need' (Leader of Council Interview). Another Leader of Council suggested, 'I don't think that they have any special needs'. A Member of the same Council said, 'they haven't expressed a need to me … They wouldn't be able to stay … We have a strong Green Belt policy'. However, such assumptions within Councils, without the support of needs surveys should be viewed as opinion rather than fact.

The Practice of Compromise?

Despite the differences between Councils, all sides were aware that 'problems' existed and that policy and practice worked against a satisfactory solution. There was no consensus between National Government and Local Authorities despite Circulars and Guidance to reconcile the harsher aspects of the CJPO Act 1994 with Gypsy/Traveller need. Within Councils there was also a difference of opinion. Bearing in mind the difficulty of formulating a satisfactory policy solution to a problem that is inaccurately framed, the next set of questions sought to examine 'the problem' more closely to see if a compromise could be reached.

When asked how Gypsies/Travellers might make life easier for LAs the main responses were (multiple responses were permitted and the question was 'open'):

By not making a mess/not tipping rubbish/clearing site afterwards	7
By not coming here	4
Being more responsible where they set up sites	2
By seeking consent before occupying land	2
By being more conscious of people around them	2
By controlling their behaviour	2
If they could read and write it would make communication easier	1
By looking at land-use planning laws	1
By helping themselves so that we can help them	1
By moving via negotiation rather than Court Order	1
The problems they create are structured in terms of their culture	2

Whilst rubbish loomed large in responses, many of the categories raised could have been applied to non-mobile groups. Some of the responses were unreasonable in terms of expectation and possibly might be applied to others who were not Gypsies/Travellers. Some of the responses took the issue to a different level, suggesting non-belonging, and otherness, together with an inability to communicate. Since communication relies on a mutual exchange of information, it could be said that the inability to communicate was mutual. Would the counter question: 'How could this LA make things easier for Gypsies/Families?' suggest a remedy? The responses are below:

Provision:
A site in each district could be considered – if there was a policy and resources to do it.

The government should take a lead on this to provide sites and then make rules. I don't think any Local Authorities are keen to have sites, even those with land.

The Council didn't realise when it built the site that they were going to stay.

Transit sites would help. (This point was mentioned at least three times.)

Site Management:
Housing Associations are willing to run sites but they don't like setting them up. It's also a question of the basis on which they are managing them and whether they would be handed back in the same state as they were received.

Some suggestion of providing water/toilets and refuse facilities. We ought to provide more information about what we're going to do in terms of evictions.

Land Allocation/not moving them on:
By not getting them to move on. As a Council if they could find them somewhere where they could make their own provision. Land locally is expensive. That's the problem. If land can be used for a caravan it can be used for housing. Brownfield sites are a possibility but that's where they don't want to go. They want to be in the Green Belt. Until the Green Belt policy is relaxed it will just continue.

There could be a certain amount of land set aside … I would expect it to be used properly.

By not moving them on and allowing them to do what they want to do.

If we find a new site it's not going to be in the town. It's got to be somewhere away from the town.

Other:
Leave them alone or adopt an overarching policy of toleration to persuade the local community it's the right thing to do. But it's not going to work.

We could raise awareness of Traveller culture and problems and try to get that over to the settled community so there is more tolerance.

My job isn't to make their life easier. My job is that once land has been illegally occupied is to move the occupants from it. It's not to make their life more difficult. It's to do a job.

We carry out government legislation. We're not proactive.

Whilst some respondents were aware of how the issue could be dealt with in a more positive way, many of the responses exhibited a resistance and a hardened attitude which some Local Authorities adopt – because they are The Authority and irrespective of whether their decision on an issue is right/just, or not. There also appeared to be a lack of recognition of the Councils' own contribution to the problem. When asked if more sites would solve the issue there was no consensus although common sense would dictate that it might ease the situation. Responses to this question are set out in Table 8.3. The 'yes' questions came with caveats phrased in negative terms – although the permanent sites established ceased to be an issue within the wider community (see Duncan 1996 on this point) – and the expectation that Gypsies/Families would default. There also appeared to be an underlying apprehension that Gypsies/Travellers wouldn't settle, despite evidence to the contrary. One Senior Officer pointed out that the increasing mobility of the homeless, young people and those on low incomes were equally 'a problem' which would have to be addressed by the new Community Strategy process.

Table 8.3: Would More Sites Solve 'the Problem'

	Yes	No	Don't Know	No Response
Senior Officers	4	3	3	2
Junior Officers	4	2	3	2
Leaders of Council	1	4	1	-
Members of Council	1	1	2	-
Total	**10**	**10**	**9**	**4**

I don't see how transit sites could be managed without a bottomless management problem.

Would Travellers be prepared to move onto them?

If they were charged for occupation.

It may be helpful to relieve other Local Authorities of their problem.

They don't want permanent sites, they just want to roam the world.

The Practice of Protest

A persistent thread through the responses was the effect that sites would have on local residents and what their reaction would be because this would disturb any local equilibrium. Given that elected Members would bear the brunt of any local opposition, only Councillors were asked if local opposition to Gypsies/Travellers was strong. Of the ten asked this question, nine said yes. The no response came from a Member of a Council which had limited experience of Gypsies/Travellers. Some respondents felt that the reasons for the opposition were the rubbish left, the location of the site and the general chaos caused. However, this would not explain the same level of opposition to sites where this did not happen. Some Councillors claimed that residents were 'frightened'. One said that, 'It varies from site to site how it's perceived'. Another said that 'If they settled in a derelict marl hole we wouldn't have complaints'. Three Leaders of Council felt that 'people's perceptions are based on ignorance'. Two felt that opposition began in 'a concentrated way with a vociferous minority' and this then moved 'out' as the matter was taken up by the local media. Indeed, there were some Councillors who had been elected on an anti-Gypsy/Traveller-site platform. Two Councillors claimed that they had nearly lost their seats because they supported a permanent site in the area.

Councillors were then asked if they ever went against public opinion. The majority (8) said that they did and mainly in the Planning context. However, when pressed two said that they would never 'make a stand on Gypsy/Traveller issues'. Another claimed that he would speak out 'on a personal level, for individual families' but on reflection did this mean Gypsy/Traveller families or his constituents? Did this mean that local opposition affected Local Policy and its implementation? The responses to this question ranged from no to 'everything affects Policy'. In between, the following comments were made:

> We take into account local opposition and complaints and try to rectify complaints of nuisance. If Travellers are not a nuisance they can stay.

> If there is opposition to anything, we listen.

> It can if individual members are not strong enough.

> Yes. In the siting of a Gypsy site, we have to consider all aspects. We want to ensure that Gypsies are secure wherever they are going to locate them and we have to ensure that neighbours are secure.

> It shouldn't do.

> We consult with people. Council policy is set by Councillors. It's very much influenced by pressure groups within local areas. We go through the spectrum of consultation (whether we have to or not) to see how it fits in with Local Plans.

> No, not on racial matters.

Councillors and Officers were then asked how they dealt with local opposition. Local people were usually first to discover unauthorised encampments. The majority of

Councillors felt that they had to listen to local people when they complained. Some admitted that at times this 'could be over-powering'. Officers claimed that they 'listened', investigated all complaints they received, since some complainants exaggerated the situation, 'mediated', 'liaised' and attempted 'to explain that Travellers also had rights'. One Officer stated that 'the public are only interested in the removal of illegal encampments. Locals can take things into their own hands, so we point out to Travellers that they are in danger (in some areas). Officers then 'follow procedures' and this is where a Policy was useful. It was explained to both parties in the hope that both sides would act 'responsibly'. However, any complaints would tend to trigger eviction and Officers would attempt to carry this out as quickly as possible to avert trouble' (LA Officer Interview). It would appear that such situations require leadership. Chisholm (2001:46) believed that 'a component of leadership is to do desirable things'. An even greater test of leadership might be to do what is right and necessary – although it might be unpopular - which sometimes involves not taking the line of least resistance. This might have been expected since several paid and elected Officers of the Council appeared to be aware of the action that *needed* to be taken in order to ensure that the rights and needs of all parties were satisfied.

To this end Officers paid and elected were then asked what they were doing to change public attitudes towards Gypsies/Travellers. This task was not high on any Council's Agenda, thus the response was either 'nothing' or 'it is not up to the Council' (Elected Members Interviews). Some Councillors ventured the view that it was 'up to the Travellers to change the attitudes of the public (Leader of Council Interview). Thus it appeared that Councils were not taking a lead on this, or intended to which meant that attitudes would remain unchanged. This should be a cause for concern since this suggests that LAs were failing in their statutory duty to promote good (race) relations and equality of opportunity between different groups. This failure would also be running counter to EU directives and National Government's Policies and Directives.

The Internal Mechanisms of Practice

Officers were asked a series of questions on this issue. For example, 'Does the Council have a (collective) view of Gypsies/Travellers? Do Councillors interfere in what you do with regard to Gypsy/Traveller issues? 'Is there ever a Councillor/Officer clash of view on this issue?

The first question attempted to discover if Councils had a collective/uniform view of Gypsies/Travellers which, together with perception and notions of identity might influence practice and service delivery. The general response to this question was that there was no formal corporate view. Nevertheless, informal, personal views were expressed and whilst these might not be voiced openly in Council they did have the potential to influence any action. During interviews 'views' did emerge which ranged from 'aggressive' to 'We don't look on them any differently to other residents or travellers through'. One Officer claimed that a view was formed 'when they create a problem. We react to nuisance' (Council Member Interview). Some said that they had 'never heard a view expressed' (Leader of Council). Another commented that 'everyone sees them as a bit of a nuisance' (Council Member Interview). One said that 'the word Traveller is wrong, some don't travel' (Council Member Interview). Some interpreted the question as a view of action to be taken so comments were: 'Our view is that we don't tolerate unauthorised sites. Swift enforcement action is taken' (Enforcement Officer Interview). One Leader of Council stated that the Council had less of a view and 'more of a custom in that certain Travellers were not harassed. Any others we try to ensure don't occupy land belonging to the Council because we have had so many problems in the past'. Another Councillor claimed that 'even if Council did not have a view of Gypsies/Travellers the local population does', and that local Councillors were 'representing public opinion and we're all very anti-itinerants' (Elected Member and Chair of the Council's Planning Committee).

Paid Officers only were asked the next question: Do Councillors interfere in what you do? The responses are listed below:

They let us get on with it unless they're under a lot of public pressure.

Councillors make the decisions and make their views known outside the Council Chamber.

If Travellers are on their patch, yes we get pressure.

Every member wants sites moved as soon as possible. They want it to be given a high level of priority. Members do make representation on behalf of residents to remove them.

Local Members get involved by … asking us what we're doing about it. We are expected to get on with it. They would only get involved if there were problems arising from continued occupation – violence, litter …'.

They try to, but no. To be fair they get people ringing them up, but once they know what the situation is they're quite happy. Locals just want them to move. The CJPO Act raised expectations re powers but there are limits to those powers.
No, provided we put into practice the policy as it stands, we're doing what Members want.

The only real history of practice here, is getting rid of unauthorised sites. They ask us can we do it quicker and we say 'no, this is the policy'.

They question why they are not moved on when they should be.

If the problem is in a Councillor's ward, then yes. They are our political masters … they have the power to do as they wish.

Even where no corporate view existed there appeared to be strong accord between elected Members and residents with regard to the presence/entry of 'others' who did not, or were thought not to toe the line. In order to test the strength of this 'agreement between paid and elected Officers they were then asked if there was ever a clash of view on this issue? The responses were:

There is between individual Councillors and some Officers. Individual Councillors may also have a clash of view with other Councillors.

Officers would have a fair idea how things will work and Councillors will be dragged screaming to change.

The only fall out is when they ring us up at the week-end and want us to remove encampments.

Yes, there has been. When we tried to allocate a piece of land there was a long, on-going fairly heated debate about certain areas being used a s a possible site.

There are the odd occasions when there is a balancing exercise. I don't see this as a clash of view. I see it as a difference of opinion.

Several respondents claimed that there was never a clash of view, whilst other elected and paid officers in the same Council said that there was. It was deduced that any clash' might have been as a result of personal/individual differences. There was an acknowledgement that elected Members had the last word. Nevertheless, Officers tended to have the most information so losing one battle did not necessarily mean losing the war on any issue. Generally, both parties would, simply, agree to differ.

Feed Back on Practice

During interviews it appeared that LAs and Gypsies/Traveller each rehearsed particular views which were often incorrect. For example, Interviewees felt in the main that Gypsies/Travellers knew what the rules were and how the system worked. Gypsies/Travellers felt in the main that they were doing nothing wrong. It would appear that neither party were innocent in each other's predicament. From the above responses it was shown that rules were not always explained to Gypsies/Travellers and that any knowledge of 'the system' appeared to be based on their particular experience of 'the process'. Thus the next question sought to discover how far families had recourse to 'the system' and how they interacted with it. Thus Council Officers (only) were asked if there were channels for feedback from Gypsy/Traveller families (see Table 8.4).

Table 8.4: Were There Channels For Feed-back From Gypsies/Travellers

	Yes	No	Don't Know	No Response Given	Yes But
Senior Officers	-	9	1	1	1
Junior Officers	4	5	1	-	1
Total	**4**	**14**	**2**	**1**	**2**

Eight of the ten Councils did not have formal feed-back mechanisms for complaints from Gypsy/Traveller families. One LA claimed that it had moved from a 'complaints' system to one where 'comments' were welcomed. Additional information was offered:

> When we give them notice there is a number they can ring. There is nothing to stop them.
>
> We get informal feedback from visiting sites. They will talk to the site manager … The site manager would tell me and I would tell my line manager.
>
> They have access to politicians and community leaders. On permanent sites they would have exactly the same access as any other resident in the borough.
>
> There are no formal procedures at the moment, but under best value there could be.

> They complain when we deal with them on sites but not in a way that forms part of Council's official complaints procedure.

There appeared to be no consensus between or within Councils on this issue. Officers indicated that whilst Gypsies/Travellers might have had some rights to the complaints procedure, there was no encouragement by Councils to move beyond families complaining to the Officer in charge or the Site Warden in the hope that this would work its way up they system to a resolution. Given that some Councils only received complaints on officially accepted formats, this appeared unlikely. It was noted during site visits, that families would articulate what they wanted/needed on site, or the way in which they were treated by their Council. Some Officers interpreted this as 'just moaning', 'wanting more' or 'never being satisfied'. This process appears to have become 'a game', which both parties subscribed to, with neither taking the other seriously. On one site visit, a request was made to the accompanying Officer re the repair of the long, badly pot-holed, unadopted, tarmacked drive leading to the site. He listened and said he would mention it. Afterwards he said that this was a continual complaint from this site but the pathway would never be repaired by the Council. A Senior Officer later confirmed this. A young resident on one site said, 'We're used to being treated badly'. Another resident said, 'We've rung up so many times, but they comes down and says it's nothing to do with us'. One resident took the view that 'In my life I've never asked anyone to show me how to do nothing. I've looked after meself'. For those on temporary/permitted sites, the fear was that if families complained or made demands the Council would remove them. Not knowing how the system operated in effect rendered them powerless. However Gypsy/Traveller families were not alone in this dilemma.

Evaluation of Practice

Officers and Members were asked to evaluate their practices and to give their Councils marks out of ten. As this was an open question respondents were given a free-hand to interpret the question as they wished. The Officers and Members who viewed the practice of eviction from a constituent point of view gave themselves high marks for this practice. Where this practice was perceived from a Gypsy/Traveller point of view, low marks were awarded. Some responses were more candid than expected.

Staffordshire County Council: The County Council respondents claimed that their practices 'were as reasonable' as they could be 'under the circumstances and we try'. It was also suggested that, 'If there were more resources we might have more sites'. The self-score was zero for mobile groups and 6 for settled groups.

Staffordshire Moorlands District Council: this Council felt that its practices had not been sufficiently tested to evaluate them since the Council did not have many Gypsies/Travellers frequenting the area. However, one Officer did claim that, 'Even if we had more resources, I don't think we would have more sites. We've got so many other things we need to do'

Stoke-on-Trent City Council: '(Our practices) seek to put over the Local Authority's standpoint and the transit site provision. The transit site has been a huge success. There is a balance when they camp on Council land. We take into account welfare issues. We don't want to go and do something that's incorrect and be challenged in the Courts (Senior Officer Interview). The Officers of this council rated its practices highly and gave an average mark of 9.

Newcastle-under-Lyme Borough Council: This Council claimed that its practices were 'reasonable but not innovative'. However, some Officers had also described them as 'aggressive' and 'non-tolerant'. It was also claimed that given the success of the permanent site, more sites might be possible. It was also stated that mobile groups were 'illegal occupiers of our land and are treated as such. They are perfectly fair practices'. This Council awarded itself an average of 8 marks on the basis of the provision of a permanent site and carrying out prompt evictions which pleased local constituents.

Stafford Borough Council

This Council deemed its practices to be fair. One Officer claimed that he did not 'measure practices as to whether they were fair or not. On our land we keep them informed and we don't turn up with gangs of heavies … we follow our legal rights. We're doing what we can'. However, another Officer claimed that 'our policies are pretty effective in practice. I think our practices are by and large fair. I think the Council would want to adopt a more tolerant approach than it is able to do in reality. If the behaviour of the families we get from time to time was more moderate … We are often cast in the role of wanting to get them out but that is caused by the behaviour of the families, by and large. I don't think it's a very satisfactory position (Senior Officer Interview). This council awarded itself an average mark of 6.

Lichfield

'I think the help we give them isn't enough. There is low tolerance by residents. I don't think our practices are fair' (Junior Officer Interview). A mark of 3 was mentioned.

Tamworth

Overall, Officers and Members felt that 'the Council tries to do its utmost within the powers they have to assist the residents of the town. From a Gypsy point of view, Tamworth isn't much for the welfare of Travellers'. Another view expressed was that 'Local Authorities are struggling with a problem with no obvious solution. I would say we are fair. The marks given by this Council ranged between 2 and 6.

Cannock: Whilst this LA felt that its practices were 'fair' as far as residents were concerned, in terms of human rights for Travellers, not particularly fair'. Officers declined to give a mark.

East Staffordshire:

This Council felt that it was 'reasonable' in that it 'saw problems that others (LAs) have, so we must be dealing with it fairly well' (Senior Officer Interview). In terms of Council response to residents' complaints against unauthorised sites it gave a mark of 9 and for its response to Gypsies/Travellers 1.

South Staffordshire:

This Council declined to assess itself. However, the following comments were made: 'They are treated the same as any other individual from a licensing point of view (Senior Officer Interview). 'More sites wouldn't solve the problem' (Elected Member Interview) and 'Transit sites don't work, they stay on them' (ibid).

Practices, thus, varied from Council to Council – as did proportionate levels of response to unauthorised encampments. However the gap between thought and deed can be great. To test this, four case studies were selected within Staffordshire to show not only how Gypsies/Travellers were treated in practice, but also to bring together the several threads which have wound their way through the narrative of this chapter. Unfortunately, it was beyond the scope of this discipline to assess the psychological and physical impact of such practices on Gypsy/Traveller families. Several women on unauthorised sites said that they suffered from 'nerves' and stress. Once evicted, families tended to move out of the area. And there is every indication to suggest that once back on the road families enter a vicious cycle of forced mobility. The four case studies below represent the kind of difficulties encountered by families who attempted to remain in a particular area.

A Reality Check
Case Study A

In 1992 land was purchased to set up a caravan site for four caravans. Although the site had previously been part of a disused railway and used as an infill site for inert material, it was in the Green Belt on the urban fringe. The site was reported to have 'no established use in the past (Report of the Planning Committee 16 November 1993:7.4.1, pp:17) and the area 'contained a mix of land use'. The family were described by the Agent assisting with the application as 'having lived, been to school and worked in the area for five generations'. Their main business locally, was in carpets and bed-linen and in summer visits 'may' be made to fruit and potato growing areas in the south of England.

The first application was refused on the grounds that it was 'Green Belt land', and on 'highway and land contamination grounds'. In 1993 the application was made for a temporary 3-year change of use of the site to a residential Gypsy site for two families. This was also rejected on Green Belt and amenity grounds. In October 1992 the Council had issued enforcement notices. A planning re-application attempted to satisfy previous objections.

Before the planning application had been considered by the LPA, 73 standard letters and 4 individual letters of objection (many third party objections) had been received. Objections had also been received from two Parish Councils and the local MP. The County Council also objected. A Report from the LPA on 16 November 1993 stated that: 'This latest submission was an attempt to demonstrate that the development is acceptable in policy terms and that a safe access could be constructed … . An enforcement notice was currently under appeal and the Planning Inspectorate was awaiting the determination of the current application.' The Planning Committee claimed that the main planning considerations were 'Policy including need, and use, amenity and access to highways'. The 22 page Report of the meeting indicated that 'it may reasonably be said that this Gypsy caravan site is not an inappropriate use in this urban fringe area' (7.4.3). The Report also considered that 'no harm would be created by this development. There would be no significant obtrusive, visual impact, no noise, no dust, no working on site, no significant traffic movement, no loss of agricultural land and no significant effect on the Green Belt as such'. Additionally, 'the applicants would be willing to enter into a legal agreement with the Council (or otherwise accept conditions attached to any permission that may be granted' (8.11). It was also noted elsewhere that 'objectors have not made a case on Planning grounds that would warrant refusal of permission'

Despite the 21 pages of what could be reasonably construed as a 'favourable' report on the application, Members of the Planning Committee recommended refusal on the grounds that (i) 'the site would be contrary and harmful to the Development Plan and insufficient reason to justify departure from the policy of not permitting inappropriate development in the Green Belt; (ii) that insufficient land within the applicant's control to construct and maintain a satisfactory visibility splay at the site's access onto (the main road) resulting in danger to other highway users from vehicles emerging from the site' (ibid:22).

On 27 November 1993 a site visit was made by Members and Officers of the Planning Committee. From correspondence received from the applicant's Agent and from the Chief Executive of Council, it would appear that more than 60 members of the public turned up to the meeting. In anticipation of trouble one of the Officers had requested a police presence. Two anonymous notes were in circulation prior to this event, one circulated to all local people requesting that they attend the site visit meeting and the other was sent to the applicant. In the event it was reported that Officers were 'harangued', 'jostled' and 'intimidated' by some of the protesters.

Another Planning Meeting was held on 6 December 1993. The highway visibility splay objection had been resolved. However, at this meeting the County Council objected to the site. It was revealed that the families had been offered a space on the nearby permanent site, which they refused. The planning application was therefore refused on the grounds of being 'contrary and harmful to the Development Plan and insufficient reason to justify departure from the Policy of not permitting inappropriate development in the Green Belt'.

Since no further amendment to the planning application could be made, the family sold the land and the matter was taken to the Court of Human Rights. In the summer of 2001 an out of court settlement was made on the understanding that had the case gone to Court the families would have won. A sum of around £65000 was quoted as the settlement, which apparently did not go far enough to cover the families' legal costs.

The above might have been considered a case where Councillors were attempting to protect the Green Belt and placate local residents to the point that the Officers' advice had been ignored as a matter of 'principle', not according to Planning rules. However, the land was sold to a bus company. Almost immediately after the land had been vacated by the family, buses were moved onto the site and letters of complaint were sent to the local Council. The local MP wrote in support of the new ownership. The then Minister of Transport (S Byers) felt that he could not rule against the site on grounds that to do so would mean the Company going out of business and job losses would be incurred. The records then show a flow of letters and petitions supporting the site. Although the matter of nuisance from the site was periodically brought to the attention of the Council it remained.

Given the location of the site and if the legal test of 'reasonableness' had been taken, the records make it difficult to fathom why one site was refused and the other was permitted. Both applicants were small business people. The letters of objection submitted suggested that the second usage was more detrimental to the Green Belt than the Gypsy/Traveller site might have been. The questions could be asked, was the Council response 'proportionate? Was the Council response in line with its duty of Equality of Opportunity and did the Council buckle under pressure to discriminate – which would also have been unlawful? When questioned about these issues the Senior Officer interviewed claimed that this case had been 'an opportunity missed'.

Case Study B

A Gypsy/Traveller family had lived in/resorted to the area of this LA for ten years. Under the 1968 Caravan Sites Act, the local Council had not provided sites on the grounds that it had no suitable land. The family ran a successful block paving business. The LA adopted the strategy of eviction, so the family was moved around the local area continuously on a weekly/fortnightly basis (depending on the location of the site and the number of complaints received from the local community). Much of the land in the borough was said to be in private ownership, some of which awaited development. The unauthorised sites were therefore industrial parks or disused factory/warehouse car parks. The Council paid for the eviction and clearance of these sites which amounted to a quoted estimate of £30-40000 per annum. It was the only Council to do so in Staffordshire.

I visited the family in November 1999 where they were being allowed to stay on a disused factory site until January 2000. There were seven caravans. The family were very suspicious and only the husband would be interviewed. The site was not 'a mess'.

A major complaint against the family was the business rubble left on site when enforced removal took place. There appeared to be no negotiation between the Council and the family for the rubbish to be removed, and the Council did not appear to charge the family for clearance. The Enforcement Officer told me that the family had just moved and the Council was about to take out an injunction against them. It seems that the wife had been captured on CCTV piling carpet in a corner of the site where they were parked. She was taken to Court and given a conditional discharge. In the early Summer she had been fined £750 for returning to land within three months of being directed to leave it (CJPO Act 1994), £500 for clear up costs and £200 for Court costs. In June/July 2000 an injunction was issued against her by the High Court. The family would have needed a Barrister to represent them (at a cost of around £2000). The family did not want to do this so they did not attend the Court hearing. In their absence the injunction against the wife was made official 'barring her from the roads, highways and private and public land within the Local Authority district for the rest of her life', on the grounds of repeated nuisance and trespass. The family left the Borough without contesting the injunction. They could have done so.

During their time in the area, the family had not approached the Council to ask for provision to be made for them or to ask if there was suitable land available to purchase for a site. The family claimed that they would remain until the Council provided for them. The Council claimed that it couldn't/wouldn't act until they made a formal request to the Council. County Officers believed that an offer of land had been made. It appears that the relationship between the family and the LA was confrontational/conflictual; the only inter-play was that of removal and resistance. Entrenched positions had been taken embedding negative attitudes on both sides which produced a lose-lose situation.

After the injunction the family moved into the neighbouring LA and were being regularly moved from site to site. This Council claimed that it would have taken a more 'tolerant' view had the local community not made complaints accompanied by cam-recorder evidence and had the police not become involved on the grounds of alleged criminal activity.

In the summer of 2001 the LA was considering evicting the family from their area. A Council Officer had been working with the family because they had expressed a wish to move into a house. However, recently, these negotiations had begun to unravel. In November 2001 the Council had gone to Court to obtain a re-possession Order. In the Summer of 2002 the family were awaiting removal from the LA. The cycle of enforced removal for this family continued.

Case Study C
On 17 July 2000 a single caravan was stationed outside the entrance to the local permanent Gypsy/Traveller site. Its owner was a 19 year-old girl who was about to give birth. Her grandmother and aunt lived on the site. There was no room on site for any more caravans. The family claimed that health forms had not been issued (as per Circular 18/94) to the daughter (although it appears that her condition might have been taken into account as the caravan had not been forcibly removed).

On 7 August two more caravans arrived and were stationed on the opposite side of the road. When I visited the site on 9 August 2000 the daughter, after a difficult labour had had the baby by caesarean section. She had been discharged from hospital on 8 August 2000 and her parents with siblings had come to look after her. The daughter's caravan was moved from one side of the road to the other to join her parents' vehicles. The family had been issued with a Court Order S24 and the Court hearing had been arranged for 11 August 2000. The mother said that her daughter was not fit to leave since she was suffering from post-natal depression, the baby had contracted an eye infection and the mid-wife was still visiting. The family was using the grandmother's facilities on the site. The midwife had written a letter to the LA to say that the mother and child were unfit to travel. The mother delivered this, together with a letter asking for leave to remain, to the Court before the hearing. The family did not attend the Court hearing on 11 August 2000. The Judge granted the family another 48 hours on the site. The day before the Court hearing the police had visited the family (reportedly in three police cars) and quizzed the daughter as to when she would be leaving, saying that they would return. The daughter had been very distressed by this visit.

In informal conversation with her mother, I was told that she had put her name down on the LA waiting list for a house 'a long time ago', but it had been taken off when she had gone to live on a site up north to look after her sick in-laws. When they died the family had left the site because they didn't like it and began travelling again, moving from site to site. The mother said that she 'would like to settle somewhere and if there was a house with a place for the caravan' she 'would be happy'. She said the family travelled because 'there was nowhere to settle permanently'. She wanted to be near her parents who were now elderly and had health problems. She asked if she would get a house if she went to the Housing Department. I took her there. Because she had not been in contact her name had been removed from the list. The mother told the Officer that she was about to be evicted from the unauthorised site and that the family would become homeless. The Officer offered her a place on a site in the adjacent Local Authority. The daughter refused to go there. Once a refusal had been made the Housing Officer claimed that the family were voluntarily homeless and that nothing more could be done for them. The mother was told by the Officer that she 'wouldn't want to go into a house'. The only alternative for the family was to return to the road.

After the Court hearing on the 11 August, the bailiffs arrived on the 14 August. They were not unsympathetic. However, they said that they would evict them on Thursday. The family left on Wednesday and temporarily 'disappeared'. I was informed a few days later that they had camped near the entrance to the local University not far from the permanent site. They said that they had spent the last few days at the motorway service station car park but it had been dirty, noisy and not suitable for the baby. They said they wanted to stay in the area until the daughter had had her final check-up with the midwife.

I was present when the University served a Repossession Order on the family. The matter was dealt with amicably and both sides behaved as if this was a matter of course. After some negotiation with the University the family was 'allowed' to stay until the beginning of September. The sites that the family had used were kept clean and tidy - they were just conspicuous. The University contacted Social Services on their behalf 'to see if there was any advice or assistance they or the Borough Council could offer and which could be passed on to the family. Other than being 'happy to see them on request' neither agency was able to offer the family 'anything that would be immediately useful'. The family left on the date agreed with the University. As a result both sites used by the family were 'secured' so that they could not be used again.

Case Study D

A recent planning application for a private (Gypsy/Traveller) caravan site in the north of the County was first refused on the grounds of contravention of the Development Plan on 4 January 2002. Prior to the Planning Meeting local residents had expressed their 'fears' via the local media and had established a defence group even though the applicants had not identified themselves as Gypsies/Travellers. The applicants were not at the Planning Meeting; no-one spoke in defence of the application and one local Councillor opposed it. The Planning Committee took less than ten minutes to reject the application, although there appeared to be few Planning grounds to do so: the site was not in the Green Belt, neither was the application retrospective and the site was one of mixed use. The family had hired a Planning Consultant and had expressed a wish to remain. When the first application was refused it was withdrawn, amendments were made and the project was resubmitted. The Council's Planning Committee had no alternative but to approve the application.

As planning applications go this one was not exceptional. Neither was the initial response of the Planning Committee. What was exceptional was that the family had followed the correct planning procedure. It was not a retrospective application and the family were not living on the land when the application was made. Had a Planning Consultant not been involved then the family might have given up at the first refusal and moved on. The decision, however, was not well received by local residents, something the media was keen to report.

SUMMARY

This and the previous chapter have attempted to show how Policy and practice are bonded together: Policy often becomes whatever is 'doable' or workable in practice. However, in many instances, expediency can become 'The Policy' and management becomes a euphemism for muddling through - perfected to 'a science' by some LAs (after Lindblom 1995).

Of late, and currently (2012) National Policy has been a framework for managing the issue at the local level, rather than finding mutually acceptable and workable solutions. At the time of writing the Thesis (in 2003), an impasse had been reached, which, without major adjustments and compromises on both sides, would be sustained. The Good Practice Guide (1998) and its amendments were about management and exemplified the ways in which national policy and local practice converge. It is questionable how far the amalgamation and sifting of everyday poor practice in terms of non-toleration, non-settlement, removal and exclusion can be recycled as good practice and advocated as 'good management'. The danger here is the creation of 'Policy monsters' (Majone and Widavsky 1995:147) whereby the 'right' or envisaged outcomes do not materialise but worst case scenarios become 'accepted' over time (ibid:152). At times it was clear that National and Local Policy did not always 'fit', or in some cases was ignored at the local level – and this practice appeared to be written off at the National level.

The fieldwork revealed that all the operational mechanisms listed by Stoker (1991) – 'negotiation, persuasion, manipulation, regulation and coercion' were used in Staffordshire to varying degrees in the management of mobile groups, which in the main were employed to remove and to prevent non-settlement. Whilst the overall group of Gypsies/Travellers appeared to be separated crudely into the settled ('the good') and the mobile ('the bad') there were no mechanisms to sift through the latter group. The assumption re the mobile grouping was that none wished to settle and neither were they worthy of being integrated – unless they were prepared to legally argue their case.

Paralleling these mechanisms were the 'strategies and tactics' used by LAs to resist any National Government pressure and control (after Bardach 1995:137). To ensure removal, most LAs played the game by interpreting and applying the negative aspects of the rules. If Gypsies/Travellers had a better knowledge of the rules then challenges could be made. However, LAs did little, at the time, to familiarise families with their rights or the rules of engagement, thus LAs were able to maintain the upper hand. Resistance was interpreted as a nuisance not to be tolerated – families were viewed as squatters on land – rather than as citizens, or residents who had lived in and/or had resorted to the area for decades, whose needs were not being met.

Although Policy to encourage self-help and privatisation has been in place since 1994, local practices in Staffordshire (and beyond) coupled with lack of knowledge and lack of adequate means, in many cases, tended to preclude Gypsies/Travellers from availing themselves of opportunities. This means that national policy has not been able to be translated into more positive action at the local level. It was only in the last five years of the 21st Century that Gypsy/Traveller families have been awarded the same security of tenure on LA authorised sites as families living in social housing (Circular 1/2006). Unfortunately, this could be short-lived since the Conservative-Lib Dem coalition administration appear to be attempting to revoke this via various Policies to curb and regulate those living in social housing (eg 'the Bedroom Tax'). This means that 'unless officials in the implementing agencies are strongly committed to the achievement of the objectives, then the attainment of statutory objectives that seek to significantly modify target group behaviour is unlikely' (Sabbatier and Mazmanian 1995: 160). It is necessary, then, that any ambivalence and/or lack of commitment at the National level between toleration/non-toleration, provision/exclusion needs to be resolved, since this provides loop-holes for some LAs.

Stewart (1983:102) claims that 'different skills, values and assumptions and beliefs within a Local Authority are united to constitute an ideology which powerfully influences action'. The 'personality' of any LA is an amalgamation of the individual agents operating within it and carrying out its functions in a manner acceptable to those who have authority over them. Given the hierarchy within such organisations it would not be a quantum leap for individual influence to be negative as well as positive. Until the last decade and the mantras of joined-up thinking and partnership working, many Departments within LAs operated as almost separate entities bordering on the medieval fief system. Old habits and attitudes die hard. Sanctions afforded by national policy to induce LAs to comply can take on a life of their own to become 'the Policy' – as designation demonstrated.

The irony appeared to be that, as with the issue of Policy, Officers paid and elected *were* aware of the practical solutions to the issue and since many of these were enshrined in National Policy, Circulars and Guidance. Some Councils chose to seemingly ignore, or worked around these. The cost of implementing Policy was often used as an excuse for negative game play along with 'fears', often irrational, with regard to outcomes which masked a deeper, historical irrationality which has attached to Gypsies/Travellers over the centuries ensuring that the higher costs of removal and eviction are the accepted preference. Gypsies/Travellers equally expressed 'fears' of majority society and its influences on their lives preferring exclusion to integration. It appeared that most families recognised the futility of engaging with LAs. Such circles of fear, feelings of pointlessness coupled with mutual assumptions and misperceptions, preclude useful dialogue/negotiation between Gypsies/Travellers and officialdom. Until such attitudes are changed, Policy will remain difficult to translate into practice.

One of the biggest obstacles to implementation of Policy appeared to be local and vocal constituents, often a minority who opposed any kind of settlement or integration. In a majority of the Councils in Staffordshire little appeared to be being done with regard to changing attitudes and promoting good relations between different ethnic groups. Such attitudes were present in the Council Chamber, particularly around the issue of Planning, where personal prejudices and party politics were allowed to override professionalism reasonableness and fairness and perhaps where it was unlikely that families making an application would not be able to supply any capital for S106 Agreements. Thus little might be gained from granting any planning permission. Whether the amended 1976 Race Relations Act 2000 and the more recent Equalities Act (2010) will provide a more positive 'third way' to facilitate the implementation of positive Policy for minority and disadvantaged groups, remains to be seen.

The next chapter will examine service delivery and equality of opportunity for Gypsies/Travellers in Staffordshire. Attainable - or forever a 'working towards'?

CHAPTER NINE
EQUALITY OF OPPORTUNITY AND SERVICE DELIVERY

Chapters 6, 7 and 8 have attempted to show the way that Policy and practice intertwine to produce numerous structuring structures which gradually become mutually supportive and influential in regulating individual behaviour and, ultimately, 'a relationship' between Authority and the target group bringing about a group formation. In a liberal society (which the UK claims to be) service delivery is attached to Policy and practice and thus may not be divorced easily from equality of opportunity (EO). Policies, practices and service delivery can act, with the aid of the media, to maintain (and even to establish) boundaries and stereotypes, creating 'the deserving' and 'non-deserving' within society unless notions of fairness and equality of opportunity are utilised to temper and occasion self-reflection. That said, ultimately it is Authority, with power group input, which decides who is equal - or more equal - and to whom services will be delivered first.

The rhetoric on diversity and its management at the time of writing the Thesis permeated many Policy documents (see Chapters 6 and 7) in an attempt to include individuals from legally defined disadvantaged groups so that they could, in practice, equitably access 'opportunity' in terms of access to goods, facilities and services. To this end a duty has been placed on LAs to promote equality of opportunity (Race Relations Act 1976: S.71 and its Amendment 2000). The 2000 amendment to the Act extended the duty to other statutory and voluntary organisations in an attempt to address exclusion as a result of 'institutional racism'. This was important given the evolving role of LAs which obliged them to contract out services to arms-length Agencies on their behalf. However, the quality and equality of service delivery are predicated on an (agreed) understanding of equality of opportunity and increasingly, notions of citizenship (Heater 1999; Kirton and

Greene 2000) and responsibility (Lister 1998). Exclusion of some groups and individuals from the resource queue can occur via a series of mechanisms and games (interactions) which range from the simple to the convoluted (Chapter 10 will elaborate on these phenomena).

EQUALITY OF OPPORTUNITY

Positioning EO

In the 1980s equality centred around fair and equal shares and equal treatment (Dine and Watt 1996; Boxhill (1990). Equal respect and value became added (Young 1992) as the notion of responsibility and citizenship came to prominence. Positive action in UK and positive discrimination in the USA for some defined groups were advocated as a means to achieve this (Jewson and Mason 1992) but seemed difficult concepts to grasp particularly in the employment arena and by Trade Unions at a time of high unemployment, who interpreted positive action as 'quotas' (positive discrimination was deemed unlawful under Irish and EU equality law (Employment Equality Agency (Dublin) 1998). As EU Directives gradually took effect, and as immigration from the New Commonwealth countries declined, interpretation of EO in UK has moved from *equitable division of resources* (1970s/1980s) to equality of *access to opportunities* (1990s/2000s) as advocated by Dine and Watt (1996) and Cairns (1988). Contract compliance changed to competitive tendering and a new vocabulary and discourse which centred around 'human rights', 'duties and obligations' and 'responsibilities' (Lister 1998), 'citizenship' and the issues surrounding the definition and role of 'the citizen' in the 21st Century (Heater 1999; Kymicka 2000) emerged. As the welfare state downsizes, individual responsibility has become extended and in 2013 is being supported by economic independence from the State and personal responsibility for Health, Welfare and Higher Education. However, being propelled from subject to citizen might take some time to establish in the minds of the UK population. Marshall and Bottomore (1992) assisted the debate by identifying three types of citizenship: civil, political and social. Heater (1999:2) sums up the discourse surrounding Marshall's view of citizenship ie civil citizenship as 'establishing rights against the State' and necessary for personal freedom (ibid:13 and after TH Marshall (1950); political rights – the right to vote and to stand for political office; and social citizenship as 'establishing rights provided by the State (eg Education, Healthcare, Welfare etc.). Thus like EO, the notion of citizenship and individual responsibility are also expanding.

Gradually, and as the nature of discrimination has become understood (in terms of racisms (Anthias and Yuval-Davis 1993), and as ethnicities (Hall 1992) which can cross-cut other perceived disadvantages, equality now embraces a plethora of other exclusions along the fissures of gender, disability, sexual orientation and more latterly religion, which have been harmonised under the umbrella of diversity. In England and Wales diversity is seen via the five categories mentioned above, whilst Ireland has combined these into one Equalities Authority which 'works horizontally across many grounds' (Harvey 2002:18). This method of working was advocated and encouraged by the EU Commission so that today (2013) England, too, has its own Equalities Commission (after the Equalities Act 2010).[104] In many ways this has served to remove the sting from race and ethnic differences since these are now in competition with so many others.

In an attempt to combat discriminatory practices, service deliverers, from the 1970s were obliged to draw up Equality of Opportunity Policies (EOPs) as both statements of intent and as a blue print for action and practice. Diversity management agendas were promoted nationally. Success however, depended on good EO policies, good practice, monitoring service delivery and political will (Kirton and Greene 2000; Rees 1998; Kandola and Fullerton 1994) if a 'long' agenda (Cockburn 1989; Colling and Dickens 1998) of structural change was to be effected as opposed to a 'short' agenda of tinkering and tailoring (Rees 1998). It is recognised, too, that the adoption of a policy does not necessarily lead to its effective implementation (Jenkins and Solomos 1987; Lustgarten and Edwards 1992). Thomas and Krishnarayan (1994) found that in the early 1990s, of the 135 LAs surveyed, few were properly implementing their EOPs. This led Young (1992:267) to conclude that the 'history of EOPs is what people have learned to say rather than being a history of concrete accomplishments'. Indeed, in 2001 the Audit

---

[104] Ireland's Equalities Commission protects nine classes: gender, marital status, sexual orientation, religious beliefs, age disability race and members of the Travelling community. The commissioned EU Report suggested that countries such as Britain were 'considering making their approaches more horizontal.

Commission found that 'around two-fifths of Councils in England and Wales had not reached the first level (Level 1) of the CRE standard on Racial Equality. The Commission suggested 'commitment', 'involving users', and 'mainstreaming equality, diversity and 'sustainability'.

Although all Policies 'work to some extent' (Glazer 1975) one of the greatest stumbling blocks to the successful implementation of EOPs has been understanding and agreeing a workable definition of equality of opportunity (Young 1987; Jewson and Mason 1992) that would be acceptable to all and which would not infringe the 'autonomy' of others (Dine and Watt 1996). There was varying opinion as to its meaning and intent. For some it was bound up with benevolence whilst for others it was viewed as a human right (Jenkins and Solomos 1987; Banton 1994). For those to whom the EOP would be applied it was more a matter of changing entrenched colonial/imperial/class attitudes which had combined over time with embedded procedures within organisations and institutions (Ollearnshaw 1983) to produce an equity/equality blindness. This had implications for resource distribution. For some these were more a matter of entitlement - ie 'the rights which in *theory* citizens should have; provision is what in practice citizens are *allowed* to have' (Heater 1999:21). Bound up with this was the notion of the deserving and the non-deserving, the latter being relegated to the end of any resource queue or excluded altogether. Whilst Policy as statements of intent might be commendable and admirable, the practices which they inform tend to lag far behind to the point where service delivery as an outcome is often frustrated. This gives rise to a tiered society of rich and poor which, if taken to extremes, can be a threat to national stability in that 'too great a disproportion weakens any State' (Glennerster 2000:160; Parker 1975). The spates of riots around UK, the most recent in August 2011 were a cause for concern.

At the time of completing the Thesis (in 2003), an attempt was being made to present EOPs as business cases to be embedded in any agency structure with 'Opportunity 2000' and 'Race for Opportunity' attempting to promote diversity as an untapped resource (Kirton and Greene 2000) with employers rather than the State taking responsibility to deliver this policy. At the time the then Commission for Racial Equality (CRE)

'Standard for Racial Equality for Employers' (1995) was a blueprint for good employment practices which a few LAs in Staffordshire said that they had begun to adopt. Whether this would lead to socially just outcomes for Gypsies/Travellers in Staffordshire or, indeed, nationally, remained to be seen.

This chapter will now proceed to examine the notions of EO, the way it is understood and translated into practice, and service delivery in Staffordshire and the game play employed. The data was collected via fieldwork, interviews and documentation research between 1999-2001.

Equality of Opportunity - The Staffordshire Scenario

All Councils in Staffordshire subscribed to EO in theory to a greater or lesser extent. Some had members of staff who dealt with EO issues as part of another job, whilst larger LAs had special units with dedicated Officers. Interviews were conducted to see how theory was understood and translated into practice. Of the ten Staffordshire LAs, five EO Officers agreed to be interviewed, one Officer sent in a cursory written response, four sent their EOPs, and two, despite telephone calls and letters requesting them to do so, did not respond to a postal questionnaire or forward their EOP. The telephone manner of some did not inspire confidence in any written Council statement on EO. The questionnaire for EO Officers centred on their Council's meaning of equality and EO and how this related to Gypsies/Travellers. This was supported by interviewing Officers who dealt with Gypsies/Travellers on a regular and practical basis.

EO Policy

All Councils claimed that they had an EO Policy in place. Some Councils were more advanced within the EOP cycle than others – one Council said that they were just writing theirs. However, not all Officers and Councillors were aware of its existence (see Table 9.1). The majority claimed that the Policy had been in place 'for a long time'. It was also claimed that the EOP related to employment and to internal personnel issues. Some recognised that it should permeate all areas of a council's work – although some Officers

Table 9.1 Does This Council Have an Equality of Opportunities Policy

	Yes	No	Don't Know
Senior Officers	10	2	-
Junior Officers	7	2	2
Leaders of Council	5	-	1
Council Members	4	-	-
Total	26	4	3

thought it 'unworkable'. From interviews with the five EOP Officers and from the eight EOP statements submitted the policies appeared comprehensive covering employment, service delivery and practice and access to services, special needs and harassment and bullying. Some Policy statements were impressive, ranging from overarching statements of intent to highly prescriptive procedural documents covering recruitment, staff behaviour and discipline. All Councils said that they offered induction courses to new staff and regular training. In some LAs this had been extended to elected Members. The County and Stoke-on-Trent as Unitary Authorities had embarked on the Equality Standards trail which included race – although the majority of respondents were aware that EOP included race. The EO Officers interviewed said that although EO had always been on the agenda, the Macpherson Report (1999) had concentrated the minds of LAs to 'encourage' new interest. The European Parliament, too, had conveyed its determination via the European Social Policy Agenda, by requiring all Member States to submit an Action Plan by June 2001 which would cover a two-year period and would define indicators and monitoring mechanisms capable of measuring progress. This information would feed in to the EU Strategy on race and equality to be completed by 2003. This would account for Staffordshire LAs having some form of Plan by 2000/2002, which some were working on at the time. Table 9.2 charts the then current progress. It also shows the variability in compliance, some having begun the process late and as a response to National Government direction, and underachievement. Four LAs had not achieved Level 1 of the CRE Equality Standard which indicated that there was not a policy in place. For example, Newcastle-under-Lyme in terms of its Local Target BV2 the target was 'yes' but the performance between 1999 2002 was 'no'. The target level for 2000 -2001 was 2 and the target for 2001-2002 was 1 – neither of which was achieved. South Staffordshire claimed that it would not be adopting BV 2 – the CRE Equality Standard, yet it had the highest number of Gypsy/Traveller caravans in the

County. So what *did* EO mean to each LA, did Officers and Members agree on its meaning and did their EOP translate efficiently into practice?

All EO Officers saw their EOP permeating all LA functions. Although one LA did not apply it to service delivery, they were about to rewrite the policy to do so. Most had a harassment/bullying Policy in place or were about to ratify one. Overall, and at the time of interviewing, the EOPs were strongly aligned to recruitment and employment procedures – at least in theory. The term 'inclusion' was widely used in all forward plan documents. References to 'diverse needs' were also prevalent as a way to 'eliminate unfair discrimination' (Staffordshire County Council EOP). However, terms such as living *within* the borough/district, 'all sections of *the community*' and 'in consultation with *local communities*' were stressed which tended to 'ring fence' those eligible for inclusion. Such sentiments serve to reinforce the close kin and friendship networks and

Table 9.2 Best Value Performance Plan Indicators for Staffordshire in Terms of BV1, BV2, BV17a and BV17b.

LA	Indicators and Results			
	BV1*	BV2**	BV17a^	BV17b^^
Staffordshire County Council	yes	2	1.2	2.2
Staffordshire Moorlands	yes	0	2.0	0.5
Stoke-on-Trent	yes	2	0.8	1.4
Newcastle-under-Lyme	yes	0	0.3	0.6
Stafford	yes	0	1.6	0.9
Cannock	yes	1	0.6	1.4
Lichfield	yes	1	2.6	n/a
Tamworth	yes	1	1.5	1.1
East Staffordshire	yes	2	2.4	2.8
South Staffordshire	yes	0	1.1	0.8

Source: ODPM 3/1/03

Key: BV1*   Local Agenda 21 adoption of a Strategy Plan for sustainable development of local communities.

BV2**   Level of CRE Equality of Standard achieved.

BV17a^   Percentage of staff from ethnic minorities compared with percentage of economically active ethnic minorities in the local area.

BV 17b^^   Percentage of economically active people from ethnic minorities in the LA area.

ties which, whilst they bind communities together and create belonging, also create notions of the outsider and the non-belonger.

EO Policy into Practice – An Understanding of EO

When Council Officers with responsibility for Gypsy/Traveller issues were asked if EO extended to service delivery the majority thought it did (see Table 9.3). Two Senior Officers qualified this by stating that it was *supposed* to extend to service delivery or that it only extended to certain services. The overall impression was one of lack of clarity with regard to the scope of EO.

Table 9.3 Does Equality of Opportunity Extend to Service Delivery

	Yes	No	Don't Know	Other
Senior Officer	8	2	-	2
Junior Officers	6	3	2	-
Leaders of Council	5	-	1	-
Member of Council	3	-	1	-
Total	**22**	**5**	**4**	**2**

Respondents were then asked for their interpretation of EO and multiple responses were allowed (see Table 9.4). All Senior Officers spoke in terms of equal access and equal treatment. One Senior Officer spoke of each group needing 'to be aware of others' needs and rights'. Another claimed that 'all people no matter what their gender or creed, have a right to work and to be treated properly' (Senior LA Officer Interview). Information was

Table 9.4 What Do You Understand by EO?

Employment	7
Equal Treatment	11
Access to Services	6
Non Exclusion	2
Regard for Human Dignity	1
Don't Know	2

offered that 'existing staff are given vacant positions to cut costs' (Elected Member Interview). This was reiterated by another Member in a different LA who claimed that 'everyone has a chance to advance in this Council … we put in-house people in rather than bring new people in'. Only one Leader of Council approached the notion of positive action by stating that the same opportunities to apply for jobs 'existed as for any other person' and 'the ability to train if necessary and the right to be trained' existed – which recognised and acknowledged that not everyone started from the same position (Leader of Council Interview).

The impression given from the above Tables was that LAs did not have a clear idea or understanding of EO. Some felt that it was unachievable. It also became obvious that some LAs had overestimated their achievements in that practice appeared to fall far short of Policy and there seemed to be no mechanisms which ensured that outcomes matched Policy.[105] Indeed, at the time, although some Councils had an EOP in place it was not monitored to see if it was working satisfactorily. Thus the conclusion drawn was that for some Councils this was just another paper exercise and a box ticked and that Policy written, appeared to be both the beginning and the end of the exercise in all but a few LAs in Staffordshire.

Who is Included in EOP?

Respondents were then asked if Gypsies/Travellers were included in their Council's EOP (see Table 9.5). Some Officers claimed that Gypsies/Travellers would be included although they were not especially mentioned. Others claimed that they had a specific

Table 9.5 Are Gypsies/Travellers Included in This Council's EOP

	Yes	No	Don't Know	Other
Senior Officers	4	1	3	4
Junior Officers	5	1	5	-
Leaders of Council	3	-	1	2
Members of Council	2	-	1	1
Total	**14**	**2**	**10**	**7**

Policy for the treatment of Gypsies/Travellers – but this mainly related to eviction procedures. Additional information came in statements such as, 'The rule is for everyone', (Leader of Council Interview) and 'Arguably, yes' (Senior LA Officer Interview) or other more cryptic remarks such as, 'It wouldn't affect Travellers in terms of jobs but any dealings with this Office it would' (Senior Officer Interview), to 'EOP

---

[105] One Council claimed in its official newspaper that it had achieved Level 2 in its Race Equality Scheme and that it was now embarking on Level 3. When this was checked it became clear that not only was this 'news' within the LA but also it had barley achieved Level 1.

has never been considered (for Gypsies/Travellers) they're just a band of people who wander around' (Junior Officer Interview). The yes responses referred, primarily, to those settled on sites, although there was some acceptance (in theory since this did not appear to be born out in practice) that those on the road could be included if certain criteria were met.

The implications of the above responses were that despite the rhetoric or the imagined outcome, Gypsies/Travellers had appeared to have slipped under the EOP net. Additionally, during the course of interviewing even Senior Officers it was clear that any form of positive action for Gypsies/Travellers would be construed as awarding them an unfair advantage.

Equality in Practice
The next set of questions examined how far EOP translated into practice. Respondents were asked if any Gypsies/Travellers were employed within the Council (see Table 9.6). A majority thought not. This did not appear to cause concern. Additional information from LA Officers was: 'I don't know but I don't think so'; 'We don't ask if they are Gypsies/Travellers when they apply for jobs'; 'I don't think we keep records on that'. Gypsies/Travellers interviewed, who said that they had applied for jobs (not necessarily

Table 9.6 Are Any Gypsies/Travellers Employed by This Council

	Yes	No	Don't Know
Senior Officers	-	7	5
Junior Officers	-	7	4
Leaders of Council	-	2	4
Members of Council	-	3	1
Total	**0**	**19**	**14**

in the Council) claimed that they had been refused when it was discovered (from their site address) that they were Gypsies/Travellers (Gypsy/Traveller Interview).

The response to the question 'Does this Council employ Gypsies/Travellers, was unanimously 'no' – all Council respondents were asked this question. This was qualified mainly with, 'As Gypsies/Travellers were not a category on the EO form then they wouldn't know'. EO Officers who responded also claimed that Gypsies/Travellers did not apply for jobs. One EO Officer stated that the Council went out to ethnic minority groups to discover why they did not apply for jobs. This Council also ran workshops to explain application procedures, assisted with form filling and interview procedures and outlined the standards expected. Officers, however did not visit Gypsy/Traveller sites, neither did Councils have a positive action plan for Gypsies/Travellers. The majority of EOs interviewed did not know the number of Gypsies/Travellers within their administrative district, and had not heard of the DTLR/ODPM Gypsy/Traveller twice yearly caravan Count. There were no plans to attract Gypsy/Traveller applicants. One Social Inclusion Officer claimed not to be aware of the Gypsy/Traveller site within the borough.

Officers were then asked if Gypsies/Travellers would be welcomed as small businessmen – given the then encouragement offered to other small businesses in the County/LA. The response was unanimously negative. Further information was volunteered:

> They are not asked about business. We are not staffed to make that kind of enquiry.
> We see them as people causing a problem.
> No, they are not welcome here.

When asked if their Council was taking any positive action to assist those families who wished to settle in the area the response was generally negative. Where permanent Council sites existed, respondents were asked if Gypsies/Travellers had the same tenure rights as house dwellers. The general response was 'no, they rent a licensed pitch but they don't have the same security of tenure (LA Officer Interview). The explanation for this was that, 'Travellers regard themselves as being able to leave when they want to. They don't have security of tenure, but they are statutorily protected from eviction. We have to give them notice to leave and if they don't we obtain an Order from the Court. When the site was first opened they said, 'We're not staying here'. But most have become permanent (LA Officer Interview). Some families and members of the same family have been on the same site for 20-30 years (Gypsy/Traveller Interviews and conversations). However, if the site land was needed by the Council for another use, then the families would be removed. At the time of interviewing it was discovered that one Council site did not even have a proper licence.

Overall, it would appear that whilst EO and EOPs include Gypsies/Travellers in theory it does not necessarily embrace them in practice. Mobile groups particularly appear to be excluded – regarded as someone else's responsibility. Examining this further, respondents were asked if mobile groups had rights. Several viewpoints were expressed within and between Councils. The yes responses were qualified thus:

> Settled groups have the same rights as council tenants.
>
> They would have the same responsibilities and rights to access services as anyone else.
>
> Those settled are treated the same as any other member of the community. The policy is the same for all whether resident on sites or not.
>
> We recognise that some Gypsy families are permanent and we treat them the same as anyone else.
>
> They are treated the same as anyone else.
>
> In planning they have the same rights as any other mobile home dweller … . They don't want traditional housing they want sites where they can move on and off.

The no responses were qualified as follows:

> No trespasser has a right to land.
>
> Mobile groups can't be treated the same because the issue is different.
>
> Rights are not written down in policy documents.
>
> They are passing through so it's transitional help.
>
> They should have, but they are not terribly well considered within this authority.

The tension between statements and between the two sets of responses is noted, as is the tension between policy and practice and service delivery. What was most notable was the lack of awareness in some Officers that their practices could actually be contravening not only Guidance and Circulars but also the Law. Some in charge of practice and service delivery did not appear to know what their Council's policies were: EOPs, discrimination laws and human rights seemed somewhat dispensable with regard to families not living in an area on authorised sites. And this seemed to hark back to medieval times where responsibility was taken only for those deemed to belong to a particular area, the rest were removed. Thus two groups of Gypsies/Travellers were being created - the settled who were more acceptable and had some entitlements and the mobile who were not.[106] It was also questionable, at the time, whether the settled families were receiving and or claiming all their entitlements.

Monitoring Policy

Respondents were asked if their EOP was regularly monitored (see Table 9.7) Validity was checked by comparing the EO Officers' responses with those of paid and elected Officers and against their own Council's EO policy documents.

Table 9.7 Is the Council's EOP Regularly Monitored

	Yes	No	Don't Know
Senior Officers	4	5	3
Junior Officers	3	4	4
Leaders of Council	3	2	1
Memebers of Council	3	-	1
Total	**13**	**11**	**9**

Some EO Officers qualified their yes responses with:

> It's monitored re jobs. This is a reactive rather than a proactive process at present.

> It's stringently monitored with regard to employment. The District Auditor comes in each year to do that. Service delivery is more difficult to monitor. That tends to be a departmental responsibility.

> We analyse the information for each job. That information is then sent to each department to see how the job offers are being made.

> Yes by me (Leader of Council)

whilst the no responses were qualified with:

> No clear monitoring is done at the moment. The whole policy framework is being devised this year.

---

[106] It appeared that mobile groups tended to be excluded.

We have no full time staff to monitor it.

It's only just been set up so it's not done properly yet.

Not totally

It's monitored by word of mouth – if we get complaints.

There are no set procedures for monitoring any of the planning outcomes.

It was noted via documentary research that, for example, one Borough Council in its response to Indicator ACP1-A3b (1999-2000) 'Does the Authority formally monitor how it carried out this policy' stated in its published performance Plan 2002-2003 that their performance was 'no' for the years 1999-2002 although their target was 'yes'. This Indicator was removed altogether in 2002-2003. It appeared that in Staffordshire the Unitary Authorities tended to be more conscientious re monitoring this Policy than their Borough or District counterparts. It also appeared that provided the paper work was correct, the Audit Commission did not appear to interfere unduly in LA affairs and where any expenditure was not incurred. Also if Gypsies/Travellers were not entered as an ethnic group on the Local Authority's EO forms then they did not appear to be a consideration and were generally not included as part of the monitoring process. The perceived fuzziness around ethnicity seemed to inform procedures here (see Chapter 4). Few LAs travelled the extra mile to redress these omissions/slippages. All EO Officers interviewed stated (at the time) that ethnic groups were under-represented in their work force and that Gypsies/Travellers did not feature at all. This did not appear to be of great concern, particularly as families, if not employed in conventional ways, would seek alternative means and ways in order to survive – appeared to be the assumption. Whilst this could be construed as a dereliction of duty, it was pointed out that this duty possibly sank under the weight of all other duties (LA Officer personal comment).

The Bi-annual Caravan Count was one way of monitoring Gypsy/Traveller mobility. LAs were asked if any other records were kept (see Table 9.8). Only one LA claimed that it kept records to assist them with service delivery. However, in the main, records which emphasised events rather than people – for example, evictions from Council land, illegal encampments and complaints tended to be kept. Health and education records were kept as were police records and land clearance records after encampments. Some LAs and sites kept more records than others and some sites kept records of families and

Table 9.8 Which Records on Gypsies./Travellers Does Your Council Keep

Type of Record	Number of Councils
Evictions from council land	4
Site files	3
Bi-annual count	3
Illegal encampments	2
Complaints	2
Environmental health	2
Site records	2
None	3

NB: Private sites would not be required to keep the same records as LA sites

of vehicle registration numbers also photographs of illegal encampments – usually for Court proceedings. At the time (2002-2003) LA and Police Officers said that such records that were kept were not generated systematically or as a matter of course. At the time of writing the Thesis, no family names were taken, except for Court proceedings, although some LAs said that they would consider taking more details where illegal encampments were concerned – ie number of caravans on site, where they had come from and where they were going. This information was already being collected in Scotland (The Scottish Executive 2002). It was difficult to discover if this information from the various agencies was shared. One could only assume that the Inter Agency Group established in North Staffordshire to deal with Gypsy/Traveller issues, shared such information.

EOP Self Evaluation

Respondents were asked to evaluate their EOP in relation to Gypsies/Travellers. Within the ten Councils the marks out of ten ranged from zero to ten. Leaders and Members of Council and junior Officers tended to give the highest scores, whilst Senior Officers awarded the lowest scores. The number who said that they did not know or 'no comment' was significant. Some of the highest scores related to EO and employment.

Where the score was ten, Officers pointed out that this mark was for the Policy overall and not specifically in relation to Gypsies/Travellers. Scores given specifically for EOP in relation to Gypsies/Travellers were consistently lower ranging from zero to three. The accompanying comments exemplify any ambivalence and are worth recording below:

> I don't know that we're active in promoting EOP.
>
> Council is beginning to take these issues seriously.
>
> Those outside the law can't be treated equally.
>
> Policy is largely irrelevant. It's how you apply it that's relevant and whether you seek to meet the needs of individuals.

One Gypsy/Traveller responded, 'Because we're Gypsies they just don't care'. However, although this may be true in one sense, who LAs care for is often defined in legislation.

SERVICE DELIVERY

Elcock (1994:296) claimed that the central reason for the existence of LAs was to ensure the democratic control of service provision. An arrangement also exists between LAs and their constituents re service delivery in exchange for payment of local and national taxes/charges. With regard to Gypsy/Traveller families, even on settled sites, there is a local assumption that they do not pay tax or the Community Charge. This assumption tends to preclude them, at least perceptually, from any entitlements which would apply to other members of the community who may, similarly, not pay tax or the Community Charge. This brings Parker's (1975) notion of 'free-riding' and 'fair distribution' into play. And whilst a blind eye is turned to some who free ride, it is not to others. Similarly, fair distribution is rendered to some but not to others and Gypsies/Travellers would appear, in the minds of some, to fall into the two latter categories. Although not enough is known, generally, about Gypsy/Traveller financial affairs, via interview it was found that in Staffordshire, where families were settled on sites, their dues were paid both to the LA and to the State.

Parker (ibid: x) claimed that 'in practice the distribution of goods and services in Britain' was 'associated very tenuously with need' and that 'needs have to be recognised before programmes are delivered to meet them' (ibid:3). Unfortunately, those with special needs were often overlooked in the past since for ease of operation, the system tended to be 'one size fits all' only. During the 1990s and early 2000s, and as groups and categories of people became sifted and sorted, difference and diversity have become the philosophical drivers to meet need. Whilst this might be admirable in theory, it is more difficult to deliver in practice and some groups can become excluded altogether. Most services are delivered to a particular address. However mobile Gypsies/Travellers who are assumed not to have a permanent place of residence, can be excluded from Health, Welfare and Education rights or have difficulty in accessing them.

The then LA Community Strategy directives were an attempt to oversee and to ensure the well-being of local communities. The term 'communities', however, presupposes insiders and outsiders. Mobile and even settled families have historically been designated outsider/non-belonger status and some are deemed non-deserving too. Protracted exclusion can result in disconnection from the social/economic hinterland and from service entitlement and provision - given that the rules for services and their delivery change constantly. There is also a presumption that LA services are delivered uniformly in terms of type and degree across the UK and that state agreed provision is always delivered. This is not always the case. Some Gypsy/Traveller exclusion is justified by some Councils on the grounds that they do not 'live' in the area. However, as the previous chapters have shown, if families are constantly moved on they could never 'live' in any area. And since no records are kept and no questions asked to see if they 'live' anywhere else, families may never be provided for, even where entitlements exist. Until recently (ie the last six years) needs assessment of Gypsy/Traveller accommodation, for example, was not considered. If Gypsy/Traveller need assessments were not undertaken then it would be difficult for LAs to know what their needs might be and what provision to make. If this information is not fed in at the local level then the needs of this grouping will never rise to make it onto national Agendas.

At the time, the Thesis suggested that needs assessments, delivery and persuasion needed to be targeted sensitively since not all services would be wanted, welcomed or needed. Raising awareness of need and what was available so that choices could be made were also necessary. Equally important are trained personnel to carry out such duties. At the time of interviewing in Staffordshire, none of the personnel interviewed who were dealing with Gypsies/Travellers, had had any special training. Site Wardens and Enforcement Officers tended to come via the police force, or debt collection. Only one Site Warden had had some experience of people management.

The fieldwork identified some of the services which would impact directly on Gypsy/Traveller families and which could have positive/negative effects depending on how they were delivered. Whilst many services are statutory, like Education, others are more demand-led such as Health and Social Welfare. These will now be discussed.

Positive Service Delivery for Gypsies/Travellers?

A National View of Site Provision

The ODPM circulated an Interim Report in 2002 focussing on the provision and management of Gypsy/Traveller sites which offered an overview of the situation in England (http://www.housing.odpm.gov.uk/information/gypsy/provision/01.htm). It claimed that 'site management was more intensive than for social housing' (ibid: Chapter 1.2). It also stated that overall '1000-2000 residential pitches' and '2000 -2500 transit stopping places' would be needed over the next 5 years (ibid) and that an expenditure of £16.78 million would be needed over the next five years to achieve the necessary provision levels. The Report also suggested a 'strong' National Government lead. At the time, 324 sites existed with 5005 pitches in England (ODPM January 2001) although the Interim Report of 2002 believed that this was an overestimate of provision.

Site Provision, Amenities and Management – The Staffordshire Scenario

Site Provision and Amenities: the fieldwork attempted to match actual provision with formal statements and perceived need. At the time of interviewing, none of the Staffordshire LAs had undertaken needs surveys of Gypsies/Travellers. Did LAs have any pro-vision for Gypsies/Travellers? Within Staffordshire there were around 300 caravans 'properly settled' (Senior LA Officer Interview) on 37 authorised sites, three of which had been created by LAs and were, until recently, Council run (see Chapter 1 on sites and Chapter 5 on numbers).[107] The County estimated, at the time, that there were around 200 pitches needed in order to meet accommodation provision, current and projected. For the purpose of service delivery, Gypsies/Travellers had been sub-divided into two groups – the settled (the deserving) and the mobile (the non-deserving).

Where sites had been provided respondents claimed that they met the basic needs of the residents in terms of electricity, running water, hard standing and bathroom and kitchen facilities provided in separate amenity blocks. Newcastle-under-Lyme and Stoke-on-Trent had provided a brick amenity block for each double pitch. Rubbish was collected weekly, each caravan had its own rubbish bin and skips were used for other waste material.

Stafford admitted that the facilities provided did not meet residents' needs and were in poor condition: they were port-a-cabins and more than twenty years old. Residents had complained over a long period of time about them and at the time of fieldwork they were about to be replaced. Residents had not been consulted on any refurbishment. The skips on site were emptied only when they were full. Stafford did not appear to know about the DTLR/ODPM grant aid scheme for refurbishment. When an application was made retrospectively it was rejected on the grounds that it was work in progress and that the site was not a permanent site with only a temporary permission.

Cannock claimed that it had undertaken a 'survey' of mobile groups who had expressed an interest in transit sites. However, the Council 'had not taken the matter any further' (Senior LA Officer Interview). Cannock had one private site, one permitted site with no amenities and regular unauthorised sites.

---

[107] Stoke City site at Linehouses, is run by the City Council in partnership with the (N)GC and the Site Warden, an Irish Traveller. Newcastle site, Cemetery Road, is run by Aspire Housing Association (formerly the Housing Department of the LA). The Stafford site at Glover Street, is run by Stafford Borough Council on behalf of the County Council.

On the three sites where LAs had an interest, residents paid for all their amenities. The rents were higher to cover the cost of refuse collecting, public lighting and grass cutting. The rate for a double pitch with an amenity block was then around £40-50 per week on some sites. Higher rates were also levied for water and electricity since these were metered to each pitch via a pre-payment card, supplied by the Site Warden. Residents permanently settled on sites, also paid Council Tax. Apart from the Stafford site, these sites were self-financing with some having a healthy surplus. It was said that any 'profits' from the site were ring-fenced for the site. None of the sites had play areas for children and appeared as self-contained communities separated from the mainstream by combinations of fencing, open space, planting and wire.

The views of residents living on LA sites who were interviewed were:

> The lane is so bad doctors, ambulances and the postman don't come. We've rung up so many times but they comes down and says its nothing to do with us

> I've got everything here, bath, toilet, washing machine, electricity. It's clean. It's okay on here.

> This is a good site for me. Wouldn't get no better. We're away from people's houses.

> Problem is all you can see is wire. It just looks like a prisoner of war camp. It doesn't look homely does it? You look out your back door and you've got a ten foot wall at the back and this shed. (the amenity block). It should be at the back then we'd have space. It's their fault we've got a fire hazard … but they just don't listen.

> For the old on this site, going into the shed in winter is not very nice. They've all got arthritis I should think half of it is that. They should have somewhere warm to go to and wash. Even the young ones have got 'flu' all the time, so I don't know how the old ones cope. I don't like going out into that shower, but I force myself. You come out shivering and you have to run from here to there and you've got 'flu' straight away. Because we're Travellers they think we're going to tolerate it, but we're not. We've been to school, we know what our rights are. We've been waiting 21 years.

Whilst some were content with their p(lot) there was an indication that some residents' needs were not being met and that some residents were more aware than others that they were being disadvantaged.

Site Management:

Granting licenses rather than tenancies pertained in Staffordshire, since this was deemed more suited to Gypsy/Traveller needs. The ODPM Report of 2002 suggested that if this was where inequality existed, then it should be corrected. The Report also highlighted housing benefit anomalies for families living on sites. This issue had been raised in 2001 by a National Gypsy Council Report. Officers claimed that this was not apparent for families on LA sites in Staffordshire.

All LA sites had a Site Warden with varying degrees of responsibility and discipline. Some ran their site whilst others presided only over the day to day maintenance of it. Where the Site Warden was a Gypsy/Traveller on LA sites, there was usually a part –time of full-time non-Gypsy/Traveller site manager who linked the site into the line management of the LA. Sites appeared to be more efficiently run where Site Wardens were paid, worked full time and lived on site. One Site Warden claimed that he did 'everything' for the residents, giving the impression that the role was to be 'in charge' and 'in control' not only of the site but also the residents on site. This tended to compare with the ODPM (2002) findings on site management.

There were site rules for both private and Council run sites and some sets of rules were more comprehensive than others. Private sites tended to have fewer site rules, and procedures appeared more informal than on Council run sites. Whilst these might have existed informally, site residents' associations did not appear to be encouraged and the Site Warden appeared to be the main link with the LA. Site Wardens claimed that they were scrupulously fair, although some residents did complain of favouritism. Wardens had the power and authority to choose and vet those who would live on site. It was claimed that this was done in consultation with the site residents. On private sites, the owners had the last word. From interviews and site conversations, it appeared that residents, in the main, had a good relationship with the Site Warden/Manager, although this, in many cases, was based on a kind of subordination and possibly fear of being removed from the site if residents did not toe the line.

Private sites in Staffordshire were mainly family run and whilst other family members and friends might be welcome, others would not. Some private sites had spaces reserved for Gypsies/Travellers as part of their site license. LA Officers said that they did not interfere with the running of private sites unless complaints were received. They also said that private sites were better run than LA sites. However, as some private sites improved and became upgraded, Gypsies/Travellers were forced off and were not being replaced (Senior LA Officer and Site Warden Interviews). This suggested that even within the Gypsy/Traveller grouping exclusion operated.

Families on permanent sites expressed fears of violence from mobile groups or those on unauthorised sites who were competing for space. How safe and peaceful a site was depended on the calibre and management skills of the Site Warden/Manager. Several site Wardens and residents also claimed that families passing through confirmed their worst fears and served to perpetuate the then current negative perceptions of Gypsies/ Travellers.

Future Prospects?

Whilst some site provision existed in Staffordshire much of it had reached capacity leaving little room for growing families or newcomers. LA respondents were asked in what other ways Gypsy/Traveller families *could* be accommodated. Officers and Councillors listed sites (transit and permanent) 'on their own land' or housing. When asked if Councils encouraged families to buy their own land and helped them to do so the replies were less than encouraging:

> We don't offer land as such.

> Travellers don't get more or less assistance than anyone else.

> If they want their own site they submit a planning application and that will be dealt with by the relevant committee. We would give them help to complete a planning application form. … to run a site of their own they have to comply with planning rules and regulations.

> We would give them advice on how to make a planning application. We would tell them a site that might get approval if they didn't have one in mind. We are keen to talk to people prior to applications being submitted.

> Anyone can come in and request assistance. When out on site we sometimes get asked.

We don't encourage Travellers to buy their own land.

If Travellers come into the area my job is to get a planning application out of them. They start off on the wrong planning foot by living on land before they have planning permission to do so. They don't have to own the land in order to put planning permission in.

Travellers are by their nature less bureaucratic and they do what they want to do. They will buy the land and move onto it and then … wait for us to regularise the position. If they want to change the sue of the land then they need planning permission. They tend not to ask for advice, that's the difficulty. We would go out to advise people.

Councillors and Officers were asked how families *should* be accommodated. Multiple comments were allowed (see Table 9.9). Responses divided themselves into negative and positive. The negative responses displayed an apathy and lack of concern which, if transferred to other minority groups would be deemed unacceptable.

The positive responses from Officers tended to be practical and summed up the dilemmas involved with accommodating mobile groups. However, when compared with Councillor responses it was clear that Officers knew what to say, either because they had more knowledge and information on the subject or their arguments were well rehearsed. What did emerge was that unless the National Government took a lead or unless accommodation of families was statutory or unless families pressed the matter, then LAs did not intend to take the initiative. Transit sites were mentioned as a need. Currently, the County has two occupied transit sites – one in the north and the other in the south. At the time, the Stoke-on-Trent site had received a DTLR/ODPM refurbishment grant of £24,000 to upgrade the amenity blocks on the permanent site and more transit pitches had been created. The rule for this site was that families could remain on the transit site for two weeks at a time, and that this was a renewable arrangement. During the winter months some families were allowed to stay longer. Some families then chose to move onto the permanent site when pitches were available. On a visit to one of the temporary sites in the south of the County it was found to be abandoned and the amenities vandalised.

Table 9.9   How Should Gypsy/Traveller Families be Accommodated?

Councilors

Positive:

Create a reasonable site and ensure they keep their side of the bargain	3
In a caravan if that's what they want	1
However they want to be accommodated	1
If it was a statutory duty then we would have to accommodate them	1
Thy have never come to the council to say that they want land	1

Negative:

They can't be that's the problem	1
If they don't intend staying how can we accommodate them	1
They are breaking the law when they are trespassing	1
We have no land	1

Officers

Positive

More provision	13
Short term sites	6
On their own and	5
Need for a national strategy on accommodating families	3

Negative:

Don't know	3
Don't know what they want	2
We don't accommodate them	2
Offer them a house	1
They can't be accommodated under the present legislation	1

Nevertheless, the overall practices and policy indicated that whilst LAs were prepared to meet the minimum needs of families, they were generally not encouraged to remain or to settle in the area and some LAs were prepared to spend large amounts to ensure this. Some Officers said that they did not want to appear too welcoming. That said, some Officers were aware of human need as opposed to just space for caravans but this tended to be a theoretical concern with the consensus view being, 'somewhere else, but not here'.

Negative Service Delivery as Management of Unauthorised Sites

When Officers were asked to summarise their relationship with mobile groups their responses were as follows:

> They have to find somewhere to camp and we try to make sure they don't. The minute they arrive we hassle them.

> We don't try to charge them for clearance.

> Council has a low tolerance and doesn't want them there. I have to follow procedure.

> Because there are no sites there are always unlawful sites. We are always approaching them to leave.

> It's almost a set routine with regard to what happens: we don't provide a site for them or allow them to park where they want.

> The majority don't know what they're entitled to.

> They know all the rules of the game so they don't want to seek support or advice.

By their own admission actual service delivery to mobile families was poor to non-existent, with any LA resources channeled into removal and/or eviction. Few LAs offered rubbish collection or lavatories, but then did families ask for them and if offered did they accept them? This tended to indicate that 18/94 had had little impact. It also meant that rubbish built up on sites. Some families disposed of this when they left, but others did not and this had become a contentious issue in many LAs. Although this was described as a big problem, few had figures of the clearance costs – partly because the costs were spread across several departments and it depended on who the land owner was. Table 9.10 attempted to quantify the costs for Staffordshire. Morris (1999) and Morris and Clements (2002) estimated a figure of around £6 million for England. Table 9.10 suggests that this might have been a great under-estimation.

At the time Gypsy/Traveller waste was only part of the wider and escalating problem of trade waste disposal and fly-tipping which LAs had to address. Staffordshire appeared, at the time, to be under-achieving in terms of waste management and recycling. Table 9.11 shows the general costs for other types of waste removal and it is likely that Gypsy/Traveller waste was amalgamated with this.

Table 9.10 Unauthorised Encampments in Staffordshire 2001/02

Local Authority	Number of Sites	Estimated Costs
Staffs Moorlands	None	-
Stoke-on-Trent	18*	Not Known+
Newcastle-u-Lyme	16**	Not Known
Stafford	1	-
Lichfield	11	£500 -£1000 per site
Cannock	13	£8000 for one site
Tamworth	10/15 (same group)	Not Known (£30-40,000 in previous year)
South Staffordshire	several (one large)	Not Known
East Staffordshire	5	Not Known

Key:
* These are February to May (2001) figures and compare with 61 sites in the previous full year. In terms of unauthorised caravans: the sites represented 256 unauthorised caravans in 2000 and 97 for the year February to May 2001. These are to be compared with the bi annual returns for Stoke-on-Trent: January 2000 – 5; July 2000 – 6; January 2001 – 4; July 2001 – 5. Some families stayed for only a few days others were moved from site to site over a period of months. Stoke-on-Trent City Council appears to be the only local authority in Staffordshire to systematically collect this information (although not the costs involved). Newcastle LA has just begun.

** These are February to October figures and constitute 108 unauthorised caravans numbers of caravans were not recorded on all sites), compared with the bi annual return for January 2001 – 23, July 2001 - 28. This compares with 26/27 in the previous year (April to October). Some families stayed only for a few hours, others were moved from site to site.

+ Before the transit site was created and the permanent site extended to provide with a long-term unauthorised site, the cost of skips, standpipes and evictions, securing sites and clearing up afterwards over a twelve month period was c £90,000 (Document 5c P3, Planning Department) 1996/97.
(Source: Councils' own Records)

The then Crispin Blunt Private Members Bill (2002) was intended to ensure that families on unauthorized encampments paid the clear up costs. Should Best Value gather momentum then LAs will have to justify the cost of clearing sites.

Overall, communication with families on unauthorized sites was perfunctory and focused on ensuring that families would move – or would be removed. Officers felt that they could not be seen to condone infringements of the Law. Leeds was one of the first LAs to have a negotiating strategy for leaving which involved signed agreements.

Table 9.11 BV85 Cost of Keeping Land Clear of General Refuse and Litter in Staffordshire.

LA	Cost PA (£)
Staffordshire	1783
Staffordshire Moorlands	62364
Stoke-on-Trent	159311
Newcastle-under-Lyme	90142
Stafford	52206
Cannock	66504
Lichfield	n/a
Tamworth*	n/a
East Staffordshire	173003
South Staffordshire	51700
Total	**657013**

Source: Best Value performance Indicators for 2001/2002 (collated by ODPM)

* If Tamworth had made a response the figures would have been much higher since Tamworth was the only LA to pay for removal of rubbish after an unauthorized encampment on private land. This was estimated at £35000 to the end of 2002 (Senior LA Officer Interview)

Other Related Management Issues

Accommodation

Choice was limited for Gypsy/Traveller families. For those wishing to remain and who wanted housing, an affiliation with the area had to be proved, and a need to reside locally whilst their application moved through the system had to be arranged. This has not changed. Given the structures in place these criteria would be impossible for some families to meet. For those who wished to remain on a site, this could only be achieved via the planning system and on their own land. This is equally a long process and would need families to reside/resort to the area for that time. All the LA sites at the time of interview were full and had waiting lists. One Gypsy/Traveller responded:

> They told us they'd extend the site as families grow. Three got married on site and had to move off. One got married a year ago and she's moving up and down waiting for a site, looking. Some are waiting ten years for a slab (pitch).

Some families said they would consider housing. However the fears attached to this decision were that they would end up on 'sink estates', they would feel 'closed in' in a house, and the regular incoming bills coming in when employment was not regular appeared to be a daunting prospect. If bungalows were an option and if families had a regular income housing might be an alternative. Some of the objections and fears raised relating to housing appeared to be as much practical and economic as they were cultural. When families were asked what their ideal home might be, a significant number said a bungalow on their own land in the country. They also indicated that they would like to be on their own and left alone (formal interview and informal conversation). Such comments perhaps indicate the psychological wear and tear of constant eviction, exclusion and rejection.

Land

Land seemed to be at the crux of the LA/Gypsy/Traveller situation. The majority of LAs had land registers and 'vacant' land for sale/development. None of the Officers thought that Gypsy/Traveller families had ever come in to enquire about this. Neither was the register openly advertised. When LA respondents were asked if they helped families to identify sites, they said they did not. Some respondents offered additional information:

> No but we would if they requested us to.
>
> If Travellers came to us we would put them in touch with a planning officer.
>
> We expect mobile groups to move through…
>
> Planners would assist them, but I suspect not. They're not very helpful to anyone.
>
> We have never been approached.
>
> It's not my job to do that. The Travellers have generally chosen Green Belt site and I have suggested that they look at sites outside the Green Belt. The Green Belt is the urban fringe where they want to be.

The costs to both LAs and Gypsy/Traveller families in relation to removal, and eviction and Appeals remain high and yet little is done to avoid these routes.[108] Agreeing suitable land in forward LA Plans could be a useful beginning to any negotiations.

Employment

Employment of families is another management issue on some sites. Councils were not approached by Gypsies/Travellers re business start-up or business development, although most families on sites appeared to be involved in a small business (see also Chapter 4). All Councils had formal business support agencies (at the time of fieldwork it was Business Link) and business promotion/development units where advice was given for prospective new and expanding businesses. Although the service and grant aid was geared toward high-tech, large labour force enterprise, particularly manufacturing (Business Link Interview), these agencies did run classes and give advice on a range of issues connected with starting up and running a small business and how to deal with paperwork. These were free of charge.

The Lack of Paperwork

This was a persistent issue raised in relation to Gypsy/Traveller business. However, the general perception was that Gypsy/Traveller business did not 'fit' the criteria. Agencies did not 'target' this group as possible clients for their services and neither did Gypsies/Travellers approach them. Indeed, none of the respondents perceived Gypsies/Travellers as small business people. One respondent said that, 'For us to deal with bona fide businessmen there have to be accounts, trading accounts and a business plan' (Business Link Interview). Another interviewee stated, 'One of the remits of the Business Units was to 'work through the planning system ... (new businesses) which usually requires planning permission and we smooth that process. We work closely with the people in Planning to agree the use of a particular site that is acceptable in planning terms and if not what the outstanding issues are – car parking, highways, access, environmental assessments etc., (and) to flag these up early in the process before the planning application comes in so that the applicant is aware of the issues' (LA Officer, Business Centre Interview). It was considered that Gypsies/Travellers would not fit into this system. Overall, Gypsies/Travellers were perceived as 'odd jobbers' in the informal sector economy. However, this would not apply to all Gypsies/Travellers.

---

[108] Basildon LA, at the time, was setting aside a quarter of a million pounds to evict families from their Dale Farm site because the site had the wrong planning permission for the type and size of site it had become. The site was partially cleared in 2011 and some families have now encamped nearby.

Officers expressed the difficulty of attempting to provide suitable services for a 'moving target group'. Nevertheless, in Staffordshire, some LAs had attempted to reach families by outsourcing some services.

Outsourced Services and Delivery
Today, many LA functions are devolved to arms' length Agencies. At the time of writing the Thesis, different agencies were joining together in North Staffordshire on Gypsy/Traveller issues. Although education is freely accessible to all, Staffordshire was at the time part of the West Midlands Consortium which provided an educational service for mobile Gypsy/Traveller children. Although the funding streams for this changed in 2009 and the Consortium has considerably reduced, some Councils have retained at least one teacher to continue this function.

Education
The education of Roma and Gypsies/Travellers has become an issue of international concern. European research on this subject had been commissioned by the Save the Children Fund which produced the 'Denied a Future Report' in in 2001. This highlighted the gap between legislation, practice and service delivery and the problems involved in setting up successful education programmes. The main recommendations emphasised the need to monitor and ensure the following:

- Specially trained teachers, teachers assistants and teachers of Roma/Gypsy/Traveller descent;
- The safety of the school environment;
- That the curriculum reflect the language and culture of Roma/Gypsies/Travellers;
- The cost of attendance to families, the numbers attending special schools;
- The number reintegrating into mainstream schooling from segregated provision;
- The number completing basic education and employment options when compared to other groups;
- The number accessing and completing further and higher education;
- The degree to which provision is 'mainstreamed' over time in overall national and education policies and budgets. (ibid :60).

A list of more UK specific recommendations were to be found at the end of Chapter 8 Volume 2 (ibid: 278) which will not be replicated here, but which suggested that the UK had some way to go in order to begin to successfully educate Gypsy/Traveller children.

National Government policy for the education of Gypsy/Traveller children in England, at the time, is framed below and which should have influenced, if not set out clearly, what must happen at the local level:

> 'Traveller children should be given the same opportunities as all other to profit from what schools can offer them. This is reflected in the fundamental legal duty on local education authorities (LEAs) to ensure that education is available for all children of compulsory school age in their area appropriate to their age, abilities and aptitudes and any special needs they may have. The duty applies whether families are residing in the area permanently or temporarily and therefore includes Traveller children. Similarly, all parents are under a legal duty to ensure that their school-age children receive appropriate full-time education, either by regular attendance at school or otherwise. Where such children are registered at a school, LEAs are responsible in law for enforcing their regular attendance. (School Inclusion and Wider Social Policy Team (e-mail 27 July 2001)

In 2001-2002 the total grant for Traveller children education was £15.7 million, to support the work in over 3400 schools in over 130 LEAs. At the time 60 per cent of the grant came from National Government with LEAs providing the remainder. However, the national contribution was regularly decreasing. The grant was made to support specialist teachers, education welfare officers, and classroom assistants. A raft of legislation and Circulars supported the Education Act 1996 which ranged from a duty on parents to school their children (Section 444), to a duty on LEAs to school all children in their area (Section 14 together with Circular 1.81 Para.5). Section 14 also placed a duty on LEAs to provide sufficient places in suitable schools. Section 411 dealt with parental choice of school and Section 437 was concerned with the duty of LEAs to register each child. Section 466 pertained to school attendance, its recording and subsequent action for non-attendance. However, for all mobile groups a process of dual registration (where a child can be enrolled in more than one school) was allowed in order to facilitate continuity for mobile families. Children were permitted to have only 200 attendances in order to complete the school year. Circular 18/94 requested that the education needs of families on unauthorised sites be taken into account before eviction took place. Thus in theory at least, at the National level, some encouragement had been given for the education of Gypsy/Traveller children.

The Local Response

The West Midlands Consortium supported by 13 LEAs in the West Midlands had the task of providing education for Gypsy/Traveller children on sites and whose families were mobile. It employed 22 teachers and covered an area of 10 000 square miles. Each teacher covered a designated geographical area and around 200-300 children were involved in Staffordshire. An OFSED Report in 1999 claimed that the support of children in this Consortium was 'disproportionate' in that the average ratio was one teacher to 157 children, whereas the national average was around one teacher to 50 children (Senior Teacher Interview). The budget for its activities in 2000 was approximately £935 000. The money was ring-fenced. At the time of interviewing the Consortium was beginning to employ Gypsy/Traveller teaching assistants and mentors. At the time the Consortium liaised with other similar groups and had formed a bench marking club for raising attendance and attainment standards. The West Midlands Consortium was also involved in EU projects (Senior Teacher Interview).

The West Midlands Consortium (and presumably others) was set up to counter some of the factors that hinder Gypsy/Traveller children's education and progress. These were:

Insufficient school places for families moving into the catchment area short term;

Schools reticent to accept children starting school as late learners or who have had intermittent school experience;

...prejudice and discrimination in schools both overt and subtle and public hostility towards them;

Parental anxiety at their children's missing schooling and the well-being of their children in institutions which are often strange to them or which they have often have only negative experience and memories of. (West Midlands Consortium)

The expectation was that children who lived on sites for however long, would be able to access mainstream education in local schools via home tuition at some point. The Consortium dealt with the harder to reach families who were constantly being evicted, finding schools which would take them at short notice, for the short term, and assist them in settling in.

Whilst some families were able to access schools themselves, others needed 'encouragement'. This took the form of taxis to school or the school bus picking up children from the site where the sites were distant from the school, and ensuring that children attended regularly and on time. Although some site rules stipulated regular school attendance this was not always enforced. It was also noted that Education Welfare Officers did not always pursue Gypsy/Traveller parents re non-attendance as they did other families. At the time it was the responsibility of the school to contact Welfare Officers if children failed to attend. The West Midlands Consortium had its own Welfare Officers. There was also the expectation that Gypsy/Traveller children would attend less frequently than other children (see above). The Consortium was contacted weekly by the LA Enforcement Officer checking on roadside encampments. Most LEAs complied with this and 11 of the 13 were said to be proactive (Senior Teacher Interview). However, some evictions took place before the families could be contacted by staff and some families felt that they did not require this service.

Some reasons given by parents for non-attendance or home tuition at secondary level were bullying, drugs and getting into bad company. Some parents questioned the curriculum, particularly sex education. This tended to be viewed by LEAs as a 'cultural' objection rather than a dissatisfaction with the ethos of the school or the education system or genuine parental concerns. One parent stated that she had sent her child to a private school because the local state school was 'too rough'. Another said that during the interview with a Head Teacher she had asked what her daughter was going to be taught. When the Head Teacher said Geography and French, the mother had replied, 'Are you going to teacher how to cook, drive, about money and the banks and where to get the best interest?' The reply was that, 'We don't teach them things like that'. The mother responded with , 'You're not much good at teaching are you?' 'That's why I'm teaching my daughter. So I took her home. By the time she was 16 she could tow a trailer, she taught herself to drive, and two days after she was 17 she passed her driving test. She towed her trailer to the farthest end of Scotland. She can bake anything you want, she's always got money' (Gypsy/Traveller Interview). Such differing views on education and what it is for, could be amalgamated to produce a more relevant model of education for Gypsy/Traveller needs.

Whilst primary schooling initiatives appear to have been successful, the poor secondary school uptake was a cause for concern. In a recent interview (October 2012) whilst inroads were being made and parents and children were realizing the importance of a good education and literacy and numeracy levels beyond those of the elementary school, still too few children were accessing conventional secondary schooling. However, where parents and children have been engaged with the system, success has been achieved and some children are now going on to Further Education via college and in some cases to University. At the time of writing the Thesis the Consortium did not keep records of what happened to children after they had left secondary school.

In 2002, funding for Gypsy/Traveller education was being gradually reduced and merged with that for other minority groups – the Ethnic Minority Achievement Grant (EMAG) and particularly where take up was failing to reach set targets. By 2012 the funding stream for this activity had altered considerably. The West Midlands Consortium is now considerably reduced in size, each LA is now responsible for its own service re the education of Traveller children and deciding whether or not specialist teachers are required. Most LAs are awaiting the results of their budget allocations expecting that in the current economic climate cuts in certain service will have to be made (Interview LA Officer October 2012). Adding to the complexity of the situation is the fact that Roma from Eastern Europe who come to the UK have different education needs in that they are able to access housing and schools and are eager to 'get on'. The stumbling block here would appear to be language, a need for fluency in English, whilst maintaining their own language too.

The process of education is bound up with leisure and out-of-school activity and this involved some form of integration and 'mingling'. To this end LA Officers were asked if they made any provision for young people on sites – in the form of play areas on site, holiday activities etc.. Six Officers claimed that they did, 12 did not know and 5 said that they did.

When asked if there were problems with young people on sites, the response was generally, no (see Table 9.12 and additional comments). Adult literacy classes were available under various initiatives but the take-up was described as poor (Consortium Teacher Interview and HAZ Project Worker Interview). Reasons for this had not been explored.

Tale 9.12 Are There Problems With Young People on Sites

	Yes	No	Don't Know
Senior Officers	3	8	1
Junior Officers	4	6	1
Leaders of Council	1	2	3
Members of Council	1	3	-
Total	**9**	**19**	**5**

We are trying to get them involved in local activities.

They go to school.

The Play council provides a scheme on site in the summer.

There is no room on site for a play area.

We only make provision for those on site.

Health

Van Cleemput and Parry (2001:133) found that 'Travellers' health status was poor, in comparison with the lowest socio-economic groups'. Hawes (1997) gave an overview of the health needs of, and problems faced by Gypsies/Travellers with particular reference to those in the Southwest which supported other studies elsewhere – that Gypsy/Traveller health was below the national average (Pahl and Vaile 1988) with higher death rates from cardiovascular disease, higher proportions of babies with low birth weight and a higher rate of childhood accidents (Feder 1989; Beech 1999; Hajioff and McKee 2000; Van

Cleemput and Parry 2001). High mortality rates were also reported to Van Cleemput 2001:129) by Health workers. Maternal death rates have also been studied (CPHVA 2002)[109] as has the exclusion of men's health from research studies (Acton et al 1998). A report prepared by the Southwest Public Health Observatory (SWPHO 2002) claimed that research undertaken on Gypsy/Traveller health tended to be 'one-off studies', many of which were 'anecdotal' and few which 'compare 'Travellers' (health) to the general population'. Additionally, 'focus is almost exclusively on primary care and evaluations of interventions, lack rigour and impartiality' and that Gypsy/Traveller families were excluded from needs surveys (SWPHO 2002:iv).

Health Visitors interviewed reported similar health issues and concerns in Staffordshire. Although the Health Authority did try to ensure that families were able to access GPs this was not always successful (see HAZ section below). At the time, Health Visitors were instrumental in assisting families in Staffordshire to access health care. The immunisation programme in North Staffordshire was described as 'successful', particularly when families on unauthorised sites were given their own record cards so that they were able to keep track of their child's immunisation history, thus taking ownership of the process. The West Midlands (branch) of the Association of Health Workers/Visitors with Travellers was attempting at the time to build on this work. However, as a respondent from the organization stated, their work was more difficult if GPs did not cooperate.

Twelve years on research indicates that much of the above applies, still.

The Health Action Zone (HAZ)

This initiative began in North Staffordshire in 1999 as part of a national scheme to improve health via access and information in targeted areas and was geared towards prevention. An advice project in conjunction with the CAB in Stoke-on-Trent for North Staffordshire Gypsies/Travellers was set up in 2000 (and was due to end in March 2002). The project took under its wing the ailing Inter-Agency Working Group (see Drakakis-

---

[109] This report was based on a confidential enquiry into maternal deaths in UK – 'Why Mothers Die 1997-1999 (Quoted by Joanne Dais NAHWT 2002).

Smith 1997 for a critique of this). By 2003 this Group had become the North Staffordshire Advisory Group for Gypsies/Travellers. This (combined) project had a budget of £10 000 for two years and it employed one project worker. Its work was described as follows:

'Subgroups now look into particular issues. The aim of the group is to improved and homogenise services for Gypsies/Travellers. Group members are expected to go back to their own organization and lobby for change where necessary'.

The respondent could not think of any instance where this had happened. When asked about health issues the response was,

'There are issues around health that have not been resolved. If the project continues GPs is probably something that we will look at. It's on the back burner at the moment. I haven't experienced many refusals, although I have experienced people who are not happy with their GP … but we are limited if Gypsies/Travellers don't want to make a formal complaint. I would encourage them to but they don't want to do it.'

The issue of GPS excluding Gypsy/Traveller families from their lists was on the North Staffordshire Inter-Agency Group agenda in 1997. A Compromise effected was the introduction of an allocation system whereby if a GP Practice refused to accept a family onto its list, the family could contact the Allocations Service which would find them a GP within 2-3 days. This system was described as not ideal but an improvement. A Primary Care Pilot Scheme had also been funded to enable one surgery to employ a nurse/practitioner and a GP for Gypsies/Travellers. This exercise was described as 'working on paper but not in practice'. Whilst a nurse practitioner had been employed a GP had not. Families who had been steered towards the surgery from the nearby transit site had not been taken on as patients. The Health Authority was believed to be monitoring the scheme (Health Visitor Interview).

Although the advice worker assisted families to access health care, the focus appeared to be on community development and benefit advice. A women's group which included Gypsies/Travellers had been set up and trips and outings organised. It also helped to find funding for those wishing to move into housing and for holidays. Since few mechanisms appeared to have been put in place for Gypsies/Travellers to help themselves, when the project ended in March, it was likely that families would be left to their own devices once more.

It was questionable whether separate health care provision for Gypsies/Travelers was a solution. However, given the above it appeared to be a necessity if health care was to be provided at all. Although Health and Education were important topics of concern gaining access depended, too, on other important material factors – eg adequate income, a good diet, a secure job, and a secure and permanent place to be. The inter-linkage of these factors need to be appreciated by all parties including Gypsies/Travellers.

Social Services and Care

Social Services are Statutory Agencies providing services which are need and referral-led. The onus is either on clients to recognize their own needs or allows professional SLBs such as Teachers, Health Visitors, GPs to refer families on or to make them aware of their rights/entitlements, if they so wish. However those not au fait with the system might not be aware of available services since these are not always widely advertised. The elderly on sites interviewed appeared to rely on their families for assistance. One person said, 'I don't know what a social service is, I've never seen them' (social workers, health visitors). Clark (1999:14) claimed that there is a perception that Gypsies/Travellers looked after themselves. Perhaps this is an area that needs further research since it was similarly assumed that Asian families cared for each other. However, on closer scrutiny this was found not always to be the case.

Although several Officers claimed that they contacted Social Services prior to an eviction taking place, they also claimed that Social Services rarely responded (if at all). The question was raised – that Under Circular 18/94 were evicting Officers supposed to *make* enquiries re the need for Social Services involvement, or were Officers supposed to simply *contact* Social Services as a matter of course, who would then come and make their own assessment of need? Since no-one seemed clear about this it was difficult to know if LAs or Social Services were being remiss. This led to the scenario in North Staffordshire whereby when the CAB began outreach work on two sites in the area, it was found that a large proportion were either not claiming benefits at all or they were not given all that they were entitled to. Neither were families aware of the appeal procedures if they had been refused.

At the time of fieldwork in 1999/2001 the County Council Social Service Department was putting together a number of 'inclusion' initiatives one of which was cultural/racism awareness in the form of a Report (1999) entitled 'Diversity' which was updated in 2001. The Report recognised the need for consultation (P7) the need to respond to multiple disadvantage (P14) and the need to advertise services more widely to those who might need them (P7). No mention was made of resolving the difficulties faced by mobile groups to access welfare benefits (see Clark 1999:196 on this issue). In similar vein the Staffordshire Children's Service Plan Review (April 1999) wished to extend its services further to ethnic minority children, to target need areas, to begin ethnic monitoring and record keeping and to improve ethnic minority recruitment of foster carers, residential and day care, and field work staff. Whether this included Gypsies/Travellers would remain to be seen. Although at County level there was a stated commitment to EO and anti-discrimination practices, when the County was asked to lead on the Social Inclusion Strategy the response was that as there were no resources it wasn't done (Senior Officer Social Services Interview).

After the Audit Commission's Review of Social Service in Staffordshire (n/d) it was understood that moves were afoot to implement its recommendations for partnership working between different agencies and community groups. It was admitted, at the time, that Social Services in Staffordshire 'did not have a lot to do with Gypsies/Travellers'. It was difficult to know whether this was due to a wary or arms-length approach by Gypsy/Traveller families, a lack of encouragement to do so or that there was no need for any intervention by Social Services. Resources also played a part. In 2001/2002 the funding for Social Services was £113.4m, £10 m lower than for other English shires (Officer Interview). Whilst Staffordshire had a population, then, of around 800,000, Birmingham with a population of around 1 000 000 received three-times the funding. The Audit Commission reckoned that Staffordshire would be £10 m short. It also appeared that Gypsy/Traveller families had not been included in the standard spending assessment (Senior Officer Social Services Interview). The view of the respondent at the County Social Services department was, 'You can't force people to be included if they don't want to be'. However, this should be an established fact rather than a cultural assumption (see also SWPHO 2002 on this issue).

Cemlyn (1998:38) found that Social Services did not have a particularly high standing with Gypsy/Traveller families and that there was 'a generally low level of Social Service provision across England'. Clark (1999:197) claimed that Gypsies/Travellers have not received fair treatment in the past given the practice of making Gypsies/Travellers provide identification in order to access services since they were marked as a high risk 'group' in terms of making potentially fraudulent claims. This tended to indicate that an improved line of communication was needed on all sides. The response to this suggestion at the time was, 'there is no policy relating to Travellers. We tend to operate on the basis of individual assessment based on individual need … We can't always see particular sets of issues coming from particular communities … the Traveller community is quite small and doesn't feature in our statistics in a way that we can say yes, they use this particular service' (Senior Officer Social Services Interview). Respondents did recognise that their 'responsibility for Gypsies/Travellers was the same as for any other family in need'. Another Officer stated that, 'Just because they are Traveller families does not mean that they are in need of Social Services. An eviction might take place without us knowing anything about it'.

In North Staffordshire there were only four cases that Social Services were dealing with and two in South Staffordshire. Thus it would appear that Social Services in Staffordshire were aware of the 'low demand for services', from Gypsy/Traveller families but this was not seen as a particular problem. As Gypsy/Travellers do not appear to participate in Forums where issues are raised (Cemlyn 1998:85) then it would be unlikely that their issues would be picked up to be acted upon or appear on Social Service agendas. Social Services at the time was either self-referral or demand led and not necessarily pro-active in its approach.

The Police – National Intent

The Association of Police Officers of England, Wales and Northern Ireland (ACPO) in their Blueprint for Policing in the 21st Century (August 2001) believed 'that the public should continue to have an independent Police Service which contributes fully in providing safe and peaceful communities, and works with others to build a safe and just society' (ibid:1.1) and 'within which members of the public can go confidently about their lawful business' (ibid:1.2). ACPO has also compiled a comprehensive Race Hate Manual (www.acpo.police.uk/policies/index.htm) to assist Officers in their day-to-day policing. Trust was mentioned as an important factor in partnership working between the police and the community/communities. However, as with most policy it was questionable how far this was this being translated into practice and service delivery, particularly in relation to Gypsies/Travellers.

The Local Response

At the time of writing the Thesis, the Staffordshire Police Force had recently been divided up into Local Policing Units (LPUs). Interviews were undertaken in Leek, Newcastle-under-Lyme and Stoke-on-Trent LPUs and the Staffordshire County Police Headquarters in Stafford. I was informed that the role of the police was described as 'the protection of life and property and the prevention/reduction in crime' (LPU Officer). The respondents claimed that the Police did not intervene in matters of crime unless crime had occurred or public order was threatened. Thus police were present at evictions with a watching brief at the request of LAs. Liaison rather than action appeared to be increasingly important. Some LPUs appeared to be better at liaison and did more of it than others. However had the Crispin Blunt Bill been passed then LAs would have been able to request the Chief Constable to 'take action', which the officers would then have been required to do.

Overall, the Officers interviewed claimed that they saw Gypsies/Travellers as being no different to the rest of the community in terms of criminal activity. When families moved into an area and onto an unauthorized site, the matter was left to the LA (or the private landowner if the site was on private land) to initiate proceedings – unless the site was highly sensitive – ie on the road or in a school or playing field. Section 61 of the CJPO Act (194) had been used only once by one Council to remove a 'sensitive site' (Senior Officer LPU Interview). The reason given for not using Section 61 appeared to be bound up with the practicality of Police involvement. As one respondent put it, 'If we were to use Section 61 we have to take them into custody until we find who they are – finger-printing, past criminal records if any etc.. It is very difficult to do that with 30 or 40 people and impound all their vehicles (Section 62). We have the power to arrest, but we wait for the Local Authority to do it (take action), or the land owner'. Section 61 was seen as 'a last resort'. Section 78 of the Act gives LAs the power to remove. The enforcement end play of this Section is 'non-imprisonable'. This might have explained the reluctance of the Police to be involved and why LAs thus took the initiative. However, LAs tended not to use the CJPO Act because time-consuming investigations had to be carried out before eviction could take place thus Order 24 was quicker. This is not to say that these rules were strictly applied or adhered to at all times as Case Study C in Chapter 8 demonstrated. The then view was that, 'There are few evictions now because it is worth allowing people to stay an extra few days, rather than invoking the full weight of the '94 Act. It's expensive and it begs the question, where do they go?' (Senior LPU Officer Interview)

… And Crime

When asked if crime increased when unauthorised sites were set up (a common local complaint and a reason given why removal should take place) respondents claimed that they 'monitored the situation'. 'We monitor crime levels daily at the LPU. If crime erupts near an unauthorised site then we have to ask questions. Is it the site or is it somebody just released from prison, nearby?' (Senior LPU Officer Interview). One LPU claimed to keep registration numbers stored of vehicles on unauthorised sites which 'is there to be used if they commit an offence'. This respondent connected this scenario with the way in which illegal immigrants and asylum seekers were perceived and treated: 'We don't know who they are. It's impossible to know where they've come from. It's impossible to do any checks on their background. Most are decent people but some could have committed a crime. No-one knows' (Officer LPU Interview). However, the overall response was that the Police 'did not keep records' and 'did not ask if families on unauthorized sites were local or not' (Officer LPU Interview). LPU Officers claimed that generally Gypsy/Traveller crime was 'not a big problem any more'.

LPU Officers explained some incidents of violence in terms of 'young men feeling their feet' or to family feuding. Nevertheless, all reported incidents were checked. Officers claimed that it was impossible to get to the bottom of any dispute on site. It was felt that families on LA sites were, to some extent, 'protected' from any unruly mobile groups.

When crime was/is reported on unauthorised sites the general reaction was/is to move families on.

Alcohol and soft drugs were mentioned although this was not viewed as 'a problem'. More concern was expressed for violence and vandalism on some Council sites. The site problems encountered in 1997 by Stoke-on-Trent City Council have largely been resolved with a new Site Warden and the employment of an LGO. It was reported that any drinking tended to take place off site and in the form of binge drinking by 'the men'.

There were incidents on sites, sometimes, of a horrendous nature (Senior LPU Officer Interview) which was confined to one or two families. When the police had been involved victims had been reluctant to prosecute or to give information/evidence to the Police. 'Often the law is taken into their own hands rather than go with the law of the land'. One respondent gave a figure of 26 assaults that he knew of over a six month period in 2000 (when fieldwork was being undertaken). However, it was also stated that crime rates on sites of all types were no higher than for the housed population. Another Senior LPU Officer claimed that of the 1500 crimes committed over the last year, 750 were attributed to 'itinerants'. It was difficult to know given the way in which crimes were reported and classified how far this included Gypsies/Travellers, specifically. Unfortunately, when such incidents are reported in the local press the finer distinctions are not always explained to, or appreciated by, the general public.

Operation Liberal

This was a regional Police initiative set up in 1998 to combat bogus and distraction crime across the Midlands region. The victims were usually elderly and involved one person distracting the victim whilst the other ransacked the house for cash and valuables. It was termed 'itinerant' crime because teams moved into an area for a short period of time and then moved on elsewhere. In Staffordshire the term itinerant was also used to describe Gypsies/Travellers. In the mind of the public the two had become conflated and these crimes had become associated with mobile Gypsy/Traveller groups passing through the area. When this was pursued to Chief Constable level and to the Head of the Operation I was told categorically that this was not an initiative aimed at Gypsies/Travellers. In a letter from Headquarters I was informed that: 'from the content of your letter, you have been misinformed about the activities of the Operation to tackle the crime of Distraction/Bogus Official Burglaries. As such the activities of the Operation are directed towards that specific area of criminality and no particular section of the community. None of my Officers have dealt with any Gypsies/Travellers in the Staffordshire area'. Access to any statistical information was denied. That which was volunteered was vague and 'off the record'.

… And Protection?

The Police have a multiple role – to prevent and detect crime and to protect the community at large from crime, ensuring public safety. Although Gypsies./Travellers were included in this remit, families felt that they were not being sufficiently protected. When I raised this with LPU Officers their view was that families 'did not wish to complain to the Police and they did not wish to give evidence. We can't take any action without evidence'. I was shown a computer print-out for response times to reported incidents on one particular site. These were from 2-5 minutes. Some of the calls had proved to be either hoax calls, or when the police arrived families questioned on site denied any incident. Clearly there was much work to be done to ensure that families understood what the Police could and could not do and what their responsibility might be to assist when crime occurred.

PARINS

A PARINS (Partnership Approach to Racial Incident Reporting) Group had recently been established as a County-wide initiative to encourage ethnic minorities to report hate crimes. In North Staffordshire 7 incidents were reported between April to November 2001 – one of verbal abuse, one of assault, and five of harassment which involved being followed in shops and leisure facilities (PARINS Project Officer Interview). The success of this project relied on reportage of incidents, how those incidents were reported and classified and how they were, ultimately, dealt with.

The Crown Prosecution Racist Incident Monitoring Scheme Annual Report 2002 showed a marked increase in race-related Court cases in North Staffordshire (reported in the

Sentinel Newspaper 14/3/03) the increased activity of the British National Party (BNP) in Stoke-on-Trent and Newcastle-under-Lyme and its stated intent to contest seats in the then forthcoming local elections, was a cause for concern (reported in the Sentinel Newspaper 17/3/03). This implied a need for improved community relations which must also include Gypsies/Travellers – one of the most vulnerable groups in this area.

Other Service Issues

Regeneration as a Service Issue

In the past, regeneration had been a top-down exercise of moving people from place to place to make way for redevelopment and deciding the changes to be made with little consultation with those affected. The Community Strategy process was a possible attempt to redress this unbalanced paternalism. However, the way in which this was conceived at the local level meant that little had changed and Community Forums (set up to drive the Community Strategies) were dismal failures in some LAs. Staffordshire was no exception. More latterly, the Localism Act of 2011 whilst stating more power would be devolved to localities, and that as a result of the Act local people would have more say in the decision-making process, is also proving difficult to put into practice, hampered mainly by too many powerful elites, elected Members and paid Officers with vested interests who do not wish to relinquish either their power or control. Additionally, very little has been done to prepare localities to take a responsible role in local governance – much of which appears to involve interpreting National Policy, creating compliant Local Policy which can be further translated into workable/compliant practice and service delivery. Presently, Local Area and Enterprise Partnerships (LAP/LEPs) serve to regulate public engagement with the decision making process, limiting this to a small number of stakeholders and seemingly uncritical 'friends'. Consequently unpopular projects are railroaded through with residents being 'consulted' or informed when everything has been decided. Such processes involve a greater emphasis on literacy and technology in order to access the relevant documents and to understand what is being proposed. Groups who are less than literate or whose English is not a first language are immediately peripheralised and are potentially excluded. Similarly, anyone without access to the internet could be increasingly marginalized. It was no surprise that

Gypsy/Traveller sites (other than in Stoke-on-Trent) had not been suggested as part of any forthcoming regeneration programmes.

At the time of writing the Thesis, a plethora of regeneration schemes funded by National Government and the EU were enacted in the names of City Challenge, SRBs, Objective Funding etc.. Some of this funding was specifically and tightly targeted often down to identified post codes. Within one LA, whilst the Traveller site had been included in the statistical evidence to support a grant application, once the funding had been awarded, the site was excluded from the project. SRB projects were running in both Stoke-on-Trent and Newcastle-under-Lyme at the time. When Officers were asked if there were any projects specifically for Gypsies/Travellers which had been included in the bids, the response was categorically, 'no'. The North Staffordshire Play Council did begin summer Projects on both the Newcastle and Stoke-on-Trent sites and these were running well. Respondents at the Play Council whilst hoping that their activities would be mainstreamed, were not optimistic. The Play Council (partly funded by HAZ) eventually folded.

The Media – A Service or Power and Influence Without Responsibility?

The then Commission for Racial Equality (CRE) made guidelines for media coverage of Gypsy/Traveller issues available on line: http://www.cre.gov/media/guidetj.html. The impression given by the local newspapers in their reportage in the past of Gypsy/Traveller issues was that those guidelines were afforded a passing nod, only. Editors and journalists were bound, at the time, by large quantities of Guidance and Codes of Conduct which they were supposed to follow. The Editor of the local daily newspaper in Staffordshire produced a very thick folder stating that one of his duties was to 'ensure that everything printed' was 'within the Law'. He said that a 'standing rule' was that 'where there was a difference of opinion' a journalist had to present both sides of any story 'unless that was impossible to do'. The Editor claimed that Gypsies/Travellers were given opportunities to put their view but that they rarely spoke to reporters. Neither did families take newspapers or journalists to the Media Complaints Authority or to the CRE. It was noted that whilst national newspapers might attempt to comply with the Codes of Conduct, local newspapers tended to get around these Codes by 'reporting' local and often antagonistic views. This served to both encourage and further embed local prejudices. The local media present an aura of 'community' acting as glue binding it together, creating a 'like mind' and constantly reflecting back 'the local/vox pop' view of the world – simplistic and often black and white, them and us – thus maintaining the status quo of the locality they serve (see Drakakis-Smith 2007 on this point). Thus despite the infrequent feature article on Gypsies/Travellers, local newspapers in Staffordshire have tended to uphold and even inadvertently support anti-Gypsy feeling in the way that thy report such issues. That said, local newspapers were condemnatory of the then BNP activity in North Staffordshire in those areas where there were relatively high numbers of ethnic minority groups and Gypsies/Travellers.

SUMMARY

This Chapter has attempted to show the way in which Equality of Opportunity is understood, interpreted and applied at the local level to the issue of Gypsies/Travellers. Operating within this frame and influencing and driving services and their delivery are perceptions and evaluations of the target group. It was found that although services were delivered to Gypsies/Travellers and that this group was not excluded entirely, families on sites were provided with much less than those who lived in houses. Mobile groups who were thought to be 'nomadic' received even less, if anything, and this was linked with an evaluation of 'worth'. Any measures taken or services delivered were negative and geared towards ensuring that mobile families did not remain.

Those on sites were regarded to be more deserving. However, the location of many sites meant that they were not always physically/geographically/socially or economically integrated. Nevertheless, those settled on sites were regarded to belong more, and were more acceptable than those who were perceived to be just passing through. The general view forwarded by LAs was that Gypsies/Travellers were 'non-belongers'. The manorial mind-set prevailed – those who paid could stay, strangers were unwelcome. Families living on sites often paid more for less yet did not receive the same entitlements or services. This did not strike LA respondents as particularly unfair or as unequal treatment.

The findings suggested that services and delivery to Gypsy/Traveller families on sites was less than adequate and for mobile groups almost non-existent. Only one LA in Staffordshire had used its powers to make provision despite demonstrable and expressed need. Neither had LAs envisaged anything for Families beyond authorised 'sites' or 'pitches'. Thus families who had moved onto sites had remained there, which meant that new-comers were faced with a 'log jam'. The then ODPM site refurbishment grant tended to foster the status quo rather than attempting to support aspirational need. Provision for Gypsy/ Traveller families appeared to be narrowly focussed. The lack of a unified voice in Staffordshire to make demands for change and/or improvements had led to a certain complacency in terms of positive delivery of both sites and services by LAs. This would also bear out Lustgarten and Edwards' claim (1992:277-8) that 'the law imposes the minimum standards. Compliance is satisfied by strict adherence to the law. It is illegal to do anything more, therefore no-one is legally bound to do anything other than the least that is demanded'. The case studies and fieldwork tended to demonstrate that in some LAs it was questionable whether even the minimum standards had been reached. At the time, few if any LAs had attempted to assess need and mechanisms had been adopted to obfuscate need (eviction and moving on). There seemed to be little in place to fathom or assess Gypsy/Traveller intent. Little if any communicative dialogue appeared to take place with mobile groups.

Constant, forced mobility and eviction has tended to militate against any positive long-term service delivery where a permanent address is a prerequisite particularly for Education and Welfare, Housing and Employment. In Staffordshire, Education had been outsourced and somewhat removed from the mainstream. The same course appeared to have been taken with regard to Health particularly registration with a GP. The original reason for this was that schools and GPs were reluctant to take mobile families, particularly, onto their rolls/lists. This was not seen as an EO/race discrimination issue to be dealt with. Instead, families had been seen as the issue and any remedies devised had been to further remove families from the mainstream.

Although the EOPs in Staffordshire were largely comprehensive documents committing the LA to 'good' and 'fair' practices, these were not always translated into practice or delivery. Whilst the duty remains for LAs to promote and foster good community relations, in areas where the ethnic population is small, the prevailing attitude appears to be to 'leave well alone'. Those who do not lobby or engage tend to be left to their own devices.

The fieldwork demonstrated that in Staffordshire monitoring EOPs was not a systematic exercise. Indeed, staff were unsure if Gypsies/Travellers were included in their policy or if their EO extended to service delivery. Few if any Gypsies/Travellers were known to be employed by the LAs and there was no positive action to change this. None of the LAs evaluated or rated their EOPs highly in relation to Gypsies/Travellers.

At the time, EO remained 'a contested notion in society' as in the past (Jenkins and Solomos 1987:217; see also Jewson and Mason 1992; Gibbon 1992) its meaning constantly readjusted to move with the times and changes on the ground eluding realisation. The early 21st Century notion of EO was concerned with access to opportunity rather than to equal shares. In 2013 this has changed again to the notion of 'equity' or fairness – which in essence is what EO was all about anyway. However, within each time space, standardisation of meaning is important so that it is understood by all those who refer to it and who attempt to implement it. In Staffordshire EO was understood differentially with the result that EO and Service Delivery tended not to match. Much of the joined up thinking hoped for, operated largely with regard to exclusionary processes and much less to positive service delivery for Gypsies/Travellers. Today in 2013, EO is cited at the bottom of job adverts (if at all) more as an aspirational aim than a realisable outcome.

Poor communication meant that Gypsies/Travellers did not always ask for services: mobile groups did not ask for skips, lavatories or water from LAs and when they did it was unlikely that these would be delivered. Instead, notices to quit were the more usual response. Some authorised sites resembled reservations and the measure of a good site for some was for it to be out of sight and out of mind. Services which might have assisted families to improve their business, or to find employment which went beyond cleaning and gardening and 'recycling', seemed not to be delivered to Gypsies/Travellers partly because they were not perceived as small businesses. LA respondents claimed that families did not approach them and these services were not advertised on sites.

LAs have a duty to provide. However, citizens have to take some responsibility to avail themselves of what might be on offer since these offers do not remain open for long. Apart from Education, few opportunities are compulsory and as far as Gypsies/Travellers are concerned Education was, then, not particularly compulsory for them. Some families thought it irrelevant, and some schools did not follow up frequent absences. A secondary duty is for citizens to indicate deficiencies in services. The delivery of services is not benevolence on the part of the State but a right which citizens pay for (Parker 1975) and can demand. If such rights are not exercised then they become lost. A third duty is that which is exacted from citizens. The 21st Century notion of EO is a deal between State and citizen which dates back to manorial times along the lines of protection and reward in exchange for cooperation and active participation. Some of the earlier Blair speeches updated this pact (see Lister 1998:222) which envisaged 'the ideal of a community where the rights we enjoy reflect the duties we owe', and 'to all should be given opportunity, from all responsibility demanded'. The idea of the 'Big Society' (2012) brings to the fore, the wish of the State that citizens selflessly 'give' and not necessarily count the cost of giving. This might be a harder concept to 'sell' – particularly to those who have not received. The increasing low turn-out in national and local elections and the more recent shunning of the Police Commissioner elections (November 2012) with only an average 14 per cent voter response demonstrates a widening gulf between citizen and State which needs to be bridged - and via politics might not be the remedy. It would seem that, possibly, politics and politicians, constantly working on seemingly circular and backward looking policies, have become their own nemesis.

CHAPTER TEN

CONCLUSION

Primarily, the project was an area study of the LA/Gypsy/Traveller relationship in
Staffordshire which attempted to answer the question 'What is going on here?' The study
and fieldwork also attempted to respond to the questions raised and to address the larger
issues outlined in Chapter 2. The findings of the localised research have been
summarised at the end of each chapter and will not necessarily be repeated here. Instead,
this chapter will examine more closely some of the themes and mechanisms which have
emerged in the game and play which perpetuate the LA-Gypsy/Traveller situation in
Staffordshire.

The driving hypothesis of the project has been: that the way in which individuals and
groups are identified, perceived and represented (accurately or otherwise) will influence
the way in which they are treated by majority society and officialdom. To this end an in-
depth study of specific administrative habita was undertaken to examine their treatment
of Gypsies/Travellers who live in and/or resort to their area.

It was found that National Government has attempted to counter some behaviours of
some Gypsies/Travellers via special treatment, rules, regulations, with Guidance for
practice and service delivery with the expectation that these will become enacted and
implemented at the local level. Some of the measures are punitive/regulatory on the one
hand and re-distributary on the other. These have encouraged and produced responses
from Gypsies/Travellers which have tended to lead to a strengthening of boundaries
which create and/or support a separate habitus. Those within ultimately believe in it to
the point where its norms become 'the norms', and so it takes on a life of its own.
Protracted disengagement leads to differences (eg language, language registers, way of

life etc.) becoming established and entrenched which further distances individuals. Groupness was confirmed, strengthened (and often exaggerated) by exclusion from the mainstream, thought trajectories often diverging to run in parallel – all of which serve to create a separate habitus for some Gypsy/Traveller groups, which, once established nurtures a counter-exclusiveness. National Government perceiving the dangers of detachment has more lately introduced legislation and policies, to accept and deal with diversity and to cater for diverse needs. These are being enacted (with varied success) to the present. Some Gypsies/Travellers, particularly mobile groups, however, are excluded from their remit in practice at the local level. In some instances this is being read as self-exclusion.

The study showed, too, that in Staffordshire,[110] the structuring structures of governance have equally spawned administrative habita which can and do strive for themselves and for their own independence from National Government.[111] LAs can also take on a life of their own and become separated from majority society via language codes, rules and norms of behaviour. Such constructs on both sides tended to reveal the perverse and often negative ways in which LA and Gypsy/Traveller habita interact to support each other's structuring structures in a helixial configuration (see Figure 3.1) which are difficult to break down and separate. Bourdieu's theory of habitus was used, as a means of looking at and analysing, the LA-Gypsy/Traveller situation. This theory alone was found to be insufficient to explain how differences become identified, valued, hierachicised and politicised. To bridge this gap, theories of race, status group, ethnicity and identity were used. The LA-Gypsy/Traveller impasse was viewed against the Habermasian notion of commensurate/communicative dialogue. Together, these theories provided a useful backdrop against which the agency of the power group – LAs in Staffordshire – and its relationship with Gypsies/Travellers could be analysed and evaluated.

---

[110] There is also evidence to show that this has occurred elsewhere and on a larger scale eg Scottish and Welsh devolution, with suggestions of more regional devolution.
[111] Bovens (1998) claims that some complex organisations take on the form of a 'franchise'. LAs could be construed as such an enterprise.

In the struggle between hegemony and the push for a place to be, game strategies with zero-sum lose-lose outcomes (after Luce and Raifa 1957) appear to have produced a nominal negative equilibrium which in some LAs passes for 'peaceful coexistence'. However, before games and strategies are discussed, the LA-Gypsy/Traveller situation will be reformulated in the light of the fieldwork study.

We Need to Talk - Reformulating the LA-Gypsy/Traveller Situation

The LA and Gypsy/Traveller habita come into conflict when Gypsy/Traveller families demand what LAs cannot or do not wish to provide. Punitive measures are reserved for families who are regarded not to belong, whilst re-distribution becomes a reward for those willing to 'come in' and conform to the norms of majority society. The manner in which some families arrive and demand entry (via trespass) can lead to antagonism and a punitive response. Such scenarios are often predicated on a protracted history (or habit) of exclusion (rather than need satisfaction). Solutions have become stylised: either Gypsies/Travellers conform or move elsewhere to find what they are seeking - or they are forcibly removed. The accepted 'solution' often exacerbates 'the problem' and serves to perpetuate mobility.

Chapters 1-5 discussed the (mis)perceptions, (mis)representations and misunderstandings which have helped to create the LA-Gypsy/Traveller situation. Chapter 6, 7 and 8 discussed the 'problems' faced by National and Local Administrations and Gypsies/ Travellers, and highlighted the difficulties involved in policy-making and finding a workable solution, particularly if the 'problem' has been inexpertly formulated. Systematic and objective data collection can provide the necessary base for sound policy. The fieldwork research revealed that in Staffordshire 'the problem' had crystallised into entry, settlement and support issues. These will now be discussed.

Entry

When Gypsies/Travellers entered they claimed that there was nowhere to park their caravans since unlike other visitors, tourists and workers, they bring their homes with them. This led to a second contentious issue, that of trespass on land not their own, and/or occupying unauthorised sites (sometimes on land which families own), and often leaving rubbish on sites, the clearance of which is paid for by the local community. The question of 'a contribution' - financial and civic - is deeply entrenched at the local level and was traced back to manorial/feudal times - the general perception being that Gypsies/ Travellers take from, but do not contribute financially to the local community.

Entering the boundary of an LA was usually without warning. Numbers of entrants varied as did entries per year. Some years in Staffordshire high numbers were reported,[112] in others, few.[113] There were no mechanisms to investigate the reasons for arrival. Some were passing through, having a permanent place elsewhere and were visiting and/or seeking work opportunities. Others, however, wished to settle in the area or claimed they had nowhere else to go. LA Officers pointed to the difficulty in providing for a moving and unpredictable client group. The solution was not to provide anything (or at least very little) for families perceived to be mobile. Clouding the issue (whilst at the same time being the crux of the issue) is the fact that because Gypsies/Travellers live in caravans, the caravan is regarded as 'home' thus families are not regarded, legally, to be homeless. The current debate centres around the issue that if families have nowhere to legally place a caravan then they are homeless in a wider context since place can also be 'home' (see also Valentine 2001 on this point).

Gypsies/Travellers are not the only people to move about in caravans. House dwellers also use this mode of dwelling on a temporary basis for holiday accommodation and permanently as affordable accommodation. Provision is made for these caravans via the Caravan Club for holiday accommodation which may or not close during the winter months, and caravan sites (private or LA run) for more permanent accommodation. Almost all LAs in Staffordshire had this type of provision. This raises the question: if this type of temporary and permanent accommodation is available for others why is it not used by Gypsies/Travellers? This might prove an interesting line of inquiry.

---

[112] At a recent Local Plan enquiry it was revealed by the Senior Planning Officer that in the year 2000/2001 as many as 800 caravans had passed through Newcastle-under-Lyme. This borough has no transit sites.
[113] In a majority of LAs in Staffordshire there were none reported in 2002.

The special provision made for Gypsies/Travellers by some LAs, and/or privately, in terms of permanent sites, is often oversubscribed which indicates that sites are in demand and that a quota for entry and settlement (which limits both) is covertly or overtly being imposed (akin to that for immigration/asylum etc).[114] LAs which had provided for some were adamant that they would not make any further provision.[115] The overall number of Gypsy/Traveller caravans is monitored nationally by the ODPM and now the CLG (see Chapter 5). This census, whilst useful was, then, overdue for amendment.

If Gypsy/Traveller families, for whatever reason, do not/cannot use the accommodation that is already provided for caravans, then their entry involves unlawful/unauthorised settlement, which is met with resistance and rejection/refusal. Almost immediately families are placed in a disadvantaged position which makes it difficult to access rights and privileges or to occupy the moral or legal high ground when it comes to removal/eviction (and humanitarian grounds (via the Human Rights Act) were then only recently being tested in the Courts). Presently, there are few if any mechanisms to explore reasons for entry and the type of accommodation required – given that entry into one LA indicates an exit from another. Such information could form the basis of a Staffordshire needs survey, in the first instance.[116] In 2005 A Needs Survey had been undertaken but the results had yet to be announced with regard to implementation.

The, then, line assumed by LAs in Staffordshire was that if there was no place within the LA where Gypsies/Travellers could legally go then settlement should not occur or be tolerated. In 2013 this view appears extant. None of the LAs in Staffordshire had identified land for sites within their Local Plans and the criteria for 'inclusion'[117] were highly exclusionary – leaving few alternatives where families could go. The Local Plans examined by Todd and Clark in 1991 and Wilson in 1998 were not materially different in this respect from the new Local Plans being drafted in Staffordshire for the 21st

---

[114] Some LAs in Staffordshire were working to a quota system devised in 1979.

[115] Unless they were instructed and resources were available – and even then some were doubtful.

[116] This information would be gathered not by Eviction Officers but by trained personnel, probably Gypsies/Travellers. It would be important to ensure that the line of questioning did not and could not be used to infringe the human rights of individuals. This information is currently gathered in Scotland (Scottish Executive 1999).

Century.[118] This suggests that inclusion or acceptance of mobile Gypsies/Travellers is not a serious consideration. Thus the habit of exclusion is strengthened and perpetuated[119] bending backwards to the 14th Century.

Entry into mainstream society by settled families has also been problematic and challenging for some families since permanent sites are often created on the frontiers and fringes of urban development and therefore isolated, awaiting development. Education for some at the secondary level also takes place on site. Attempts to integrate are often met with hostility whether this is via use of communal facilities such as play areas or families moving into conventional housing. Entry into paid employment is similarly difficult without a permanent address, the attainment of paper qualifications, without contacts or 'patrons' or with a caravan site address.

Settlement

Although LAs do not have the power to prohibit entry, they can, via the legal bind, (Drakakis-Smith 1997; 2003) frustrate settlement. The histories compiled by Crofton (1908), Mayall (1988) and Fraser (1992) and the 1952/3 Staffordshire County Report (Chapter 7, Table 7.13) suggest attempts by Gypsies/Travellers at settlement and inclusion. Within mainstream society, there are varying degrees of settlement from short-stay to long term which LAs and private enterprise cater for.[120] However, the accommodation needs of Gypsies/Travellers have yet to be established by LAs - which could be the basis for a useful dialogue between LAs and Gypsies/ Travellers. For those without access to space and/or place, mobility becomes, in fact, prescriptive. [121]

Settlement involves the use of land - and land use, too, appears to be a contentious issue. Families denied entry and use of land are perceived as forcing entry via unlawful trespass

---

[117] Ie the criteria where sites should/not be - should there be 'a need' to create them.
[118] And despite the Good Practice Guide recommendation on this issue (3.10; 3.13) and Circular 1/94)
[119] Some LA officers claimed that special provision in Local Plans was unnecessary since land for housing development could also be used for caravan sites – in theory.
[120] And again questions need to be asked eg why Gypsies/Travellers do not use these facilities – although signs on premises prohibiting their entry would not encourage use.

or attempting to evade and/or subvert planning rules and regulations by unauthorised use of land (which may be their own). Over the centuries Gypsies/Travellers have included themselves via trespass (although some families would not view it as such – merely occupying land which is not being used – which challenges the norm of ownership) or purchasing land for future use (which could be construed as speculation). Such land is usually in the Green Belt or in the countryside and would be cheap because the likelihood of planning permission being granted for any development would be slim (although not impossible). In the past Gypsies/Travellers were permitted settlement within the Green Belt. Increasingly, development demands made upon this category of land by large scale developers meant that Gypsies/Travellers settled on this land, or granted permission for sites on this land, were regarded as setting a precedent. This resulted in the withdrawal of any caveats permitting this.[122] The Midlands Planning Guidance Draft Review (2001) suggested that Gypsy/Traveller sites be permitted in the countryside - which placed Gypsies/ Travellers once more on 'the edge' and at 'the frontier' of settlement in 'new space'. LA Planners claim, and their justification for planning refusal for sites in the Green Belt is, that Gypsies/Travellers are pushing the frontiers of development by occupying and opening up green field sites for development. Perpetually placed at the margins and the frontier, it is supposed that Gypsies/Travellers are positioned to challenge other 'frontiers' and limits.

Currently, the tendency is for planning permission to be given to small sites (1-6 caravans) and on land that would have little commercial value and which would prohibit future large scale development. Indeed, larger sites are being broken up and families dispersed (eg the site in Mid Bedfordshire and Dale Farm are cases in point).[123] In

---

[121] Silk (1999) speaks of 'place free' or 'stretched out' communities whilst Valentine (2001) uses the term 'communities without propinquity' – terms which could apply in some senses to Gypsies/Travellers – although they suggest choice rather than bounded choice and prescription.

[122] It is unclear whether this is to remove the issue of legal precedent and to ensure that all development of land is placed on an even footing given that land for site development is also suitable for housing development. However the notion of evenness (discussed in Chapter 9 (EO)) has demonstrated that this creates *inequality* and would do so in the land/development arena. Additionally with-holding land from development tends to increase competition and places an added scarcity value on it.

[123] Planners expressed a fear that land which has gained planing permission for a site would be sold on at a profit. However, this is not an uncommon practice for land generally (LA Planning Officer interview and Local Plan Enquiry (Senior Planning Officer).

granting planning permissions, often LAs have the unenviable task of balancing the protection of the Green Belt and the countryside against urban sprawl, with the demands and management of sustainable development of the local community - which involves the encouragement of new enterprise. Developers favour green field sites. Chapters 5 and 7 noted that LAs attempted to maintain, although not always successfully, land in the Green Belt. However, a system did pertain where the Green Belt was penetrated and restored at will. It would need further research to discover whether or not Gypsies/Travellers are afforded an equitable and/or proportionate share of this trading process.

Given the evidence, the term 'nomad' has been used to justify non settlement/non provision. The ODPM data in Chapter 5, although sometimes air brushed by LAs, suggested that the majority of Gypsies/Travellers are now settled on sites, or in more conventional ways, which indicated that entry was not impossible, that boundaries were penetrable and probable if needs were met. Chapter 5 also found that Gypsies/Travellers were, like majority society, attracted to the prospering areas where competition for place and space would be enacted. However, unless there is more provision, and/or those on sites are encouraged to move to another level of accommodation (which need not be housing) then log jams occurred, perpetuating mobility in the search for space and place.

Settlement requires some organisation. LAs 'select' locations and 'design' sites. The setting up of a site can take many years (and those in need have to wait somewhere). Resistance to top down organisation and having to wait for urgent need to be satisfied was evident in Staffordshire. Avoidance strategies by Gypsies/Travellers on the one hand spawn more stringent regulatory policies by LAs on the other. There were few mechanisms in 2002 in place in Staffordshire to de-escalate or resolve this situation.

Support
Although within national law there was some support for Gypsies/Travellers this was not always translated into practice at the local level. The fact that there were few, if any, resources to support national intent made implementation more problematic, especially in LAs where there were high numbers of caravans and unauthorised sites. Whilst attempts

by national government are made to gather evidence for, or to amend policy, this evidence can be trimmed to what National Government deems to be expedient to their own purposes or what they are prepared to respond to as fact. Chapter 6 attempted to show the way in which legislation is a historical precis of habit/practice/negotiated rights and freedoms which have become codified. However, the act of codification can also be 'the enactment of an ideological statement' (Collins 1998:2) or of an embedded value system. As such policy is rarely 'new' or 'fresh' but a tightening or slackening of past laws/regulation. Further research might reveal whether this is based on genuine practical reasons or whether it is an excuse for a lack of imagination.

Complex organisations are not structured to 'engage' easily with individuals (Bovens 1998), thus the singularity of Gypsies/Travellers is often exploited by LAs.[124] It was found in Staffordshire that small numbers and the families' tentative knowledge of 'the system' and the rules (and the sometimes LA confusion with regard to the rules) were factors excusing poor or non delivery of services. Officers, in the main, felt that mobile groups were not entitled to LA services or support, and that the Race Relations Act and EOPs did not necessarily apply to them, particularly those who flaunted, or were regarded to be, outside the law.

The attempt at the national level to remove the loop-holes of retrospective planning and adverse possession means that Gypsies/Travellers will find it more difficult to access self-help, and without professional assistance, it could be impossible for many to gain entry and settlement. In general terms this will perpetuate both exclusion and mobility. Without a permanent address some services are impossible to access.

Chapter 9 found that whilst not all Gypsies/Travellers were totally excluded from access to essential and statutory services there was some resistance both to provide (eg primary health care via GPs) and to accept (eg education where attempts had been made to tailor it to Gypsy/Traveller need – particularly for mobile groups). Without education some

---

[124] Who in turn appeared to be just as individualistic in their administrative approaches and ways in which they carried out their duties.

families would find it difficult to access the information required in order to be more independent and more confident in dealing with, and tackling, bureaucracy. Separate education for any minority group including some Gypsy/Travellers could mean that children are distanced further from mainstream society (see also Kymlicka 2000 on this point). This is an area for new negotiation and compromise, and where computers could have a role – particularly where families are hard to reach and are mobile.

Improving support and services for Gypsies/Travellers might be difficult in Staffordshire since it was found that, at the time of the study, few, if any, channels for feedback from Gypsies/Travellers on services existed and few services were advertised to them. The duty to reach isolated groups and make LA services and support more relevant and available to them might improve this situation. This gap tended to be filled by voluntary agencies carrying out temporary and ad hoc projects. There were no projects for Gypsies/Travellers featured in any of the main regional, national or EU funded projects for Staffordshire at the time. Neither had they been included in any specific or meaningful way into the then Community Strategy Plans. Efforts to include settled families have also been limited. LAs in Staffordshire were aware that service delivery to Gypsies/Travellers needed improvement on sites (and that for some mobile groups it was non-existent).

The above scenarios have been brought about by a series of games and strategies which have tended to exacerbate rather than improve the LA-Gypsy/Traveller relationship. These will now be discussed.

Game, Set and Patch – The Need for a Bigger Picture?
Games, used here, denote a series of actions/strategies used in given situations which elicit responses, spawning counter-strategies. Repeated over time, these become *the game* – learned, internalised, habitualised.

Game play is not always approached in an entirely rational manner. Weber (1978:12) conceded that rational action could be prompted by irrational motives. Brandt (1990:405)

318

believed that not all action was 'prudent' and that 'imprudence' can be built into game strategies to the extent that not all decision/making includes the 'welfare function' (Luce and Raifa 1957:328). Abell (1992:196) similarly concluded that 'emotion is affective in the process of decision-making, which can elude rational control' in that 'likes and dislikes can over-ride rational control' and 'weakness of will prevents people acting according to their better judgement'. Discriminatory behaviour could be placed in this category which, when coupled with habit, forms a powerful barrier to inclusion. For the excluded, game strategies are those of survival, based on risk and uncertainty. The fieldwork revealed that a series of games were being played out by both Gypsies/ Travellers and LAs. Such games were often counter-productive, leading to impasse and, at best, patched rather than long-term remedies.

Winning is predicated on a full 'knowledge' of the game and a 'feel' for it (see Chapter 3). Games of risk and uncertainty (Luce and Raifa 1957:275) appeared as the main game play. Uncertainty arises from imperfect or incomplete information - not knowing what 'the other' will do. A strategy of this game is to discover what the other *will* do without disclosing one's own strategy, in order to maximise the chances of gaining the upper hand. These are risk strategies and can lead to other kinds of non-productive games which can, at best, produce 'maxi-min' outcomes – the best worst state (ibid). Government attempts to reduce risk and uncertainty by formulating rules with which players are expected to comply. [125] However, as this thesis has found, rules also *initiate* defection and a series of other games which cause the relationship between power and target groups to unravel. It was also found that rules unless clearly articulated can cause defection amongst power groups too – eg National Government and LAs.

Games of Misperception, Misinformation and Bluff – Signs of breakdown in social relationships is often a failure to communicate. This is not simply a case of non-communication but part of a process which includes misperception and the conveyance of mis-information and insufficient information as strategies to disadvantage the other

---

[125] Power group strategies can take the form of pre-emption ie making rules, forcing individuals and groups to act in predictable ways so that non-compliance is minimised and defection pre-empted.

player. When players think they are in a different game and where players do not correctly perceive each other's strategy and act upon these misperceptions and misinformation, this becomes a game of misperception (Luce and Raifa (1957:270). Withholding information is an important bargaining strategy in the relationship enabling both sides to gain some ground. However, games of deceit tend to unravel as misinformation and bluff are revealed – usually in the court-room. Revelation leads to further bad feeling and retaliatory strategies so that the games escalate to those of non-cooperation. Entwined in these games are the *assumptions* of perfect/complete information, whereby both sides believe they have the level of knowledge of the rules of the game and know the pay-off function of the other players. Where false assumptions pertain and need satisfaction is not met, games of non-cooperation are generated. This type of game is being played out continually in the field of eviction/settlement. It would help all parties if Gypsies/ Travellers and LAs knew the rules of engagement, negotiated which land could be used/purchased and discussed how a successful outcome could be achieved. This would remove the major basis of uncertainty thus making space for the establishment of a better relationship,[126] communicative dialogue, respect and cooperation on all sides.

Games of Non-Cooperation - In these games neither player has a solution strategy, (Hansanyi 1990). This encourages, and is 'the justification for, forms of socially undesirable non-cooperative behaviour' (ibid: 92) from both sides. Such games are evident in the refusal to provide and in the eviction/removal process - countered with rubbish dumping and other forms of behaviour regarded as anti-social. This tends to raise the game to that of competition and conflict – for space and place and settlement/ inclusion versus non-settlement and exclusion.

Games of Competition/Collusion - Once rejection is evident, games of competition ensue, producing zero-sum outcomes. Here, each player perceives the preference patterns to be the opposite so that behaviour is ordered accordingly. Any improvement

---

[126] The misinformation circulating within LAs about Gypsies/Travellers and within Gypsy/Traveller groups about majority society, acting as a strategy keeping both apart, could be minimised.

for one player results in a loss for the other. Although Luce and Raifa (1957) claim that cooperation and collusion are impossible in such games, the research found that, perversely, a kind of cooperation and collusion did take place as both sides attempted to maximise their own interests (utilities). Both Gypsies/Travellers and LAs (in the main, in Staffordshire) wished to avoid the open conflict of the 1960s. Thus a 'give and take' which passed for 'cooperation' re the eviction/moving on process (for some LAs) was evident.[127] This could also be construed as collusion, whereby both sides obtained their maxi-min utility as a pay-off. The game between LAs and Gypsy/Traveller groups could also be termed 'variable sum' (Elster 1986:8) whereby a mixture of conflict and cooperation is involved and neither party knows when either might occur. When the players begin to suspect each other and to adopt maxi-min strategies, the 'equilibrium point' unravels and the relationship deteriorates to one of non-cooperation.

Games of Attrition - are accelerated when players use *tit-for-tat strategies* -construed as actions of stimulus and response. Bad behaviour on one side is rewarded with bad behaviour from the other, taking the interaction on a downward spiral, creating 'a situation'. Each side blames the other and the game quickly becomes one of *attrition* and *survival* – the worst-case scenario (Moser 1990).

To avoid such games both sides must change their strategies to produce games of cooperation. Lohmann (1995) suggests that to do this, *knowledge* of the game is important - involving knowing the rules, knowing the players and how they will act. It also involves an exchange of information and a willingness to compromise. The State, in its rhetoric and via its legislation, could be offering a tentative first step in this process. Resources have been allocated to refurbish sites, and (recently) to create new ones. Government research is taking place to 'find out', nationally, what is needed.[128] Similarly education is being offered to Gypsy/Traveller families which could enable them to raise their game play in order to match their 'opposition'. Such 'opportunities' if not

---

[127] Gypsies/ Travellers agreed to move on before the date of the Court hearing or before the bailiffs arrived and before fines and the threat of imprisonment were imposed. Correspondingly LAs agreed not to take immediate legal action provided families left by an agreed date.

[128] Although this is small-scale and piece-meal at present, it is a tentative step forward.

taken or negotiated at the time of offering, are usually retracted. These strategies of compromise could be extended to other 'nice' strategies (Luce and Raifa 1957:312) whereby reciprocity and good will on both sides is relied upon as a strategy to bring about games of cooperation.

Games of Cooperation - are concerned with an exchange of knowledge and information as a pre-play strategy and from which joint binding agreements can be derived. Whilst some LAs are changing their game plan to more cooperative game strategies, LAs as 'institutions' still find it difficult to respond to 'individual' demands: one size is used to fit all. Whilst group representation is advocated for Gypsies/Travellers, this is often difficult – although not impossible. Fieldwork revealed that some LAs are exploiting Gypsy/Traveller singularity in order to avoid service delivery and inclusion of some families. If LAs dealt with families on an individual basis then some issues might be better resolved.[129]

The 'big' question is, do communities want to include Gypsies/Travellers - and given the hostility that Gypsies/Travellers experience, do they want to be included? The term 'Gypsy/Traveller' in Staffordshire/UK is used not necessarily to identify people *per se* but to describe a mode of perceived behaviour. Those operating outside majority society are not trusted – primarily because they are not known. This fear is reciprocated by those 'outside'. Thus what appears to be missing is trust. This projects the study onto a larger canvas where the bigger issues of trust, citizenship, responsibility and communicative dialogue become salient.

Trust, Citizenship, Responsibility and Communicative Dialogue - The Big Picture

Williams (1998:174) believed that:

> 'the cycle of trust and betrayal … reveals an alternation of the desire for inclusion and the impulse to separatism that emerges in response to the actions of the dominant elements of society.

The desire for inclusion is prompted by actions which give hope that meaningful inclusion is possible and the impulse of separatism is brought on by actions which disappoint that hope.'

Although this refers to a broader political canvas, it might also apply to the Gypsy/Traveller situation at the micro-level in Staffordshire (and probably UK).

In terms of tit-for-tat strategies, the historical lack of respect for Gypsies/Travellers is often reflected back at hegemonic society. For some Gypsies/Travellers to participate in society freely as full citizens and for majority society to accept them as such will now take an act of faith on both sides. The construction of trust on all sides will have to begin if communicative action is to take place. Again, I concur with Williams (1998:149) and Jetten et al (2002) that 'by definition, marginalised groups stand in an uncertain relationship to other citizens, one in which they can have little confidence that others take an interest in their well-being'. However, the study found that some LAs were attempting to forge links with mobile groups, but this would have to be more widespread and more intensive if Gypsies/Travellers are to be included into majority society, and at all levels. It was found that good relations *were* being fostered with families who had settled on sites and attempts had been made by some LAs to include them. A system of representation needed to be established that Gypsies/Travellers would feel comfortable with and would be able to trust to act on their behalf.[130] A knowledge of the system might also help build a more trusting relationship with Authority. In this, LAs needed to be pro-active given that the Gypsies/Travellers in Staffordshire lacked an effective political voice. The claim of Kymlicka (2000:39) is relevant here – that it should not be assumed that 'the motivation, capacity and opportunity to participate as a virtuous citizen already exists'. Citizenship needs to be fostered – something that New Labour and subsequent governments attempted to do via Community Strategy Plans and Community

---

[129] If this is impossible then community development and encouragement should be a priority.

[130] The disagreements between some Gypsy/Traveller organisations who claim to represent the Gypsy/Traveller view/voice can be counter-productive at times. The sprint from a local base to national representation often can be premature. Few in Staffordshire had heard of or were members of the Gypsy Councils that existed then. A need for localised group leadership is pressing which could create a national forum/leadership – along the lines of Residents' Associations. This bottom up rather than top down approach might reflect more truly the plethora of groups (and their views) which make up the Gypsy/Traveller grouping.

Engagement, although in many LAs the compilation of these Plans appeared to be side-stepping Gypsies/Travellers.

LA Officers believed that the Gypsy/Traveller voice was weak. There was no acknowledgement that majority society might have contributed to make it so.[131] Williams (1998:181) takes the view that:

> 'For members of marginalised groups, the injury caused by voicelessness is magnified because the refusal of others to hear attaches not to them as individuals in particular circumstances but to attributes they did not choose to bear and cannot control. … Action based on prejudice and stereotypes about such involuntary traits is an affront to a person's agency and frequently operates to suppress that agency by denying its existence.'

Being moved on constantly means that some families are unable to 'move on' in other ways since they are constantly dealing with the basics of human subsistence – seeking a space and place to shelter. It is not necessarily a lack of ambition which places Gypsies/Travellers at the end of the resource queue but a two-way fear and lack of trust. The behaviour of some LAs in Staffordshire reinforced what Gypsies/Travellers believed – that they were being excluded. Equally, the behaviour of some Gypsies/Travellers reinforced any resolve that they should be included – thus reaching an impasse. Lack of trust drains confidence. A lack of confidence means that individuals in marginal groups find it difficult to compete (Jetten et al 2002). The circle of inequality and exclusion becomes a downward spiral. The space for representation shrinks. LAs have both the power and duty to address this scenario.

Cairns (1988:34) claims that:

> 'stigmatising state policy underlines the central significance of citizenship … . when a people is divided into citizens and others, and the latter are also systematically denigrated, the fellow-feeling that binds a people into a common society is deliberately fractured. To be put outside the community of full citizens is an official public badge of inferiority – an official statement that one is unworthy. The stigmatised group is variously defined as childlike, or incompetent, or

subhuman ... . The privileged majority ... has a remarkable capacity to accept its privileges as natural and deserved. ...

Special treatment underlines difference, and difference invites judgement that begins with the premise that the recipients of preferential recognition or treatment are not standard members of the 'we' community. The extent and nature of the institutionalisation or recognition of difference inform the reaction of the rest of society' (ibid:35).

This appeared to be the state of play for mobile groups in Staffordshire. Media and official reports indicated that this also pertained to other counties in England, Scotland and Northern Ireland.

Communicative dialogue is, however, a two way process and pre-supposes a willingness for cooperation and a mutual desire for resolutions which will satisfy all parties. This implies compromises and probably some sacrifice on all sides. Citizenship and 'responsibility' are also, now, double-edged. The paternalistic State of subjects is fast disappearing to be replaced by one of self-reliant, self-disciplined, empowered citizens who take responsibility for their actions. Williams (2000), Kymlicka (2000:6) and Nickel (1997) were of the view that 'the stability of modern democracy depends not only on the justice of institutions but also on the qualities and attributes of its citizens' sense of justice and commitment to a fair distribution of resources'. It is also about 'showing respect for diversity in a pluralistic society without, at the same time damaging or eroding the bonds and virtues of citizenship' (ibid:15). Thus a 'different' way of life should not be translated as a 'separated' way of life and (the assumption of) choosing that way of life should not mean that individuals are relegated to 'partial citizenship' status. Neither should it be 'an inward looking ... form of group identity which inhibits wider political cooperation, dialogue and solidarity' (Kymlicka 2000:11). Whilst rights are said to be what 'citizens take out of the civic system' an expectation exists that citizens will be 'dutiful and responsible' in return (Heater 1999:29) making some positive contribution to the State.

---

[131] Several LAs in Staffordshire have refused to work with the Gypsy Council

In similar vein organisations such as LAs have a duty to demonstrate an inclusive responsibility to all constituents and citizens. The Staffordshire study revealed that governance was not necessarily the seamless whole of Kantian/Weberian/Bauman bureaucratic rational perfection.[132] Neither has technology made it more efficient. At present, the impression given of LAs (and even of National Government) is that of 'muddling through'.[133] The question raised here is, does rational perfection or 'organised chaos' as styles of governance, produce the same outcomes for vulnerable groups? The thesis suggests that it might. In the power struggles between National Government and LAs, small groups such as Gypsies/Travellers slip through to become disadvantaged and discriminated against by the very institutions established to 'protect' them.

Responsibility for Gypsies/Travellers has been constantly contested between National and Local Government. LAs have been handed the baton for change by National Government – itself taking tentative steps towards change – via the Race Relations Act 1976 and its Amendment (2000) and the Human Rights Act 1998 and more latterly, and supposedly, the Localism Act 2011. It is time for LAs to set these initiatives into motion and move on if they wish to change the current state of play and the current Gypsy/ Traveller/LA habitus.

****

POSTSCRIPT 2013

Over the decades resources have been allocated by National Government for local level provision and refurbishment of sites in England. In 2010 a list of the latest grant allocations via the Gypsy Traveller Site Grant Programme (Annexe 1)[134] was produced. This suggested that £16,953,465 had been allocated to various LAs in England for both extra pitches on existing sites, refurbishment of sites and the creation of a site. One grant

---

[132] However, the latest changes were attempts to make it more so.
[133] Which possibly disguises the reservoir of power (individual and collective) which could be tapped and utilised if necessary.

was for a 'pitch loan' amounting to £77,250 for 5 pitches. Table 10.1 below summarises the distribution of this grant aid. However, of the total pitches only 90 were new or

Table 10.1: To Show the Distribution of the Allocation of Site Provision 2010

Region	Number of LAs	No of Pitches	Grant Aid
East Midlands	2	25	£1,723,571
East of England	4	64	£2,181,992
North East	3	33	£2,030,565
North West	2	27	£1,819,362
South East	4	41	£1,685,930
South West	4	39	£2,291,320
West Midlands	2	39	£2,062,600
Yorkshire and Humberside	4	52	£2,418,125
TOTALS	**25**	**320**	**£16,953,465**

Source: Based on the table produced by the HCA 24 February 2010

additional. Whether this total is sufficient to satisfy pitch need in those LAs/Regions remains to be seen as does the issue of how far need is satisfied if it is not articulated in terms of pitch or site but another type of accommodation. How soon such provision will be made available is another challenge for both Gypsy/Traveller families in need and LAs. For example Stoke-on-Trent attempted to implement their power to provide:

On Thursday 22 August 2013 a large headline on the front page of the local newspaper proclaimed: 'GYPSY SITE PLAN NEXT TO SCHOOL: 600 sign petition against proposals to create traveller pitches'. A local MP was reported to be supporting the protestors. It was 'revealed that Stoke-on-Trent City Council was considering creating a 30 pitch caravan site as part of its duty to provide sites for Gypsies/Travellers and in order to back the findings of their Needs Assessment Exercise for North Staffordshire undertaken in 2005 with some eventual positive action. To this end a strategic partnership had been set up between the City Council, Brighter Futures HA and the Homes and Communities Agency (HCA) and £1.8 million had been awarded for the

---

[134] CLG website: http:/www.homesandcommunities.co.uk/gypsies_travellers downloaded 16/7/2010

project, which Brighter Futures would manage. Forty- four sites had been examined for suitability. From a short-list of ten, three had been selected for further consideration. From this list the Longton site had been 'ear-marked' and this was the site that caused the public 'outrage'. The City Council proceeded to withdraw their support from the project stating that a more up-to-date assessment of need was required. The money was returned and the project came to a halt. It had taken around eight years to get to this stage. The two Council Officers contacted on 30 October 2013 did not appear to recognise that pressure to discriminate might have taken place. It is likely that this scenario will be replicated in many LAs where attempts are made to find land and create sites for Gypsy/Traveller families as the law prescribes and policy allows.

Possibly shadowing the duty to make provision is a new raft of proposals to control mobile groups currently being considered, redolent of the former 1968 Caravan Sites Act. The CLG in its document entitled, 'Dealing with Illegal and Unauthorised Encampments: A Summary of Available Powers, released in August 2013, is a guide reminding LAs of all the powers of removal currently at their disposal – there are 14 which pertain to LAs and an extra three for use by the Police. These presuppose that LAs have not been using their available powers. It is true that some LAs avert their gaze from families 'passing through' but this is usually tied to behaviour on the site – ie a proportionate line is taken. What appears to be advocated in the current document is a heavier hand, possibly to prevent settlement so that it does not get out of hand to reach Dale Farm proportions.

It also advocates 'being prepared' by having all the necessary paperwork for Possession Orders or Injunctions ready 'in advance'. Identifying sites which might be vulnerable to illegal encampments and sites where protests could be directed and or permitted is also advised. Thus, once again legislation is taking a broad swipe at 'protest' which could/would include Gypsies/Travellers within its remit. Such legislation also appears to be aimed at any kind of dissent[135] which appears to have become bound up with terrorist

---

[135] In a Borough Council 'Newspaper' dated August 2013, in a small paragraph on the bottom of page 6 the following was noted: 'A new policy proposing how customers who make unreasonable demands on the borough council will be dealt with, has been introduced. … The Customer Case Management Policy contains procedures for dealing with difficult behavior …'. The policy could not be found on the Council

threats and terrorist groups – making all dissent unacceptable and possibly, eventually, unlawful. And so legislation far from being propelled forward has catapulted backwards to the paranoia of the 16th Century (Yungblut 1996). Whilst policy remains with its feet stuck in the cement of history it is likely that groups such as Gypsies/Travellers will remain on the fringes of society, kept in motion until society fathoms what to do with them. For Government, the waiting game is more cost-effective than attempting to resolve the Gypsy/Traveller situation.

****

---

website, so it was impossible to discover how the terms 'difficult behaviour; ' and 'unreasonable demands' might be defined – and who or which 'groups' might be implicated in this policy.

BIBLIOGRAPHY

Abell P 1992 Is Rational Choice Theory a Rational Choice Theory? In J C Coleman and T J Fararo Rational Choice Theory: Advocacy and Critique, Pp183-206

ACERT 1999 Private Gypsy Site Provision, ACERT

Acton T 1974 Gypsy Politics and Social Change, Routledge and Keegan Paul, London

Adams B et al 1975 Gypsies and Government Policy in England, Heinemann, London

Albrecht L and W Denayer 2001 Communicative Planning and Emancipatory Politics and Post Modernism in R P Padison Handbook of Urban Studies, Sage, London, Pp 396-384

Anderson B 1983 Imagined Communities: Reflections on the Organsation and Spread of Nationalism, Verso, London

Anthias F and N Yuval-Davis 1993 Racialised Boundaries:Race, Nation, Gender, Colour and Class and the Anti-Racist Struggle, Routledge, London

Anwar M 1990 Redressive Action Policies in UK in S K Mitra The Politics of Positive Discrimination: A Cross National Perspective, Sangam Books, India

Arnold H 1970 On the Assimilation of Gypsy Populations and Speech in Central Europe, *Journal of the Gypsy Lore Society*, Series 3:49: 61-64, (transl. by A M Fraser)

Atkinson R and G Moon 1994 Urban Policy in Britain: The City, the State and the Market, Macmillan, London

Back L 1996 New Ethnicities and Urban Cultures: Racism and Multiculture in Young Lives, UCL, London

Balibar E and I Wallerstein 1991 Race, Nation, Class: Ambiguous Identities, Verso, London

Banton M 1994 Discrimination, Open University Press, London

Baharoglu D and J Leitmann 1998 Coping Strategies for Infrastructure: How Turkey's Spontaneous Settlements Operate in the Absence of Formal Rules, *Habitat International,* Vol 22:2: 115-135

Bardach E 1995 The Implementation Game, in S Z Theodolou and M A Cahn, op cit: 137-139

Barth F 1969 Ethnic Groups and Boundaries, Allen and Unwin, London

Bastinier A 1994 Immigration and the Ethnic Differentiation of Social Relations in Europe in Rex J and B Drury op cit

Benn T 1980 Manifestos and Mandarins, in Policy Practice and the Experience of Government, RIPA

Ben Tovim G et al 1986 The Local Politics of Race, Macmillan, London

Bernstein B   1960 Language and Social Class, *British Journal of Sociology,* Vol IX (3): 271-276

Billig M 1995   Banal Nationalism, Sage, London

Bindman G   1980 The Law, Equality of Opportunity and Affirmative Action, Vol11(8): 248-260

Blaut J M   1993   The Colonizers Model of the World: Geographical Diffusionism and Eurocentric History, Guildford Press, London

Bloul R A D   1999 Beyond Ethnic Identity: Resisting Exclusionary Identification, in *Social Identities,* Vol 5(1): 7-32

Borrow G   1907 (4th Edition) Romano Lavo-Lil, John Murray, London

Bourdieu P   1977   Outline of a Theory of Practice, Cambridge University Press, London

-          1987   In Other Words: Essays Towards a Reflexive Sociology, Polity Press, Oxford

-          1990   The Logic of Practice, Polity Press, Oxford

-          1993 a   The Field of Cultural Production, Polity Press, Oxford

-          1993 b   Sociology in Question, Sage Publications, London

Bourdieu P (and Loic J D Waquant) 1992   An Invitation to Reflexive Sociology, Polity Press, Oxford

Bourn C 1996 Equal treatment and Management Prerogatives in Dine, J and B Watt (eds) Discrimination Law: Concepts, Limitations and Justification, Longman, London, Pp 37-48

Boxhill B R   1990 Integration and Equality, *New Community* 17 (1): 5-18

Boyne G A 1998 Public Choice Theory and Local Government: A Comparative Analysis of the United Kingdom and the United States of America, Macmillan, London

Brand C M 1985 Carrying out the Duty to Provide Gypsy Caravan Sites, New Law Journal, 27 September

Brandt R B 1990 The Concept of Rational Action in P K Moser op cit: 398-415

Bubenik V 1995 On Typological Changes and Structural Borrowing in the History of the European Romani, in Matras Y (Ed) Romani in Contact: the history, Structure and Sociology of a Language, Current Issues in Linguistic Theory 126:1-25, John Benjamin's Publishing Company

Burgess R G 1984 In the Field: An Introduction to Field Research, Routledge, London

Cairns D 1988 In Search of Racial Equality: Indirect Discrimination and Equality of Opportunity Policies Twelve Years On, *Local Government Studies* Vol14(2): 15-29 November/December

Campbell S 1995 Gypsies and the Criminalisation of a Way of Life, *Criminal Law Review,* January 1995: 28-38

The Caravan Club 2001   Annual Profile

Cemlyn S 1998 Policy and Provision by Social Services for Traveller Children and Families, Nuffield Foundation Report, Bristol

Chisholm M 2001 Financing Community Leadership in H Kitchen (ed) op cit: 46-49

Circular 1/94 Gypsy Sites and Planning, Department of the Environment, HMSO, London

Circular 18/94 Gypsy Sites Policy and Unauthorised Camping, Department of the Environment, HMSO, London

Clark C 1998 Counting Backwards: The Roma Numbers Game in Central and Eastern Europe, *Radical Statistics,* 69: 35-46

- 1999 Race, Ethnicity and social Security: The Experience of Gypsies and Travellers in the United Kingdom, *Journal of Social Security Law,* 6(4): 186-202

Clebert J-P 1963 The Gypsies, Readers' Union, London

Clements L 1997 The Criminal Justice and Public Order Act and its Implications for Travellers in Acton T (ed) Gypsy Politics and Traveller Identity, Hatfield, University of Hertfordshire Press

- and R Morris 2001 The Traveller Law Reform Bill: A Brief Guide, TLRU, Cardiff Law School, Cardiff University, Cardiff

- and R Morris 2002 The Traveller Law Reform Bill, TLRU, Cardiff Law School, Cardiff University, Cardiff

Cobb R W and C P Elder 1995 Issues and Agendas in S Z Theodolou and M A Cahn op cit: 96-104

Cochrane A   2001 Modernisation and Accountability in H Kitchen (ed) op cit: 36-40

Cohen P   1992   It's Racism What Dunnit: Hidden Narratives in Theories of Racism in Donald J and A Rattansi (Eds), Race, Culture and Difference, Sage, London, Pp 62-103

Cornell S and D Hartmann 1998 Ethnicity and Race: Making Identities in a Changing World, Pine Forge Press, London

Comninel G C 2000 English Feudalism and the Origin of Capital, *Journal of Peasant Studies,* Vol 27 (4) July, Frank Cass, London

Cowan D 1998 Reforming the Homelessness Legislation, *Critical Social Policy,* Vol 18 (4): 435-464, November

Craib I   1998   Experiencing Identity, Sage, London

Crewe I   1983 Representation and Ethnic Minorities in Britain, in Glazer N and K Young (eds) Ethnic Pluralism and Public Policy: Achieving Equality in USA and UK, Gower, London, Pp 258-284

The Criminal Justice and Public Order Act 1994, HMSO, London

Cripps   J 1977 Accommodation for Gypsies, Department of the Environment, HMSO, London

Crofton H T 1908 Affairs of Egypt 1892-1906, *The Journal of the Gypsy Lore Society*, April 1908

Department of the Environment   1984   Defining Gypsies, HMSO

Department of the Environment for Northern Ireland 1999 New Policy on Accommodation for Travellers, Dublin

DETR 1998 Housing Research Summary No 91, http:/www.housing.detr.gov.uk/hrs/hrs090.htm

DETR 1999 Planning Policy Guidance (PPG) 12 Planning, December 1999

DETR 2000 Planning Policy Guidance (PPG) 3 Housing, March 2000

DETR 2000 Amendment to Paragraph 6-9 of DETR Circular 18/94 (Welsh Office Circular 76/94) – Revision of Advice on Toleration – July 2000

DETR 2000 Chapter 5 Revision of the Good Practice Guide – Managing Unauthorised Encampments – Housing, August 2000

DETR 2001 Local Government Act Factsheet: Community Well-being 11/12/01 http://www.local-regions.dtlr.gov.uk/lgbill99/factsheets/wbeing.htm

DETR 2000 Local Government Act 2000 11/6/01 http://www.local-regions.dtlr.gov.uk/lgbill99/wellbeing.htm

DETR 2001 Power to Promote or Improve Economic Social or Environmental Well-being 11/12/01 http://www.local-regions.dtlr.gov.uk/consult/wellbein/01.htm

DETR 2001 Power to Promote or Improve Economic Well-being 11/12/01 http://www.local-regions.dtlr.gov.uk/consult/wellbein/03.htm

DETR 2001 Preparing Community Strategies: Draft Guidance to Local Authorities 11/6/01 http://www.local-regions.dtlr.gov.uk/consult/lgbill99/pcsdraft/04.htm

DETR 2001 New Ethical Framework: General Background 11/6/01 http://www.local-regions.dtlr.gov.uk/ethical/general/index.htm

Dine J and B Watt 1996 Discrimination Law: Concepts, Limitations and Justifications, Longman, London

Drakakis-Smith A 1997 Killing Them Softly?: An examination of the recent legislation framework which directly affects Gypsies/Travellers (with particular reference to the Criminal Justice and Public Order Act 1994); the way that such legislation has been informed; and an evaluation study of the response by two local authorities in North Staffordshire in terms of policy, practice and service delivery for Gypsies/Travellers, MA Thesis, Ethnic Studies, Department of Sociology, Social Policy and Social work, Liverpool University

Drakakis-Smith A and K Mason 2001 Out for the Count: A critical examination of the DETR/DTLR bi-annual count of Gypsies/Travellers in England with special reference to Staffordshire, *Radical Statistics,* Issue 78, Autumn

Drakakis-Smith A 2003 Moving On? An Examination and Analysis of the Representation of Gypsies/Travellers and How This Informs and Perpetuates tier Socio-Economic Exclusion via Policy, Practice and Service Delivery in the County of Staffordshire, Unpublished Ph D Thesis, Department of Sociology, Bristol University, Bristol, UK

Drakakis-Smith A, G Day and H Davis 2007 Portrait of a Locality? The Local Press at Work in North West Wales, *Contemporary Wales* 21:25-46

Donison D V 1967 The Government of Housing, Penguin, London

Duncan T 1996 Neighbours' Views of Official Sites for Travelling People: A Survey Based on Three Case Studies, The Planning Exchange, Glasgow and the Joseph Rowntree Foundation, York

Elcock H 1994 (3rd Edition) Policy and Management in Local Authorities, Routledge, London

Elmore R E 1993 Organisational Models of Social Programme Implementation in M Hill (ed) op cit: 313-348

Elson M J and A Ford 1994 The Green Belt and Very Special Circumstances, *Journal of Planning and Environmental Law*, July 1994: 594-901

Elster J 1986 Rational Choice, Blackwell, London

Engels F 1969 The Condition of the Working Class in England, Panther, London

Eriksen T H 1993 Ethnicity and Nationalism: Anthropological Perspectives, Pluto, London

Fanon F 1970 Black Skins, White Masks, Paladin, London

Fenton S 1999 Ethnicity Racism Class and Culture, Macmillan, London

FFT (Friends Family and Travellers Support Group) 1996 Confined, Constrained and Condemned: Civil Rights and Travellers, FFT, Glastonbury

Foddy W 1992 Constructing Questions for Interviews and Questionnaires: Theory and Practice in Social Research, Cambridge University Press, London

Foucault M 1972 The Archaeology of Knowledge, Tavistock Press, London

-        1977 Discipline and Punish, Allen Lane, London

-        1980 Power Knowledge (ed C Gordon), Harvester Press, Sussex

Fraser A   1992   The Gypsies, Blackwell, London

Galtung J 1994   Human Rights in Another Key, Polity Press, London

Gay P and K Young 1988 Community Relations Councils, Policy Studies Institute with the Commission for Racial Equality, London

Geary R and C O'Shea 1995 Defining the Traveller: From Legal Theory to Practical Action, *The Journal of Social Welfare and Family Law,* 17(2): 167-78

Gentleman's Magazine 1787 Review, Vol 57: 896-9, London

Ghai Y 2001 Public Participation and Minorities, *Minority Rights Group International*, London

Gheorghe N 1997 The Social Construction of Romani Identity, in Acton, T (ed) Gypsy Politics and Traveller Identity, University of Hertfordshire Press, Hatfield

Gibbon P 1992 Equal Opportunities Policy and Racial Equality in Braham P, A Rattansi and R Skellington, Racism and Anti-racism: Inequalities, Opportunities and Policies, Sage, London, Pp 235-251

Gillborn D 1995 Racism and Anti-Racism in Real Schools, Open University Press, London

Gilroy P 1987 There Ain't No Black in the Union Jack, Hutchinson, London

Ginsburg N 1992 Racism and Housing: Concepts and Reality in Braham P, A Rattansi and R Skellington, Racism and Anti-racism:Inequalities, Opportunities and Policies, Sage, London, Pp: 109-132

Gist N P and A G Dworkin 1972 The Blending of Races: Marginality and Identity in World Perspective, Wiley, New York

Glazer N 1975 Affirmative Discrimination: Ethnic Inequality and Public Policy, Harper, New York

- 1995 Individual Rights Against Group Rights in W Kymlicka op cit: 123-158

Glennerster H 2000 (Second Edn) British Social Policy Since 1945, Blackwells, London

Goulbourne H 1991 Ethnicity and Nationalism in Post-Imperial Britain, Cambridge University Press, Cambridge

Grant A 1995 Plagiarism and Lexical Orphans in the European Romani Lexicon, in Matras Y (Ed) op cit: 53-68

Greenslade M W 1990 A History of Lichfield Part One: General History, Extract from the Victoria County History of Staffordshire Vol XIV

- and D G Stuart 1998 (Third Edition) A History of Staffordshire, Phillimore and Co, Chichester

Grellmann H M G 1782 A dissertation on the Gypsies being an historical enquiry concerning the manner of life, economy, custom and condition of these people in Europe and their origin. (Transl. by M Raper 1787), Elmsley

Guy W 1975 Ways at Looking at Rom: The Case for Czechoslovakia, in F Rehfisch (ed) Gypsies, Tinkers and Other Travellers, Academic Press, London

- 1977 The Attempt of Socialist Czechoslovakia to Assimilate its Gypsy Population Part 1 and 2, Unpublished Ph D Thesis, Department of Sociology, University of Bristol, Bristol, UK

- (ed) 2001 Between Past and Future: The Roma of Central and Eastern Europe, University of Hertfordshire Press, Hatfield

Habermas J 1981 The Theory of Communicative Action Vol 1: Reason and the Rationalization of Society, Heinemann, London

- 1991 Moral Consciousness and Communicative Action, Polity Press, London

Halfacree K 1996 The Distribution of Gypsy Caravans in England 1979-1994, *Geography,* Vol 81 (1): 37-46

Hallam S 1975 Fire and Hearth, The Australian Institute for Aboriginal Studies, Canberra

Hall S 1992 New Ethnicities in Donald J and A Rattansi (Eds), Race, Culture and Difference, Sage, London, Pp 252- 259

Hambleton R 2001 Enhancing Local Democracy in H Kitchin op cit: 21-25

Hammersley M (ed) 1993 Social Research Philosophy, Politics and Practice, Sage, London

Hanafin P J and M S Williams (eds) 1999 Identity, Rights and Constitutional Transformation, Ashgate, Aldershot

Hancock I 1970 Is Anglo-Romani a Creole? *The Journal of the Gypsy Lore Society* Third Series, Vol XLIX (1/2): 41-44

- 1987 The Pariah Syndrome: An Account of Gypsy Slavery and Persecution, Ann Arbor, USA

- 1997 The Struggle for Control of Identity, *Transitions*, Vol 4 (4): 36-44

Hansanyi J C 1990 Advances in Understanding Rational Behaviour, in P K Moser op cit: 271-293

Harvey P 2002 Advancing Equality and Diversity in the North Western Health Board (NWHB), in *Equality News*: Spring 2002, The Equality Authority, Eire

Hawes D 1997 Gypsies, Travellers and the Health Service, Policy Press, Bristol University, Bristol

Hawes D and B Perez 1996 The Gypsy and the State: The Ethnic Cleansing of British Society, Policy Press, Bristol

Henwood K and N Pidgeon 1993 Qualitative Research and Psychology in M Hammersley (ed) op cit: 14-32

Hetherington K 2000 New Age Travellers: Van Loads of Uproarious Humanity, Cassells, London

Hill M (ed) 1993 The Policy Process: A Reader, Harvester-Wheatsheaf, New York

HMSO 1960 The Caravan Sites and Control of Development Act 1960, HMSO, London

HMSO 1968 The Caravan Sites and Control of Development Act 1968, HMSO, London

HMSO 1976 The Race Relations Act 1976, HMSO, London

- 2000 The Race Relations (Amendment) Act 2000, HMSO, London

HMSO 1986 A Report on the Analysis Responses to Consultation on the Operation of the Caravan Sites Act 1968 by Professor G Wibberley, Department of the Environment, London

HMSO 1991 Gypsy Site Provision and Policy, A Report by Todd D and G Clark, DETR, London

HMSO 1994 The Criminal Justice and Public Order Act 1994, HMSO, London

HMSO 1998 Managing Unauthorised Camping: A Good Practice Guide, DETR, London

Hogwood B and L Gunn 1995 Why Perfect Implementation is Unattainable, in M Hill (ed) op cit: 238-247

Hogarth T and W W Daniels 1988 Britain's New Industrial Gypsies: Long Distance Weekly Commuters, PSI, London

Holstein J A and J F Gubrium 1995 Qualitative Research Methods , Series 37, Sage, London

Home R 1993 Planning Aspects of the Government Consultation Paper on Gypsies, *Journal of Planning and Environment Law*, January 1993: 13-18

- 1995 Gypsies and Development Plans after 1/94, *Journal of Planning and Environment Law*, November 1995: 1002-1006
-

Hooks bel 1981 Ain 't I a Woman?: Black Women and Femininism, Southend, Boston, Mass.

Hoskins W G and L Dudley Stamp 1963 The Common Land of England and Wales, Collins, London

Howe K R 1977 Race Relations: Australia and New Zealand, a Comparative Study 1770- 1970s, Methuen, London

Human Rights Act 2000, HMSO, London

James W and C Harris 1993 Inside Babylon, Verso, London

Jenkins R and J Solomos (eds) 1987 Racism and Equal Opportunities Policy in the 1980s, ESRC Centre for Research into Ethnic Relations and Comparative Ethnic and Race Relations Series, Cambridge University Press, Cambridge

Jetten J, Branscome NR and R Spears 2002 On Being Peripheral: Effects of Identity Insecurity on Personal and Collective Self-esteem, *The Journal of Social Psychology* 32(1): 105-124

Jewson N and D Mason 1992 The Theory and Practice of Equality of Opportunities Policy: Liberal and Radical Approaches in Braham P, A Rattansi, R Skellington, Racism and Anti-racism: Inequalities, Opportunities and Policies, Sage, London, Pp 109-132

Joinville Jean de and J de Villehardouin 2008 Chronicles of the Crusades, (Transl. C Smith) Penguin, London

Jones K 2000 Social Policy in Britain: From Poor Law to New Labour, Athlone Press, London

Jones T 2001 the Human Rights Act and Travellers, Report on ECHR, Chapman vs Others UK, 18 January 2001

Jorgensen D L 1989 Participant Observation: A Methodology for Human Studies, *Applied Social Research Methods Series,* Vol. 15, Sage, London

Keane L and R Scase 1998 Local Government Management: The Rhetoric of Reality, Open University Press, Buckingham

Keith M and S Pile (eds) 1993 Place and Politics of Identity, Routledge, London

Kenrick D and G Puxon 1972 The Destiny of Europe's Gypsies, Heinemann, London

Kenrick D and C Clark 1999 Moving On: The Gypsies and Travellers of Britain, University of Hertfordshire Press, Hatfield

Kenrick D 1993 Gypsies From India to the Mediterranean, Interface Collection Vol 3, CGRU, University of Hertfordshire Press, Hatfield

King D and G Stoker (eds) 1996 Rethinking Local Democracy, Macmillan, London

Kitchin H (ed) 2001 A Democratic Future, Local Government Information Unit, London

Klimova I 2000 The Current Academic Debate on the Political Aspects of Romani Migrations and Asylum Seeking. Prepared for the Roma Migration in Europe: Trends. Roundtable of the Academy of Sciences of the Czech Republic and the Prague Institute of Ethnology, 24-25 November 2000, Prague

Kymlicka W 1995a Multicultural Citizenship, Clarendon press, London

-          1995b   The Rights of Minority Cultures, Oxford University Press, London

Laquian A A   1969   Slums are for People, D M Press, Philippines

Liegeois J-P   1994   Roma, Gypsies and Travellers, Council for Europe Publication and Documentation Service, Strasburg

Liegeois J-P and N Gheorghe   1995   Roma/Gypsies: A European Minority, *Minority Rights Group International*

Lindblom C E   1995   The 'Science' of Muddling Through in S Z Theodolou and M A Cahn op cit: 113-127

Lipsky M   1993   Street Level Bureaucracy in M Hill (ed) op cit: 381-398

Lister R   1998   From Equality to Social Inclusion: New Labour and the Welfare State, *Critical Social Policy,* 55 Vol 8(2): 215-225

Lohmann S   1995   The Poverty of Green and Shapiro in J Friedman (ed) the Rational Choice Controversy: Economic Models of Politics Reconsidered, Yale University Press, USA, Pp 127-154

Lomax D, S Lancaster and P Gray 2000   Moving On: A Survey of Travellers' Views, Scottish Executive Central Research Unit, Edinburgh

Low-Beer R 1996 Challenging Gypsy Planning Policies, Occasional Discussion Paper No 1 (October) TLRU, Cardiff University Law School

-     2001   The Human Rights Act http://www.cf.ac.uk/claws/tlru/publications/odp1.html 9/10/2001

Low R and W Shaw 1993 Travellers: Voices of New Age Nomads, Fourth Estate, London

 Lucassen L , W Willems and A Cottar 1997 Gypsies and Other Itinerant Groups: A Socio-historical Approach, Palgrave, New Hampshire

Luce R D and H Raifa   1957 Games and Decisions: An Introduction and Critical Survey, Dover Publications, London

Lustgarten L and J Edwards 1992 Racial Equality and the Limits of the Law in P Braham, A Rattansi and R Skellington (eds) Racism and Anti-racism: Inequalities, Opportunities and Policies, Sage, London, Pp 270-293

Mac an Ghaill M   1999 Contemporary Racisms and Ethnicities: Social and Cultural Transformations, Open University Press, Buckinghamshire

MacEwan M 1994 Anti-discrimination Law in Great Britain, *New Community* Vol 20 (3) April: 353-370

Macpherson Report   1999 The Stephen Lawrence Enquiry: Report of an Enquiry by Sir William Macpherson of Cluny, Stationery Office

MacRitchie D 1890 Scottish Gypsies Under the Stewarts, *The Journal of the Gypsy Lore Society,* Vol 2, January 1890-1891

Main H A C 1990   Housing Problems and Squatting Solutions in Metropolitan Kano in Potter RB and A T Salau (eds) Cities and Development in the Third World, Pp 12-31

Majone G and A Widavsky 1995 Implementation as Evolution, in S Z Theodolou and M A Cahn, op cit: 140-153

Mangin W   1968 Latin America Squatter Settlements: A Problem and a Solution, *Development Digest,* Vol vi:3: 41-49, July

Marshall T H and T Bottomore 1992 Citizenship and Social Class, Pluto Press, London
Martin   G 1998 Generational Differences Amongst New Age Travellers, *Sociological Review*, November Vol 46 (4): 735-756

Mason D   1996   Qualitative Researching, Sage, London

Mason D 1996 some Reflection on the Sociology of Race and Racism, in R Barot (ed) The Racism Problematic: Contemporary Sociological Debates on Race and Ethnicity, Edwin Mellen Press, London

Matras Y 2000 Language and Origin: The Contribution of 18th Century German Scholarship in Gypsy/Romani Studies, Conference Paper Presented at Liverpool University, Organised by the Department of German, September 2000

-      1999   John Rudiger and the Study of Romani in the 19th Century Germany, *The Journal of the Gypsy Lore Society,* Vol 9: 89-116

-      1995   Romani in Contact:The History, Structure and Sociology of a Language, *Current Issues in Linguistic Theory 126*, John Benjamin's Publishing Company, Amsterdam

-      1998   A Response to the paper by A Mirga and N Gheorghe: the Roma in the 21st Century: A Policy Paper, *The Journal of the Gypsy Lore Society,* Vol 8(2): 151-4

Mayall D   1988   Gypsy Travellers in the Nineteenth Century, Cambridge University Press, Cambridge

McGee T G   1967 The Southeast Asian City: A Social Geography of the Primate Cities of Southeast Asia, G Bell and Son, London

McVeigh   R 1997 Theorising Sedentarism:The Roots of Anti-Nomadism in T Acton (ed) Gypsy Politics and Traveller Identity University of Hertfordshire Press, Hatfield, Pp 7-25

Midlands Regional Planning Guidance Review (Draft) November 2001

Miles R and R D Torres 1999   Does 'Race' Matter? Trans-Atlantic Perspectives on Racism after Race Relations in R D Torres, L F Miron and J X Inda, Race, Identity and Citizenship, Blackwell, Oxford,   Pp 19-38

Miles R 1996   Racism and Nationalsim in the UK: A View From the Periphery in R Barot (Ed) The Racism Problematic: Contemporary Sociological debates on Race and Ethnicity, Edwin Mellen Press, London, Pp 231-255

Mingay G E 1968 Enclosure and the Small Farmer in the Age of the Industrial Revolution, Studies in Economic History, Macmillan, London

Ministry of Housing and Local Government Wales Office (MHLG) 1967 Gypsies and Other Travellers, HMSO, London

Minogue M 1993 Theory and Practice in Public Policy Administration, in M Hill (ed) The Policy Process: A Reader, Harverter-Wheatsheaf, new York

Minority Rights Group Report 1990 The Bedouin of the Negev, No 81

Mirga A and N Gheorghe 2002 The Roma in the 21st Century: A Policy, http://www.per.usa.org/21st_c.htm

Modood T et al 1994 Changing Ethnic Identities, PSI, London

Modood T and P Werbner 1997 Debating Cultural Hybridity: Multi-Cultural Identities and the Politics of Anti-racism, Zed Books, London

Modood T 1996 If Race Does Not Exist, Then What Does? Racial categorisation and Ethnic Realities in Barot R (Ed) The Racism Problematic: Contemporary Sociological Debates on Race – and Ethnicity, E Mellen Press, London, Pp 89-105

-         et al 1997 Ethnic Minorities in Britain: Diversity and Disadvantage, Policy Studies Institute, London

Montague A (1942) 1997 (6th edition) Man's Most Dangerous Myth: The Fallacy of Race, Altermira Press and Sage, USA

Morris R 1998 Gypsies and the Planning System, Occasional discussion Paper No 4, *Journal of Planning and Environment Law*, July, Pp 635-643

-         1999 The Costs of Unauthorised Encampments, Report by TLRU, Cardiff Law School

Morris R and L Clements (eds) 1999 Gaining Ground: Law Reform for Gypsies and Travellers, University of Hertfordshire Press, Hatfield

Moser P K 1990 (ed) Rationality in Action: Contemporary Approaches, Cambridge University Press

Murdoch A 1998 The Impact of the Criminal Justice and Public Order Act 1994 on Britain's Travellers, unpublished Ph D Thesis, Department of Sociology, University of Bristol, Bristol

Murphy P 1995 Murphy on Evidence, Blackstone Press, London

Nickel J W 1997 Group Agency and Group Rights, in W Kymlicka and I Shapiro (eds) Ethnicity and Group Rights, New York University Press, New York, Pp 235-256

Okely J 1994 Traveller-Gypsies, Cambridge University Press, London

O'Leary P 2002 Theorising Equality in Equality News (Ireland) Spring 2002, Dublin

Ollearnshaw S 1983 The Promotion of Employment Equality in Britain in N Glazer and K Young Ethnic Pluralism and Public Policy, Gower, London, Pp 145-161

O'Nions H 1995 The Marginalisation of Gypsies, http://www.ncl.ac.uk/~mlawwww/articles3/onions3.html

Office of National Statistics (ONS) 2002 Social Trends Survey, No 32, London

Office of National Statistics (ONS) 1996 The Classification of Local and Health Authorities of Great Britain, (M Wallace and C Denham) HMSO, London

Office of National Statistics (ONS) 2011 Census: Digitised Boundary data (England and Wales) (Computer File), UK Data Service Census Support, Downloaded from http://edina.ac.uk/ukborder

OPCS 1991 The Gypsy Count, A Report Commissioned by the DETR by S Green et al

Organisation for Security and Cooperation in Europe (OSCE) 2000 A Report on the Situation of Roma and Sinti in the OSCE Area, High Commission on National Minorities, The Hague

Ousley et al n/d The System, The Runnymede Trust and the South London Equal Rights Consultancy

Parekh B 2000 The Commission on the Future of Multi-Ethnic Britain, The Parekh Report, The Runnymede Trust, Profile Books, London

Pischell, R 1908 The Home of the Gypsies (Transl. from German by Dora E Yates) *The Journal of the Gypsy Lore Society*, Vol 2: 292-320, New Series 1908/9

Ratcliffe P (ed) 1994 Race, Ethnicity and Nation: International Perspectives on Social Conflict, UCL Press, London

Rattansi A and S Westwood (Eds) 1994 Racism, Modernity and Identity: On the Western Front, Polity Press, London

Reid W 1997 Scottish Gypsies/Travellers and the Folklorists in Acton, A (ed) Romani Culture and Gypsy Identity, University of Hertfordshire Press, Hertford

Rex J 1983 Race Relations in Social Theory, Routledge, London

Rex J and B Drury 1994 Ethnic Mobilisation in a Multi-Cultural Europe, Avebury, UK

Ringold D 2000 Roma and the Transition in Central and Eastern Europe: Trends and Challenges, Health Communication Network, World Bank Report, Washington DC

Robbins D 2000 Bourdieu and Culture, Sage, London

Roberts J 1978 From Massacre to Mining: The Colonisation of Aboriginal Australia, CIMRA and War on Want

Rowley C D 1972a Outcasts in white Australia, Penguin, London

-        1972b The Destruction of Aboriginal Society, Penguin, London

Russell J C 1972 Medieval Regions and their Cities, David and Charles, Newton Abbot, Devon

P A Sabbatier and D A Mazmanion 1995 A Conceptual Framework of the Implementation Process, in S Z Theodolou and M A Cahn op cit: 153-172

Said E 1978 Orientalism, Penguin, London

Sampson J n/d The Welsh Gypsies, Lecture Given at University College, Wales, Scott McFie Collection, University of Liverpool

-        *The Journal of the Gypsy Lore Society*, January 1911: 2-24

Sandford J 1973 Gypsies, Secker and Warburg, London

Sarre P, D Phillips and R Skellington 1989 Ethnic Minority Housing: Explanations and Policies, Avebury Press, Aldershot

Savage S P, Atkinson R and L Robins 1994 Public Policy in Britain, Macmillan, London

Save the Children Fund   2001 Denied a Future: The Right to Education of Roma/Gypsy/Traveller Children-   Western and Central Europe, Volume Two, Save the Children Fund, London

-       2001 Denied a Future: The Right to Education of Roma/Gypsy/Traveller Children - International Legislation Handbook, Save the Children Fund, London

Scottish Executive 20002 The Twice Yearly Count of Travellers in Scotland: The First Three Years, http://www.csotland.gov.uk/cru/kd01/blue/tytcs-03.asp

Shamir R 1996   Suspended in Space: Bedouin Under the Law of Israel, *Law and Society Review,* Vol 30:2: 231-256

Sibley D   1981   Outsiders in Urban Society, Blackwell, London

-       1984a   A Robust Analysis of a Minority Census: The Distribution of Travelling People in England, *Environment and Planning A*, Vol 16:1279-1288

-       1984b   Travelling People in England: Regional Comparisons, *Regional Studies,* Vol 19.2:139-47

-       1990   Urban Change and the Exclusion of Minority Groups in British Cities, *Geoforum,* Vol 21.4: 483-488

Sigler J A   1983   Minority Rights: A Comparative Analysis, Greenwood Press, Connecticut

Silk J   1999   The Dynamics of Community, Place and Identity, *Environment and Planning A,* 31(1) :5-17

Simmel G   [1908] 1971 *The Stranger* in D N Levine (ed) On Individuality and Social Forms: Selected Writings, University of Chicago Press, Chicago

Simmie J   2001 Planning Power and Conflict in R Padison (ed) A Handbook of Urban Studies, Sage, London, Pp 385-401

Solomos J and L Back   1995 Race Politics and Social Change, Routledge, London

Spivak G C   1994 Can the Subaltern Speak? Colonial Discourse and Post-Colonial Theory, Harvester Wheatsheaf,

Stapeley L A 1996   The Personality of the Organisation: A Psychodynamic Exploration of Culture and Change, Free Association Books, London

Stationery Office (TSO) A Report into the Culture, Practices and Ethics of the Press (Part 1), Presented by Lord Leveson, 29 November 2012

Stevenson G G 1991 Common Property Economics: A General Theory and Land Use Applications, Cambridge University Press, London

Stewart J 1983   Understanding the Management of Local Government, Longman, London

Stewart M 1997 The Time of the Gypsies, Westview Press, Oxford

Stoker M 1991 (2nd Edn) The Politics of Local Government, Macmillan, London

Sway M B S 1983 Gypsies as a Middleman Minority, Ph D Thesis, Sociology Department, University of California, Los Angeles, USA

Swingler N 1969 Move on Gypsy, *New Society*, 26 June 1969, Pp 985-7

Theodolou S Z 1995 The Contemporary Language of Public Policy: A Starting Point, in S Z Theodolou and M A Cahn op cit:1-9

- and M A Cahn (eds) 1995 Public Policy: The Essential Readings, Prentice Hall, New Jersey

Thomas H and V Krishnarayan 1994 Race Equality and Planning in the 1990s: Recent Survey Evidence, in *New Community* Vol 20 (2) April:287-300

Thompson N 1998 Promoting Equality, Palgrave, Hampshire

Todd D and G Clarke 1991 Gypsy Site Provision and Policy, Department of the Environment Research Report, HMSO, London

Traveller Advice Team (TAT) 2012 Newsletter, Spring Edition, Produced by the Community Law Partnership, Birmingham

- 2013 Newsletter, Spring Edition, Produced by the Community Law Partnership, Birmingham

-
Traveller-net@jiscmail.ac.uk, 29.3.01:12.29 pm

Trevelyan G M 1964 Illustrated English Social History: 1, Penguin, London

UNSC (Economic and Social Council Commission on Human Rights) 1999 Racism, Racial Discrimination, Xenophobia and all Forms of Racial Discrimination, Res 1998/26, 56th Session item 6, Mission to Hungary, the Czech Republic and Romania, 19-30 September 1999 GE 00-10626(e)

UNESCO 1980 Social Theories: Race and Colonialism, UNESCO, Paris

Van Hear N 1998 New Diasporas: The Mass Exodus, Dispersal and Regrouping of Migrant Communities, UCL Press, London

Vermeersch P 2002 Ethnic Mobilisation and the Political Conditionality of European Union Accession: the Case for Roma in Slovakia, *The Journal of Ethnic and Migration Studies,* Vol28 (1):83-101

Wallerstein I 1991 the Ideological Tension of Capitalism: Universalisms vs Racism and Sexism in E Balibar and I Wallerstein Race, Nation, Class: Ambiguous Identities, Verso, London, Pp29-36

Watson J D 1968 the Double Helix: A Personal Account of the Discovery of the Structure of DNA, Weidenfeld, London

Weber M 1978 Selections in Translation (ed) W G Runciman (Transl.) E Matthews, Cambridge University Press, Cambridge

- 1968 On Charisma and Institution Building: Selected Papers, (ed) S N Eisenstadt, University of Chicago Press, London

- 1967 Essays in Sociology, (transl) H H Gerth and C Wright Mills, Routledge and Keegan Paul, London

Webster L and J Millar 2001 Making a Living: Social Security, Social Exclusion and New Travellers, The Policy Press, University of Bristol, Bristol

Werbner P 1997 Introduction: The Dialectics of Cultural Hybridity in P Werbner and T Modood (eds) Debating Cultural Hybridity: Multicultural Identities and the Politics of Anti-racism, Zed Books, London, Pp1-26

Wibberley G 1986 A Report on the Analysis of Responses to Consultation on the Operation of the Caravan Sites Act 1968, Department of the Environment, London

Wieviorka M 1994 Racism in Europe: Unity and Diversity in Rattansi A and S Westwood (Eds) Racism, Modernity and Identity: On the Western Front, Polity Press, London, Pp173-188

-       1995 The Arena of Racism, Sage, London

Willems W 1998 In Search of the True Gypsy: From Enlightenment to Final Solution, Frank Cass, London

Williams M S 1998 Voice, Truth and Memory: Marginalized Groups and the Failings of Liberal Representation, Princeton University Press, Princeton, USA

Wills J 1991 A Site for Some Citizens, *Local Government Chronicle*, 15 November, Pp15-16

Wilson M 1998 A Directory of Planning Policies for Gypsy Site Provision in England, Policy Press, Bristol

Wright Mills C 1995 The Power Elite, in S Z Theodolou and M A Cahn op cit :72-85

Wrightson K 2000 English Society 1580-1680, Routledge, London

Young E 1995 The Third World in the First, Routledge, London

Young I M 2000 Inclusion and Democracy, Oxford University Press, London

Young K 1987 Ethnic Pluralism and the Policy Agenda in Britain in N Glazer and K Young Ethnic Pluralism and Public Policy: Achieving Equality in USA and UK, Gower, London, Pp287-300

-       1992 Approaches to Policy Development in the Field of Equal Opportunities, in Braham P, A Rattansi and K Skellington , Racism, Anti-racism: Inequalities, Opportunities and Policies, Sage, London, Pp252-269

Young M and P Willmott 1962 Family and Kinship in east London, Penguin, London

-       1973 The Symmetrical Family: A Study of Work and Leisure in the London Region, Penguin, London

Young R 1990 White Mythologies: Writing History and the West, Routledge, London

Yungblut L H 1996 Strangers Settled Here Amongst Us: Policies, Perceptions and the Presence of Aliens in Elizabethan England, Routledge, London

APPENDICES

APPENDIX ONE: THE SEMI-STRUCTURED QUESTIONNAIRE SUITE

(A) LORD AVEBURY QUESTIONNAIRE

1. How did you come to be involved in Gypsy/Traveller Issues?

2. Can you take me through the Policy process which led up to the implementation of the 1968 Act?

3. Can you take me through the process which led to the 1994 Act?

4. Why were the positive elements of the 1968 Act withdrawn?

5. Why did you insist that designation be included in the 1968 Act? Do you regret that?

6. What does National Government do to ensure compliance with its Statutes at the Local Authority level?

7. How successful is National Government in making Local Authorities comply?

8. What is the purpose of Guidance and Circulars? Are they enforceable?

9. Is there any lobbying on behalf of Gypsies and Travellers at present?

10. Does the House of Commons/House of Lords have a view on Gypsies/Travellers? What is it?

11. What is the meaning of toleration in relation to Gypsy/Traveller sites?

12. How can the dilemma of illegal encampments and of provision be resolved, in your view?

13. How heavily does the DTLR rely on the bi-annual count data?

14. Should more information be collected on Gypsies/Travellers?

15. How can Gypsies/Travellers make their needs/aspirations known to Local and National Government?

16. Do G/Ts have a voice at present? How strong is it?

17. Would you say that the DTLR is negative/positive in its approach to G/Ts?

18. What is the current Government's view of G/Ts?

19. Would more pitch provision solve the problem?

20. How does England compare with Northern Ireland, Eire, Scotland and Wales with regard to policies and provision for G/Ts?

21. How does the UK compare with other EU countries in terms of policies and provision for G/Ts?

22. Is there any likelihood of a more positive attitude to G/Ts being encouraged?

23. Is there a likelihood of the 1994 Act being changed to include more positive action for G/Ts?

24. Has the Human Rights Act had any positive effects for G/Ts? Will it?

25. If you had the power to make any changes what would they be?

26. What would an ideal policy for G/Ts be?

(B) MP QUESTIONNAIRE

1.   How long have you been an MP?
2.   Which political Party do you belong to?
3.   Within the Commons system, what is your role?
4.   How does the Parliamentary system work?
5.   If people want to get things aired in the House of Commons what is the line management for this?
6.   Have you ever been involved with G/T issues/
7.   Is there any MP involvement at the moment with G/T issues?
8.   Do you know how and why the 1994 CJPO Act was passed?
9.   Has it made a difference?
10. What is Government Policy for G/Ts at the moment?
11. Is there much liaison between MPs and LAs?
12. Do you know what Local Policy is for G/Ts?
13. Are there any G/Ts in your Constituency?
14. Do you visit them?
15. Do you canvass them at election time?
16. Does the House of Commons have a view of G/Ts?
17. Do you get any complaints about G/Ts from other constituents?
18. What sort of complaints?
19. How do you deal with these?
20. If you were making legislation for G/Ts what would it be?
21. How could Governments improve the current situation for G/Ts?
22. How could this Government improve the current situation for G/Ts?
23. Would you say that National Government Policy for G/Ts is working?

(C) DTLR QUESTIONNAIRE

1.   Explain to me how the DTLR fits in to the Government scheme of things and what its relation is to Local Government?
2.   What is the relationship between National and Local Government generally?
3.   What is the relationship between National and Local Government specifically with regard to G/T issues? Is there d'accord and how is this achieved?

4. What is your role within the DTLR and what is your role with regard to G/T issues?

5. Does the Government have a view of G/Ts?

6. Does the Government have any responsibility for G/Ts?

7. Does the Government have any intentions with regard to G/Ts?

8. .Does the National Government/DTLR recognise G/Ts as small business men/women?

9. What was the purpose of the Good Practice Guide?

10. Guidance and Circulars form National Government appear to attempt a balanced approach. How does Government ensure that balance is achieved at the local level?

11. What is Government Policy at the moment for G/Ts/

12. Is there any special policy for New Travellers?

13. Does the DTLR distinguish between Gypsies and Travellers?

14. How is government Policy informed? What is the process? Who inputs and how?

15. When Reports are commissioned, who chooses the researchers and the research topic?

16. Scotland and Ireland have their own Advisory Committees and Policy and Guidance for G/Ts is there an English Welsh equivalent?

17. The term 'toleration' is used in conjunction with G/Ts what is the Government's/your Department's definition of this term?

18. What use does the DTLR make of the bi-annual counts. How are they taken seriously?

19. Are they monitored for accuracy?

20. Are G/Ts recognised by the DTLR as an ethnic group?

21. With regard to G/Ts what is your understanding of ethnicity?

22. Is there agreement between Whitehall and the National government re G/Ts?

23. Is Local Government expected to conform to National Government Guidance and Circulars?

24. Does the DTLR enforce and monitor compliance? If so how?

25. What happens if LAs don't comply/

26. Does the LA experience inform National Legislation with regard to G/Ts?

27. How can the DTLR overcome the dilemma of illegal encampments/lack of provision for G/Ts?

28. During the lifetime of the 1968 Act when provision was funded by national Government how much was spent on provision of sites in England and Wales. How did this compare with the amount spent on social housing?

29. How does the UK compare with other EU countries in terms of toleration/expenditure/ provision for G/Ts?

30. Does the UK and other EU Governments liaise with regard to G/Ts in terms of movement/migration/provision/toleration/strategies?

31. Are G/Ts granted the same freedom of movement as other EU citizens?

32. Is there a G/T voice within the UK? Is it effective? Does National Government listen?

33. What could National Government do to improve the lives of G/Ts?
34. What could G/Ts do to help themselves?
35. If you could change of make policy for G/Ts what would it be?
36. Has the Human Rights Act had any positive impact? Will it?
37. Does the DTLR keep records of planning permissions granted and planning permission refused with reference to G/Ts setting up sites on their own land?
38. In my research I have noted that expenditure for G/T provision has been phased in England Wales Scotland and Ireland. Would you like to comment on that?

(D) QUESTIONNAIRE FOR LEADERS OF COUNCIL AND COUNCILLORS

WARM UP QUESTIONS

1. How long have you been a Councillor?
2. What do you do when you are not being a Councillor?
3. Do you have any qualifications?
4. Do you bring any particular expertise to this Council?

EQUALITY OF OPPORTUNITY

1. When was the Council's EOP introduced?
2. How does it operate?
3. What is your understanding of equality of opportunity?. How does Council interpret EO?
4. How is it monitored? How often?
5. Is there any reason why an EOP was introduced?
6. Was training given to staff for its implementation? Is there an EO Officer in post in this Council?
7. Does it relate to G/Ts?
8. Does it extend to service delivery/practice for G/Ts?
9. Does it include service delivery for G/Ts?
10. Does the Council employ any G/Ts?
11. How many marks out of ten would you give your EO policy and its implementation?

POLICY

1. Is there a formal policy for G/Ts? What is it? If written (copy please)
2. If no policy how do Officers/staff know what to do?
3. Does Council have a view of G/Ts? Would you say this has any influence on policy?
4. When policy making for G/Ts does the Council know what their needs are? How does it find out?
5. In its policy for G/Ts has the Council tried to be positive/inclusionary?
6. Do you have a policy for self-help re G/Ts? If so how does this operate?
7. What is the Council's response to National Policy for G/Ts?
8. What has been the Council's response to the GPG? Has the Council implemented it yet? What has been the effect?
9. What is the Council's policy for unauthorised sites - toleration/non-toleration?
10. Would you say that G/Ts coming into the area/County have special needs? Are these taken into account?
11. With regard to G/Ts was the CJPO Act 1994 an improvement.
12. Would you say that National Policy works at the local level? How much notice does Local Government take of National Policy?
13. Are local Councils able to influence National Policy in any way? How is this done?

14. Does the Council welcome the recommendation for more Police involvement in the eviction process?
15. Does the Council encourage G/Ts to move into housing?
16. Does Council provide housing for its constituents? Would it provide caravans/mobile homes for G/Ts sites? Would it allow G/Ts to purchase their own pitches?
17. Have G/Ts been included in the SRB/EU/city challenge bids? What input did they have?. Were they consulted? How will they benefit from these budgets/grants?
18. Give a mark out of ten for this Council's policies for G/Ts.

PRACTICE

1. What is the practice of the Council in dealing with unauthorised sites?
2 . Is removable the best way of dealing with them?
3. What happens to G/Ts after they are evicted.?
4. Would a greater police involvement be helpful in practice or not?
5. If the Council had more resources would it set up more sites?
6. Would more sites solve the problem of illegal camping? Has the Council considered short-stay sites?
7. How much does it cost the Council per annum to evict/remove and clear unauthorised sites?
8. What happens if G/Ts don't want to leave? How does Council deal with this?
9. Are National Policies effective in practice at the local level?
10. Does Council adhere to National Policy for G/Ts? How do you rate National Policy re G/Ts?
11. How does Council deal with local opposition?
12. Has Council heard of the Race Relations Act? Is the Act applied to practice and service delivery for G/Ts?
13. Does Council work with/seek advice from the CRE/Local CRE?
14. Can local opposition affect policy? How/Why?
15. Would you say that local opposition is strong? Why?
16. Are there circumstances where Councillors/Council make a stand against local opposition?
17. Is Council doing anything to change public attitudes towards G/T?
18. Has Council implemented the GPG yet?
19. Did it find the GPG useful/helpful? In what ways?
20. If you were making policy for G/Ts what would it be?

SERVICE DELIVERY

1. How could Council improve service delivery to G/Ts coming into the borough/district/area?
2. If G/Ts wanted to remain in the borough/district/area how could they go about it?
3. Does this Council help G/Ts find their own land/set up their own sites?
4. How do you decide if a site is suitable or not?
5. Does Council assist G/Ts with identifying suitable sites/land/with planning permission for land/sites/buying land?
6. What is the Council's measure of a good site?
7. Does Council ever engage the services of bailiffs? Under what circumstances?
8. What are the major problems the Council has in dealing with G/Ts?
9. What are the major problems that G/Ts have in dealing with the Council?
10. How would you rate/evaluate site facilities provided for G/Ts by this Council?
11. Do the facilities meet their needs/requirements?
12. How many marks out of 10 would you give this Council for Service delivery?

LINE MANAGEMENT

1. What is the line management for dealing with G/Ts?
2. Where do Councillors fit into line management?
3. Who manages whom?
4. Is Cabinet-style administration being introduced by this Council? How will it work? Will it work?
5. Does the advice from paid Officers and the views of Councillors ever conflict? How is this resolved?
6. Do Councillors take a hands-on approach re G/Ts ie visiting sites/initiating eviction etc.?

7. Will the relationship between Officer and Councillor be affected by Cabinet-style administration?
8. Do you ever visit the G/T sites?

QUOTAS

1. How many sites are there in this LA? What are their status?
2. Would the Council like to see more G/Ts settled in the district?
3. Are there waiting lists for sites? How are these managed?
4. Does Council intend to increase/decrease site provision in the near future?
5. Is there any reason for the consistency of numbers within the district? Reason for changes in number of sites in the district?
6. Did this Council ever apply for designation?
7. Is your Council involved with the biannual count?
8. After the count are the numbers of unauthorised sites assessed with a view to increasing provision?
9. Has the Council identified/made provision for more sites in its Local Plans?

IDENTITY

1. How does Council define Gypsies/Travellers?
2. How are Gypsies identified? Is there a rule of thumb for identifying them? How would you describe a typical Gypsy?
3. How are travellers identified? Is there a rule of thumb for identifying them? How would you describe a typical traveller?
4. How do you know if G/Ts are passing through or they want to stay?
5. How does the Council view G/Ts - as nuisances, scroungers, small business men/women?
6. If G/Ts used traditional wooden waggons would they be more acceptable?
7. What would they have to do to become more accepted?
8. What could they do to make your life easier?
9. What could you do to make their life easier?
10. How do you think they ought to be accommodated?
11. How would you describe the relationship between the settled community and G/Ts?
12. How would you describe the relationship between this Council and mobile groups?
13. How would you describe the relationship between settled and mobile group?
14. Does the Council's view of G/Ts influence the way they are treated?
15. Does the settled community's view of G/Ts influence the way that G/Ts are treated by the Council?
16. Do you think that G/Ts are an ethnic group?
17. Where do you think they came from originally?
18. Are they covered by the Race Relations Act? Should they be?
19. Do you differentiate between the different groups? How?
20. Would you say that their way of life is chosen?

THE GYPSY/TRAVELLER VOICE

1. Would you say that there is a G/T voice? Is it heard by this Council?
2. How could the G/T voice be more effective?
3. Are policies for G/Ts made known to them?
4. Does this Council work with the NGC/with any other G/T organisation?
5. Is there a forum in the LA where G/Ts can be heard and where Councillors can listen?
6. Would the Council have approved housing estates where the G/T sites are?
7. Did any Councillors campaign on G/T issues at the last election? If so were they voted onto the Council?
8. Do G/T issues come up on Council's agendas? Often?
9. Are there any problems with young G/Ts on sites - eg petty crime/violence/drugs?
10. Has Council made any provision for the young on sites eg play areas/holiday activities?

(E) QUESTIONNAIRE FOR CHIEF EXECUTIVES/DEPUTIES

1. Is cabinet-style administration up and running in your Council yet?
2. Have there been any problems?
3. How has this initiative been received by: Elected Members
                                               Officers
4. At what stage is the Local Plan at for this Council?
5. How is the Community Strategy different to the Local Plan/
6. How will the Community Strategy affect the content of the Local Plan?
7. What stage is this council at with its Community Strategy?
8. Has this Council begun the process of assessing need for G/Ts? How is it going about it?
9. Are G/Ts included in the Community Strategy and its processes?
10. Have elected Members received any training with regards to the changes in the new Local Government Act?
11. What will this Council do re an elected Mayor?
12. Have resources from National Government been received by this Council to assist with these changes?
13. What percentage of the Community charge does this Council receive back from National Government?
14. How much does this Council need to meet its obligations and statutory duties?
15. In terms of the community Strategy has this council identified priorities yet? What are they?
16. Has this Council received all the Notes and Guidance from National Government re the drawing up of the Community Strategy yet?
17. Has your Council found National Government guidance for the Community Strategy/best value helpful/useful?
18. What is this Council doing in terms of Best Value for G/Ts?
19. Which is the majority party in this Council?
20. How helpful are the national Government Regional/National Offices? DTLR?
21. Do you have an ideal model in your mind for the delivery of policy and practice for this Council? What is it?
22. How close is this Council's workings to that model?
23. What are the current functions of this Council in terms of Service Delivery?

(F) QUESTIONNAIRE FOR PLANNING AND ENVIRONMENT DIRECTORS AND SENIOR SUPPORT OFFICERS

WARM UP QUESTIONS

1. What is your role in dealing with G/Ts?
2. Have you had any special training/experience?
3. What did you do before you took up the post?
4. Qualifications degree/HND/A levels etc..
5. When you were first appointed to the post what was your title/role/name of department to which you were appointed?
6. What qualities did you feel you bring to the post?
7. What qualities do you think are needed in dealing with G/Ts?
8. How much time do you allocate to G/T issues?
9. How much official time is allocated for dealing with G/T issues?

EQUALITY OF OPPORTUNITY

1. Does this Council have an EO policy?

2. How does this operate within your department?
3. Does it extend to service delivery and practice?
4. Are Gypsies and Travellers included?
5. What is your understanding of equality of opportunity. Do you think that EO is workable?
6. Is the policy monitored regularly? By whom?
7. Do settled G/Ts have the same tenancy rights as council tenants?
8. Do mobile groups have rights? What about those who resort to the area?
9. Are G/Ts who arrive in the area treated the same as other prospective businesspeople? If treated differently why?
10. Other than conventional housing is there any other way that G/Ts could be accommodated?
11. When G/Ts arrive in the area and say they want to stay, how are they advised/treated?
12. How much regard is given to Circulars 1/94 and 18/94 by this Council?
13 How does this Council assist G/Ts who wish to buy their own land and apply to do so?
14. How do you deal with G/TS who wish to run their own sites and apply to do so?
15. Are there formal procedures for this (written) (unwritten)?
16. When dealing with G/Ts which of the available legislation is followed?
17. Does this department work with or seek advice/assistance from the CRE?
18. Has this department heard of the local CRE? Do you work with or seek advice/assistance from the local CRE? Such as?
19. Does this Council work with the National Gypsy Council (NGC)? Does it consult with/seek advice from the NGC? Such as?
20. Is the Council taking any positive action to include G/Ts? If so what?
21. Is the Council taking any positive action to assist those who wish to settle in the area/County?
22. How many G/Ts are employed by this Council?
23. How many marks out of 10 would you give to this Council for its EOP?
24. Who is the Council's EO Officer?

POLICY

1. Does this Council have a formal/written policy for all G/Ts? What is it? For settled G/Ts. Copy please
2. If no policy how do you know what to do? Where do your instructions come from?
3. Does Council Policy for G/Ts comply with National Policy?
4. What is the Council's view on unauthorised sites? Is it formal/informal? Is it toleration/non toleration
5. What is the Council's formal policy for dealing with unauthorised sites?
6. Is the policy the same for Gypsies and Travellers or does the Council differentiate between the different groups?
7. What are the rules for eviction? Do the rules for eviction have to be followed to the letter or is there room for discretion by Officers?
8. Who makes the policy for G/Ts? How is this done? Are G/Ts involved in the process?
9. Do G/Ts ever resist eviction? What happens then?
10. Are there formal site rules? And for transit sites? Copy please
11. Would you say that National Policy conflicts with Local Policy?
12. Would you say that Local Policy meets the accommodation needs of settled G/Ts/mobile G/Ts?
13. When formulating policy for G/Ts what takes priority:
    the needs of G/Ts
    the needs of local residents
    the needs of local Councillors?
14. Given your experience with G/Ts if you were formulating policy what would it be and how would you go about making it?
15. Would you say that policies for mobile groups are fair/unfair?
16. How many marks out of ten would you give to this Council's policies for settled G/Ts
                                                                for mobile G/Ts?

PRACTICE

1. Has National Policy for G/Ts been effective in practice? Where is it most effective/least effective?
2. Is Local Policy effective in practice? Where is it most effective/least effective?
3. Does what happens at the local level in terms of practice feed into National Policy?
4. Re practice are there channels for feedback from G/Ts?
5. Once policy has been translated into practice do Councillors interfere?
6. What are the major practical problems when dealing with settled G/Ts/mobile G/Ts?
7. Are site rules enforced? How?
8. Are rules for transit sites enforced?
9. How does this Department deal with local opposition?
10. Do G/Ts ever refuse to be evicted? How is this dealt with?
11. Has the GPG been implemented by this Council yet? Is it going to be? If yes any effects on practice?
12. Did the CJPO Act 1994 have any major impact on local practice?
13. What is the procedure from the time that G/Ts arrive in the district to the time that they leave?
14. Is it possible for G/Ts on unauthorised sites to remain? Under what circumstances can they do so?
15. Are G/Ts aware of the rules for eviction? Are the rules explained to them?
16. Who contacts Social Services, Education, Health departments, when G/Ts arrive?
15. Would the Council welcome involvement by the Police in the eviction process?
16. Have many G/Ts moved into housing from sites? From illegal encampments? Since the CJPO Act 1994?
17. Are they encouraged to do so? In what ways?
18. What records do you keep of G/Ts?
20. Have G/Ts been included in any SRB/City Challenge/EU Grant bids? Have they been consulted? Has any provision been made for them in the Local Plans? Have any sites been identified for them locally/County wide basis?
21. Is there liaison between other LAs and this one? How much liaison and co-ordination takes place between this Council and the County? On what matters do you liaise with regard to G/Ts? How does the Interagency Group work?
22. Does this department liaise with any other department in this Council re G/Ts?
23. How many planning applications have been received from G/Ts? How many have been approved/refused?
24. How often are sites visited?
25. Are sites profitable/self-financing? How is this achieved? How much rent is charged per plot?
26. How could G/Ts make your life easier?
27. How could you make the lives of G/Ts easier?
28. How many evictions have taken place this year? How many last year?
29. How much has been spent this year on the eviction process? Is this more than last year? How much is spent on any cleaning up processes in any one year?
30. How would you evaluate the practices of this Council for G/Ts. Would you say they were fair/unfair?
31. How many marks out of ten would you give the practices of this Council?

SERVICE DELIVERY

1. What are the major challenges this Department experiences when dealing with G/Ts who are resident in the area?
2. What are the major challenges that resident G/Ts in the County /district face from this Department/generally?
3. What are the major challenges this Department faces with mobile G/Ts?
4. What is the major challenge that mobile G/Ts face when dealing with this Department/generally?
5. Do Officers follow any written Guidelines/Procedures when dealing with G/Ts?
6. Do your staff find it stressful serving notices on unauthorised encampments? Have they ever refused to do so?
7. Does this Department advise Council on G/T issues? How are G/T issues driven within Council?
8. Is there ever a clash of view over G/T issues between Councillors and Officers? What happens then?
9. Does this Department regularly assess the accommodation needs of G/Ts on sites and when they enter

the area?
10 Who decides where sites should be?
11. What is the Council's measure of a good site? Is that the same as a G/T measure of a good site?
12. How would you rate site facilities provided by this Council for G/Ts? Do these facilities meet their requirement/needs?
13. Is it part of Officers' brief to assist G/Ts to find/choose land/sites to develop for themselves?
14. Do G/Ts ever come to you/your Department to ask for suitable land for sale to develop sites/to assist with finding land/sites?
15. Does this Council have a Land Register of available vacant land?
16. If G/Ts come to you/this department re land/sites are they made aware that a Register exists?
17. Has the Register been used by G/Ts to your knowledge?
18. Are any inducements to settle offered to G/Ts?
19. Are all sites in the district/borough fully occupied?
20. Do you keep a waiting list? How many on the waiting list? How does this List operate?
21. What facilities do you provide for G/Ts resident on sites?
23. How often are skips emptied? Who pays?
24. What do you provide for groups in transit eg water/loos/skips?
25. Has the CJPO Act 1994 affected the way that this Council works with G/Ts? In what ways?
26. Does this Council find the Circulars and Guidance from National Government concerning G/Ts useful/helpful/confusing? In what ways?
27. Has the GPG influenced the way you deal with G/Ts? How?
28. What, for you, were the most useful/helpful guidelines in the GPG?
29. What happens to G/Ts after they have been evicted?
30. Has the Inter-Agency Group been effective? Has it assisted you with the work that you do?
31. Has Cabinet-style administration been adopted by this Council?
32. Has it effected the relationship between Officer and Councillor?
33. How does it work?
34. Has the new style administration affected service delivery overall/with regard to G/Ts?
35. Why were Site Wardens/GLO chosen? Which qualities did the Council regard as being important for the posts? Job description (copy please)
36. Do you think you could improve Service Delivery to G/Ts? How?
37. Do G/Ts make any enquiries re starting up new business in the area? How is this dealt with?
38. How many marks out of 10 would you give this Department for service delivery to G/Ts?

LINE MANAGEMENT

1. In dealing with G/Ts what is the line management within this Council?
2. When G/Ts approach this department directly for assistance are they dealt with directly or are they referred to other departments?
3. Are G/Ts made aware of procedures for complaint?
4. How formal/informal is the line management structure of this Council?
5. Are there ever conflicts of interest ie between liaison and eviction for example?
6. How has Cabinet style administration affected the line management?
7. Are there written guidelines for site management? What are they?
8. Is site management overseen by the Council (for Council and private sites)?
9. Are there channels for G/Ts to articulate their needs to the Council? What are they and how is this information dealt with?
10. When G/Ts enter the County/district who is their first point of contact?
11. How efficient is the line management structure of this Council? At what point do problems arise (with regard to G/Ts)?
12. Before G/Ts are evicted are they offered the opportunity to go on waiting lists (site/housing) which are they offered?
13. How easy/difficult is it to get G/T issues onto the Council's agendas? When staff dealing with G/T matters raise issues about G/Ts are they listened to? Are their suggestions made into policy? Are staff working on G/T issues regarded as being side-lined or as mainstream members of staff?
QUOTAS

1. How many caravans/G/Ts are there on sites in this borough/County? How many sites are there? Site status?
2. The numbers of caravans have been consistent over the years in this area/County? How has this been achieved?
3. Do you keep records of evictions?
4. Has this Council ever applied for designation?
5. Does this Council intend to increase/decrease its provision for G/Ts in the foreseeable future?
6. How secure are the current sites? Are any licences/permissions due to expire? What happens when this occurs?
7. Have sites been identified in the Local Plan?
8. Does this Council have a formal/informal quota system in operation?
9. Have there been any evictions from permanent sites in the last year or so? Under what circumstances?
10. Have any sites been closed/open this year/last year?
11. Who undertakes the biannual count?

IDENTITY

1. Do you think that G/Ts are an ethnic group?
2. Where do you think that they came from originally?
3. For the biannual count, how do officers know who to include?
4. How are Gypsies identified, generally? How would you describe a typical Gypsy? Are they different from Travellers? How would you identify Travellers?
5. Does the LA recognise them as small business men/women?
6. Are the settled G/Ts self/employed? What do they do? What do mobile groups do? Is there competition between groups?
7. Are different groups regarded/treated differently?
8. How do you know if G/Ts are just passing through or intending to stay?
9. How do you think G/Ts ought to be accommodated.?
10. How would you describe the relationship between the settled groups and this Department?
11. How would you describe the relationship between the mobile groups and this Department?
12. How would you describe the relationship between settled and mobile groups in this district/County? Can you explain the reasons for the difference?
13. How does this Department deal with small business men/women who come into the area?
14. Would you say that the G/T way of life is chosen?
15. Are the legal definitions of G/Ts accurate?
16. Are those on permanent sites still regarded as Gypsies/Travellers?

THE GYPSY/TRAVELLER VOICE

1. Is there a G/T voice? How effective is it? In relation to the Council how could it be made more effective?
2. Does Council listen to what G/Ts have to say? How?
3. What are the main complaints that Council receives from G/Ts?
4. Are policies for G/Ts made known to them? Do you know their views on the Council's policies?
5. Does Council consult with G/Ts/ G/T organisations? How are their needs assessed? By whom? Are There channels for them to articulate their needs?
6. Do you liaise with the National Gypsy Council? Are there other organisations you would prefer to work with? What is your view of the NGC? Is it effective?
7. Would the Council approve a housing estate where the current sites are? If not why not?
8. How many G/Ts in this borough/County own their own land/run their own sites? Do you assist them with site layout?
9. Does this Council keep records of those on permanent sites who can read and write, those unemployed/employed/ number plates/criminal convictions/children in school?
10. Does this Council have contact with young G/Ts? How are they treated by this Council? Are there problems with drink/drugs/violence/crime?

(G) QUESTIONNAIRE FOR LEGAL DEPARTMENTS OF COUNCILS

1. What is your role in dealing with Gypsies/Travellers?

2. What are the rules used by this Council to deal with illegal encampments?

3. What is the law with regards to Gypsies/Travellers as it is understood by this Council?

4. Which are the laws used by this Council to deal with G/Ts?

5. Does the Council take account of Circular 18/94?
   The GPG?
   Human Rights Act?

6. Do you advise the Council on good practice re illegal encampments or do you carry out orders?

7. Does this department get involved in the process of barricading G/Ts on to the illegal sites?

8. As a Barrister how would you attempt to solve the problem of illegal camping in this LA?

9. Anything else you would like to add?

(H) QUESTIONNAIRE FOR GYPSY/TRAVELLER LIAISON OFFICERS

WARM UP QUESTIONS

1. What is your role in dealing with G/Ts?
2. Have you had any special training/experience?
3. What did you do before you took up the post?
4. Qualifications - degree/HND/A levels etc.?
5. When you were first appointed to the post what was your title/role and name of Department to which you were appointed?
6. What qualities did you feel you were bringing to the post?
7. What qualities was the Council looking for?
8. What qualities do you think are needed for dealing with G/Ts?
9. How much time do you allocate to G/T issues?
10. How much time is officially allocated to G/T issues?

EQUALITY OF OPPORTUNITY

1. Does this Council have an EOP?
2. Does this operate within your department?
3. Does it extend to practice and service delivery?
4. Are G/Ts included?
5. What do you understand by equality of opportunity?
6. Is the policy monitored regularly?
7. Are mobile G/Ts treated the same as settled G/Ts?
8. Do settled groups have the same tenancy rights as Council tenants?
9. What does the Council regard its obligations to be re accommodation for G/Ts?

10. In terms of treatment and provision does the Council differentiate between G/Ts living in the area and those resorting to the area?
11. Are G/Ts assisted if they wish to purchase their own land/run their own sites?
12. How do you deal with G/Ts who wish to buy their own land and apply to do so?
13. Does this Council encourage G/Ts to buy their own land/run their own sites?
14. Do Circulars 1/94 and 18/94 favour G/TS (or not)?
14. When dealing with G/Ts which legislation do you follow ie EOP/Race Relations Act/CJPO Act? In what ways/how?
15. Have you heard of the CRE/local CRE/National Gypsy Council? Have you worked/sought advice etc from any of these groups?
16. Are any G/Ts employed by this Council?
17. Who is the EO Officer for this Council?
18. How many marks out of ten would you give this Department for EOP for G/Ts?

POLICY

1. Does this Council have a formal policy for G/Ts? (If written copy please) What is the policy?
2. If none how do you know what to do?
3. What is the formal policy for dealing with unauthorised sites - written policy for eviction procedures?
4. Are there written guidelines for dealing with local opposition?
5. Is there policy for dealing with G/T resistance to removal?
6. Does politics get in the way of what you do?
7. What are the informal procedures for eviction?
8. Do you work to Circulars 1/94; 18/94? How useful are these Circulars?
9. Would you say that Council Policy reflects the needs of G/Ts?
10. Is this Council implementing the DETR GPG - all/part/which parts? Was/is this easy to pass through Council?. Most difficult bits to implement/least difficult to implement?
11. What are the formal rules for the site? (Copy please)
12. Would you say that policy for settled G/Ts is inclusionary?
13. Would you say that policies for mobile groups are inclusionary?
14. How would you rate the Council's Policies relating to G/Ts - fair/unfair/poor/good?
15. If you could devise your own policies for G/Ts, in the light of your experience, what would they be?
16. How many marks out of 10 would you give this LA for its policies for G/Ts?

PRCTICE

1. How effective would you say that National Policy is with regard to G/Ts? Could it be improved? How?
2. Are there channels for feedback from G/Ts with regard to policy, practice and service delivery?
3. What are the major practical problems with the !994 CJPO Act?
4. Would/does the GPG improve current practice? Which sections are the most useful?
5. How do you rate the CJPO Act 1994 - strengths/weaknesses?
6. How does this Council treat G/Ts from the time they arrive in the district to the time they leave?
7. How do you know when they have arrived and what do you do if they want to settle here?
8. Do you recognise purpose of visit/health/education/needs of G/Ts?
9. Would you welcome the recommendation that there should be more police involvement with evictions?
10. Would more sites in the authority reduce illegal camping?
11. Do you assist G/Ts with planning applications? How?
12. Do you assist them to find land/suitable sites/accommodation elsewhere?
13. Do you know how many G/Ts have moved into housing since the 1994 Act? Are records kept?
14. Is moving into housing encouraged by the Council?
15. Is there a waiting list for sites? Who operates this? Procedure for reservation of pitches?
16. Would /do transit sites work in practice?
17. Is provision made for the accommodation of G/Ts in the Local Plan/Structure Plan? Did you have any input into these Plans?
18. Are there written guidelines for the management of sites?

19. When the Site Warden was chosen what qualities were the Council looking for? Is there a written job specification (copy please)?
20. Who undertakes the biannual count? Do you receive any feedback from the DETR re the count? What is it?
21. How does the Inter-agency group work? How useful is it to you? How useful is it for G/Ts?
22 Do you liaise with other GLOs? What about?
23. How often do you visit the sites in the LA?
24. Are sites profitable/self-financing? How is this achieved?
25. How could G/Ts make your job easier?
26. How could you make their life easier?
27. How many evictions have taken place over the last year? More/less than last year? Do you consider evictions to be sensible/counter-productive?
28. How much was spent on evictions last year?
29. Describe the process of eviction as carried out by this Council?
30. Do you/your Officers find evictions stressful? Have you/your Officers ever refused to evict/turned a blind eye?
31. The new legislation calls for more police involvement in this process. Will this help/make matters worse?
32. Would you say the practices of this Council are fair/unfair to G/Ts?
33. How many marks out of ten would you give for practice with regard to G/Ts?

SERVICE DELIVERY

1. What are the major problems you face when dealing with G/Ts?
2. What are the major problems you face when dealing with Council with regard to G/Ts?
3. Are there formal guidelines for dealing with all G/T issues? Are they written (copy please) or left to discretion of Officers. Which are discretionary?
4. Are any inducements offered to G/Ts to settle?
5. Who decides where sites should be? Do you have an input into the process? What is your measure of a good site?
6. Do you assist G/Ts with the planning application for Council sites?
7. Does this Council have a land register? Is it used by G/Ts?
8. Since the CJPO Act 1994 has demand for sites increased/decreased? Has demand for pitches in this authority increased/decreased?
10. Has the GPG improved the situation for G/Ts/ for you in your dealings with G/Ts?
11. Does this department assess the needs of G/Ts regularly on permanent sites/when they move into the area?
12. Do G/Ts make enquiries re starting up businesses?
13. Do you keep track of G/Ts once they have been evicted/removed?
14. What happens to those on the waiting list especially when sites are full?
15. Are there any New Travellers on sites? Are they treated the same/differently? How do they interact with the residents on site?
16. What kinds of problems do New Travellers have?
17. How are they different from the more traditional G/Ts?
18. Do you find that G/T issues are marginalised by Council? Is it easy/difficult to get G/Ts issues onto the agenda? Do you feel marginalised within the Council structure?
19. How many marks out of ten would you give this department/Council for service delivery to G/Ts?

LINE MANAGEMENT

1. In dealing with G/Ts what is the line management within the Council?
2. When G/Ts approach you directly for assistance do you deal with them directly or are they referred from /to other departments?
3. Are G/Ts made aware of the procedures for complaint? How is this done?
4. How formal/informal is the line management structure of this Council?
5. Are there written guidelines for officers who deal with G/Ts? (If so copy please)

6. Are there written guidelines for site management?
7. Who deals with the waiting list?
8. Are there channels for G/Ts to articulate their needs? How is this information dealt with?
9. Who/ is the first point of contact when G/Ts enter the area?
11. How efficient is the line management structure of this Council ie does it work? Any problems with lack of communication? At which point along the line do problems tend to occur?

QUOTAS

1. How many caravans/G/Ts are there on sites in this Council? How many sites are there? Site status?
2. Would you say that numbers of caravans in the authority have been consistent over the years? Is there a reason for this? How is this achieved?
3. Is there much movement on and off sites? When does this occur? What is the procedure? Are records kept?
4. Do you keep records of evictions? How many in the last 12 months?
5. Has this Council ever applied for designation?
6. Does this Council intend to increase/decrease its provision for G/Ts in the near future?
7. How secure are the current sites?
8. Have any more sites been identified in the Local Plan?
9. Does the Council have a quota for numbers of G/T caravans?
10. Have you evicted from permanent sites?. Under what circumstances?
11. What records do you keep concerning G/Ts?
12. Who undertakes the biannual count?

IDENTITY

1. Do you think that G/Ts are an ethnic group? Where do you think they came from originally?
2. How would you identify G/Ts generally? For the biannual count how are G/Ts identified - how do you know who to include? Any DETR Guidelines for this?
3. Does this Council recognise G/Ts as small business men/women? Are allowances made for them in this context?
4. Are the settled G/Ts employed? What do they do? What do mobile groups do? Is there competition between and within groups workwise?
5. Describe a typical Traveller (different to Gypsies) is there any rule of thumb?
6. Describe a typical G/T?
7. Are different groups treated differently?
8. How do you know if G/Ts are just passing through or intending to stay?
9. Should G/Ts be accommodated differently?
10. How would you describe the relationship your Council has with settled groups?
11. How would you describe the relationship you have with mobile groups?
12. How would you describe the relationship between settled and mobile groups?
13. Would you say that their way of life is chosen?
14 Are those on permanent sites regarded as G/Ts?
15. Are legal definitions accurate?

THE GYPSY/TRAVELLER VOICE

1. How effective is the G/T voice? How could it be made more effective?
2. What are the main complaints that you receive from G/Ts?
3. Are there channels for the G/T voice to be heard? Does the Council listen?
4. Are policies for G/Ts made known to them? How? Do you know their views on Council policy?
5. Are the G/Ts on permanent sites on the Electoral Register?
6. Does the Council cater for the needs of G/Ts on permanent sites? How are those needs articulated? By whom? Does the Council cater for the needs of mobile groups?
7. Are you in contact with the NGC? How effective is this organisation? Are there more effective organisations working for G/Ts?

8. How would you rate/evaluate the site provided by this Council? And its facilities? Do the site and facilities meet the requirements/needs of G/Ts?
9. Would the Council have built housing estates where the current sites are?
10. Are there many in the Borough/District who own and live on their own land?
11. Are there problems with drink/drugs/violence on site? How do you tackle these?
12. Do children on site go to school?

(I) QUESTIONNAIRE FOR SITE WARDENS

WARM UP QUESTIONS

1. How long have you been a Site Warden?
2. Why did you apply for the post?
3. What did you do before you became Site Warden?
4. What qualities are needed for the job?
5. Do you like the job/do you find the job stressful?
6. Who is your line manager? Do you get on well with the line manager?
7. Is the NGC involved in the running/management of the site?
8. Does the NGC visit the site? How often?
9. How often does your line manager visit the site?
10. Do local Councillors ever visit the site? How often?
11. Do you live on site? Are you a Gypsy/Traveller? Is this an advantage/disadvantage?

DUTIES

1. What are your duties as a Site Warden? Have they changed since you became Site Warden?
2. Is everything that you do covered by your job description?
3. What are the major problems that you encounter?
4. If there are problems who sorts them out?
5. Do you have to cope on your own?
6. Are you involved in the eviction process? Have you ever evicted anyone form the site?
7. Are the police involved in the eviction process? Would this help matters or not?
8. Is there a waiting list for the site? How does it operate? Do you deal with this?

SITE ORGANISATION

1. How is the site organised? Do the residents own their own caravans/mobile homes?
2. Was the system of organisation in operation when you took over the post?
3. Have you introduced any new rules/ideas? Where did these come from? Is Council/your line manager? Are they open to new ideas/suggestions?
4. What are the major problems with the site /organisation of the site?
5. Are there any changes you would like to make to improve things?
6. Do tenants have a say in how the site is run/residents committee etc?
7 Do you receive complaints from tenants? How do you deal with these?
8. Are there formal rules/regulations (copy please)?
9. Who drew these up? Have they changed recently?
10. Do the tenants ask to change things? What kind of things? How is this dealt with?
11. Who decides who comes onto the site?
12. How do you deal with groups who just turn up?
13. How do you deal with visitors? Are there spaces on site for them?
14. How do you deal with trouble makers?
15. Do people move from this site into houses? Do you assist them to do this? Are they encouraged to do

so? In what ways?
16. Do residents here get on well together? What tends to cause trouble between families?
17. Is there a complaints procedure for residents/against residents? Written/formal or informal/unwritten?
18. Are tenants suggestions taken on board? How are they dealt with?
19. Do tenants on this site approach the Council through you/individually/or a s a group?
20. Would you say that residents on this site are part of the local community? In what ways?
21. Do you receive complaints from the settled community? How do you deal with these?
22. Are there any new Travellers on site? Do they get on with the other residents?
23. Have the new good practice guidelines affected the work you do and how it is done? Has it improved matters on site?
24. Is the site self-financing? Cost of rent per pitch? What do residents pay for?
25. Do residents get good value for money?
26. How would you rate the facilities on this site?
27. Are residents on the electoral register?
28. Are there problems linked to the location of the site?
29. Are all tenants in employment?
30. What kinds of work do they do?
31. Can all residents read and write?
32. What records do you keep of tenants on site? What do you do with these records?
33. Do all children on site go to school regularly?
34. How are young people catered for on site?
35. Is there any violence/problems with drugs/alcohol on site? How are these dealt with?
36. What would be your idea of a perfect site? Where would it be?
37. How many marks out of ten would you give this site?
38. Do you live on site?

IDENTITY

1. Do you think that Gypsies/Travellers are an ethnic group?
2. Where do you think that Gypsies/Travellers came from originally?
3. How would you describe a Gypsy/ a Traveller? Are they the same? How are they different?
4. Does a true Gypsy exist? How would you define a real Gypsy?
5. Are those on permanent sites still considered to be Gypsies/Travellers?
6. How often do people move off site? How long are they away for? For what reasons do they move?
7. Do you think that the Gypsy/Traveller way of life is chosen?
8. How could the Local Authority make your life/job easier?
9. How could the residents on site make your life easier?
10. How could National Government make your life/job easier?
11. How do you rate the law for Gypsies/Travellers? Could it be improved? How?
12. Do New Travellers ever come on site? How do the different groups interact with each other?
13. Is there anything else you would like to add?

(J) QUESTIONNAIRE FOR GYPSIES/TRAVELLERS

INTRODUCTORY QUESTIONS

1. How long have you been a Traveller/travelling?
2. When did you come to this area?
3. How long have you been on this site?
4. Where did you live before you came here?
5. When did you last leave this site? Circumstances? For how long? Did you manage to keep your pitch?
6. How did you get onto this site?
7. What do you like about living here?

8   What do you like about living in a caravan? Would you prefer a house? Why?
9. What would be your ideal home and where would it be?
10. Were your parents Gypsies/Travellers?
11. Do you work? What work do you do?

EQUALITY OF OPPORTUNITY

1. Have you ever been evicted/moved on? When was this? What happened?
2. Do you ever visit the Council offices? .How are you treated when you go there?
3. Have you had any problems with the Council?
4. What is your opinion of the Council?
5. If there is a problem what do you do? Does anyone help you?
6. Are there any problems with this site? Have you told the Council about them? What did they do/say?
7. If you have any complaints where do you go?
8. Do you get on well with the Site Warden? Is he/she a traveller? Is this good/ not good?
9. Who is your local Councillor? Does he/she ever visit the site?
10. Do you vote in local elections?
11. Are you on the Electoral Register?
12. Have you ever tried to buy land for a site of your own? What happened? Did you know the rules for doing this?
13. How did you go about doing this? Did you ask the National Gypsy Council for help? Did you ask the local Council to help you? What happened?
14. Do you own this site? How did you go about finding it/buying it etc.?
15. Is there anything that Gypsies/Travellers do that really annoys the Council?
16. Is there anything which the Council does/not do that really annoys you?
17. Have you ever gone onto a site, not your own and want/ask to stay?. Did anyone help you? Did you go to Court?
18. Do you find it easy to find work? If not why not?
19. Have you ever asked the Council to help you with your business? Have you ever received a grant, asked them for suitable land and or premises? What happened?

SOCIAL ISSUES

1.   How old were you when you left school?
2.   Can you read/write?
3.   Do your children go to school? How do they like it?
4.   Do you think education/school is a good idea? If there was a school on site would you send your children? Even if they were over 12 years old?
5.   Do social services/education doctors/health visitors come to the site?
6.   When did you last visit the doctor/hospital?
7.   Has a doctor ever refused to treat you? What happened?
8.   Does the health visitor call to the site regularly?
9.   Do you mix at all with the settled community? How do you get on with them?
10. Are there any problems with violence/drink/drugs on this site? What is being done about it?
11. Have you ever lived in a house? How did you come to move into a house?
12. Do you think this is a good site? If you were looking for a better site where would it be?
13. What would make it a good site for you?
14. What is the best thing that has ever happened to you?
15. What is the worst thing that has ever happened to you?

IDENTITY

1. How do you describe yourself? Do you think of yourself as a Gypsy or a Traveller …?
2. Do you speak Romanischal? What about your children?
3. Where do you think Gypsies came from? Do you think they came from India?
4. Do you think that Gypsies are an ethnic group?

5. Are you a member of the National Gypsy Council?
6. Have you ever asked for help from the NGC? What happened?
7. Is there a committee/spokesman who speaks on behalf of all the residents on this site to the Council?
8. Has there ever been any trouble between residents on this site and the local community? Circumstances
9. How would you describe a typical Gypsy/Traveller?
10. Do you think that Gypsies/Travellers have changed? In what ways?
11. If you lived in a house would you still feel that you were a G/T? Would other Gypsies and Travellers think of you as a Gypsy/Traveller? If children marry non Gypsy/Travellers would you still see them as Gypsies/Travellers?
12. What do you like about living in a caravan?
13. If you could change anything about your life what would it be?
14. What would best improve your life at the moment?
15. What kind of life would you like your children to have?
16. If you were granted one wish what would it be?
17. If there was one thing that you would say to the Prime Minister, what would it be?

(K) GYPSY/TRAVELLER COUNT QUESTIONNAIRE

Name of Council:

Counting Officer

1. Does the DETR set out clear guidelines for the biannual count?
2. Are they in printed form?
3. Is there any criteria re those who are to be counted?
4. Who decides who is to be counted?
5. How is it decided who should be counted?
6. Who takes overall responsibility within the LA for the count?
7. What is the criteria for inclusion/exclusion?
8. How do you identify Gypsies/Travellers/NewTravellers? Methods used?
9. How does the LA ensure accuracy of the count?
10. What is your procedure for the count?
11. Do you visit each caravan?
12. Is the information recorded on a standard sheet or into a notebook?
13. Does the Counting Officer visit all sites?
14. Does the count include privately owned site by G/Ts?
15. Does the count include unauthorised sites?
16. Are unauthorised caravans moved on before the count?
17. Are New Travellers included?
18. Are Irish Travellers included?
19. Do you count visitors?
20. Do you count tents?
21. Does the count take place all in one day?
22. Does the count take place on the day designated by the DETR?
23. Who do you collect information from:

site wardens
GLO
LA records
family members
neighbours?

24. Do you ask G/Ts if they want residential accommodation (if on unauthorised sites at the time)
transit accommodation (if on unauthorised sites at the time)?

25. Do you have maps of the location of sites?
26. Is the information monitored by anyone for accuracy eg the LA/County?
27. What is done with the information?
28. Do you get any feedback from the DETR/County afterwards?
Do you keep the following records of G/Ts on permanent sites:

age of G/Ts
gender of G/Ts
number of persons in family
number of school-age children
employment status
vehicle registration numbers?

29 Do you keep the following information on G/Ts on temporary/unauthorised sites:

age of G/Ts
gender of G/Ts
number of persons in family
number of school-age children
employment status
vehicle registration numbers
where they have come from
where they are going to?

30 What do you do with this information?
31 Do you collect any other information?
32 Do you identify unauthorised sites regularly?
33 Are they marked on a map?
34 Do you check traditional stopping places regularly?
35 Are these marked on a map?
36 Does this LA keep a file on possession orders/evictions/dealings with the Court?
37 Are G/Ts allowed to work on site? Reasons for yes/no answers?

(L) EQUALITY OF OPPORTUNITY QUESTIONNAIRE

1. In what ways is this Council's EOP put into practice?

2. Does it cover service delivery/practice?

3. Does it include Gypsies/Travellers?

4. Do you require applicants to complete an EOP form? What do you do with the information?

5. How do you monitor the EO Policy?

6. Does the Council have an EO Committee?

7. Are any members of the EO Committee on appointment panels as a matter of course/occasionally?

8. Are any Gypsies/Travellers employed by this Council?

9. Do any apply to this Council for jobs?

10. Does this Council have a Racial Harassment Policy?

11. Are any Gypsies employed to deal with Gypsy/Traveller issues?

12. Does this Council have a positive action plan for Gypsies/Travellers?

(M) SMALL BUSINESS UNIT QUESTIONNAIRE

1. What is your role?

2. What is the remit of this Unit?

3. How do you help small businesses?

4. If grants are available how do you inform small businesses and prospective businesses?

5. What do you give grants for?

6. Do you assist minority groups either to start or to improve their businesses? Is there much take up?

7. What is the kind of business that ethnic minorities do in the area? Is there much competition?

8. What is the kind of business that G/Ts run?

9. Do you regard Gypsies and Travellers as small business men/women?

10. Do you do anything to encourage Gypsies and Travellers to start their own businesses?

11. Do they ever come to you for help or advice about starting up a business/improving their business?

12. Do you ever go to sites to disseminate information about this unit and what is available?

13. If Gypsies and Travellers came to this unit how would you be able to assist them?

14. How would you rate the businesses that G/Ts carry out in the area?

15. Would you say that the work that G/Ts do fills a gap in the market?

(N) EDUCATION SERVICES QUESTIONNAIRE

1. With regard to Gypsies/Travellers who deals with what and how does the system work?

2. What are the responsibilities of the Council re the education of G/T children?

3. What are your specific responsibilities?

4. What are the policies for non-attendance at school? What are the procedures for non-attendance?

5. Does equality of opportunity operate within the education section?

6. What is the budget for education?

7. Is anything ring fenced for G/Ts? How much?

8. Is Section 11 still operating?. Are G/Ts included?

9. How does the Council educate G/T children on permanent sites/ on unauthorised sites?

10. How many children are in the SOT education catchment area?

11. Are records of G/T families kept by the education department?

12. Are specific schools earmarked to teach G/T children? If so do they receive special funding?

13. When education polices for G/Ts are being discussed are they included in the discussions?

14. Does the Education Department make any distinction between Gypsies and Travellers?

15. How could the Education Department best educate G/T children?

16. Do you think that G/Ts are an ethnic group?

APPENDIX 2

28 May 1968

Mr Macdonald:- 'The object of the Bill is to note that gypsies have a nomadic way of life and it seeks to ensure that proper provision shall be made so that that way of life is not offensive to other people. The Amendment goes a step further and seeks to impose a change in their way of life. It assumes that they ought necessarily to be integrated in the community. But the amendment would require local authorities to make special provision and, in a sense, gypsies would be given priority over other sections of the community ... while it may be right that gypsies should be integrated into the rest of the community it is a long-term process and we ought not to rush it'.

6 February 1987

Mr N Ridley: On Review of Gypsy Sites Policy:- 'Government has decided there should be no amendment of legislation at this stage. ... No practical alternative solution to the problem has been proposed, although there is some scope for private sector provision which will be encouraged. The total number of local authority sites is 236 at the beginning of 1986, 3,850 pitches. ... Private sites are capable of holding 2000 and more gypsy caravans ... but 3000 families are unaccommodated on authorised sites. £5 million has been reserved for grants to local authorities. ... proper identification of numbers is vital.'

He asks for regular and more frequent counting by local authorities. He also claims that the 'interpretation of the statutory definition of gypsy is also crucial. The local authorities have generally been able to decide who meets the statutory definition but there is increasing concern that it may be extended to members of other groups'.

'It has proved difficult to find satisfactory solutions to the problems of long distance and regional travellers. Progress continues to depend on the willingness of local authorities to find suitable locations for stopping [places which can be designed to simpler standards than the settled sites needed by more locally based gypsies.

The Government believes that conventional housing on a selective and voluntary basis can contribute usefully to meeting needs of gypsy families.

The need for gypsy sites will continue to be a material consideration with local authorities. ... I urge gypsies to recognise the importance of getting planning permission before purchasing land

and to cooperate with District Councils to identify sites which might be suitable ... I hope the District councils will recognise ... that their development control policies need to take account of the serious need for gypsy sites'.

13 March 1987

Peter Lilley:- This House calls for a thorough reform of legislation requiring local authorities to provide caravan sites for so-called travellers; believes that no special privileges such as the right to build permanent sites in the Green Belt should be granted to one section of the population whilst the rate paying settled majority is rightly prevented from doing so; ... believes that official caravan sites should be available only for those pursuing a general nomadic lifestyle rather than semi-permanent residents in one place. ... Local authorities are caught up in a Catch 22 situation under the present legislation. Without designation local authorities do not have adequate powers to move on gypsies using illegal sites and are forced to tolerate them. To obtain powers to move them on, local authorities must create official sites so one way or another we have to have gypsy caravan sites in our area. ... Circular 28/77 specifically states that caravan sites can be built in the Green Belt (however, if special circumstances can be proved gypsy sites can be established in these areas) ... only gypsies are granted that privilege ... despite the fact that they are not conspicuously noted for paying rates or taxes or for abiding by the law, as most of my constituents do. ...when privilege was granted people may have thought of gypsy sites as a few rustic wooden caravans nestling among the trees like a Constable painting – but in practice that is not the case. They can look like dumps. Indeed even well regulated sites are not attractive with their modern garish caravans and vehicles. Indeed, they look all the more unattractive as the activities in which gypsies frequently engage and on which they depend for a living such as car breaking, the provision of aggregates and laying tarmac are unsightly, require unsightly machinery and equipment and leave residues which destroy the environment.

Gypsies themselves by their culture want to live apart from the rest of society. They want to be different, separate and distinct. ... that is reciprocated by the majority of the public. They do not want to live cheek by jowl with gypsies either.

I am sure that, like everybody else, the majority of gypsies are decent law abiding folk but a significant number do not abide by our laws. There is often crime and problems associated with gypsy caravan sites. ... the laws are weighted too heavily towards gypsies ... there is a great danger that others will learn of their privileges and seek to define themselves as gypsies under the loose definition that operates'.

19 November 1987

Merlyn Rees:- 'I do not know what a gypsy is although I remember that years ago I thought I knew what a gypsy was. What is a gypsy? These people in my constituency (South Leeds) have JCBs, E-reg cars and patio furniture but they do not pay taxes. They do not fit into the category of gypsy that I thought I knew about years ago'.

Marion Roe, Parliamentary Under-Secretary of State for the Environment:- 'We have a legislative package which balances the duty to provide sites with the availability of special controls on unauthorised camping … we are convinced that it can be made to work, if there is a will to make it work … we are considering what further general advice we can give to local authorities to help them do the job … the current framework for provision allows suitable sites to be set up with little financial cost to the local authority'.

28 June 1989

K Vaz:- 14050 petitioners against gypsy and traveller sites in a densely populated area of the eastern part of the city (Leicester).

28 June 1989

K Vaz:- that his 'petitioners are against gypsy and traveller sites in densely populated areas of the eastern part of the city (Leicester). … Should the matter come before the Secretary for the Environment he must take appropriate action to prevent the sites being used for these purposes'.

26 July 1989

? Opposition to creation of a gypsy site in South Woodham Ferriers on an old concrete batching plant. Essex County Council in 1974 promised it would be a public open space. … The residents of SW1 have been since the new town was developed prevented by restrictive covenant from parking caravans on their own property. Yet there is now a proposal to bring in caravans belonging to strangers from outside the area. The riverside and rural nature of the environment will be spoiled by bringing a gypsy site to the town.

2 November 1989

K Vaz:- presents a petition from residents in Leicester re traveller sites in their area.

10 July 1990

R B Jones:- Above all there is the problem of visual pollution. To some, gypsies may be historic Romany folk with brightly painted caravans towed by horses but those of us who have experienced the problem in recent years know that it is more to do with tumbledown caravans and beaten up vehicles and piles of scrap and rubbish and that those people often occupy inappropriate sites that are extremely visible to the general public.

Genuine travellers ought to be provided with a decent lifestyle and somewhere to live so that education can be provided for their children but the law needs to be reformed to deal with the remainder.

Max Madden:- This is not a party political issue but one of good local government and community relations.

Sir Hugh Rossi:- My constituency has been subject to a plague of gypsies for about 7 years. I call them gypsies but they are not the true Romanies. Possibly some of them are Tinkers. They may be itinerant scrap metal merchants but mostly they seem to be motorised squatters. That is probably the best term I can use. … It is of some interest that the council which is reluctant to use its power to remove trespassers from its property seems to anticipate travellers moving from one site to another, because overnight a water standpipe and portaloos suddenly appear, and lo and behold they remain for several months.

Anthony Coombs:- The number of caravans is rising all the time … and we have not taken into account … the increasing number of European travellers who are likely to come here after 1992.
